Contemporary Applied Management

Skills for Managers

Contemporary Applied Management

Skills for Managers

Andrew J. DuBrin
Rochester Institute of Technology

Fourth Edition

IRWIN
Burr Ridge, Illinois
Boston, Massachusetts
Sydney, Australia

To Douglas

Sponsoring editor:	Kurt L. Strand
Marketing manager:	Kurt Messersmith
Project editor:	Stephanie M. Britt
Production manager:	Jon Christopher
Art cordinator:	Mark Malloy
Typeface:	10/12 Times Roman
Printer:	Malloy Lithographing

Library of Congress Cataloging-in-Publication Data

DuBrin, Andrew J.

  Contemporary applied management : skills for managers / Andrew J. DuBrin. — 4th ed.

    p.   cm.

  Includes bibliographical references and indexes.

  ISBN 0-256-10528-6

  1. Management   2. Organizational behavior.   I. Title.

HD31.D79   1994

658.2—dc20   93-13311

Printed in the United States of America

1 2 3 4 5 6 7 8 9 0 ML 0 9 8 7 6 5 4 3

Preface

Management thought and action has been influenced by the work of organizational behaviorists and other behavioral scientists. Many students of organizational behavior, management, and human resources management have been exposed to general information about behaviorally based techniques and concepts. Examples of these include team building, influence tactics, creativity improvement, and employee empowerment programs.

This book provides managers, aspiring managers, and staff professionals with a look at the application of a current selection of both behavioral science and management techniques, methods, and strategies. (*Management* in this context refers to the classical, functional, or process approach.) Toward this purpose, each chapter begins with a brief statement of why a technique was chosen and a hands-on description—in a job setting—of the technique or method under consideration.

The underlying theme of this book is that applied management techniques serve such useful ends as increased productivity, quality, and job satisfaction, despite some of their disadvantages and shortcomings. In support of this theme, each chapter considers both the advantages and disadvantages, or strengths and weaknesses, of the technique or method. In addition, guidelines are presented for the appropriate application of each technique or method. Each chapter also contains a specific skill-building exercise. Skill development is thus enhanced by descriptions of techniques, exercises, and guidelines for applying techniques.

This book is written for two audiences. One is students of organizational behavior, management development, human relations, organizational psychology, introduction to management, and human resources management. The other audience is managers and professionals seeking development on their own or within internal management development programs. This book is designed to be used as a supplement to a formal text, alone in application courses, or in management development.

Generally, the user of this book will have some understanding of or will have completed some reading in organizational behavior, management, supervision, or human resources management. *Contemporary Applied Management* intentionally does not duplicate the theoretical and conceptual background contained in texts in organizational behavior, introduction to management, and human resources management. Current texts in those fields provide the student with an adequate theoretical background and research orientation for benefiting from an application text of this type.

In addition to providing a concise look at the application of current applied management techniques and methods, this book has several other objectives. One major objective is to explain techniques that can be applied by managers acting alone or with assistance from specialists in organizational behavior or human resources management. Two examples would be a career-development specialist or an organization-development specialist. Some of the techniques described, such as negotiating or crisis management, can be implemented by the individual without the assistance of a formal program sponsored by the organization.

Another objective is to offer a balanced presentation of the methods described, looking at both strengths and potential pitfalls. If a technique is considered of neutral or negative value, it is not included here. Still another objective is to provide readers an opportunity to enhance their managerial skills. One approach to this objective is to discuss managerial skill development at various places in the text. A second approach is to provide a skill-building exercise in each chapter. A third approach is to provide the reader with concrete guidelines for the effective use of the techniques described. We provide a Guidelines for Action and Skill Development section at the end of each chapter to keep the reader focused on skill development.

A final objective is to increase the self-awareness of the reader in relation to such key aspects of job behavior as work habits and time management, creativity, ethical conduct, career self-sabotage, negotiating skills, teamwork, and intrapreneuring. To accomplish this, self-examination quizzes are included as appendixes to appropriate chapters. These instruments can serve as launching points for personalized discussions about the technique under examination.

CHANGES IN THE FOURTH EDITION

The fourth edition has substantial changes in content, and it updates research evidence and opinion about the methods and techniques described in the book. Seven new chapters have been added and seven old ones deleted. Deleting certain chapters makes room for new, leading-edge techniques. By deleting a chapter, we are not implying the technique is no longer in use or has proved unreliable. About half the case illustrations from the 13 remaining chapters are new. The seven new chapters deal with overcoming and preventing career self-sabotage, developing ethical conduct, using influence tactics, improving customer service, employing fun and humor in the workplace, empowering employees, training for cultural diversity awareness, and balancing work and family demands.

Part I, Improving Individual Skills, describes four techniques individuals can use to improve personal productivity and enhance their careers. Part II, Improving Interpersonal Relationships, deals with four techniques, methods, and programs designed to overcome or prevent problems among people in organizations. Part III, Improving Work Group Skills, describes four methods designed to enhance both productivity and satisfaction.

Part IV, Improving Quality and Productivity at the Organizational Level, describes four methods for boosting productivity, enhancing innovation, and sometimes elevating job satisfaction and morale. Part V, Human Resources Management Skills: Improving Human Potential, describes four programs typically administered through the human resources department.

The five-part structure of this text helps the reader organize and conceptualize the information. However, several of the chapters could be logically placed in more than one part. For example, employee empowerment programs could be conveniently placed into Part IV or Part V.

ACKNOWLEDGMENTS

Producing a book of this nature is a team effort. Among the key contributors to this project were my sponsoring editor Kurt Strand and my project editor Stephanie Britt. Professor M. Ivancevich of the University of Houston receives my appreciation for presenting me with the basic concept for the first edition of this book. The outside reviewers for previous editions provided major suggestions for improving the structure and content of this book. In alphabetical order they are: M. K. Badaway, Virginia Polytechnic Institute; John D. Blair, Texas Tech University; Lawrence G. Brandon, The American Institute for Property & Liability Underwriters, Inc.; Angelo S. DeNisi, University of South Carolina; Bill Fannin, University of Houston; William G. Hahn, Savannah State College; Richard D. Hodgetts, Florida International University; Pamela A. Posey, University of Vermont; and Mary Van Sell, Oakland University.

The many professors, management development professionals, and students who had kind words about the three previous editions also receive my appreciation. Thanks also to the people close to me: Carol, Drew, Douglas, Melanie, Molly, Rosie, Tom, and Kristine.

Andrew J. DuBrin

Contents

Improving Individual Skills

The four chapters in this section concentrate on developing skills, techniques, and attitudes that can help the individual perform more effectively on the job. As a consequence, organizational performance is simultaneously improved. Frequently, these same skills, techniques, and attitudes can be applied to improving effectiveness in personal life. These four chapters provide insight into overcoming problems that face many managers and professionals. The four major problems covered here are low personal productivity, insufficient job creativity, poor crisis management, and career self-sabotage (or self-defeating behavior).

Chapter 1, Work Habits and Time Management, covers the always current topic of improving personal productivity. The goal of improving organizational productivity and quality can often be partially met by improving the work habits and time management of employees. Improvement of work habits and time management results in control of time and work. Such improvement often prevents stress caused by feeling overwhelmed.

Chapter 2, Improving Your Creativity, presents many do-it-yourself techniques for making better use of creative potential. A case description of how brainstorming works is included. The chapter concludes with an instrument for measuring creative potential.

Chapter 3, Crisis Management, presents information about one of the most demanding tasks facing managers—gaining control in a crisis. Crisis management has emerged as an important topic as organizations continue to deal with turbulent environments. Although crisis management might be regarded as a special case of problem solving, it warrants separate attention because of its consequences for organizational survival.

Chapter 4, Overcoming and Preventing Career Self-Sabotage, is a topic of major significance that has received only minor attention in the professional and trade literature. The premise for including this topic here is that many managers and professionals engage in self-defeating behavior (such as acting out faulty life scripts) that severely limits their careers.

Chapter One

Work Habits and Time Management

> To achieve his high-level goals, the executive described below developed finely tuned work habits and time management practices.

Mark H. McCormack walked into the room, and I sized him up. I knew right away I had never met anyone so organized. A picture of the well-organized executive began taking shape in my mind. Over the past 25 years, McCormack has built an empire, and he runs it with a personal touch. His International Management Group specializes in sports and entertainment around the world.

"Mark is so organized it is frightening," says Lodwrick M. Cook, chairman and chief executive officer (CEO) of Tichfield. "He sets standards all of us should emulate. He prepares as if he were an athlete and doesn't leave anything to chance."

The rudiments of McCormack's success system are the 3-by- 5-inch index cards he carries in his jacket and on which he writes meticulous notes. He copies these notes onto legal pads, which he divides down the middle, with "People to Call" on the left and "To Do" on the right. He dates the pages several months into the future, he says, "so when someone asks you to call next Wednesday at 10:30, go to the sheet for that day and put the name and number about one third of the way down on the left side of the sheet."

Another empire builder, Alexander the Great, said the secret of his many accomplishments was never putting off anything until tomorrow. Similarly,

McCormack says that if you get behind on your agenda, "don't eliminate any-thing—you'll just have to do it tomorrow. Pick up the pace a bit, and you'll catch up." McCormack stresses that you should write down everything you intend to do, then forget it until it turns up on your pad on the appropriate day and time.

Emperors in ages past lacked telephones and jet planes, which McCormack uses to an extraordinary degree. He logs 250,000 miles a year in the air. He keeps his 15 offices around the world hopping with his practice of "manage-ment by phoning around." McCormack says, "The well-timed phone call can be a great management tool, forcing people to act, to get answers they've been avoiding, or simply to learn they are not forgotten."

I've heard that genius lies in combining unlike elements in new ways. Mc-Cormack, a lawyer, combined the sports hero with the marketing needs of the modern corporation and created a new era in product endorsements. His list of 500 clients includes top athletes in every field from golf to windsurfing who en-dorse everything from perfume to tires. Other clients include the Olympics, Wimbledon, the Nobel Prize Committee, and the Pope, to name a few. [1]

STRATEGIES FOR PERSONAL PRODUCTIVITY

Why improve your work habits and time management? One major reason is to increase your personal productivity, as measured by the formula: Produc-tivity = Units of output / Units of input. If you achieve more good-quality out-put without additional input (such as more hours worked), your productivity increases. Good work habits and time management can also improve your pro-ductivity ratio by decreasing the amount of input you require to achieve the same output. For example, if you are just as productive, but now work 50 in-stead of 60 hours a week, your productivity ratio has increased.

Saving time is not the only justification for improving your work habits and time management. What really counts is what you do with the time saved. [2] The time can be invested back into your career for such things as creative problem solving. People with good work habits and time-management practices tend to be more successful in their careers than poorly organ-ized individuals.

Good work habits and time management are valuable for another impor-tant reason. Some of the time saved can be invested in your personal life. By be-coming better organized, you will enjoy your personal life more because you are not preoccupied with unfinished job assignments.

Our discussion of suggestions for improved personal productivity is di-vided into three major categories: productive attitudes and values, productive skills and techniques, and overcoming time wasters. Practicing these sugges-tions should lead to improved productivity as a manager or individual contrib-utor. [3] Readers with work experience will be familiar with many of these attitudes, skills, and techniques, and this discussion can serve as a reminder to put into practice familiar ideas. However, the reader should also be on the alert for the fresh ideas contained in this chapter.

Productive Attitudes and Values

Developing good work habits and time-management practices is often a matter of forming the right attitude toward your work and toward time. If, for example, you think your job is important and time is precious, you will be on your way toward developing good work habits. This section summarizes a group of attitudes, values, and beliefs that can help a person make good use of time and develop productive work habits.

Be Aware of the Dangers of Procrastination. Procrastination is the major way in which employees at all levels lose productivity. People procrastinate for many reasons. [4] One reason is that they perceive the task as unpleasant, such as conducting a performance appraisal with a problem employee. We procrastinate also when we perceive the job as overwhelming, such as preparing a strategic plan for the department. Procrastination also occurs when we fear the consequences of our actions. One possible negative consequence is a poor evaluation of your work and bad news is another. For example, if an executive thinks a budget analysis will reveal a deficit, he or she may delay preparing the report.

A deep-rooted reason for procrastination is self-defeating behavior. For instance, a person might have the chance to make a presentation to top management that could represent a major career boost. Yet the person delays preparing the report until top management loses interest or assigns the project to someone else. The person has thus worked against his or her own best interest. (Self-defeating behavior is described more fully in Chapter 4.)

Self-defeating behavior is related to another reason some people procrastinate—fear of success. The person who fears success will sometimes procrastinate to avoid taking on the added responsibilities brought by success. Self-defeating behavior in this instance may be a symptom of fear of success.

People frequently put off tasks that do not appear to offer a meaningful reward. Suppose you decide your computer files need a thorough updating, including deleting inactive files. Even if you know it should be done, having updated files might not be a particularly meaningful reward. Finally, people often procrastinate to rebel against being controlled. Rather than submit to authority, the person might say to himself or herself, "Nobody is going to tell me when I should get a report done. I'll do it when I'm good and ready."

Procrastination is a major hindrance to personal productivity. The following suggestions can help you deal with the problem. First, calculate the cost of procrastination. [5] For example, by not having a résumé prepared on time, a person may miss out on a high-paying job opportunity. The cost of procrastination includes the difference in salary between the job the person finds and the one really wanted. Another cost is the loss of potential job satisfaction.

Another way to overcome procrastination is to create momentum. A useful tactic is to find a leading task (an easy, warm-up activity) to perform. If you have to prepare a strategic plan, you can get momentum going by performing such tasks as getting a new file folder and reaching for a text dealing with the subject.

Breaking the task into manageable units can conquer procrastination caused by facing an overwhelming task. The problem is more acute when you face more than one of these elephants. A well-accepted principle in this situation is to "Eat the elephant one bite at a time." Break the project down into logical parts and begin with a few simple parts of the project. For example, a manager in charge of an office relocation might begin by scheduling an interview with a commercial real estate broker.

Settling for less than perfection can also reduce procrastination. Striving for perfection can block completion of a project. You can also fight procrastination by rewarding yourself for your progress in not postponing the activity. If you schedule the performance appraisal with the problem employee, treat yourself to a new sweater or pair of athletic shoes. Making a commitment to other people that you will accomplish something by a certain date may help you curb procrastination. If you miss the deadline, you are likely to experience embarrassment or guilt.

For those who enjoy *psychotechnology*, subliminal messages can be used to help overcome procrastination. *MindSet* software flashes positive reinforcing messages across the menu bar on your computer. [6] You can adjust the frequency and duration of the suggestions. The message can flash by subliminally (below the level of conscious awareness) or remain on the screen for a few seconds. The procrastination message is: "My goals are obtainable. I am confident in my abilities. I make and keep deadlines."

Finally, procrastination can sometimes be overcome by counterattacking the problem task. Forcing yourself to do something overwhelming, frightening, or uncomfortable helps to prove that the task was not as bad as initially perceived. [7] Assume you presented a budget proposal that was rejected and sternly criticized by management. You must resubmit your budget, but first you want to express your disagreement about the criticisms to your boss. Set up a time to call your manager and schedule an appointment. Force yourself to show up for the budget discussion appointment. After you break the ice with a statement such as, "I have strong reservations about your perception of the budget I submitted," the task will be much easier.

Avoid Attempting Too Much.   Many managers and professionals become disorganized and fall behind schedule because they assume more responsibility than they can handle. Especially significant is when the beleaguered person has voluntarily attempted to handle too much. An executive already loaded with responsibility, for example, might accept an invitation to join yet another board of directors or another community activity. His or her work schedule becomes all the more cramped, and the list of unfinished tasks mounts.

To avoid attempting too much, you must learn to say no to additional demands on your time. You cannot take care of your own priorities unless you learn to tactfully decline requests from other people that interfere with your work. If your boss interrupts your work with an added assignment, point out how the new task will conflict with higher-priority ones and suggest alternatives. When your boss recognizes that you are motivated to get your major tasks accomplished and not to avoid work, you will have a good chance of avoiding unproductive assignments.

A word of caution: Do not turn down your boss too frequently. Much discretion and tact is needed in using this approach to improving personal productivity. Knowing *when* to say no is very important.

Avoid Workaholism. An extension of attempting too much is the problem of workaholism. True workaholics are not simply people who work long and hard to achieve important organizational and personal goals. Instead, workaholics are addicted to work to the point that nonwork activities yield no pleasure. Workaholic behaviors include the inability to delegate work or to complete a project. Workaholics overschedule time, can work any place or any time, and use work as the primary source of satisfaction in life. [8]

Workaholism interferes with productivity in several ways. Workaholics are often perfectionists who cannot get projects completed on time because it is difficult for them to believe anything is ever finished. Also, people who take very little time off from work may be less productive than employees who do not work on weekends and during vacations. In extreme situations, workaholics fall victim to heart disease or death. Many Japanese managers in recent years have fallen victim to death from overwork, or *karoshi*.

Thomas R. Horton's career included positions as the CEO of the American Management Association and as an IBM executive. He presents this personal analysis of the pitfalls of attempting too much and avoiding rest and relaxation:

> At one time in my career at IBM, I became so committed to succeeding that 14-hour days and 7-day weeks became my regular schedule. I was not really a workaholic (so I kept telling myself). It was just that the job demands required this dedication. As I dug myself deeper and deeper into the rut I had created, I finally realized how stale I had become. Lacking perspective, I simply plowed ahead, my efforts on the job becoming less and less effective.
>
> When I faced the fact that I was mismanaging my time and my life, I forced myself to break away and devote some time to my family and myself. Not surprisingly, this made me more productive on and off the job. [9]

Although work addiction can lower productivity, some workaholics find so much pleasure in their jobs that work becomes a form of relaxation. One observer notes that people can work themselves to death only when they are working laboriously and without excitement. [10]

Appreciate the Value of Your Time.   People who place a high value on their time are propelled into making good use of time. If people believe their time is valuable, it will be difficult to engage them in idle conversation during working hours. The value of one's time can be calculated in several ways. The most straightforward method is to divide your income for a unit of time by the number of hours in that unit. A professional earning $50,000 per year therefore earns about $25 per hour.

A more accurate estimate of the value of your time is to include the contribution productive work might make to your future earnings. If the person who is earning $25 per hour is highly productive, he or she may be earning "promotion credits" that could double his or her income in the near future. The value of that person's time therefore approaches $50 per hour.

Value Cleanliness and Orderliness.   An orderly desk, file cabinet, computer file, or attaché case does not inevitably indicate an orderly mind. Yet it does help most people become more productive. Less time is wasted and less energy is expended if you do not have to hunt for information you thought you had on hand. Knowing where information is and what information you have available is a way of being in control of your job. When your job gets out of control, you are probably working at less than peak efficiency.

Become Self-Employed Psychologically.   A distinguishing characteristic of many self-employed people is that they care deeply about what they accomplish each day. [11] Most of their job activities directly or indirectly affect their financial status. Additionally, many self-employed people enjoy high job satisfaction because they have chosen work that fits their interests. Because of the factors just mentioned, the self-employed person is compelled to make good use of time. Also, the high level of job satisfaction typical of many self-employed people leads them to enjoy being productive.

If a person working for an employer regards his or her area of responsibility as self-employment, productivity may increase. To help regard employment by others as self-employment, keep this thought in mind. Every employee is given some assets to manage to achieve a good return on investment. Assume you are managing a distribution center for your company. You would be expected to manage that asset so that it is profitable.

Appreciate the Importance of Paperwork and Electronic Work.
Office automation has increased the amount of printed and electronic information to be handled. Even routine information requires efficient handling for you to remain productive and to avoid slowing down others. Correspondence has to be sorted and answered; faxes require responses (unless they are

unsolicited menus from delicatessens); expense reports must be filed; and internal questionnaires must be answered.

Unless paperwork and electronic work is efficiently attended to, a person's job may get out of control and lead to stress. Ideally, a small amount of time should be invested in paperwork and electronic work each day. Some productive people spend an occasional few hours on weekends sorting through paperwork to unclutter their offices. Nonprime time (when you are at less than your peak of efficiency, but not overfatigued) is the best time to handle routine work. Save prime time for the creative aspects of your job.

Challenge Your Use of Time.   A major tool for improving productivity is to ask, "What is the best use of my time right now?"[12] This question helps you justify every action. A particularly good time to ask this question is when you have been interrupted by a visitor or phone call. When it's over, check whether you should go back to what you were doing or go on to something new.

Your answer to the best-use-of-time question may be different even in comparable situations. One day you are waiting for an elevator in your office building. You ask, "What is the best possible use of my time right now?" Your answer is, "Certainly not waiting for an elevator. I'll jog up the stairs and get some exercise."

One week later you are again waiting for the elevator. You ask the same question. This time your answer is, "Waiting for the elevator is a good use of my time right now. It's about time I interacted with a few employees from different departments."

Productive Skills and Techniques

In addition to developing the right attitudes, values, and beliefs, you also need the right skills and techniques to become productive. Below is a summary of the skills and techniques that willl help you work smarter, not harder.

Clarify Your Objectives.   Knowing what you want to accomplish—having specific goals—can improve your use of time. For example, students with specific occupational goals often make better use of time than other students. Knowing what your boss thinks you should be accomplishing is also important. It helps prevent you from ignoring activities your boss thinks are important, thus making you appear unproductive. A careful review of your job description and objectives with your boss is of fundamental importance.

Build in Quiet Time for Planning.   An essential first step in personal productivity improvement is to find uninterrupted time to plan your work and devise tactics for improving your work methods. For some people who work in busy offices, this quiet time is best found at home or while commuting. Others have the luxury of informing others that they are not to be interrupted during planning time. Quiet time is frequently used for making up a To Do list, which is essentially short-range planning.

Ernest C. Huge contends that every worker, from the CEO on down, should invest at least 5 percent of work time pondering how to work better.[13] Established routines should be challenged and new approaches formulated. During one such planning session, a marketing manager for laptop computers decided on a new way of boosting sales. Any company employee who referred a person who actually bought a laptop would receive a $50 bonus. Sales of laptop computers increased 9 percent the next year.

Prepare a To Do List.   Few people are so innately well organized that they can make good use of time without preparing a list of activities that need doing. You will recall that Mark McCormack, similar to many other busy people, uses 3-by-5 index cards to establish his To Do list. Many people make their lists on a combined desk calendar and planner. These planners are orderly systems of allocating your time among various activities. Some planners suggest apportioning your time into 30-minute or one-hour chunks. In addition to time allocations, such planners keep records for luncheon engagements, expense account items, and important dates. Figure 1 presents two pages from a representative planner.

Assign an A, B, or C rating to each item on the list. Items with an A rating have the higher value; B items have medium value; and C items have the lowest value. Taking care of a few C items first can be a morale booster because it feels as if progress is being made. Many people describe a therapeutic feeling when they knock off a few C items from a formidable To Do list. See Skill-Building Exercise 1 to get started assigning priorities to your activities.

The To Do list has been extended into elaborate variations. A variation developed by time-management consultant Jeffrey Mayer is the master list. Instead of rewriting a list every day and attempting to establish priorities, the master list is ongoing. You note all your work to be performed on a lined sheet of paper. As you accomplish each task, you cross it off. When the sheet is full, transfer the old items to the next page and add new items. The master list resembles the directory on a computer disk. It becomes your primary document for indicating the work that needs to be performed.[14]

A popular extension of the To Do list is the Franklin Planner, a way of integrating life planning with daily tasks. To use the Franklin Planner, you must first attend a workshop offered by the developers of the planner. Participants in the session draft mission statements for their lives. Daily tasks are then tied to long- and intermediate-range goals. For example, the To Do list item "schedule career development review with boss" might be tied to the long-range goal of becoming a vice president.

AMA

39
Week

Meeting,
Appointments, Projects,
and Tasks

Plans get you into things but you got to work your way out.

—Will Rogers

Thursday 27
Annual Membership Meeting
New York Headquarters

Friday 28

Saturday 29
Yom Kippur

Sunday 30
3rd Quarter Ends

Be careful not to become too attached to a plan. It is sometimes easy to forget that the plan is not reality. Rather it is a combination of best educated guess and best wish. Having it before us, however, is seductive because it's concrete while the future is abstract. Reality has a way of humbling us, though. Try to defend the plan when reality signals the need for change. Though some people have attempted to fit reality to plan, it is usually an exercise in futility. Be flexible and remain ready to moderate plans when change is required.

**Monday September 24
thru
Sunday, September 30**

September	October	November
M T W T F S S	M T W T F S S	M T W T F S S
3 4 5 6 7 8 9	1 2 3 4 5 6 7	1 2 3 4
10 11 12 13 14 15 16	8 9 10 11 12 13 14	5 6 7 8 9 10 11
17 18 19 20 21 22 23	15 16 17 18 19 20 21	12 13 14 15 16 17 18
24 25 26 27 28 29 30	22 23 24 25 26 27 28	19 20 21 22 23 24 25
	29 30 31	26 27 28 29 30

Meeting,
Appointments, Projects,
and Tasks

Monday 24
Upcoming This Week

Reports/Tasks Due:

Tasks To Be Delegated:

Personnel/Projects To Follow:

Tasks Carried Forward:

Tuesday 25

Wednesday 26

SKILL-BUILDING EXERCISE 1
The To Do List

Here is an opportunity to organize your current activities for work, school, and personal life, or a combination of the three. In column 1, list all the tasks to be accomplished in the next 30 days. In column 2, assign the activity an A, B, or C rating in terms of importance (value). In column 3, establish a deadline or due date for each item. In column 4, describe in a few words the action to be taken. As you complete each item, indicate the date in column 5. If the system helps you organize your efforts, prepare a new list 30 days from now. People facing many tasks to be accomplished in a short period may choose to make a 7-day or 15-day list.

	(1) Item or Task	(2) A, B, or C Priority	(3) Dead- line	(4) Action to Be Taken	(5) Follow Up
1.					
2.					
3.					
4.					
5.					
6.					
7.					
8.					
9.					
10.					

Schedule Activities Carefully.   Use of a To Do list and a desk planner enables a person to schedule activities in a productive manner. Four other important scheduling suggestions are described next:

1. *Allow time for emergencies.* Because many managerial and professional jobs require handling emergencies, slack has to be built into a schedule for handling these unpredictable problems. The careful scheduler creates room for unscheduled events. Similarly, a household budget must allow enough room for the inevitable miscellaneous category.

2. *Schedule similar tasks together.* To accomplish small tasks efficiently, group them together and perform them in one block of time. To illustrate, you might make most of your telephone calls in relation to your job from 11 to 11:30 each workday morning. Or you might reserve the first hour of every workday for correspondence. When you visit down-

town, think of all your errands that can best be done downtown. Over a period of time, you save a number of wasted trips.

By using this method, you develop the necessary pace and mind-set to knock off chores in short order. In contrast, when you flit from one type of task to another, your efficiency may suffer.

3. *Schedule yourself by computer.* Software is available that enables a personal computer to be used as an electronic calendar to help keep track of appointments and To Do items. The first step in implementing these programs would be to enter into the computer's memory your appointments, tasks, and errands. For instance, a person might use these items as input:

April 2   Meet with Brady to discuss budget.

April 17   Get strategic plan for department started.

May 3   Lunch with Rachel to discuss cultural diversity program implementation.

May 18   Make request for new office furniture.

From this point forward, the computer's information-processing capabilities could be tapped. Suppose you couldn't remember the date of your lunch with Rachel. You would command the computer to "Find lunch date with Rachel." Or, if you were an extremely busy person, you might ask the computer to tell you when you had the next opening for lunch. This type of software can also flag key appointments and tasks. An indicator such as **URGENT** might be used. Several of these programs have an alarm-clock feature to alert you when it is time to take a certain action.

4. *Set time limits for certain tasks.* Another important aspect of scheduling is to decide how much time to allot for each item on your list. As managers and professionals become more experienced with certain projects, they can more accurately estimate how long a project will take to complete. A department head might say, for example, "Getting this cause-and-effect diagram ready to show to my boss should take seven hours." A good time-management practice is to estimate how long a job should take and then proceed with a strong determination to get that job completed within the time estimate.

A productive variation of this technique is to decide that some low- and medium-priority items are only worth so much of your time. Invest that much time in a project, but no more. Preparing a file on advertisements and announcements that cross your desk is one example.

Work at a Steady Pace.   In most jobs, working at a steady pace pays dividends in efficiency. The sprint worker creates many problems for superiors, co-workers, and team members. With the steady-pace approach, you accomplish much more than someone who puts out extra effort just once in a while. Trying to catch up for lost time may result in a high error rate even in managerial work.

In the steady-pace approach, you strive for a constant expenditure of energy every working day. (As one person describes this strategy, "Every day is Monday.") Part of working at a steady pace is to begin the day strong and continue with this reasonable pace. The "I'm not a morning person" attitude soon disappears under the discipline of the steady-pace approach.

The payoff from working at a steady pace is that you develop a precious supply of bonus time that you can use for planning and thinking creatively about your job. If you find yourself with an afternoon of discretionary time, you can figure out ways of doing your job more effectively. Such improvements should ultimately enhance your reputation wherever you work. Despite the advantages of maintaining a steady pace, some peaks and valleys in your work may be inevitable. The seasonal demands of public accounting firms are a prime example.

Concentrate on High-Output Tasks.   To become more effective in your job, you have to concentrate on tasks where superior performance could have a big payoff for the organization. This is the familiar distinction between breakthrough versus routine or trivial tasks, or the Pareto principle. This principle (also referred to as the 80–20 principle) states that 80 percent of the results of most transactions derive from 20 percent of the activity. If you work on the right 20 percent of your job, you will achieve bigger results.

In following the A-B-C system, you should devote ample time to the A items. You should not pay more attention than necessary to the C items. However, if you find that working on C items reduces tension, proceed. Recognize, however, that you must return to A items as soon as you feel relaxed. When working on high-output items is suggested, many managers respond, "I don't think that concentrating on important tasks applies to me. My job is so filled with routine. I have no chance to work on breakthrough ideas." True, most jobs are filled with routine requirements, but a person can spend some time—even one hour per week—concentrating on tasks that may prove to have high output.

Concentrate on One Task at a Time.   Whether you are performing a high-output or low-output task at the moment, it is best to concentrate on one task at a time. Effective executives have a well-developed capacity to concentrate on the problem or person facing them, however swamped with obligations they are. Intense concentration leads to crisper judgment and analysis. It also minimizes major errors. The thousands of fingers lost each year by the owners of home power tools attest to this! Concentration also helps reduce absentmindedness. If you concentrate intensely on what you are doing, you decrease the chance of forgetting what you intended to do.

Stand Instead of Sit for Certain Tasks.   Merrill E. Douglass says that standing rather than sitting is an overlooked secret for getting more done during working hours. People tend to take longer to accomplish things when they sit down. If forced to stand, they will answer you more quickly rather than become engaged in long conversation. Because of this, many managers schedule stand-up meetings when an agenda is not too long or complicated. Also, some companies have experimented successfully with stand-up conference tables. [15]

Standing is perceived by most people as more formal than sitting. Because people tend to respect time more in formal than informal settings, they make better use of standing time. Also, they waste less time than when slouched in chairs. People also get things done more quickly while standing because they find it less comfortable than sitting. To avoid personal discomfort, they get to the point quickly.

Delegate when Feasible.   A manager who does too many tasks alone eventually becomes overwhelmed and less productive. A sounder approach is to delegate work that can be properly handled by a team member. To delegate effectively, it is necessary to have competent and willing subordinates. Even under such conditions, it is important to exercise some control on work that is delegated. If the team members do not produce results, *you* are still responsible.

Delegation boosts productivity in another important way. Charles D. Pringle observes that managers who delegate wisely have higher-performing team members, and hence more effective departments, than do poor delegators. In turn, this leads to a personal benefit for the manager because managers of successful departments are more likely to be promoted. [16]

Overcoming Time Wasters

Another basic thrust to improved work habits and time management is to minimize the waste of time. Many of the techniques already described in this chapter help save time. The tactics and strategies described below, however, are directly aimed at overcoming wasted time.

Use a Time Log and Track Time Wasters.   An advanced tool for managing time efficiently is to prepare a time log of how you are currently investing time. For five full workdays, write down everything you do, including such activities as answering mail and taking rest breaks. An activity calendar is ideally suited to preparing a time log. One of the most important outputs of a time log is uncovering *time leaks*. A time leak is anything you are doing or not doing that allows time to get away from you, such as stopping your work 15 minutes before you leave the office.

Another important output from a time log is to uncover bits of time being squandered. For example, while waiting for an elevator, you might be able to read a 100-word report. And if you have finished your day's work 10 minutes before quitting time, you can use that 10 minutes to clean out a desk drawer. By the end of the year, your productivity will have increased much more than if you had squandered these small bits of time.

Deal with Distracting Problems.   When you are preoccupied with a personal or work problem, it is difficult to concentrate. Poor concentration, in turn, wastes time because little is accomplished when you are daydreaming. The solution is to address the problem so its impact is minimized. Suppose a person is so far in debt there is no room for the unanticipated expenses that seem to arise every month. As dire as the solution seems, it might be to that person's advantage to obtain a debt-consolidation loan. The monthly payment might be low enough to allow breathing room. Once the consolidation load is paid off, that person might choose never to incur debt again, thus contributing to long-term peace of mind.

Sometimes a relatively minor problem such as being long overdue for a dental checkup can impair work concentration. At other times, a major problem such as a child-custody dispute between divorcing parents interferes with work. In either situation, your concentration will suffer until you take appropriate action.

Keep Track of Important Names, Places, and Things.   How   much time have you wasted lately searching for such items as the name of an important supplier, your keys, or an appointment book? A manager suddenly realized he had forgotten to show up for a luncheon appointment. He wanted to call and apologize but was unable to locate the person's name and phone number! Standard solutions to overcoming these problems are to keep a Rolodex (or competitive brand) file of people's names and companies. It is difficult to misplace such a file. Many other managers and professionals store such information in a data base program or in a word-processing file. Such files are more difficult to misplace than a pocket directory.

Two practical suggestions have been offered for remembering where you put things. [17] First, have a "parking" place for everything. This means putting your keys and appointment book back in the same place after each use. Second, make visual associations. To have something register in your mind at the moment you are doing it, make up a visual association about that act. Thus, you might say, "Here I am putting my budgeting proposal in the back section of my attaché case."

Use the Telephone Efficiently.   Much business today is conducted over the telephone, including both internal and external calls. Using the telephone efficiently can save substantial time. Many callers are slow to get to their point. A good way to handle this problem is to take the initiative by asking, "How can I help you?" or "What can I do for you?" Such an approach decreases the chances that the caller will engage in small talk. Long-distance callers, for example, particularly enjoy comparing their weather to the receiver's weather.

Telephones can also be used to prevent wasted time. A telephone call often can save a trip because the business can be transacted over the phone. Teleconferencing, a combination of telephones and videos, can cut back substantially on travel time. People in two or more geographic locations gather at local teleconferencing centers to conduct an almost-live meeting among all of them.

Telephone tag is a potential time waster and must be dealt with effectively. The tag problem occurs when you call a person who is not there; he or she calls back and you are not there; you call back and he or she is not there; and the process continues for several days. To combat the problem, ask people you call frequently the best time to reach them by telephone. If you reach a person's assistant or an answering machine, leave enough information so you might not have to call back.

If it is important to talk to the person you do not reach, inquire as to the best time to reach that person. Although it seems impersonal, leaving messages on each other's answering machine can complete many transactions. Another way to avoid the time waste associated with telephone tag is to use electronic mail or fax machines. [18]

Minimize Nonessential Socializing.   A modicum of pure socializing in the office is helpful for networking, relieving tension, and increasing job satisfaction. Nevertheless, socializing is a major time leak. Excessively long lunch hours are part of nonessential socializing. Many workers readily drift into purely social conversations during working hours, sometimes to fill the void of not having adequate companionship off the job.

To protect your privacy from small-talkers in the office, simply say: "I'm sorry, but I'm busy and can't be disturbed. I will get back to you later." If you are concerned that others will take this personally or consider you to be antisocial, you can take another step. Compensate by going out of your way to be friendly with these people at other times.

Avoid Being a Computer Goof-Off.   An unproductive use of computers is to tinker with them to the exclusion of more important work. Many people have become intrigued with computers to the point of diversion. They habitually create new reports, use exquisite graphics, and even play computer games on company time. Some managers become so involved with computers they neglect leadership responsibilities, thus lowering their productivity. In short, avoid wasting time by becoming a computer goof-off.

Be Aware of Diminishing Returns.   Staying on a project beyond the point at which you remain productive wastes time. Knowing when to stop a project is as important as knowing when to start.[19] If you can concentrate on developing a quality-improvement plan for only three hours, stop at that point. If it is not the end of your workday, move on to a less tedious task.

As you acquire more skill on a difficult task, you are likely to find you can work productively on the same tasks for longer periods. Thus, the point of diminishing returns takes longer to reach. This occurs because as people become more skilled in performing a task, they become less tense and more relaxed. Working under moderate tension, in turn, leads to fewer errors than working under high tension.

Be Decisive and Finish Things. Much time is wasted by managers who vacillate too long before choosing among alternative solutions to a problem. Indecisiveness sometimes stems from low self-confidence and thus cannot be overcome until the person becomes more confident. Indecisiveness can also stem from a penchant for overanalyzing problems. The productive individual will invest a reasonable amount of time in weighing alternatives, but then will make a decision.

A useful technique for finishing things is to maintain a follow-up file to monitor your own work and that of others.[20] Set future checkpoints in your daily planner. Suppose you have decided on a plan to investigate why certain customers have never returned to your firm. Specify how much of the project should be accomplished by different dates. in the future. If progress is behind schedule, take remedial action. A follow-up system reduces wasted time because it helps bring projects to completion. Partially completed projects do little good for you or the organization.

The Case for Good Work Habits and Time Management

Common sense and experience suggest much can be gained by improving your approach to work along the lines suggested in this chapter. Good work habits, including time management, may be as important as high intelligence and appropriate personality characteristics in bringing about career success. If you are in charge of issuing payroll checks, your employees will be more concerned about your timeliness than your charisma.

Another important reason for improving your work habits is that they contribute to your life in many ways. Good work habits can improve job performance, personal life, and mental health. A person who performs efficiently and effectively on the job has more time (and often more money) for personal life. Simultaneously, he or she escapes the stress stemming from a constant feeling of being behind at work.

Good work habits are also important because, to a large extent, they underlie the basic management functions of planning and controlling. Planning involves setting priorities, and controlling includes following up on progress toward achieving goals. Most importantly, good work habits and time management contribute organizational productivity.

The Case against Using These Methods to Improve Productivity

Almost no experienced manager or professional would say poor work habits and time management are keys to success. Yet the converse is not always true. Many successful people do not appear particularly well organized. Successful executives often behave impulsively, responding to the demand of the moment. Frequent interruptions characterize their work.

Another fundamental argument against placing too much emphasis on good work habits is that they reflect underlying personality characteristics. As such, they are difficult to change. For instance, if you are a compulsive personality (tidy or highly concerned about details), your natural inclination will be toward good work habits. If you are not compulsive, trying to behave compulsively may not be worth the effort. Also, people who are basically patient have an easier time developing good work habits than do impatient people.

Another important issue is whether the attitudes, methods, and techniques described here actually contribute to personal productivity. Some critics of this approach believe people who take time-management techniques too seriously become rigid and obsessed with making optimum use of time. In their quest for personal efficiency, they drive themselves into a stress disorder. (Note that rest and relaxation is an important time-management technique.)

Critics of popular approaches to the improvement of work habits and time management also note that these techniques do not work for everybody. Each person has to discover what works best for himself or herself. John Kotter reports that the best executives do not necessarily map out their daily schedules in advance. Instead, they react to events as they occur. [21]

While these criticisms of approaches to improve your work habits and time management may have merit, almost any manager or professional would become more productive by practicing some of the suggestions made in this chapter.

Guidelines for Action and Skill Development

As you embark on a program of improved personal productivity, guard against becoming an annoyance to everybody else; try not to convert everybody. If you become too concerned about squandering time and inefficiency, you might irritate more than motivate others. The goal of these suggestions is to improve your productivity but still retain flexibility in your work and compassion for people.

(continued)

To start improving your work habits, select the aspect of work where you are hurting the most. Next, choose an appropriate remedial technique. A good starting point for most people is to clarify their objectives or to develop a To Do list.

Practice faithfully and patiently whichever work habits and time-management approaches you select. Poor work habits and time management usually develop over years and therefore require at least several months to change. Once you have mastered one new habit or habits, proceed to another technique appropriate to your situation.

DISCUSSION QUESTIONS AND ACTIVITIES

1. Describe a work problem you have observed that was caused by procrastination.

2. How would you rate the efficiency of Mark McCormack (see the opening example) in using the telephone?

3. Some highly productive scientists and college professors work in offices that appear chaotic. How does this reconcile with statements made in this chapter about valuing orderliness and cleanliness?

4. What impact has office automation had on people's ability to keep up with paperwork?

5. In what types of work will good work habits and time management most likely lead directly to increased earnings for individuals?

6. One executive tells team members, "I want you to make as good use of time in the office as you would playing a timed sport such as basketball or football." What do you think of the validity of the analogy?

7. Some tidy, perfectionistic people never become highly successful from a career standpoint. What time-management strategy are they probably neglecting?

8. What is your reaction to the statement: "A clear and orderly desk reflects a clear and orderly mind"?

9. Interview a person you know to be highly productive. Investigate which of the time-management approaches and work habits presented in this chapter he or she uses regularly.

NOTES

1. Scott De Garmo, "The Organized Executive," *Success*, December 1986, p. 4. Excerpted and adapted with permission.
2. Alec Mackenzie, *The Time Trap* (New York: AMACOM, 1990), p. 25.

3. Strategies and tactics for improving work habits and time management are similar from source to source. Where credit to one particular source is deserved, it will be indicated by a footnote.

4. Theodore Kurtz, "Ten Reasons Why People Procrastinate," *Supervisory Management*, April 1990, pp. 1–2; and "When to Procrastinate and When to Get Going," *Working Smart*, March 1992, pp. 1–2.

5. Alan Lakein, *How to Gain Control of Your Time and Your Life* (New York: Peter Wyden, 1973), pp. 141–51.

6. Michael Maren, "Program Yourself: Software for the Right Side of Your Brain," *Success*, October 1991, p. 58. Software produced by Visionary Software, Portland, Oregon.

7. "Don't Procrastinate," *Practical Supervision*, January 1989, p. 3.

8. Ruth Haas, "Workaholics: Good News—Bad News," *Human Resources Forum*, July 1990, pp. 1–3; John W. Hodge, "Workaholic Organizations May Not Work," *HRMagazine*, March 1991, pp. 6–8.

9. Thomas R. Horton, "How Dedicated Must You Be?" *Success*, March 1987 p. 16.

10. "Confessions of a Happy Workaholic," *Success*, June 1983, p. 8.

11. Raymond P. Rood and Brenda L. Meneley, "Serious Play at Work," *Personnel Journal*, January 1991, p. 90.

12. Lakein, *How to Gain Control of Your Time and Your Life*, p. 99.

13. Quoted in Mark B. Roman, "Ultimate Output," *Success*, June 1989, p. 55.

14. Jeffrey J. Mayer, "When You Waste Time, You're Wasting Money," *Management Review*, May 1991, p. 42.

15. Merrill E. Douglass, "Standing Saves Time," *Executive Forum*, July 1989, p. 4.

16. Charles D. Pringle, "Seven Reasons Why Managers Don't Delegate," *Management Solutions*, November 1986, p. 30.

17. Peter A. Turla and Kathleen L. Hawkins, "Remembering to Remember," *Success*, May 1983, p. 60.

18. Merrill Douglass, "How to Avoid Telephone Tag," *Executive Management Forum*, February 1990, p. 4.

19. Stephanie Winston, *Getting Organized* (New York: Warner Books, 1979), p. 40.

20. Mackenzie, *The Time Trap*, p. 175.

21. Cited in "Time Management Techniques—A Rundown," *Personal Report for the Executive*, August 1, 1987, p. 4.

SOME ADDITIONAL REFERENCES

Bittel, Lester R. *Right On Time*. New York: McGraw-Hill, 1990.

Douglass, Merrill. "The Oats Formula: How to Better Plan Your Time." *Supervisory Management*, February 1990, pp. 10–11.

Fassel, Diane. *Working Ourselves to Death: The High Cost of Workaholism and the Rewards of Recovery*. San Francisco: Harper, 1990.

Fram, Eugene H. "Time Pressed Consumer." *Marketing Insights*, Summer 1991, pp. 34–39.

James, Dennis. "Simplify Your Life: Put First Things First." *Success*, September 1992, p. 48.

McCormack, Mark H. *The 110% Solution: Using Good Old American Know-How to Manage Your Time, Talent and Ideas*. New York: Villard Books, 1991.

McGee-Cooper, Ann, with Duana Trammell and Barbara Lau. *You Don't Have to Go Home from Work Exhausted*. New York: Bowen & Rogers, 1990.

Seiwert, Lothar J. *Time Is Money: Save It*. Homewood, Ill: Dow Jones-Irwin, 1989.

Stiasen, Sarah. "Making Time: How Tracking the Hours Yields Hidden Benefits." *Success*, April 1990, p. 198.

Appendix to Chapter One

IMPROVING YOUR WORK HABITS AND TIME MANAGEMENT

Casually reading this chapter will probably not lead to improvements in your personal productivity. You need to back up these ideas with a specific action plan for improvement. The checklist presented below will help achieve this end. It covers the attitudes, strategies, techniques, and tactics described in this chapter. Select the six areas in which you need the most help. For each item you select, write a one- or two-sentence action plan. Suppose you checked "Concentrate on high-output tasks." Your action plan might take this form:

> I tend to put too much effort into performing tasks well that do not have a big payoff. I'm going to review carefully my job and figure out which tasks could really have a big payoff. Then I will put more effort into tasks with a potential for a big breakthrough.

WORK HABITS AND TIME-MANAGEMENT CHECKLIST

Productive Attitudes and Values
1. Be aware of the dangers of procrastination.
2. Avoid attempting too much. _____
3. Avoid workaholism. _____
4. Appreciate the value of your time. _____
5. Value cleanliness and orderliness. _____
6. Become self-employed psychologically. _____
7. Appreciate the importance of paperwork and electronic work. _____
8. Challenge your use of time.

Productive Skills and Techniques
1. Clarify your objectives. _____
2. Build in quiet time for planning. _____

3. Prepare a To Do list. _____
4. Schedule activities carefully. _____
   a. Allow time for emergencies. _____
   b. Schedule similar tasks together. _____
   c. Schedule yourself by computer. _____
   d. Set time limits for certain tasks. _____
5. Work at a steady pace. _____
6. Concentrate on high-output tasks. _____
7. Concentrate on one task at a time. _____
8. Stand in place of sit for certain tasks. _____
9. Delegate when feasible. _____

Overcoming Time Wasters
1. Use a time log and track time wasters. _____
2. Deal with distracting problems. _____
3. Keep track of important names, places, and things. _____
4. Use the telephone efficiently. _____
5. Minimize nonessential socializing. _____
6. Avoid being a computer goof-off. _____
7. Be aware of diminishing returns. _____
8. Be decisive and finish things. _____

Chapter Two

Improving Your Creativity

To carry out the vision of a practical indoor golf course, two brothers had to make a golf simulator more realistic. Their persistence in finding a creative solution to their problem led to a successful business.

You gaze into the distance at the first green of the famous Pebble Beach golf course near San Jose, California, cradling your favorite driver. Smiling, you remind yourself that you are playing a golf course generally reserved for wealthy people and golf pros. You wind up gracefully and watch the ball soar 300 yards and bounce onto the fairway. You are impressed by your strength and precision. What a wonderful way to spend an afternoon.

The hitch is that you are not really at Pebble Beach. You're in your own basement. The course, the greens, and the sand traps are all part of a pleasant, satisfying illusion. The illusion is so satisfying that the two brothers who invented this realistic video golf simulator expect to sell 400 devices this year at $28,000 each.

That's $11.2 million in sales. Dan and Don Wilson of Optronics, Ltd., in Salt Lake City, have turned this fantasy into a highly profitable business. The Wilson brothers have accomplished this success through vision, constant innovation, and incredible persistence.

The Wilsons' *Par T Golf Simulator* allows one to drive a real golf ball into a 9-by-12-foot projection of any of seven world-famous golf courses. After your ball strikes the projection screen made of tough nylon, it slides to the floor. The simulator instantly plots where your ball *would* have gone. Through an accurate simulation, you are transported to where the ball would have landed, and you set up your next shot.

The idea for the *Par T* was born in 1975, when the Wilsons' father observed that golf was growing, yet indoor golf was not available. Indoor driving ranges had been operating for many years, but they did not simulate a golf course. Imaging technology was not yet developed.

When their father died in 1980, the Wilsons decided to act on their father's vision. While still in their twenties, the Wilsons poured energy into making a crude golf simulator more realistic. They read every article they could find on sports simulation. Don recalls that they would call universities and ask, "Are you working on anything that might help us?" The brothers dreamed about their invention at night, scrawling ideas to show engineers the next day.

Finally, in 1985, the Wilsons learned of an advanced microchip used in fax machines, video cameras, and certain missiles. The chip, called a CCD (charge coupled device), was a light sensor for detecting motion. A sudden thought hit the Wilson brothers. If you hit your ball past lines of CCD chips, you could map its motion precisely enough to "see" the course from the point of view of the ball.

The CCD chip made possible ball flight and imaging of golf courses that were strikingly realistic. By 1986, the company went into the black. Don Wilson reports that on cruise ships, *Par T Golf Simulators* are booked virtually around the clock. The product is continually improved to allow for golf variations, such as best ball.

Proving Thomas Edison's adage about invention once again, Don says, "It doesn't seem we can do anything by accident. We always have to work at everything we do." [1]

THE IMPORTANCE OF CREATIVITY IN BUSINESS

The Wilson brothers hit on a creative idea in part because they relentlessly pursued one. They also immersed themselves in their business and kept an open mind about possible solutions to their problem. The CCD chip represented a solution to their problem. Both creativity and innovation were involved in bringing the golf simulator to market. As used here, *creativity* is the generation of a novel and useful idea, while *innovation* is the implementation of that idea. [2] Many of today's writers, however, include innovation in their definition of creativity.

Creativity and innovation are important in business for such diverse purposes as developing new products, improving quality, reducing costs, and conserving the environment. The quest for creative thinking is so widespread that one fourth of all organizations that employ more than 100 people offer creativity training. [3] Most of these programs are based on the techniques presented in this chapter.

Creativity is not the province only of the inventor, product development specialist, or advertising copywriter. Managerial work also requires creativity and innovation. The manager or professional frequently faces a complex problem for which programmed alternatives are not available. By searching for a new alternative, the manager engages in creative thinking. Robert E. Kaplan, a behavioral scientist and project manager at the Center for Creative Leadership, contends that good managers are creative all the time: "They have to be to meet the confusing, fast-changing procession of demands on their intelligence, adaptability, and people-handling skills."[4]

Some of the need for creativity in management stems from the hectic nature of a manager's job. A manager's day includes such diverse activities as attending meetings, reading, writing, accessing an information system, making presentations, greeting visitors, and going on tours. Managers jump from one task to another. According to Kaplan, fashioning order out of this potential chaos is a creative act.[5]

Entrepreneurial managers continuously face the need to be creative. The entrepreneur needs to be creative in such matters as identifying a new product or service that customers will accept, getting by with a small staff, and arranging for financing.

Thus, another way of developing one's managerial skills is to improve one's creativity. The suggestions described in this chapter, the skill-building exercise, and the guidelines are directly relevant. In addition, to enhance creativity one needs to learn to search for several good alternatives to the problem before reaching a decision. The less creative manager or professional will grab at the first alternative rather than stretch his or her mind one step further.

The Stages of Creative Thought

Because of the importance of creativity, much effort has been devoted to understanding the process by which creative ideas surface. Here is a list of the five stages in a person's thinking and behavior that produce a creative result.

1. *Problem finding.* The individual discovers that something is worth working on or becomes aware that a problem or disturbance exists.

2. *Immersion.* The individual concentrates on the problem and becomes immersed in it. He or she will recall and collect information that seems relevant, dreaming up alternatives without refining or evaluating them.

3. *Incubation.* After assembling the information, the individual keeps it in mind for a while without taking action. It has been hypothesized that the subconscious mind begins to take over. It is therefore justifiable to go for a walk during working hours to engage in creative problem solving. While the problem is simmering, the subconscious may be trying to arrange the facts into a meaningful pattern.

4. *Insight.* If you have ever experienced a sudden insight about a vexing problem, you will understand this step in the creative process. The problem-conquering solution flashes into the mind at an unexpected time, while about to go to sleep, showering, or running. The circumstances surrounding the invention of the computer illustrate the insight stage of creative thought.

John Atanasoff, an Iowa State University professor, spent years performing routine math on IBM calculators. He knew there must be a better way. One night in 1937, he went for a drive in his car across Iowa. Two hundred miles later he wound up at a bar in Illinois.

On his second drink, a flash of genius hit Atanasoff. Build a computer that used base 2—a series of 1s and 0s—instead of the traditional base 10. In 1939, his first prototype appeared. It could only add and subtract eight-digit numbers. Nobody paid any attention. But Atanasoff's discovery laid the foundation for ENIAC, the world's first general purpose computer, which made its debut in 1946. [6]

5. *Verification and Application.* The individual sets out to prove the creative solution has merit. Verification includes gathering supporting evidence, logical persuasion, and experimenting with new ideas. Tenacity is usually required at the application stage of creative thought because most novel ideas are first rejected as being impractical.

SELF-HELP APPROACHES TO CREATIVITY IMPROVEMENT

Our description of self-help approaches to creativity is divided into two categories: developing creative attitudes and thinking patterns, and specific creativity-improvement techniques. The two categories overlap because most of the specific techniques, such as brainstorming and brainwriting, help you develop creative attitudes and thinking patterns.

Developing Creative Attitudes and Thinking Patterns

The self-help techniques in this section get at the underlying processes involved in creative problem solving. Most of the techniques relate to becoming a more intellectually flexible person, while the last two concern obtaining a knowledge base.

Overcome Traditional Mind-Sets.   The most important part of learning to behave creatively is to overcome familiar approaches to problems that lock us into one way of doing things. These familiar approaches have been referred to as *perceptual blocks* or *traditional mind-sets.* According to Roger von Oech, founder of a creativity consulting firm, people have become prisoners of familiarity. The more often a person manages a project, runs a meet-

ing, or designs a marketing strategy the same way, it becomes more difficult
to think about doing it any other way. Originally, he concentrated on developing creativity-training programs to help high-technology companies arrive at
more creative solutions to scientific and marketing problems. His methods
have now been applied in many different organizations and individuals. Von
Oech suggests a few ways he believes most people can overcome mental
blocks and thus get in a creative frame of mind.[7]

1. *Allow the foolish side of you to come out.* Humor has long been
known to stimulate a creative mind-set. "For example, one of my clients
manufactures satellites. They had a design meeting and everyone started
making fun of the satellites. They made weird jokes about them, bad
puns, and were just really silly with it. In the course of this they came up
with two major innovative design breakthroughs," said von Oech.

2. *Be a hunter.* Von Oech says he has worked with creative people
in many industries, disciplines, and professions. All the really good ones
are hunters. These people look outside their areas for ideas. When they
find an idea, they bring it back to their area and find an application.

3. *Use stepping-stones.* Crazy-sounding, impractical, infrequent
ideas, even though you are unable to execute them, can sometimes serve
as stepping-stones to practical, creative, new ideas. A paint company representative said a few years ago, "Let's put gunpowder in our house
paint. Then when the paint cracks and it's a real pain to get off, we could
just blow it right off the side of the house."

Von Oech notes the silliness of the idea. However, that idea was
used as a stepping-stone to ask another question: "What other ways could
we put additives in our paint at the front end so they would remain inert,
but combined with another solution a few years later, would react and
make the paint easy to get off?" The paint is now available commercially.

4. *Be a revolutionary.* Most new ideas and advances in technology,
science, and business come about when someone breaks or bends the
rules. Microprocessors and recombinant DNA break the rules. Ask yourself, "What if we tried it another way? What if we didn't do this?" One
company president says his most difficult task is getting his team members to challenge the rules.

5. *Don't be afraid to try and fail.* The late Sydney Harris contended
it is fear of failure more than anything else that separates the imitators
from the innovators.[8] If you try a large number of projects, ideas, or
things, a large number of them are likely to fail. Yet your number of
"hits" will be much higher than if you tried only a few projects, ideas, or
things. It is the absolute number of successes that counts the most—not
the percentage of successes.

Avoid Conformity to Group Thinking. Readily agreeing with the group's solutions to problems deters creative thinking. By definition, the creative person is an intellectual nonconformist. Be ready to challenge what others think and you are on the path to arriving at novel solutions to problems. However, if the group solution seems adequate after making your challenge, it is pointless to take a contrary stand.

Engage in Nonlinear Thinking. The usual logical approach to obtaining creative ideas is linear thinking, moving from one idea to another in step-by-step fashion. One moves from thought A to thought B to thought C, and so forth. According to Edward Glassman, another approach is nonlinear thinking. Ideas leap from A to J to X to F to B, and so forth. Something useful may eventually emerge out of bizarre intermediaries and remote associations. Glassman furnishes this example:

> During a discussion about how to prevent ice from breaking power lines, somebody suggested: "Let's train bears to climb the telephone poles in winter and shake loose the ice that accumulates and breaks the transmission wires." A second person, again in jest, suggested putting pots of honey on top of the poles so that the bear would make the climb in the first place. A third person humorously suggested using helicopters to place the pots of honey on the poles, another bizarre idea.
>
> All this humorous and bizarre thinking led to a practical solution, used for many years. The downdraft from the helicopters flying over the wires knocks off the ice before the wires break. [9]

Develop a Tolerance for Frustration and Ambiguity. Two related personality characteristics commonly attributed to creative people are resistance to frustration and high tolerance for ambiguity and chaos. [10] Coping with frustration and tolerating ambiguity are related because vagueness is frustrating to many people. If you want to be creative, you must learn to deal with ill-defined problems that have no apparent solution. Instead of declaring an ill-defined problem as too poorly framed to handle, seize the opportunity for finding a creative solution.

Tolerating frustration and ambiguity helped specialists at Public Technology Inc. deal with the vague problem of "how to make local government more responsive to citizens." Working with IBM, Public Technology developed an "electronic city hall" that helps local government be more responsive to citizens in a specific way. Citizens can conduct much of their business with the city (such as paying parking tickets and obtaining information) through an ATM-style computer. IBM and the cities involved in the pilot project settled on software called InfoWindows. The touch screen allows the citizen to interact with the computer to obtain information by on-screen text, printed text, audio, or video. For example, the person might be able to receive a list of nearby recycling centers. [11]

Develop a Synergy between Both Sides of the Brain. It is a generally held belief that the left side of the brain is the source of most analytical, logical, and rational thought. It performs the tasks necessary for well-reasoned arguments and working with standard applications of a computer. The right side of the brain grasps the work in a more intuitive, overall manner. It is the source of impressionistic, creative thought. People with dominant right brains thrive on disorder and ambiguity—both characteristics of creative people.

Current scientific thought indicates that any mental activity is carried out by both sides of the brain simultaneously. Joined by the corpus callosum, the two hemispheres work together in harmony. Creativity is the result of both sides of the brain working in harmony. Creative thought arises from the symbiotic cooperation of various parts of the brain in both the left and right hemispheres. Therefore, the highly creative individual achieves *synergy* (the combination is more than the sum of the parts) between the two sides of the brain. Both brain hemispheres are used as needed. Robert Gundlack, a physicist who had been awarded 128 patents in his first 30 years of work, explains this approach to creativity improvement in these terms:

> Being creative means developing synergy between the left half of the   brain—the analytical half—and the right half—the creative half. I learned that at home during my childhood. My mother was an artist, a painter of landscapes. My father was a chemist and inventor of Wildroot hair oil. Both my parents influenced me equally well.[12]

Recognize that Three Modes of Innovation Exist. Believing that true creativity or innovation can take the form only of a wildly imaginative new idea can hamper creative thinking. Recognizing that three modes of innovation exist is more reassuring and creativity-inducing.[13] According to Stephen R. Grossman and Margaret J. King, the first mode is *innovation by improvement.* This mode entails process improvements, or making things run more efficiently or cost-effectively. Innovation by improvement modifies conventional methods, products, or services. An example is the new generation of tennis racket that allows players to hit with much more power. The new rackets have wider frames and are made of stronger materials, but the basic concept of the racket has been retained.

Innovation by extension is the second mode. It involves initiating new schemes or reconfiguring product components to produce some new benefit. New product development can involve innovation by extension by using a well-developed technology for another product. One example is the creation of highly absorbent tissues and towels through the use of technology developed for disposable diapers.

Innovation by paradigm brings about new patterns or innovations dealing with products, processes, and services. An innovation by paradigm answers the question, "I know it's impossible, but I wonder if there is any way to _____ ?"

Examples of this type of innovation are found in breakthrough discoveries such as film animation, organ transplants, and frozen food. People who believe that innovation by paradigm is the only true mode of creativity are likely to be discouraged about becoming creative problem solvers.

Maintain an Enthusiastic Attitude.   A major hurdle to creativity for the manager or professional is resolving the conflict between being judicial and imaginative. Many work situations require the manager to be judicial (or judgmental). Situations calling for judicial thinking include reviewing proposed expenditures and inspecting products for quality or safety defects. Imaginative thinking is involved when searching for creative alternatives. Alex F. Osborn, a former advertising executive and the originator of brainstorming, notes how judgment and imagination are often in conflict: [14]

> The fact that moods won't mix largely explains why the judicial and the creative tend to clash. The right mood for judicial thinking is largely negative. "What's wrong with this? . . . No, this won't work." Such reflexes are right and proper when trying to judge.
>
> In contrast, our creative thinking calls for a positive attitude. We have to be hopeful. We need enthusiasm. We have to encourage ourselves to the point of self-confidence. We have to beware of perfectionism lest it be abortive.

You should project yourself into a positive frame of mind when attempting to be creative. The same principle applies when attempting to be creative about a judicial task. For instance, a manager might face the task of looking for creative ways to cut costs. The manager would then have to think positively about thinking negatively!

Become Immersed in Your Work.   More than a vivid imagination is required to be creative. A wealth of knowledge in the area in which you are working is also needed to process and combine information. The importance of having facts and details at your disposal increases when creativity is regarded as the association of previously uncombined ideas. The person who thought of an electronic city hall, for example, had to be aware of such facts as (*a*) the demands made on local governments, (*b*) the services offered by local government, (*c*) computer capabilities, and (*d*) automatic teller machines. Combining the four sets of facts allowed for the development of the concept of an electronic city hall.

Get a Balanced Cultural Media Diet.   To gather creative ideas, Stephen J. Bennett recommends you obtain a *balanced cultural media diet*. While few people can keep up with reading in their own fields, let alone a general sense of what is happening in other fields, he reasons the information glut should not act as a deterrent for expanding knowledge. Scan publications in other fields, as well as newspapers, magazines, and books. Frequently, a creative idea will jump out of an article. [15]

Using the ideas obtained in reading or in talking to others is referred to as duplication. Knowing when and which ideas to borrow from other people can help you behave as if you were an imaginative person yourself. Many useful ideas brought into an organization are lifted directly from others or are a simple combination of others' ideas. We are, of course, referring to borrowing ideas that are public information, not trade secrets. It is also important to properly credit the source of these creative ideas.

An example of a creative idea borrowed from others concerns the challenge faced by suburban department stores and fast-food restaurants in obtaining teenage help. Abraham and Strauss, an upscale department store chain in metropolitan New York, apparently originated the idea. Faced with a critical shortage of teenage help in its Westchester store (located near New York City), the company bused in teenagers from New York City. The teenagers proved to be high -quality workers. Today many other stores have duplicated this creative idea.

Specific Creativity-Improvement Techniques

This section describes how to use specific techniques for creative problem solving. As these techniques are used to solve real problems, they simultaneously improve creative thinking ability. Most of these techniques are used operationally and as part of creativity-training programs. To begin improving your creativity, do Skill-Building Exercise 2.

SKILL-BUILDING EXERCISE 2
Creative Thinking

Below are two exercises designed to give you practice in the expansive and flexible thinking required in creativity.

Unusual Consequences Test
Anticipate at least five consequences if the following happened:
a. A law passed stating that 30 days from now the United States would shift completely from the decimal to the metric system, including in the manufacture of new products and services.

b. Tobacco was declared an illegal substance throughout the world.
c. Gravity worked only half way on Monday.

Word Hints to Creativity
The object of this exercise is to find a fourth word related to all three words listed. For example, what word is related to these words?

---

	poke	go	molasses	_____

The answer is "slow" because of slow poke, go slow, and slow as molasses.

1. Surprise	line	birthday	_____
2. Base	snow	dance	_____
3. Rat	blue	cottage	_____
4. Nap	rig	call	_____
5. Golf	foot	country	_____
6. House	weary	ape	_____
7. Tiger	plate	news	_____
8. Painting	bowl	nail	_____
9. Jump	sea	priest	_____
10. Maple	beet	loaf	_____
11. Oak	show	plan	_____
12. Light	village	golf	_____
13. Merry	out	up	_____
14. Jelly	green	kidney	_____
15. Bulb	house	lamp	_____

Scoring: If you were able to think of the correct word, or another plausible one, for 10 or more of these groups, your score compares favorably to that of creative individuals. The answers are at the end of this chapter. More important than the score is that you practiced making remote associations, a characteristic of creative people.

SOURCE: The word hints tests, developed by Eugene Raudsepp, is updated and adapted from "Ideas: Test Your Creativity," *Nation's Business*, June 1965, p. 80.

Identify Your Creative Time Period.   As you begin to make creativity a habit, it helps to identify those times of the day or week when your capacity for creative thought is the highest and the lowest. For most people, creative capacity is best following ample rest, so it is best to tackle creative problems at the start of a workday. Some executives and researchers tackle their biggest thought problems while on vacation or exercising. The solution to the problem is conceptualized, and the details are worked out on the job. Among such "vacation problems" might be, "What new service might our agency offer?" or," What else can we do to improve the quality of our oldest product?"

Other individuals report that their best time for creative thought is immediately before falling asleep. Some energetic people keep a pen and notebook next to their bed to jot down nocturnal flashes of inspiration. One manager reports that he gets his best ideas during meetings conducted for other purposes. The point is to chart your individual creative time periods.

Conduct Brainwriting Sessions.   Brainstorming is widely recognized as a group method of finding creative alternatives to problems. A variation that can be used by individuals is referred to as *brainwriting*. In brainwriting, the individual works alone and writes down a number of alternatives to a problem. It often helps to give yourself a quota of ideas along with a deadline.

Much self-discipline is required to conduct brainwriting because you do not have the support of the group. Faced with a situation calling for a creative response, you might sit quietly with a pencil and pad and begin to generate possible solutions. For example, "How can I shorten the time it takes our customers to pay their bills without creating ill will?" Most people accept the first one or two alternatives to such a problem. Through private brainstorming, you can learn to search for many alternatives.

The computer program *IdeaFisher* facilitates brainwriting. The software contains over 3,000 questions designed to help the user think of solutions to business problems. Examples include developing a marketing strategy or inventing a new product or service. As part of the program, over 60,000 words, expressions, people, places, and things are cross-referenced in over 700,000 ways. Associations to your key word are broken down into subcategories.[16] Assume you are trying to develop a new service for senior citizens. *IdeaFisher* could help you develop a long list of things and ideas associated with senior citizens.

Brainstorm with Others.   The best-known method for creativity improvement is brainstorming. The accompanying chart presents rules and guidelines for brainstorming. During the idea-generating part of brainstorming, potential solutions are not criticized or evaluated in any way, so spontaneity is encouraged.

A key aspect of brainstorming is that all ideas can be stepping-stones and triggers for new and more useful ideas. Any idea might lead to other associations and connections. The idea for pet seat belts apparently came about during a brainstorming session. Somebody suggested a designer leash for pet dogs; somebody else said "pet restraint," which led to "pet seat belt." (Although pet seat belts have not become a growth industry, they can be found in a few catalogues and specialty stores.)

A recent application of brainstorming is the *pet peeve technique*. A work team brainstorms as many complaints as possible about every facet of the organizational unit. Sources of complaints could include external and internal customers, competitors, and suppliers. Imaginary complaints are also welcome. In addition to providing useful information, the pet peeve technique helps people loosen up mentally and see things from an outsider's perspective.[17]

Rules and Guidelines for Brainstorming

1. Use groups of about five to seven people.

2. Encourage the spontaneous expression of ideas. All suggestions are welcome, even if they are outlandish or outrageous. The least workable ideas can be edited out when the idea-generation phase is completed.
3. Quantity and variety are important. The greater the number of ideas, the greater the likelihood of a breakthrough idea.
4. Encourage combination and improvement of ideas. This process is referred to as piggybacking or hitchhiking.
5. One person serves as the secretary and records the ideas, writing them on a chalkboard or flip chart.
6. In many instances, a moderator can help keep the session on track by preventing one or two members from dominating the session. If the moderator takes notes, a secretary is not needed.
7. Do not overstructure the session by following any of the rules too rigidly. Brainstorming is a spontaneous process.

Use Individual Synectics. Similar to brainstorming, *synectics* is primarily a group method of generating creative ideas, but it can also be used by individuals working alone. The technique uses analogies to provide mental images to the brain. By using analogies, the unfamiliar becomes familiar. Follow these guidelines to use synectics when acting alone:[18]

1. Begin with a personal analogy by projecting yourself into the essence of the problem. The personal analogy method is also referred to as *You Are the Product*. You act out how it would feel to be the product you are trying to develop or improve. A creativity consultant had managers from a contact lens maker pair off in role-playing teams. One manager played the role of an eyeball; the other played a rigid contact lens. One eyeball kept pleading for a pillow to cushion him from the hard, "insensitive" contact lens. The output from this analogy session is a new research effort to bond a high-tech cushioning material onto the contact lens. [19]

2. Think of a direct analogy. A direct analogy looks for something that solves the same problem but in a different setting. For example, a high-speed electronic typewriter prints by moving the printing head across the page, rather than moving the carriage back and forth. Why not use this same principle in a computer printer? (This is now done.)

3. Develop a symbolic analogy. A symbolic analogy is looser and more visual. The development of Pringles potato chips involved symbolic analogy. The synectics group was asked to solve the problem of compressing the potato chips into a small place without squashing them. Part of the creative task was to find an instance in which nature had solved the problem. In the end, the group members found an analogy in leaves. Although fragile, leaves were found compressed and undamaged. This feat is accomplished because the leaves are compressed while

moist. It was decided to make Pringles by compressing moist potato chips.

4. Use a fantasy analogy. Wild and imaginative thinking is called for in this step. An example of this step was an engineer who was attempting to develop a device to link two electrical wires. Operating in the fantasy stage, the engineer visualized the wires being held in the teeth of two people facing each other. Out of this fantasy came the idea for the alligator clip.

Use the Random-Word Technique.   The random-word technique is based on the assumption that making remote associations is an important part of the creative process. The technique forces people to make a useful association to a word chosen at random. Practicing this technique helps develop flexible thinking. Here is how the approach works:

> You are a product manager at Reynolds Metals. Your boss has just read how Arm & Hammer strategists increased sales of baking soda by 70 percent. They suggested that homemakers put a box in the refrigerator to absorb food odors. The boss would like you to make a similar breakthrough for your company—come up with new uses for Reynolds Wrap.
>
> You select a concrete word at random to use as an idea hook for your associations. Selecting a word at random in your dictionary, you get *costume*. Let's think. How about putting directions on the back of the Reynolds Wrap package showing parents how to make Halloween costumes for kids from aluminum foil? "Mr. Reflection." "The Silver Wonder Woman." You get the idea. [20]

The Napoleon Technique.   Another creativity-enhancing technique is for the problem solver to assume another identity. This Napoleon technique is particularly applicable when you face a repeated, intractable dilemma. The other identity helps you look at the problem from a different perspective. Creativity consultant Roger von Oech was asked to help generate ideas for icons (tiny images that represent different functions) for the Macintosh computer. Von Oech fantasized into the exercise a number of famous participants. Of these fantasized participants, game show celebrity Vanna White contributed the most useful idea.

White's imagined presence made the problem-solving group think of turning letters, then of attractive women. Finally, the term *airhead* also surfaced. Flash. The new icon chosen was a vacuum cleaner to represent a function that collects things from one spot on the screen and deposits them elsewhere. [21]

The Superhero Technique.   A variation of assuming another identity to solve a problem is to imagine you are a superhero. According to the developers of this technique, the prospect of wielding superhuman powers tends to free the imagination. One person assumes the role of a client with a problem. The other people assume the identities of superheroes such as Superman, Wonder Woman, Batman, Catwoman, or Captain Marvel. Another choice is for participants to create their own superheroes. The client asks each super-hero for ideas, as illustrated in this anecdote:

> A regional Social Security office suffered from confused communication. A notable problem was the difficulty in locating employees. Spiderman (a superhero) came to the rescue. He stopped the confusion by throwing his spider net around every employee in the regional office. This visual image of employees ensnared in Spiderman's net triggered the idea of a local area network to ensure that employees received their messages and stayed in touch. [22]

The Excursion Method.   Similar to the other methods described so far, the excursion method requires the problem solver to make word associations that relate to the problem. The association could be to another word or object. A group of supermarket managers used the excursion technique to develop ways of saving money without sacrificing food quality or service. One of the words chosen for an excursion was *senior citizen*. Among the word associations that emerged were, "reliable customer," "slow moving," "thrifty," "affluent," "kindly," "limited budget," "careful shopper," and "bag person." The term *bag person* was then related back to the problem. In the past, older people often carried their own net shopping bags. Why not sell permanent shopping bags at cost to induce shoppers to carry their own bag, thus saving substantial sums for paper and plastic bags?

Maintain and Use an Idea Notebook.   It is difficult to capitalize on creative ideas unless you keep a careful record of them. A creative idea trusted to memory may become forgotten in the press of everyday business. An important suggestion kept on your daily planner may become obscured. Because creative ideas carry considerable weight in forwarding your career, they deserve the dignity of a separate notebook or computer file. The cautious or forgetful person is advised to keep two copies of the idea book or computer file—one at home and one in the office.

The Case for Creativity Improvement

Few people would argue that improving creativity is of no benefit to the individual and the organization. As Michael E. Porter states, "Companies achieve competitive advantage through acts of innovation. They approach innovation in its broadest sense, including both new technologies and new ways of doing things." [23]

Assuming the suggestions for creativity improvement described here worked for you, it could propel you forward in your career. Many high-ranking executives gained early momentum in their careers because they spearheaded breakthrough ideas. Bill Gates of Microsoft built his name and fortune around the development of a disk operating system (DOS) for personal computers. On a lesser scale, Spencer Silver, the 28-year-old chemist who invented Post-it Notes, was treated better by his company (3M) after the product's success. It became easier to get equipment and assistance, and "they give me a lot more support with some of the stranger ideas I come up with." [24]

A key strength of these methods of creativity improvement is that they are highly cost effective. For a modest investment of time, and virtually no money, they can yield a major return. Brainstorming, both in groups and individually, has spurred thousands of creative suggestions.

The case for using individual approaches to creativity improvement is furtherstrengthened by experiments comparing individual and group brainstorming. The results show that brainstorming groups consistently produce fewer ideas than the equivalent number of people working by themselves. [25]

The Weaknesses of Creativity Improvement

Improving creativity is not the goal of every organization. Many companies are not looking for more creative ideas. They already have more good ideas floating around than they have resources to implement them. Being imaginative is usually far removed from creating change. As articulated by a past president of a manufacturing association in reference to the developer of a new type of waterbed, "He is one of the few persons who ever invented anything who has business sense. There are no end of ideas that are going to revolutionize the world. But there are few people with the ability and patience to put them into practice."[26]

Another problem with emphasizing creativity is that it may lead to a deemphasis on mundane products and services. Yet many of these ordinary products and services are highly profitable and useful.

If an individual carries creativity improvement too far, he or she may be perceived as more of a dreamer than a realist. Most organizations are looking for an occasional good idea, not a spate of them.

Some argue against the creativity-improvement exercises described in this chapter because they are not validated by experiments. One scholar in the field contends that creative behavior cannot be taught as if it were a training ritual in watch repair.[27] (This chapter takes the position that creativity improvement requires both changes in thinking patterns and creativity-improvement exercises.)

Guidelines for Action and Skill Development

Select several or a combination of creativity-improvement techniques that seem best suited to you. Perhaps you find it comfortable to conduct brainwriting sessions. Yet you might find that trying to develop a synergy between both sides of your brain is too much of a long-term commitment. Unless you have an extraordinary gift for remembering things, using an idea notebook will be beneficial for you.

Improving your creativity requires much self-discipline and concentrated effort. The techniques and strategies described here and in the references are intended to supplement, not substitute for, diligent application of your mental efforts toward finding creative alternatives to problems.

Avoid overemphasizing creativity to the point that you develop a distaste for the repetitive aspects of your job. Every position from the data-entry specialist to the chief executive officer includes some noncreative tasks.

An idea cannot be considered truly creative until other people pass judgment on its utility. Your idea must be converted to action before it is classified as creative. Give your ideas a "pilot run" by asking others for their reactions to your innovative suggestions. To keep the process alive, establish a reciprocal relationship with those people by providing them feedback about their ideas.

If you develop a creative concept that you think will sell, the authors of a book about creativity suggest: (1) Bounce your idea off bright co-workers with different specialties, such as manufacturing and marketing; (2) find a senior management sponsor to protect and later promote your idea; (3) don't ask for too big a budget commitment too soon because a large budget request is often rejected; and (4) be persistent and don't be discouraged by naysayers and skeptics. [28]

DISCUSSION QUESTIONS AND ACTIVITIES

1. Business organizations currently emphasize creativity by such means as creativity training and hiring creativity consultants. What factors do you think are behind this renewed emphasis on creativity?

2. Which method of creativity improvement discussed in this chapter do you think is best suited for you? Why?

3. Is there room for everyone in the organization to be creative?

4. It has been said that the best creative ideas in business are magnificently simple. Furnish an example of a successful yet magnificently simple business idea?

5. Name a few periodicals you think would help people achieve a balanced cultural media diet.

6. Some creativity experts contend that doing crossword puzzles and writing poems help build creativity. Why might this be true?

7. Try one of the creativity-improvement suggestions in this chapter for 10 days. See if you actually become more proficient at searching for creative solutions to problems. Be ready to report your observations to the class.

NOTES

1. Adapted with permission from "Triumph of the Vision," *Success,*   October 1991, p. 23.
2. "Some Basic Concepts of Innovation and Storytelling," *Issues & Observations,* 1991, p. 7.
3. Charlene Marmer Solomon, "What an Idea: Creativity Training," *Personnel Journal,* May 1990, p. 66.
4. Robert E. Kaplan, "Creativity in the Everyday Business of Managing," *Issues &. Observations,* May 1983, p. 1.
5. Ibid.
6. John Hillkirk, "1939: It Was an Outstanding Year for Useful Inventions," Gannett News Service Story, December 1, 1989.
7. Roger von Oech, *A Whack on the Side of the Head* (New York: Warner Books, 1984).
8. Sydney J. Harris, "Fear of Failure Separates Imitators from the Innovators," syndicated column, October 3, 1986.
9. Adapted from Edward Glassman, "Creative Problem Solving," *Supervisory. Management,* January 1989, pp. 21–26.
10. John A. Glover, Royce R. Ronning, and Cecil R. Reynolds, eds., *Handbook of Creativity* (New York: Plenum Press, 1989), p. 10.
11. Larry Reynolds, "Moving City Hall into the Mall," *Management Review,* October 1989, pp. 32–33.
12. John J. Bryczkowski, "Invention's a Necessity at Xerox," *Rochester Democrat. and Chronicle,* January 9, 1983, p. 1F.
13. Stephen R. Grossman and Margaret J. King, "Eagles, Otters, .& Unicorns: Three Species of Innovation," *Industry Week,* March 5, 1990, p. 30.
14. Quoted in "Breakthrough Ideas," *Success,* October 1987, p. 50.
15. Steven J. Bennett, "Entrepreneurial Thinking: 5 Ways to Make It Work for You," *Business Week's Careers,* Spring–Summer 1987, p. 30.
16. Bryan M. Mattimore, "Mind Blasters," *Success,* June 1990, pp. 46–47.
17. Anne Skagen, "Creativity Tools: Versatile Problem Solvers that Can Double as Fun and Games," *Supervisory Management,* October 1991, pp. 1–2.
18. Marilyn Goldstein, David Scholthauer, and Brian H. Kleiner, "Management on the Right Side of the Brain," *Personnel Journal,* November 1985, p. 44.
19. "Brainstormers' Boot Camp," *Success,* October 1991, p. 26.
20. Bryan W. Mattimore, "Breakthroughs," *Success,* November 1988, p. 46.
21. Ibid.
22. "Brainstormers' Boot Camp," pp. 24, 26.
23. Michael E. Porter, "The Competitive Advantage of Nations," *Harvard Business Review,* March–April 1990, p. 74.
24. Ruth Hamel, "Wish You Thought of That? They Did," *USA Weekend,* October 10–12, 1986, p. 14.
25. R. Brent Gallupe, Lana M. Bastianutti, and William H. Cooper, "Unblocking Brainstorms," *Journal of Applied Psychology,* February 1991, p. 137.
26. Phil Ebersole, "Air-Water Mix Makes Bed," *Rochester Democrat and Chronicle,* November 3, 1987, p. 7D.

27. Review of Glover, Ronning, and Reynolds, *Handbook of Creativity*, in *Contemporary Psychology*, August 1991, p. 672.
28. John M. Ketteringham and P. Ranganath Nayak, *Breakthroughs!* (New York: Rawson Associates, 1987).

SOME ADDITIONAL REFERENCES

Dacey, John S. *Fundamentals of Creative Thinking*. Lexington, Mass: Lexington Books, 1989.

Etzioni, Amitai. "Humble Decision Making." *Harvard Business Review,* July-August 1989, pp. 122–126.

"Eureka! It's a Breakthrough Idea." ("Out" Sixth Annual Breakthrough Ideas.) *Success,* October 1992, pp. 18–27.

Glassman, Edward. "Creative Problem Solving: Habits that Need Changing." *Supervisory Management*, Februrary 1989, pp. 8–12.

———. "Creative Problem Solving: Your Role as Leader." *Supervisory Management*, April 1989, pp. 37–42.

Kanter, Rosabeth Moss. "How to Outsmart the Bureaucracy." *Working Woman*, September 1988, pp. 42–46.

Kirrane, Dianne, and Peter R. Kirrane. "Managing by Expert Systems," *HRMagazine*, March 1990, pp. 37–39.

Runco, Mark Andrew, and Robert S. Albert, eds. *Theories of Creativity*. Newbury Park, Calif.: Sage Publications, 1990.

Appendix to Chapter Two

The following test will help you determine if certain aspects of your personality are similar to those of a creative individual. Because our test is for illustrative and learning purposes, proceed with caution. It is not a standardized psychological instrument.

Answer each of the following statements as "mostly true" or "mostly false." We are looking for general trends. Do not be concerned if you answer mostly true, even though there is conceivably some time when the answer could be mostly false.

	Mostly true	*Mostly false*
1. Novels are a waste of time. If you want to read, read nonfiction books.	_____	_____
2. You have to admit, some crooks are very clever.	_____	_____
3. People consider me a fastidious dresser. I despise looking shaggy.	_____	_____

4. I am a person of very strong convictions. What's right is right; what's wrong is wrong.   _____   _____

5. I enjoy it when my manager gives me vague instructions.   _____   _____

6. Business before pleasure is a hard and fast rule in life.   _____   _____

7. Taking a different route to work is fun, even if it takes longer.   _____   _____

8. Rules and regulations should not be taken too seriously. Most rules can be broken under unusual circumstances.   _____   _____

9. Playing with a new idea is fun even if it does not lead to any immediate payoff.   _____   _____

10. My imagination leaves much to be desired.   _____   _____

11. Writing should try to avoid the use of unusual words and word combinations.   _____   _____

12. Detective work would have some appeal to me.   _____   _____

13. The wild thoughts of children are mostly nonsense.   _____   _____

14. Why write letters to friends when there are so many clever greeting cards available in the stores today?   _____   _____

15. I have some very unusual thoughts on many days.   _____   _____

16. If you dig long enough, you will find the true answer to most questions.   _____   _____

Scoring: The answer in the *creative direction for* each question is as follows:

1. Mostly false	9. Mostly true
2. Mostly true	10. Mostly false
3. Mostly false	11. Mostly false
4. Mostly false	12. Mostly true
5. Mostly true	13. Mostly false
6. Mostly false	14. Mostly false
7. Mostly true	15. Mostly true
8. Mostly true	16. Mostly false

ANSWERS TO *WORD HINTS TO CREATIVITY:*

1. Party	5. Club	9. High	13. Make
2. Ball	6. Dog	10. Sugar	14. Bean
3. Cheese	7. Paper	11. Floor	15. Light
4. Cat	8. Finger	12. Green	

Chapter Three

Crisis Management

A soft-drink company faced the destruction of its business when a malicious rumor spread rapidly through the community. Through judicious use of a public relations consulting firm, the company was able to restore its customer base.

Brooklyn Bottling Company was heading toward bankruptcy in the 1980s, barely surviving on the sale of seltzer, when Eric Miller inherited the firm founded by his grandfather in 1937. Thirty-three-year-old Miller revived the family business through innovative marketing. He revived a line of fruit-flavored sodas, added a few new ones, and changed the brand name to Tropical Fantasy. Miller's strategy was pricing below national brands of soft drink.

Tropical Fantasy sold briskly in small groceries from Boston to North Carolina. However, Miller could not control the counter price. The soda was sold to grocery-store owners who charged as high as 85 cents for what Miller intended to be low-priced soda. He solved the problem by printing a 49-cent retail price on the bottle cap. Another change was to increase the bottle size from 12 to 20 ounces. The new package was introduced September 30, 1990, andimmediately became a smash success.

Sales surged 50 percent in 1990 to $12 million, and Miller predicted a 25 percent increase for 1991. His optimism lasted seven months. A bizarre rumor hit April 3, 1991. Crudely printed, anonymous handbills were posted at many places in Harlem. Each handbill read:

ATTENTION!!! ATTENTION!!! ATTENTION!!! Please be advised, Top Pop and Tropical Fantasy, also A-Treat sodas are being manufactured by the Klu Klux Klan. Sodas contain stimulants to sterilize the black man, and who knows what else!!!! You have been warned. Please save the children.

Three days later, the same flier appeared in Brooklyn, and the rumor flew all over metropolitan New York. Over 20 inquiries came into the Food and

Three days later, the same flier appeared in Brooklyn, and the rumor flew all over metropolitan New York. Over 20 inquiries came into the Food and Drug Administration (FDA). Soda samples were tested for the presence of saltpeter, the opposite of an aphrodisiac. FDA investigators visited Brooklyn Bottling Co., checked the warehouse, the raw materials area, and the production line. Nothing unusual was detected.

The crisis engulfed Brooklyn Bottling. Grocers could not sell the soda, and many stopped their orders. Top Pop and A-Treat also lost orders, but they depended less on the New York market.

Eric Miller was angry. He was proud that his 125-employee company was staffed mostly by minorities. Miller also liked offering poor consumers a good deal for soda. He regarded the rumor as an absurd attack and was determined to cut it short. Miller hired Robin Verges, a public relations consultant specializing in African-American issues. Her efforts succeeded when New York Mayor David Dinkins, a black man, agreed to appear on television drinking Tropical Fantasy.

The plight of Brooklyn Bottling caught the attention of the media. The Ku Klux Klan made a disclaimer in response to the controversy. Wizard James Farrands of Sanford, N.C., told a weekly newsmagazine: "The KKK is not in the bottling business." Editorials in New York newspapers urged readers not to believe hurtful nonsense.

Brooklyn Bottling and the manufacturer of Top Pop distributed their own fliers dismissing the rumor. Miller estimated that by mid-June most of his customers had returned. "But we had three months of horror," he said. He and other bottlers battered by the rumor think a jealous competitor was responsible. [1]

CRISIS–MANAGEMENT STRATEGIES AND TECHNIQUES

Eric Miller was engaged in crisis management. Although executives and managers have dealt with crises in the past, the formal label *crisis management* emerged with the publication of Steven Fink's book, *Crisis Management*. A crisis is a turning point for better or for worse, or a situation that has reached a critical phase. [2] Crisis management is taking control of a crisis that has already surfaced or advance preparation for one. The phrase *turnaround management* also refers to managing in a crisis or a situation that requires drastic, fast improvement. Enough knowledge has been accumulated about crisis management to offer some principles and suggestions for people faced with handling crises.

Identify, Isolate, and Manage the Crisis

The core of crisis management, according to Fink's framework, is to identify, isolate, and manage the crisis. Although this statement contains three principles, they can be considered a flow of interrelated activities. Identifying the company faced losing all its customers and therefore would be forced out of business. Falling demand for Tropical Fantasy was a problem, but not the real crisis. Losing his business and source of income was the real crisis facing Eric Miller.

A classic example of a crisis is the 1982 Tylenol poisonings. Someone placed cyanide-laced Tylenol capsules in bottles of Extra-Strength Tylenol and put them on store shelves in the Chicago area. According to Fink, the real crisis facing Johnson & Johnson was the demise of the Tylenol brand and the subsidiary company MacNeil Consumer Labs. Dow Corning is another large company facing a crisis. Hundreds of women are expected to file lawsuits alleging Dow Corning hid the health risks of its silicone gel breast implants. The company faces an onslaught of shareholder class action suits, government fines, and criminal charges. Revenue from the breast implant business was less than 1 percent of the company's revenues, yet the penalties could exceed $1 billion, creating a financial crisis. [3]

Isolating the crisis contains it to avoid contaminating anything else, much like quarantining a patient with an infectious disease. Isolation in this sense means the CEO, and any other members of the crisis team, focus on the crisis to the exclusion of other responsibilities. Nothing can or should take precedence over the crisis.

Once the decision maker has identified and isolated the crisis, it becomes easier to manage because any misleading and diversionary paths have been blocked. The manager also has a clearer idea of what actions must be taken to rectify the problem. Quick and decisive action is imperative. When the Exxon *Valdez* went aground on a reef in Prince William Sound, Alaska, over 10 million gallons of oil gushed from the tanker within five hours. The environment suffered seemingly irreversible damage. The cleanup costs for Exxon have been estimated at $1.38 billion. Lawsuits from the incident still have not been settled.

After the spill, Exxon and the regulatory agencies lost precious time figuring out who was in charge. The Coast Guard officer supposedly in charge spent most of his time being interviewed by government and industry officials. Frontline action to limit the spill was hampered while the officer spoke to investigators. [4]

Adapt a Crisis Decision-Making Style

Managing a crisis centers around making the right decisions. It may prove helpful to fine-tune your decision-making style toward a crisis mode. John Ramee offers some decision-making rules: [5]

Rule 1: Avoid the quick fix. It is important to correct the underlying problem rather than grab an almost immediate solution—borrowing money at exorbitant interest rates rather than cutting costs when faced with a cash crunch.

Rule 2: Seek new information. A crisis fosters rapid change, and makes information quickly obsolete. Gathering ample new information will tell deci-

Rule 2: Seek new information. A crisis fosters rapid change, and makes information quickly obsolete. Gathering ample new information will tell decision makers if their current strategies are valid or if new strategies must be formulated.

Rule 3: Revise strategies. A vigilant crisis manager, or crisis management team, will be prepared to modify new strategies whenever new information indicates the need. A typical strategy for a company facing a profit crisis is to sell assets to raise cash. In one company facing this, the CEO decided to purchase a small company that made laser printers because of its growth potential. The gamble paid—the sale of laser printers infused new cash into the firm.

Rule 4: Have one center of authority. Without a central crisis-management authority, strategies can fragment and lower-ranking power centers can emerge. This rule is an aspect of isolating the crisis because only a few key people are concentrating on the crisis.

Rule 5: Act as the need arises. An unfortunate aspect of crisis management is that the cure often seems worse than the problem, particularly when massive numbers of employees are laid off and valuable assets are sold. Procrastination only deepens the crisis. It is important to select the best strategies and act quickly and decisively, as Eric Miller did.

Place the Crisis in a Problem-Solving Mode

A general method of dealing with crises is to regard the crisis as yet another important work problem requiring resolution. When you cope successfully with a crisis, you use the problem-solving method. In essence, it involves these familiar steps:

1. *Clarify the problem.* What is the real problem created by this crisis? Most crises can force a company out of business either through losing customers or paying fines and damages.

2. *Search for creative alternatives.* What options are open? Many managers choose stonewalling the problem over dealing with it openly, and dig a deeper hole for themselves.

3. *Make a choice.* If the crisis is to be resolved, a tough decision must be made at some point.

4. *Develop an action plan and implement it.* What steps must be taken to get out of the mess? Eric Miller hired a public relations consultant with expertise in dealing with African-American concerns. The consultant, in turn, formulated an effective action plan. An effective crisis manager is advised to explore shortcuts and innovative or unorthodox ways of getting things accomplished.[6]

5. *Evaluate the outcome.* Did the crisis-management plan work or will an alternative be required? Geico Corporation, an insurance company, once appeared near bankruptcy because it was paying out so much in claims. The

action plan Geico executives chose was to be very selective about who they insured, to coddle safe drivers with low prices and good service, and to offer cut-rate prices. It worked remarkably well. Geico is now one of the most profitable insurers. [7]

Be Honest with the Public and Employees

Adopting a bunker mentality is a trap often fallen into by decision makers in a crisis. The decision maker collects facts, hides behind them, and does not deal with the crisis publicly. The manager also avoids communicating with the public by erecting barriers. Moving aggressively to explain the problem was one of the successful strategies Johnson & Johnson used to deal with the Tylenol poisonings. An equally important strategy was taking decisive action by removing the product from the stores.

More recently, the investment firm of Salomon Brothers Incorporated was found rigging its bids in Treasury auctions—an illegal and unethical tactic. Investor Warren E. Buffett was appointed as the new chief executive officer. He quickly removed the implicated employees and publicly admitted the firm's wrongdoing. The firm still faces potential criminal charges and a steady erosion of its client base, but admitting the wrongdoing appears to be aiding its survival. [8]

Retrenchment, both in private and public organizations, is a common crisis that should be dealt with openly. However, employees should be informed before the public that resources are declining and cuts are necessary. One or two announcements concerning necessary cuts are insufficient. Top management must explain with many reports, speeches, and fact sheets that the retrenchment is necessary. Specific statements about how many employees will be laid off result in less probing than do generalities.

Deal Effectively with the Media

An inescapable aspect of making information about a crisis public is dealing with the media. The communicator in a crisis must have immediate access to top-level authority or have authority himself or herself. Without such authority, the communicator may have to hedge or act evasively. A key general principle in communicating with the media is to present the truth in the most advantageous way.

Public relations firms such as Hill and Knowlton offer crisis counseling. The crisis counselor helps the client present a balanced picture of the problem to the community. For example, it could be pointed out that although Salomon violated regulations, its clients did not lose money as a result.

Another important principle for dealing with the media is that the spokesperson must be qualified to withstand the media inquiry and present the organization in the most positive way. Also, the presentation must be carefully prepared. Lack of preparation may result in false information, misstatements, and embarrassing gaffes. [9] Aerospace company Morton Thiokol endured embarrassment over its inconsistent statements about the reliability of its O-ring seals involved in the space shuttle Challenger explosion.

Obtain Information from the Original Source

When a crisis hits, an important question to be answered is, "How bad is it?" Experienced crisis managers say customers, clients, and suppliers can provide valuable information about the gravity of a crisis. Michael D. Dingman, CEO of a company that specializes in turning around troubled companies, points out that a key principle of turnaround management is to get close to the customer. [10]

Armed with accurate information about the company's cash position, turnaround managers seek additional sources of information—customers, employees, competitors, vendors, bankers, the investment community, government agencies or regulators, and the media. The most useful information comes from the primary source, such as sitting in a customer's office and listening to complaints about product quality or late shipments. Building communications bridges to the customer is valuable as revealed by this incident:[11]

> The CEO of a troubled $50 million consumer products company made all his senior officers, himself included, take part in a 30-day sales blitz. In so doing, he learned that a $2 million OEM (original equipment manufacturer), thought to be safe, was so unhappy with the company's work, it was considering withdrawing its business. Worse, the CEO had been counting on that customer's continued support to keep a plant open. Fortunately, his timely call helped him save the customer and sparked a critical assessment of his consumer goods operation.

Turnaround managers also maintain open communication channels with some of the firm's major vendors. Because these vendors conduct business with competitors and other customers, they may be aware of trends in the marketplace. They may also provide marketing information about pricing and discount schedules. Vendors can also provide insights into the strengths and weaknesses of the company and its employees. [12]

Take Advantage of the Hidden Opportunity

An important principle of managing adversity is to look for hidden opportunities within the negative circumstances. A manager whose new product group is dismantled by the company may decide to quit and start a company to make the new product.

Crisis managers also follow this principle in managing organizational assets. After the stock market crash of 1987, many chief financial officers (CFOs) directed their firms to capitalize on the sudden downturn in stock prices. [13] IBM spent about $1 billion repurchasing its shares. Olin Corporation bought close to 300,000 shares of its own stock. By purchasing their own stocks, companies stabilize prices for the stock and take advantage of good values. When the stock market rebounds, the company can sell the repurchased stocks at a sizable profit.

Reduce Costs Drastically

Turnaround managers are usually called in from the outside by boards of directors, often under pressure from bankers who are worried about the company's deteriorating financial position. Turnaround managers' core strategy is to slash costs, including excising layers of management, to improve the firm's financial position. Once the firm's financial health improves, it is often sold at a favorable price. This cost-cutting strategy includes deciding what part of a company is healthy and then acting decisively to sell anything that is unhealthy. [14]

A representative example of a cost-cutting program enforced by turnaround managers is the approach used by James Sullivan. He zealously goes after what he describes as corporate fat. When assigned to turn around a company, he immediately enforces a temporary pay cut of 10 percent and reduces corporate overhead by 25 percent. Sullivan usually eliminates company cars and frequently sells the company headquarters building and leases it back. In one instance, the owner of the troubled company was also the owner of the headquarters building. Sullivan ordered him to reduce the rent. [15]

Decreasing the number of management layers reduces costs because payroll costs are lowered. Sometimes revenue is increased because the displaced managers are assigned to sales positions. Although flattening the structure may reduce costs substantially, other benefits may be greater. A flat organization presents fewer barriers to the flow of information and reduces the filtering effect of the hierarchy. It also opens opportunities for a dialogue between top management and those close to operations and market information. The shortened chain of command also improves mobilizing people for action, especially when task forces are used to implement new programs. [16]

Inside managers can also deal with a financial crisis. The present cadre of managers can also slash costs to combat a major financial setback. Many of the computer industry layoffs in 1992 were attempts by company officials to avert major losses due to poor sales.

Provide Counseling for Disaster Victims

Organizations also face internal disasters, such as a disgruntled and deranged employee (or recently dismissed employee) opening fire on co-workers and superiors. Frederick E. Ramsey, director of the State of Maryland Employee Assistance Program, notes, "In the last three years, we have had about

10 incidents where we had to respond to posttraumatic stress. These included two cases of employees who died of natural causes and one case where an employee was shot to death." [17]

In one grisly incident, a welfare client fatally stabbed a Department of Social Services employee. Within two hours of the murder, Ramsey had arranged for immediate on-site crisis counseling for witnesses to the incident. Counseling was also given to employees with whom the victim had previously worked at another Social Services location. A manager in the agency said, "Mr. Ramsey's attentiveness to details, his early intervention, and his compassion fostered a caring environment. This enabled employees to confront the situation and eventually return to productive employment." [18]

SKILL-BUILDING EXERCISE 3

Dealing with the Human Aspects of a Disaster

Read the following description of a disaster that hit an organization, and then decide what steps you would take to manage the crisis. After you have prepared your answer, compare it to what the managers involved did, as described at the end of the chapter.

The San Francisco earthquake hit the Environmental Protection Agency Region X office at 5:04 P.M. October 17, 1989. The building that housed the 700 EPA employees became uninhabitable. John Spafford, branch chief of EPA human resources management, described what happened:

"When the earthquake hit, we not only had effects from the earthquake itself, but we had a large cistern of water on the roof. The cistern's contents went cascading through the middle of the building, destroying the interior walls. After accounting for all the employees, we determined that the structural damage was so severe that we could not reinhabit the building.

"However, we not only had to be greatly concerned with what was happening to us, we had to fulfill EPA's overall mission of providing emergency assistance. The earthquake potentially posed an environmental crisis to public health and safety. Such concerns as possible oil spills into the San Francisco Bay and the safety of San Francisco's drinking water had to take precedence over our own logistical problems."[19]

Action Plan for Dealing with the Crisis:

Practice Transformational Leadership

An organization in crisis requires decisive and bold leadership to move it from a morass to higher ground. This type of leadership is referred to as *transformational*. The transformational leader must create something new out of something old. The transformational process aims at moving individuals beyond normal, expected performance to higher achievement and maturity levels. Charisma, individualized consideration, and intellectual stimulation are traits and behaviors that distinguish transformational leaders. Conventional leadership involves transactions between the leader and group members. Transactional leaders give team members something they want in exchange for something the leaders want. [20]

Part of being a transformational leader is to optimistically interpret facts related to the crisis. In the fall of 1992, R. H. Macy & Co. was struggling to pull itself out of bankruptcy. During June 1992, the retail giant had posted an operating loss of $33 million. The company had also lost many managers to other companies. Despite these problems, co-CEO Myron Ullman projected optimism. He admitted, "We don't think we have a victory. But it's difficult to anticipate job loss, and unrest and earthquakes in California." He insisted results would soon improve. Ullman pointed to the $42 million in savings in one quarter achieved through closing stores, inventory, management, and selling the corporate airplane. [21]

Transformational leadership is likely to benefit the troubled organization in both dealing with the immediate crisis and performing better in the long run. Some turnaround managers, however, are concerned more with the short range. The slash-and-burn manager turns around the company in a hurry and then departs to fix another broken organization.

CONTINGENCY PLANNING FOR CRISES

As management awareness of the inevitability of crises has increased, more thought has gone into contingency planning for crises. Here we describe what many firms are doing, or should be doing, to lessen the impact of future crises.

Engage in Crisis Forecasting

Contingency planning begins with forecasting. Based on past experience, senior management should estimate the type of crises that could occur. For instance, an automotive company might predict future recalls based on the percentage of previous recalls. Many consumer products now have a tamper-resistant packaging to prevent poisoning the contents of packages on store shelves.

An important part of crisis forecasting is looking for early-warning signals of impending crises. Early-warning signals can come from such sources as exceptional performance deviations, employee observations, and customer input. An internal Union Carbide report warned that the plant in Institute, West Virginia, faced a possible runaway reaction of methylisocyanate. The initial report was dated September 11, 1984—three months before the crisis at the sister plant in Bhopal, India. Dow Corning reportedly responded slowly to safety concerns voiced by employees about silicone gel implants. [22]

Develop Crisis-Management Policies and Procedures

An advanced form of contingency planning for crises is to develop appropriate crisis-management policies and procedures. An abridgment of such policies and procedures established by one university is presented in the box.

Crisis and Media Contacts Plan at a University

Definition: A crisis is a major occurrence that threatens university policy, peace, and/or safety of students and/or employees.

Responsibilities: When a crisis develops, follow this communication system: (1) Inform the president, provost, and director of communications about the crisis. (2) The communications department provides facts to the media, the public, and our university community. (3) Campus safety provides the direct linkage to the appropriate community services to alleviate the crisis.

Crisis center: The communications department will establish a crisis center for handling all requests for information and for disseminating information.

Communication principles: During a crisis, follow these communication principles: (1) When the crisis involves the threat of personal safety to members of the university, Campus Safety should take the lead in and work with the administration to control and eliminate the crisis. (2) There should be a "one voice" response from the university, such as the president. (3) In dealing with media inquiries, tell them the established facts as quickly as possible. Even if the news is bad, reporting the news to the media first gives the university the opportunity to emphasize positive points.

Informing institute administration: When a crisis develops, or threatens to develop, take the following action: (1) Make direct contact with the administrative official most closely involved. (2) Next, contact the president, provost, vice president, and secretary of the university. (3) Any major general crisis such as a health emergency or a major explosion or fire should involve the vice president and secretary of the university.

Establish a Corporate Crisis-Management Team

Another preparedness tactic is to set up a corporate crisis-management team composed of employees who are trained to take charge in a sudden disaster. United Airlines, Dow Chemical, Heinz, and Waste Management are among the companies that have crisis-management teams ready to swing into action. Some companies conduct simulate crises with the corporate crisis team and/or members of top management.

Crisis-management teams enabled Wells Fargo Bank and Chevron to resume near-normal business soon after the 1989 San Francisco earthquake. Extensive planning and practice drills enabled these firms to rapidly implement action plans that ranged from hot lines to emergency computer backups.

Build Cash Reserves

Another way of managing a crisis in advance is to build substantial cash reserves. According to one turnaround manager, nothing is more important to a successful turnaround than cash. Financial managers should devise a system for gathering accurate information about the company's true cash picture.[23]

While cash reserves can help overcome a crisis, not having enough cash can create a crisis. Many companies that have borrowed heavily to acquire other companies have found themselves without sufficient operating funds. Loan payments consumed profits. Part of Macy's problems were attributed to an overzealous acquisition program by the parent company.

THE CASE FOR CRISIS-MANAGEMENT STRATEGIES AND TECHNIQUES

The case for crisis-management techniques involves two major issues. First, are crises worth worrying about? Corporate crises can exert substantial damage to a company's operation. A crisis such as the Three Mile Island nuclear accident or the Exxon *Valdez* oil spill can have the following effects: (1) severe negative impact on company profits; (2) unwanted public and government scrutiny; (3) damage to corporate integrity and name; (4) unproductive diversion of effort to quell the crisis; and (5) employee morale problems.

Second, are crisis-management strategies and tactics effective? Evidence suggests these approaches to crisis management are useful because companies that follow them cope with crises. For example, Tylenol's market share actually increased several months after the poisonings. Johnson & Johnson acted aggressively and positively. Companies that do not follow these principles do not fare as well. For example, the Star-Kist subsidiary of H. J. Heinz was accused of shipping 1 million cans of rancid tuna to Canada. Even after the Canadian prime minister impounded the fish, Heinz executives refused to communicate with the public or the press. The episode became a major embarrassment to the firm. [24]

THE CASE AGAINST CRISIS-MANAGEMENT STRATEGIES AND TECHNIQUES

Crisis-management strategies and techniques can be criticized on philosophical, humanitarian, and empirical grounds. Philosophically, crisis management is a special case of managerial decision making. Decision making follows the same process in good times and bad times. According to this argument, crisis management has no separate existence in the same way that international management and small-business management are not really separate fields of study.

The humanistic argument is that a subset of crisis management, turnaround management, is unsavory. A turnaround can result in many lost jobs and personal hardships. Rather than shrink a troubled firm so drastically other steps could be taken, including pay cuts for all employees, shorter work weeks, decreased stock dividends, and substantially reduced pay for top managers. In addition to creating economic hardship, plant closings dramatically escalate the domestic violence and suicide rate of laid-off employees.

An empirical argument against crisis-management methods is that they often do not work—they may result in a company so trimmed down that it cannot survive in the long run. In an attempt to trim fat, muscle tissue is also sacrificed. Too many middle managers with innovative ideas are sacrificed, as is investment in research and development.

Guidelines for Action and Skill Development

Crisis management deserves every manager's thought. In addition to the ideas already presented, consider these suggestions:

Do not cry wolf too often. Forecasts of impending crises will ultimately be ignored if too many past predictions were made of crises that did not materialize. Crisis management should be reserved for legitimate crises and the early stages of a turnaround. Used unnecessarily, too often, or too long, crisis management creates fear and confusion and can lower morale. The head of a healthy company will use it judiciously and will replace it with conventional management practices and organization structures as soon as feasible.

Motivating team members during a crisis can stretch your talents as a manager. It is important to spend extra time with team members because they will need your emotional support. Avoid unnecessary meetings and reports because most team members are already overburdened during a crisis. Communicate immediately any news about the crisis that will affect your staff. Be positive but avoid giving false hope about the severity of the crisis. [25]

DISCUSSION QUESTIONS AND ACTIVITIES

1. Give an example of how several of the techniques described in this chapter might be used to handle a personal crisis.

2. How might managers in the agriculture business who were ravaged by Hurricane Andrew in the summer of 1992 have used crisis-management principles?

3. What seems to be the difference in emphasis between crisis management and turnaround management?

4. Some turnaround managers hire bodyguards. Why might such action be advisable?

5. How might customers help warn a firm about a future potential crisis?

6. Several acts of workplace violence, such as shooting employees, have been committed by workers who were fired and then sought revenge on their former employer. Should management take any responsibility to prevent such violent acts?

7. Attempt to find somebody who was working at a company during a period of crisis management, including turnaround management. Get that individual's perception of what it was like to live through those conditions.

NOTES

1. Adapted from "Soda-Pop Company Caps Rumors," Associated Press syndicated story, July 7, 1991. Reprinted with permission.
2. Steven Fink, *Crisis Management: Planning for the Inevitable* (New York: AMACOM, 1986), p. 15.
3. "Debacle at Dow Corning: How Bad Will It Get?" *Business Week,* March 2, 1992, p. 36.
4. "The Alaskan Oil Spill: Lessons in Crisis Management," Management Review, April 1990, pp. 16–17.
5. John Ramee, "Managing in a Crisis," *Management Solutions*, February 1987, pp. 28–29.
6. "Panic Project," *Executive Strategies*, January 8, 1991, p. 3.
7. "Geico's Acceleration is No Accident," *Business Week,* March 30, 1992, p. 46.
8. Leah Nathans Spiro, "How Bad Will It Get?" *Business Week*, October 7, 1991, p. 122.
9. Ramee, "Managing in a Crisis," p. 28.
10. "Mike Dingman Tunes 'Em Up, Turns 'Em Around, Spins 'Em Off," *Business Week,* October 5, 1987, p. 90.
11. Adapted from John O. Whitney, "Turnaround Management Every Day," *Harvard Business Review,* September–October 1987, p. 52.
12. Ibid.
13. Christopher Farrell, "Companies Are Staying Cool—But Moving Fast," *Business Week,* November 9, 1987, p. 37.

14. "The Green Berets of Corporate Management," *Business Week,* September 21, 1987 p. 111.
15. Ibid., p. 112.
16. Whitney, "Turnaround Management Every Day," p. 54.
17. Stephenie Overman, "You May Not Be Able to Deal with This," *HRMagazine,* November 1991, p. 46.
18. Ibid., p. 47.
19. Lucia W. Landon, "We Didn't Fall Through the Cracks," *HRMagazine,* November 1991, p. 48.
20. Bernard M. Bass, *Bass & Stogdill's Handbook of Leadership: Theory, Research, & Managerial Applications,* 3rd ed. (New York: The Free Press, 1990), p. 23.
21. Laura Zinn, "More Trouble in Store?" *Business Week,* September 21, 1992, p. 36.
22. "Debacle at Dow Corning," p. 36.
23. Whitney, "Turnaround Management Every Day," p. 51.
24. "Coping with Catastrophe," *Time,* February 24, 1986, p. 53.
25. "Company Crisis: Tactics to Keep Your Staff Motivated in Lean Times," *Executive Strategies,* November 7, 1989, p. 6.

SOME ADDITIONAL REFERENCES

Barton, Laurence. *Crisis in Organizations: Managing and Communicating in the Heat of Chaos.* Cincinnati: South-Western Publishing Co., 1992.

Briggs, William."Taking Control After a Crisis," *HR Magazine,* March 1990, pp. 60–61, 80.

Caulkin, Simon, "Dangerous Exposure," *Best of Business International,* Autumn 1990.

DuBrin, Andrew J. *Bouncing Back: How to Get Back In the Game When Your Career Is on the Line.* New York: McGraw-Hill, 1992.

Esaki-Smith, Anna. "Fighters." *Success,* July–August 1992, pp. 22- 34.

Janis, Irving L. *Crucial Decisions: Leadership in Policymaking and Crisis Management.* New York: The Free Press, 1989.

Ramee, John. "Corporate Crisis: The Aftermath." *Management Solutions,* March 1987, pp. 18–22.

Sloma, Richard S. *The Turnaround Manager's Handbook.* New York: The Free Press, 1985.

Weitzel, William, and Ellen Jonsson. "Reversing the Downward Spiral: Lessons from W. T. Grant and Sears Roebuck." *Academy of Management Executive,* August 1991, pp. 7-22.

SOLUTION TO SKILL-BUILDING EXERCISE 3–1

Dealing with the EPA Earthquake Crisis

The first thing the EPA did was to create a crisis-management team composed of 100 essential employees and place them in a satellite office. The group established the basic operational functions. A communication system was set up.

Second, systems were established for basic administrative activities such as payroll, mail, and travel arrangements.

Third, the team searched immediately for space to reunite the work force. By March 1990, 60 percent of employees were placed in interim office space.

An EPA official thinks in retrospect that the group should have been more proactive. For example, the group should have pestered suppliers to ship personal computers and other equipment more rapidly.

Chapter Four

Overcoming and Preventing Career Self-Sabotage

The manager described below unwittingly engaged in career self-sabotage by playing Jekyll and Hyde. When dealing with superiors, his interpersonal skills are superior, but he is often abrasive when dealing with team members.

Roger Nelson began his career as a management trainee in the San Francisco office of a nonprofit medical insurance company. He quickly impressed his superiors with his above-average productivity. Although abrupt with people, Roger was promoted to claims supervisor in three years. His superiors attributed his abruptness to his strong desire to achieve high levels of productivity and to satisfy clients. Roger bragged about his unit's short turnaround time on claims.

Roger continued to impress his superiors with his dedication and performance. The employee turnover rate in his unit was above average, but not high enough to sound a warning to upper management. During an exit interview, a claims processor who had worked for Roger complained about his abrasiveness toward employees. When Roger was confronted with this information by the director of human resources, he convinced the director these were the comments of a disgruntled low performer. The human resources director was reasonably satisfied and decided not to share the incident with upper management.

After three more years of satisfactory performance, Roger was promoted to director of claims. The vice president of claims, noting that Roger had a few rough edges in handling people, had some reservations about promoting him. However, because of a hiring freeze, the vice president promoted him anyway. Roger now supervised a large staff and attended administrative meetings held by the CEO. With one more promotion, Roger would become a vice president and member of the executive committee. His popularity with the supervisors, however, continued to erode. Deborah Lupiani, one of his supervisors, provides a firsthand description:

> Most of us knew Roger from before he was promoted to director. He was always a little heavy-handed with people. He used to rant and rave if a claim was disputed, or if somebody's productivity fell too far below quota. When Roger was promoted to director, he became much worse. Power must have gone to his head. Half the time in staff meetings was devoted to his reviewing any little mistake made since the last meeting.
>
> Roger would get the angriest when he thought a supervisor was not pushing employees hard enough. He didn't seem to understand that a medical insurance company was not the place for a slave driver. He once chewed out a supervisor in front of everybody else. He accused her of reading the *National Enquirer* on company time. The woman was really just taking a late lunch.
>
> What irritates me and the other supervisors the most about Roger is that he is two-faced. When he deals with the vice presidents or important visitors, he becomes Prince Charming. So tactful, so polite. It makes us gag. Roger reminds me of a head waiter I worked for when I was a teenager. He would rant and rave when he walked into the kitchen. As soon as he went through the swinging doors into the dining room, his snarl changed into a smile. He was a tyrant toward the workers but a charmer toward the guests.

Roger's career advancement with the company was soon blocked. A job satisfaction survey revealed low morale among the staff and many negative comments about his handling of people. The human resources director was then asked to thoroughly review Roger's people-handling skills. The investigation turned up so many negatives that Roger was reassigned to a position as a senior systems analyst. His pride was hurt, but his pay was not cut. Roger is now attempting to improve his interpersonal skills and hopes to someday return to a management position. [1]

WHY PEOPLE ENGAGE IN CAREER SELF-SABOTAGE

Many forces lead people to sabotage their careers. A review of the scant information on the topic points to four key reasons people in the workplace become their own worst enemy.[2] The major cause of career self-sabotage is a *loser life script*. Early in life, our parents and other influential forces program our brains to act out certain life plans. These plans are known as scripts. People fortunate enough to have winner scripts consistently emerge victorious. When a tough assignment needs doing, they get the job done. For example, they get a jammed computer program running again after the problem baffles everybody else in the office.

Unfortunately, others have scripts that program them toward damaging their careers and falling short of their potential. Much of this damage paradoxically occurs just when things seem to be going well. Roger Nelson intensified

ing in a way to preserve the position he wanted so much, he acted in a self-defeating manner. Perhaps Roger was responding to the dictates of a loser script. Fortunately, loser scripts are reversible, as described later.

The simplest explanation for career self-sabotage is that some people suffer from a personality that fosters defeat. People with a *self-defeating personality pattern* have three notable characteristics. First, they repeatedly fail at tasks they have the ability to perform. Second, they place themselves in very difficult situations and respond helplessly. Third, they typically refuse to take advantage of escape routes, such as accepting advice and counsel from their manager.

Self-defeating beliefs put many people on the road to career self-sabotage. In this context, a self-defeating belief is an erroneous belief that creates the conditions for failure. For example, some people sabotage their job campaigns before even starting. They think to themselves: "I lack the right experience," "I'm not sharp enough," "I'm too old," "I'm too young," and so forth.

Fear of success is yet another contributor to career self-sabotage. People who fear success often procrastinate to the point of self-defeat. These people worry that being successful will lead to such negative outcomes as an overwhelming work load or loss of friends. They also worry that success will bring about unrealistic expectations from others, such as winning a big suggestion award every year.

To examine your present tendencies toward career self-sabotage, do Skill-Building Exercise 4. Taking the self-sabotage quiz will help alert you to many self-imposed behaviors and attitudes that could potentially harm your career.

SKILL-BUILDING EXERCISE 4

The Self-Sabotage Questionnaire

Indicate how accurately each of the statements below describes or characterizes you, using a five-point scale: (0) very inaccurately, (1) inaccurately, (2) midway between inaccurately and accurately, (3) accurately, (4) very accurately. Consider discussing some of the questions with a family member, close friend, or work associate. Another person's feedback may prove helpful in providing accurate answers.

1. Other people have said that I am my worst enemy.   _____

2. If I don't do a perfect job, I feel worthless.   _____

3. I am my own harshest critic.   _____

4. When engaged in a sport or other competitive activity, I find a way to lose a substantial lead near the end.   _____

5. When I make a mistake, I can usually identify another person to blame.   _____

6. I have a tendency to procrastinate.   _____

7. I have trouble focusing on what is really important to me. _____

8. I have trouble taking criticism, even from friends. _____

9. My fear of seeming stupid often prevents me from asking questions or offering my opinion. _____

10. I tend to expect the worst in most situations. _____

11. Many times I have rejected people who treat me well. _____

12. When I have an important project to complete, I usually get sidetracked, and then miss the deadline. _____

13. I choose work assignments that lead to disappointments even when better options are clearly available. _____

14. I frequently misplace things such as my keys, then get very angry at myself. _____

15. I am concerned that if I take on more responsibility people will expect too much from me. _____

16. I avoid situations, such as competitive sports, where people can find out how good or bad I really am. _____

17. People describe me as the office clown. _____

18. I have an insatiable demand for money and power. _____

19. When negotiating with others, I hate to grant any concessions. _____

20. I seek revenge for even the smallest hurts. _____

21. I have an overwhelming ego. _____

22. When I receive a compliment or other form of recognition, I usually feel I don't deserve it. _____

23. To be honest, I choose to suffer. _____

24. I regularly enter into conflict with people who try to help me. _____

25. I'm a loser. _____

Total score _____

Scoring and interpretation: Add your answers to all the questions to obtain your total score. Your total score provides an approximate index of your tendencies toward being self-sabotaging or self-defeating. The higher your score, the more probable it is that you create conditions to bring about your own setbacks, disappointments, and failures. The lower your score, the less likely it is that you are a self-saboteur.

0–25: You appear to have very few tendencies toward self-sabotage. If this interpretation is supported by your own positive feelings toward your life and yourself, you are in good shape with respect to self-defeating behavior tendencies. However, stay alert to potential self-sabotaging tendencies that could develop later in your career.

26–50: You may have some mild tendencies toward self-sabotage. It could be that you do things occasionally that defeat your own purposes. A person in this category, for example, might write an angry memo to an executive expressing disagreement with a decision that hurts his or her operation. Review actions you have taken during the past six months to decide if any of them have been self-sabotaging.

51–75: You show signs of engaging in self-sabotage. You probably have thoughts, and carry out actions, that could be blocking you from achieving important work and personal goals. People whose scores place in this category characteristically engage in negative self-talk that lowers their self-confidence and makes them appear weak and indecisive to others. For example, "I'm usually not good at learning new things." People in this range frequently experience another problem. They sometimes sabotage their chances of succeeding on a project just to prove their negative self-assessment is correct. If you scored in this range, carefully study the suggestions offered in this chapter.

76–100: You most likely have a strong tendency toward self-sabotage. (Sometimes it is possible to obtain a high score on a test like this because you are going through an unusually stressful period in your life.) Study this chapter carefully and look for useful hints for removing hidden barriers to your success. Equally important, you might discuss your tendencies toward undermining your own achievements with a mental health professional.

STRATEGIES AND TECHNIQUES FOR OVERCOMING AND PREVENTING CAREER SELF-SABOTAGE

Overcoming self-defeating behavior requires hard work and patience. Here we present 9 widely applicable strategies for overcoming and preventing career self-sabotage. Choose those that fit your circumstances and personal style.

Examine Your Script and Make the Necessary Changes

Much importance has been attached to the influence of early-life programming in determining whether a person is predisposed to self-defeat. Note carefully the word *predisposed*. A person may be predisposed to snatch defeat from the jaws of victory, but that does not mean the predisposition makes defeat inevitable. It does mean the person will have to work harder to overcome a tendency toward self-sabotage.

A script is much like a set point with respect to body weight. A person whose natural body weight (the set point) is 145 pounds will experience difficulty getting down to 125 pounds and staying there. The body will fight in such ways as slowing metabolism when the food intake decreases. To stay below 145 pounds may be a lifelong struggle, but it can be done.

The set point analogy applied to self-defeating scripts means you can identify them and modify them. After asking yourself a series of penetrating questions, you can exercise conscious control over changing the script. A good starting point is to look for patterns in your setbacks:

- Did you show up late for several key appointments with upper management or important customers?
- Did you blow up at people who have the authority to make the administrative decisions about your future?
- Did you get so tense during your last few command performances that you were unable to function effectively?
- Did you give up at the late stages of several projects and say, "I just can't get this done"?

Stop Blaming Others for Your Problems

Blaming others for our problems contributes to self-defeating behavior and career self-sabotage. [3] Blaming others is self-defeating because doing so relieves you of most of the responsibility for your setback and failure. Consider this example: If someone blames favoritism for not receiving a promotion, he or she will not have to worry about becoming a stronger candidate for future promotions. Not to improve one's suitability for promotion is self-sabotaging. If you accept most of the blame for not being promoted, you are more likely to make the changes necessary to qualify in the future.

An underlying theme to the suggestions for preventing and overcoming career self-sabotage is that we need to engage in thoughts and actions that increase our personal control. This is why blaming others for our problems is self-sabotaging. By turning over control of your fate to forces outside yourself, you are holding them responsible for your problems.

Solicit Feedback on the Actions You Take

Feedback is essential for monitoring whether you are sabotaging your career. A starting point is to listen carefully to any direct or indirect comments from your superiors, subordinates, co-workers, and customers about how you are coming across to them.

Bill, a technical writer, heard three people in one week make comments about his appearance. It started innocently with, "Here, let me fix your collar." Next, an office assistant said, "Bill, are you are coming down with something?" The third comment was, "You look pretty tired today. Have you been working extra hard?" Bill processed this feedback carefully. He used it as a signal that his habit of late nights was hurting his image. He then cut back on staying out late during the week enough to revert to his normal healthy appearance.

An assertive and thick-skinned person might try another technique. Approach a sampling of people both on and off the job with this line of questioning: "I'm trying to develop myself personally. Can you think of anything I do or say that creates a bad impression in any way? Do not be afraid of offending me. Only people who know me can provide me with this kind of information."

Take notes to show how serious you are about the feedback. When someone provides any feedback, say, "Please continue, this is very useful." Try not to react defensively when you hear something negative. You asked for it, and the person is truly doing you a favor.

Stop Denying the Existence of Problems

Many people sabotage their careers because they deny a problem exists and therefore do not take appropriate action. Denial is a defensive maneuver against a painful reality. Much denial takes place in the context of mergers, acquisitions, and hostile takeovers. Some people do not start looking for jobs until it is too late. Robert Bell, who has extensively studied the problems of takeovers, suggests:

> Talk to any consultant who has advised on the staffing issues in takeovers and any manager who has lived through a takeover. One term will inevitably come up: *denial*. This is the belief that the nex person will get fired, not you. This occurs despite the overwhelming evidence that your company, division, or you are on the scrap heap. So you stay until it is too late.[4]

Another self-sabotaging form of denial is to ignore the importance of upgrading one's credentials despite overwhelming evidence that it is necessary. Some people never quite complete a degree program that has become an informal qualification for promotion. Consequently, they sabotage their chances of receiving a promotion for which they are otherwise qualified. Many people in recent years have damaged their chances for career progress by not upgrading their computer skills.

Make Positive Changes in Your Life

There is something almost mystical about making positive changes in your life as a way of overcoming self-sabotage. Although the changes you make may not have anything directly to do with self-defeating behavior, they enable you to achieve greater control over your life. For example, if you have always relied on others to prepare your income tax returns, and you now do it yourself, you have mastered one more part of your environment. You thus feel more in control of your world than you did in the past.

Feeling in control of one's life—and therefore being more in control—is the discipline the self-sabotaging person needs. People are sometimes propelled into counterproductive routines because they believe they are being dragged along by external forces. Their experience is much like that of a compact car being pushed to the side of the road by the draft from a semi passing on the left.

The person who consumes three drinks at lunch might say, "I don't know why I did it. I couldn't resist the temptation. Other people were paying for the drinks." If you are in control, you can decline the two extra drinks you don't really need—and are sure to lead to an impression-damaging wooziness back at the office.

Modify or Leave Relationships that Divert You from Your Career Goals

People sometimes blame their career setbacks on a spouse or a domestic partner who doesn't understand the importance of their work. People who blame their partner for encouraging them to engage in self-defeating career actions are partially correct. A partner who does not share your career goals and dreams can be a liability. To overcome this problem, and escape handicapping your career, you definitely have to work things out with your significant other.

Pam, a product manager, often worked much later at night than her husband, Corey, found acceptable. He claimed that when they married she never had mentioned that she would be spending so much time at the office. Pam could feel the tension whenever she prepared to leave for work. She could sense a coolness in Corey's voice when she called home to say she would be late. Pam suggested that the two of them together should see a relationship counselor.

The counseling sessions revealed that Corey felt insecure about Pam's devotion to business. He admitted to being concerned that her career was becoming more important to her than their relationship. Pam reassured Corey that her marriage and her career were both very important, and that Corey did not have to be jealous of her career. She also worked out a plan whereby she would rely more on her home computer in order to cut down on overtime spent at work. Pam now felt that she had more of the energy she needed to move forward in her career, without sacrificing her relationship with Corey.

Pam was able to modify her relationship with Corey. At other times, a relationship may be incompatible with one's career because the partner does not share the same goals and values and refuses to change. Goal incompatibility can lead to career self-sabotaging behaviors. These include being preoccupied with marital problems and withdrawing from involvement in one's career because it leads to conflict at home. Trying to arrive at a workable compromise before changing or establishing your goals is obviously the preferred solution.

Get Appropriate Help from Your Organization

A person headed toward career self-sabotage can sometimes receive help from the organization in reversing the trend. The fact that you are seeking help suggests that the process of overcoming self-sabotage has begun. Three sources of help are ordinarily available in large organizations: feedback and advice from a superior; an employee assistance program; and human resource professionals.

Solicit Feedback and Advice from a Superior.   Asking for feedback is a basic tactic for overcoming career self-sabotage. Feedback usually includes advice and suggestions. A supportive boss is likely to ask how he or she can help a team member who comes for advice.

> Alex, a financial analyst, became so nervous when making a presentation to management that he would state facts incorrectly. Consequently, he was worried about being regarded as a mediocre financial analyst. The analyst asked his boss, who was experienced at presentations, if he had noticed this problem. The boss said he had noticed a few instances in which Alex had flubbed his facts, but not to an unusual extent.
>
> Alex then asked his boss what he could do about the problem. The boss volunteered to set aside time to listen to Alex conduct a dress rehearsal of his next two presentations. Alex took the boss up on the offer, and it helped him overcome his presentation anxiety.

The rehearsals themselves benefited Alex, but the support and encouragement shown by his boss were equally valuable. Research by Donald Cole has shown that emotionally supportive managers are effective antidotes to career homicide. [5]

Use Employee Assistance Programs.   A major purpose of an employee assistance program (EAP) is to help employees overcome personal problems that drain productivity. Typically, the EAP coordinator refers the troubled employee to an outside treatment facility. Some larger organizations have their own treatment facilities located on or off company premises. The program is confidential, sometimes to the extent that the company does not know which employees have referred themselves for help.

Many of the problems EAPs deal with involve self-defeating behavior, including substance abuse, cigarette addiction, compulsive gambling, financial problems, and physical abuse of family members. Employees can also spend one or two sessions with an EAP counselor to talk about self-sabotaging problems in general. If the counselor thinks multiple sessions are required, an appropriate referral is made.

Seeking help from an EAP rather than going to a mental health practitioner on one's own has an important advantage. Employee assistance counselors work regularly with people whose personal problems are hurting job performance. Also, the company usually pays the entire fee.

Confer with a Human Resources Professional.   Another organizational resource that may help in dealing with self-sabotaging tendencies is a human resources professional who specializes in career problems. These professionals include counseling psychologists, industrial psychologists, and career-development specialists.

> Lorie, a budget analyst, requested an appointment with a career development specialist to discuss career planning. During the second session, it became apparent that *career planning* was a euphemism for *interpersonal problem*. As Lorie explained it, she often got into disputes with people she was supposed to be helping, especially managers from outside her department. Her role was to help people from other departments prepare their budgets. She bickered with operating people so often that several times they asked to work with another budget analyst.
>
> In discussing her problems with the career counselor, it became apparent to Lorie that the root of her self-defeating behavior was a strong need to challenge authority. At the same time, she had a strong need not to be challenged herself. She also came to realize that budget preparation always involved negotiation. Therefore, when she did not agree entirely with the figures presented to her, it was not a signal to challenge their authority. Similarly, when people did not immediately agree with her analysis, it did not mean they were challenging her authority.
>
> The insights Lorie gained in the sessions with the career counselor helped her improve her ability to engage in give-and-take over budgets without assuming an attack posture.

Strive toward Overcoming a Negative Self-Image

A negative image of oneself is a major contributor to career self-sabotage. Closely linked to a negative self-image is *negative self-talk*. The individual says so many negative things to himself or herself about personal capabilities that the individual loses confidence and fails. Examples include: "I know I'll look like a fool asking for a 15 percent increase in our budget." "How can I ask for a promotion when there are so many more talented and capable people competing against me?"

Some cognitive therapists believe our thoughts and assumptions, expressed by our inner voice, determine our overall functioning. Faced with a challenge or crisis, your self-talk has a powerful impact on your attitude, motivation, and performance. If your self-talk is negative, the result is a self-fulfilling prophecy.[6] You talk yourself into failure.

Converting a negative self-image to a positive one is a complex and time-consuming process. One reason for the difficulty may be that people have an inherent, biological predisposition to distort reality. For example, some people inherit a predisposition toward pessimism. They view things in a negative, unhappy manner that often encourages a negative outcome, such as a sales representative who makes cynical comments about his firm's delivery schedule, thereby losing a potential sale.

One of the first hurdles in overcoming a negative self-image is to try to see yourself in an objective and realistic light. For example, are the other people competing for promotion really more talented and capable than you? Another approach is to deliberately make more positive self-statements when thinking about yourself. Among them would be, "My qualifications are good. I deserve a promotion." "Asking for a 15 percent budget increase makes sense. My rationale is very sound." "I know I can handle this assignment. I've done quite well on many other assignments in my career." [7]

Visualize Self-Enhancing Behavior

Visualization is a primary method for achieving many different types of self-improvement and is essential in overcoming career self-sabotage. To apply visualization, program yourself to overcome self-sabotaging actions and thoughts. Imagine yourself engaging in self-enhancing, winning actions and thoughts. Picture yourself achieving peak performance when good results count the most.

To use visualization for overcoming career self-sabotage, start by identifying the next job situation you will face that is similar to ones you have flubbed in the past. Then imagine yourself mentally and physically projected into that situation. Imagine what the room looks like, who will be there, and the confident expression you will have on your face. Visualization is akin to watching a video of yourself doing something right.

> Matt, an actuary in a life insurance company, has an upcoming meeting with top management to discuss his analysis of how insurance rates should be changed to factor in the impact of AIDS on mortality rates. Based on past experience, Matt knows that he becomes flustered and acquiescent in high-level meetings about controversial topics (such as rate increases). Matt also knows that to behave in this way is self-defeating.
>
> As he prepares for the meeting, he visualizes himself calmly listening to challenges to his analysis. In response, he does not back off from his position, who challenged him changing their attitudes as he knowledgeably explains his case. By the end of the meeting, Matt is warmly thanked for his recommendations on making rate changes to meet the incidence of AIDS in the population. The president congratulates him on how well he stood up to the challenges to his forecasts.

THE CASE FOR AND AGAINST BEING CONCERNED ABOUT CAREER SELF-SABOTAGE

Career self-sabotage has received little attention in both the management and career-development literature. However, this does not limit its importance. Many people do not achieve their career goals because they work against their own purposes. With more insight into recognizing and overcoming self-defeating behavior, presumably many of these people would achieve their goals.

Overcoming and preventing career self-sabotage is also important from the organizational standpoint. Many forms of self-defeating behavior are both costly and embarrassing to the organization. Among them are alcoholism, substance abuse, and a pattern of sexual harassment. Also, many competent executives sabotage their careers and thus are no longer available to handle their responsibilities. For example, an executive who takes kickbacks from major suppliers might be forced to resign.

The case against being concerned about career self-sabotage is that the topic does not deserve separate mention outside of career management and performance management. If individuals are effectively managing their careers, they will be able to recognize self-defeating patterns of behavior. If managers are effectively managing their team members, they will work toward achieving high performance from everybody—even self-saboteurs.

Guidelines for Action and Skill Development

Career self-sabotage can take many forms in addition to those already mentioned in this chapter. One form of career self-sabotage is committing political blunders.[8] It is self-sabotaging to do such things as irritate people in power or show indifference to the company's products or services. Be alert to avoid the following nine recurring political blunders:

1. Bypassing your immediate superior. Going over your boss's head to resolve a problem between the two of you will almost always hurt your relationship with him or her.
2. Criticizing your boss in front of others.
3. Challenging your boss's judgment. Constructive and tactful criticism is helpful, but questioning your boss's judgment goes beyond the bounds of good sense.
4. Making overt signs of disloyalty. An example would be publicly criticizing your firm or bragging about your interest in seeking employment elsewhere.
5. Being a nay-sayer. People who criticize everything are perceived as poor leaders.
6. Being a pest. When assertiveness is used too often, it becomes annoying and may lead to unfavorable decisions against you.
7. Declining an offer from top management. If you turn down top management more than once, you will probably not be considered for future offers.
8. Resisting the dress code. A wider range of clothing and appearance is acceptable today than in the past, but deviating too far from a dress code can make you appear unidentified with the organization.
9. Burning your bridges. Creating ill will among former employers or people who have helped you in the past can backfire in the form of poor references and a damaged reputation in your field.

DISCUSSION QUESTIONS AND ACTIVITIES

1. How is procrastination a form of career self-sabotage?
2. How could Roger Nelson (the key figure in the opening example) have been helped before he committed career self-sabotage?
3. What appears to be the difference between a self-defeating personality pattern and other forms of career self-sabotage?
4. Describe the behavior of a person you know who appears to be following a loser script.
5. Describe the behavior of a person you know who appears to be following a winner script.
6. Identify a public figure who you think is following a winner script and justify your answer.

NOTES

1. Andrew J. DuBrin, *Your Own Worst Enemy: How to Prevent Career Self-Sabotage* (New York: AMACOM, 1992), pp. 117–119. Most of this chapter is based on various parts of *Your Own Worst Enemy*.
2. Thomas A. Widiger and Allen J. Frances, "Controversies Concerning the Self-Defeating Personality Disorder," in *Self-Defeating Behaviors*, ed. Rebecca C. Curtis (New York: Plenum Press, 1989), p. 304; John Wareham, *Wareham's Way: Escaping the Judas Trap* (New York: Atheneum, 1983).
3. Seth Allcorn, "The Self-Protective Actions of Managers," *Supervisory Management*, January 1989, pp. 3–7.
4. Robert Bell, *Surviving the 10 Ordeals of the Takeover* (New York: AMACOM, 1988), p. 123.
5. Donald W. Cole, *Professional Suicide or Organizational Murder?* 2nd ed. (Cleveland: The Organization Development Institute, 1989), p. 142.
6. "Self-Talk: Should You Listen to Your Own Professional Advice?" *Working Smart*, August 1, 1990, p. 6.
7. Hap LeCrone, "Overcoming a Negative Self-Image," Cox News Service, June 29, 1991.
8. Robert P. Vecchio, *Organizational Behavior*, 2nd ed. (Hinsdale, Ill.: Dryden Press, 1991), p. 180.

SOME ADDITIONAL REFERENCES

Bernstein, Albert J., and Sydney Craft Rosen. *Neanderthals at Work: How People and Politics Can Drive You Crazy . . . And What You Can Do About Them.* New York: John Wiley & Sons, 1992.

Karp, H. B. "Avoiding Political Pitfalls." *Management Solutions,* October 1988, pp. 9–13.

Kets de Vries, Manfred F. R. "Leaders Who Self-Destruct: The Causes and Cures." *Organizational Dynamics,* Spring 1989, pp. 6–25.

Kushel, Gerald. *The Fully Effective Executive.* Chicago: Contemporary Books, 1983.

Sondak, Arthur. "The Path to Managerial Self-Destruction." *Management Solutions,* September 1988, pp. 12–13.

Sondak, Arthur. "The Path to Managerial Self-Destruction." *Management Solutions,* August 1988, p. 27.

Speller, Jeffrey Lynn. *Executives in Crisis.* New York: John Wiley & Sons, 1989.

Appendix to Chapter Four

THE BLUNDER QUIZ

Indicate whether you agree or disagree with the following statements:

1. It's fine to criticize a company executive in a meeting as long as the criticism is valid.
2. Dressing for success is a sham. You should wear whatever clothing you find the most comfortable.
3. I am willing to insult any co-worker if the insult is deserved.
4. I see no problem in using competitors' products or services and letting my superiors know about it.
5. If someone higher up than you in the company offends you, let that person know about it.
6. Never bother with company-sponsored social events, such as holiday parties, unless you are really interested.
7. If I disagreed with something major my employer did, I would voice my opinion in a letter to the editor of the local newspaper.
8. I'm very open about passing along confidential information.
9. I openly criticize most new ventures my company or department is contemplating.
10. I always avoid office politics of any kind.

The greater the number of statements you agree with, the more prone you are to making political blunders that can damage your career. You need to raise your awareness level about blunders on the job. Review carefully the Guidelines for Action and Skill Development section.

Part II

Improving Interpersonal Relationships

The next four chapters concentrate on techniques for strengthening one-to-one relationships in organizations. However, these interpersonal relationships occur in the context of a group and also have ramifications for the entire firm.

Chapter 5, Developing Ethical Conduct, describes specific actions managers and professionals can take to develop stronger ethical codes and conduct. It Includes case histories of questionable behavior and examples of how companies are training employees to behave more ethically.

Chapter 6, Influence Tactics, pinpoints a variety of tactics managers and professionals can use to get others to respond positively to demands and requests. As with Chapter 5, the focus is ethical approaches to influencing others.

Chapter 7, Effective Negotiating, describes strategies and tactics for improving your ability to negotiate for what you want in a variety of situations. Negotiating gets attention in the organizational behavior and management literature and is the subject of many trade books, articles, and management development programs.

Chapter 8, Improving Customer Service, describes principles and techniques you can apply to enhancing service to external and internal customers.

Organizational behavior and management literature is now paying more attention to customers as a result of TQM and its emphasis on customer satisfaction. It is therefore important not to lose sight of basic techniques of pleasing customers.

Chapter Five

Developing Ethical Conduct

The entrepreneur described below founded a business by using other people's equipment without paying a user fee or royalty. Although his business activities are not illegal, objections have been raised to the basic idea behind his business.

International Discount Telecommunications Corp. (IDT) has its headquarters in a former funeral home in the East Bronx section of New York City. The small company has discovered a way to provide substantial savings on telephone calls from overseas, but many of the government-owned telephone companies in Europe are upset by IDT's method of operation.

Founder Howard Jonas, age 35, has devised a system that allows callers to use a U.S. telephone line from overseas. Using this system, the customer circumvents the more expensive phone systems of foreign countries. The company has about 150 customers including PepsiCo, the World Bank, and a major television network.

The system works in this manner: Assume a person is making a call from Barcelona, Spain. The caller dials a special number in the United States and hangs up after one ring. An electronic device attached to the line then dials the caller back. The caller in Barcelona picks up the phone again and hits the pound sign (#) on the dial. The action connects the phone to a U.S. phone company such as AT&T, Sprint, or MCI via one of the U.S. carrier's transatlantic lines. A dial tone is then produced. (Critics have likened this system to the old dodge of the person who makes a free call home indicating a safe arrival. Assume Todd Rover has traveled out of town. He makes a person-to-person phone call to his home, asking to speak to "Jack" Rover. The receiver of the operator-assisted message says, "Please call back, 'Jack' won't be home for several hours." Thus, Todd has informed his relative, friend, or spouse that he has arrived safely, without paying for a phone call.)

The IDT customer can call any number in the United States or another country. The U.S. long-distance company bills for the call, and the European telephone company receives no compensation. The savings can be substantial. A 10-minute call from Spain to New York costs about $34 when placed through Spain's phone system. Using IDT lines, the cost is about $8.

International Discount Telecommunications also offers lower rates on intercontinental calls that are routed through the United States. A one-minute call from Rome to Argentina using IDT costs about $1.55, compared to $5.80 if placed through the Italian phone system. The fee for using International Discount Telecommunications is $250 a month for the first phone line. Discounts are available for additional lines.

The service is a potential money saver. Yet some potential customers have been concerned about retaliation by the local phone company in the country in which they operate. Companies doing business overseas depend on the local phone company for such things as satellite access and microwave links.

International Discount Telecommunications faces competition from U.S. long-distance telephone companies that offer calling cards for calls from overseas. The calling card system allows an American overseas to dial a local access number and be billed at U.S. rates. Other competition stems from overseas companies that have already begun to lower their long-distance rates.

For now, IDT's business is growing. To handle the growth, Jonas has installed hundreds of his machines in a 16,000-square-foot building in Hackensack, New Jersey, that was once occupied by AT&T.

Many people will now be routing their long-distance calls from overseas to the United States through Hackensack. [1]

STRATEGIES AND TECHNIQUES FOR DEVELOPING ETHICAL CONDUCT

Ethics deals with what is right or wrong, moral or immoral, and just and unjust. Behaving ethically in the workplace is good for its own sake from a moral viewpoint and is highly valued by organizations. Business ethics today is a central leadership concern because so many executives in private and public firms have been guilty of ethical violations. Many businesses have developed extensive programs to encourage high standards of corporate conduct. [2]

Ethics programs can make an important contribution to a manager's development. With a stronger sense of ethics, the founder of International Discount Telecommunications might have developed a plan to compensate the European telephone companies for the use of their electronic equipment. This chapter incorporates many of the key ideas and principles contained in ethics programs. The emphasis here, however, is more sharply focused on skill-building actions for improving one's ethics. Philosophical and theoretical discussions about ethics should precede skill building.

Ask Yourself, "What Do You Stand For?"

According to Archie B. Carroll, the basic organizational strategy question is, "What business are you in?" The basic ethics question is, "What do you stand for?" [3] A starting point in building developing ethical conduct is to ask yourself what you really stand for. If your answer is fair business practices, your behavior will be much different than people whose answer is anything that makes money is fair play. Bad-mouthing the competition is an example of the depths to which some people will stoop to gain the competitive edge.

A couple opened a child-care center a half mile from an existing center. A surprisingly large number of clients enrolled in the new child-care center. About 10 percent of these new clients were parents who switched from the established competitor because of what they perceived to be mediocre child care.

The owners of the established child-care center decided drastic action was necessary to meet the competitive threat of the new center. The competitive tactic they chose was to plant derogatory rumors about the new center. The husband-and-wife team casually mentioned to parents that the new center served children ketchup sandwiches, had lax standards about changing diapers, and had hired a staff member who had been convicted of child abuse.

Enrollment in the target child-care center dropped precipitously. On hearing about these rumors, the owner distributed fliers denying the accusations. Although the rumors were partially counteracted, the center now faced serious financial trouble.

Small businesses are not alone in bad-mouthing the competition to gain advantage. Logitech Inc. manufactures "mouse" pointer devices for computers. Microsoft and Logitech are the key players in the $500 million market for such devices. Senior management at Logitech has written formal complaints to Microsoft that Microsoft sales representatives have bad-mouthed Logitech's products. [4]

Ethically Test Contemplated Decisions

A practical way of improving ethical decision making is to run contemplated decisions through an ethics test when any doubt exists. Many of these tests have been developed in recent years. Two of them are presented here. The first test is used at the Center for Business Ethics at Bentley College as part of corporate training programs. Decision makers are taught to ask themselves: [5]

1. *Is it right?* This question is based on the deontological theory of ethics that there are certain universally accepted guiding principles of rightness and wrongness, such as "thou shall not steal."

2. *Is it fair?* This question is based on the deontological theory of justice, implying that certain actions are inherently just and others unjust. For example, it is unjust to fire a high-performing employee to make room for a less competent person who is a personal friend.

3. *Who gets hurt?* This question is based on the utilitarian notion of attempting to do the greatest good for the greatest number of people.

4. *Would you be comfortable if the details of your decision were reported on the front page of your local newspaper or through your company's electronic messaging system?* This question is based on the universalist principle of disclosure.

5. *Would you tell your child (or young relative) to do it?* This question is based on the deontological principle of reversibility, referring to reversing who carries out the decision.

6. *How does it smell?* This question is based on a person's intuition and common sense. For example, bad-mouthing the competition would "smell" bad to a sensible person.

A decision that was obviously ethical, such as giving discounts to senior citizens, would not need to be run through the six-question test. Neither would a blatantly illegal act, such as not paying employees for work performed. But the test is useful for decisions that are neither obviously ethical nor unethical. Among such gray areas would be charging clients based on their ability to pay and developing a clone of a successful competitive product.

An ethics test developed by Laura L. Nash asks just one question, "What if we did this 20 times?" Some managerial actions might seem ethically passable because they are done only once. However, if done 20 times, the result could be quite unfair and dysfunctional to the organization. For example, a senior executive might place an unqualified relative in a high-paying position. Because the company is large and profitable, it can absorb this one bogus employee on the payroll. But if 20 unqualified relatives and friends were placed in high-paying positions, the result could be a drain on profits and morale. [6] Employees would think the amount of nepotism was beyond reason, thus blocking promotional opportunities.

Follow an Organizational Code of Conduct

Assume your organization has a printed ethical code of conduct. An easy way to develop ethical conduct is to carefully study the code and follow its guidelines. Some aspects of these codes are general, such as requiring people to conduct themselves with integrity and candor. Other aspects of the codes might be specific, such as indicating the maximum size gift that can be accepted from a vendor. In many organizations, known code violators are disciplined. At one company, a manager was suspended for a week because she used company equipment and supplies to produce fliers for her off-hours antique business.

Look at the analysis of the variables found in corporate codes of conduct in Table 5–1. Some clauses are job-specific, such as "bribes are prohibited."

Others are aimed at character development, such as "manage personal finances well."

TABLE 5–1   Clusters of Variables Found in 83 Corporate Codes of Ethics

Cluster 1: Be a dependable organizational citizen

1. Comply with safety, health, and security regulations.
2. Demonstrate courtesy, respect, honesty, and fairness.
3. Do not use illegal drugs and alcohol at work.
4. Manage personal finances well.
5. Exhibit good attendance and punctuality.
6. Follow directives of supervisors.
7. Do not use abusive language.
8. Dress in businesslike attire.
9. Do not bring firearms to work.

Cluster 2: Do not do anything unlawful or improper that will harm the organization

1. Conduct business in compliance with all laws.
2. Do not make payments for unlawful purposes.
3. Do not offer bribes.
4. Avoid outside activities that impair duties.
5. Maintain confidentiality of records.
6. Comply with antitrust and trade regulations.
7. Comply with accounting rules and controls.
8. Do not use company property for personal benefit.
9. Be personally accountable for company funds.
10. Do not propagate false or misleading information.
11. Make decisions without regard for personal gain.

Cluster 3: Be good to customers

1. Convey true claims in product advertisements.
2. Perform assigned duties to the best of your ability.
3. Provide products and services of the highest quality.

SOURCE: Fred R. David, "An Empirical Study of Codes of Business Ethics: A Strategic Perspective." Paper presented at the 48th Annual Academy of Management Conference, Anaheim, California, August 1988. Reprinted with permission.

Follow Professional Rules of Conduct

Virtually all states and provinces have boards appointed by the government to regulate certain professions, including architecture, certified public accountancy, dentistry, land surveying, massage, medicine, optometry, psychology, public accountancy, and veterinary medicine. Rules on professional conduct are developed for all professions, along with additional rules for health professions. Many of the general provisions for all professions also have relevance for managers and business owners. Table 5–2 presents some examples of un professional conduct as defined by a state agency.

TABLE 5–2   Examples of Unprofessional Conduct

1. Willfully making or filing a false report, or failing to file a report required by law, or willfully impeding or obstructing such filing, or inducing another person to do so.
2. Failing to make available to a client, upon request, copies of documents in the possession or under the control of the licensee which have been prepared and paid for by the client.
3. Practicing or offering to practice beyond the scope permitted by law, or accepting and performing professional responsibilities which the licensee knows or has reason to know that he or she is not competent to perform.
4. Delegating professional responsibilities to a person when the licensee delegating such responsibilities knows or has reason to know that such person is not qualified by training, by experience, or by licensure, to perform them.
5. Performing professional services which have not been duly authorized by the patient or client or his or her legal representative.
6. Advertising that is not in the public interest because it is false, fraudulent, deceptive, misleading, sensational, or flamboyant.

SOURCE: "Rules of the New York State Board of Regents Relating to Professional Conduct," May 1988.

Challenge Your Rationalizations about Ethical Behavior

Through creative rationalization a person can justify almost any unethical act. For example, a manager might present grossly inflated estimates of a company's future earnings to an industry analyst. Her rationalization might be, "I know I was presenting inaccurate projections. However, by presenting such an optimistic picture, the analyst might recommend our stock. This will bring us a much-needed infusion of cash that will help prevent layoffs."

Saul Gellerman believes unethical behavior stems from four questionable rationalizations often made by businesspeople:[7]

1. A belief that the activity is within ethical and legal limits, such as offering an employee a small bribe for not reporting a workplace accident.
2. A belief that because the activity is in the individual's or organization's best interest, the individual would be expected to undertake the activity. An example is accepting a substantial gift from a vendor because the buyer believes he or she is underpaid and the gift can be regarded as a form of compensation.
3. A belief that the activity is safe because it will never be uncovered. An envelope manufacturer decided to cut costs by reducing by 1 percent the

stated amount of envelopes contained in shipments, reasoning that neither wholesale nor retail customers bother to count envelopes.

4. A belief that because the unethical activity helps the company, the company will condone the activity and protect the person. For example, the managers in the envelope-shorting incident believed saving the company money would exempt them from punishment if caught.

To enhance ethical conduct, a person should be on guard against using these four rationalizations. When justifying a borderline ethical decision, ask yourself, "Is my rationalization for what I am doing faulty?" Because rationalizations are typically made almost unconsciously, self-confrontation must be done with rigor. Skill-Building Exercise 5 is used in ethics training programs.

SKILL-BUILDING EXERCISE 5
The Ethics Game

Citicorp has developed an ethics game, *The Work Ethic*. The game teaches ethics by asking small teams of employees to confront difficult scenarios such as those presented below.

Scenario I. A vice president in your organization asks you, as corporate recruiter, to find a career opportunity for a manager in his area. You know this manager is a poor performer, although the vice president has not reflected on any performance issues in the manager's performance reviews. The vice president tells you he wants this manager out of his area within three months. Your rapport with this vice president is critical to your success on the job. You:

a. Insist the manager be counseled on his job performance before any transfer process begins.
b. Present the manager to your fellow recruiters with the performance review and say nothing about the performance.
c. Refuse to help in this transfer.
d. Present the candidate to your fellow recruiters but are frank about the performance issues.

Scoring and observation: Notice that the most comfortable solution, taking the problem to your supervisor, is not an option. Teams that chose *a* receive 20 points; *b*, –10; *c*, 0; and *d*, 10.

Scenario II. One of your assignments is to find a contractor to conduct grounds maintenance for your company headquarters. You invite bids for the job. Star Landscaping, a firm staffed largely by teenagers who have been raised in abusive families, bids on the job. Many of these teenagers also have severe learning disabilities and cannot readily find employment. Star Landscaping proves to be the second highest bidder. You:

continued

a. Advise Star Landscaping that its bid is far too high for consideration, and your company is not a social agency.

b. Award the bid to Star Landscaping, and justify your actions with a letter to top management talking about social responsibility.

c. Falsify the other bids in your report to management, making Star Landscaping the low bidder, and thus the winner of the contract.

d. Explain to Star Landscaping that it lost the bid, but you will award the company a piece (of the contract because of its sterling work with needy teenagers.)

Scoring and observation: This scenario raises dozens of ethical questions, including whether humanitarian considerations can outweigh profit concerns. Teams that chose *a, (receive 0 points;) b,* 20 points; *c,* –10; *d, (10 points.)*

SOURCE: Scenario I is from Karin Ireland, "The Ethics Game," *Personnel Journal*, March 1991, p. 74. Reprinted with permission.

Conduct Audits of Ethical Behavior

Standard business practice is to conduct external and internal audits of company financial practices. Irregularities, such as overvaluing inventory, inventory shrinkage, and classifying intentions to buy as accounts receivable, are reported to management. Kenneth R. Andrews observes that purposefully ethical organizations expand these traditional audits to include corporate ethical standards.

The managers or professionals assigned to the ethical audit must have enough wisdom or experience to recognize the ethical consequences of business decisions regarding issues such as prices, equal opportunity and payoff dilemmas, and plans for downsizings. The ethical auditors must also have the respect and trust of operating people so open exchange about ethical issues is possible. [8]

Conducting an ethical audit—or being audited—develops sensitivity to possible ethical problems throughout the firm. Following are some problems uncovered through an ethical audit of a women's clothing manufacturer:

* Purchasing agents and merchandising managers were being lavishly entertained by textile manufacturers.

* Fashion models were routinely subjected to environmental sexual harassment, and sometimes company officials demanded sexual favors as a precondition for obtaining a modeling assignment.

* Many illegal aliens were doing piecework at home for less than the minimum wage.

* A line of pantsuits was imported through a broker in Asia who specialized in getting work manufactured by firms that used Chinese prison labor.

- Returns on defective merchandise received in December were often debited to the next year to present a more favorable financial picture for the current year.

As a result of this audit, many business practices were changed, several managers were disciplined, and a purchasing manager was demoted.

Andrews advises that an ethical audit must sometimes result in decisive disciplinary action.

The secretary who steals petty cash, the successful sales representative who falsifies his expense account, the accountant and her boss who alter cost records, and, more problematically, the chronically sleazy operator who never does anything actually illegal—all must be dealt with cleanly, with minimum attention to allegedly extenuating circumstances. [9]

Discuss Ethical Concerns in Small Groups

Discussing problems in small groups is an effective vehicle for changing attitudes. To improve ethical attitudes and conduct, it helps to discuss ethical issues in small work groups. Unfortunately, some ethics programs use large-group meetings that include members of top management. But according to consultant Barbara Ley Toffler, few managers are likely to talk openly about moral issues in the presence of a large number of employees, including the boss. "You need small groups of about six people, and even then the reality is that someone inside won't talk freely to someone in-house," she says. [10]

Dow Corning had an elaborate system for tracking ethical behavior in place before the suppression of information about the potential dangers of silicone gel breast implants. Part of the breakdown of this otherwise impressive ethics system has been attributed to the absence of a small-group mechanism. The Dow Corning ethics system centers around the following steps: [11]

- Six managers serve three-year terms on a business conduct committee. Each member spends up to six weeks a year serving on the committee.
- Two members audit every business operation every three years. The committee reviews up to 35 Dow Corning facilities annually.
- Three-hour reviews are held with up to 35 employees. Committee members refer to a company code of ethics as the framework. Employees are encouraged to raise ethical issues.
- Results of the ethical audits are reported to a three-member audit and social responsibility committee of the board of directors.

The Dow Corning ethics system uses large-group meetings rather than small-group discussions. The field visits by auditors may inhibit some employees from openly discussing ethical issues. Discussion in smaller groups, might uncover more sensitive ethical problems.

Resist Being Manipulated When Already Behaving Ethically

Another tactic to consider in developing realistic standards of ethical conduct is to hold fast when you are right. When you are convinced that you are behaving ethically, resist being manipulated into changing your way of doing business. Being charged with unethical behavior is certainly a time to pause and scrutinize your behavior, but the scrutiny could reveal that you are not violating any corporate, professional, or religious code of conduct.

A classic example of executives being manipulated to change already ethical business practices occurred at McDonald's. McDonald's was pressured to substitute paper for Styrofoam cups and sandwich wrappers. McDonald's executives sided with the environmentalists despite scientific evidence that paper creates more pollution problems and consumes more energy than does Styrofoam. Terence Corcoran, a social commentator, makes this analysis:

> All hail the triumph of environmentalists over McDonald's! But wait: what are we celebrating? Once the public relations material has been biodegraded and the claims of environmentalists filtered through the facts concerning plastics, the less reason there is to hoist a Styrofoam cup in a toast.
>
> In fact there is nothing to celebrate in the fast-food chain's decision to wrap Big Macs in paper rather than plastic, unless it is the exploitation of children. The major triumph in the McDonald's case is the ability of elementary school teachers to organize nine-year-old boys and girls to join a mindless and senseless campaign against a company and its products.
>
> In this era in which there is a need for corporations to be more ethical and socially responsible, what are the moral and ethical issues surrounding the overt manipulation of children to demonstrate for and join a cause they cannot even begin to understand? [12]

THE CASE FOR AND AGAINST DEVELOPING ETHICS CODES

The case for developing ethics codes is convincing. The greater the number of ethical workers, the more good organizations will do. There are also financial rewards for being ethical. Unethical behavior, such as employee theft or fraud, is costly. Theft costs American and Canadian businesses about $46 billion annually. [13] Companies can also receive substantial fines for behaving unethically. For example, Sunstrand was fined $227 million after pleading guilty to five counts of defrauding the Pentagon. Many stock brokerage firms specializing in penny stocks (low-priced stocks of start-up companies) have been forced out of business after being convicted of scams. Alan Weiss offers other reasons for examining workplace ethics and improving ethical conduct. Improving ethics improves customer satisfaction and service. An improvement in ethical behavior could also lead to improved employee loyalty. If managers behave more ethically, employees will think the company is more protective of their interests. [14] When a company executive receives $80 million in compensation the same year the company lays off workers, employee loyalty is likely to weaken.

The case against developing ethical codes of conduct centers around the idea that they are superfluous. Proponents of this idea argue that market factors function as an invisible hand that forces firms into behaving ethically. To do otherwise hurts business. If the sales practices of a penny-stock brokerage firm cause financial hardship to many of its clients, word will spread quickly about the bad deeds (unethical practices) and the firm will be forced out of business. Such reasoning reflects the classic economic argument against corporate social responsibility and regulation of business.

The traditional view holds that management's one responsibility is to maximize the profits of owners or shareholders. If ethical and socially responsible behavior leads to profits, managers will behave accordingly. Dow Corning, for example, will now listen more carefully to dissent about product hazards from within the organization. The traditional view has been softened in recent years. Economist Milton Friedman states that management should make as much money as possible yet still conform to the law and ethical customs. [15]

Guidelines for Action and Skill Development

Following the preceding suggestions for improving ethical conduct should enhance your ethical behavior. Consider also five guiding principles prepared by Philip M. Van Auken, for being an ethical manager.

1. *The mission principle.* Adhere to the mission of your organization (such as service, quality, or value to the customer) as a day-to-day guide to decision making.
2. *The consistency principle.* Demand the same fair, objective standards from every employee.
3. *The constituency principle.* Consider the needs and rights of as many groups (such as customers, employees, and shareholders) as possible in decision making.
4. *The proactive principle.* Exceed the minimum expectation or rule in taking action. Strive to deliver as much as you can for internal and external customers.
5. *The holism principle.* Keep an overall perspective in mind: the work and personal side of employees' lives, the needs of the majority as well as the minority, and the customer service side of business as well as manufacturing and sales. [16]

Another guideline for being an ethical manager is to both listen to whistle-blowers and be willing to blow the whistle yourself on unethical behavior in the organization. Report your findings on unethical behavior to the highest company executive who will listen. Proceed cautiously in reporting your findings to an outside agency or the media. You have some legal protection against job loss for whistle-blowing. Nevertheless, your reputation in the company and industry might suffer, and you might be the first to go in a downsizing.

General Electric Co., caught up in many high-profile corporate scandals during the last decade, now strongly endorses whistle-blowing. GE offers employees seminars and videos to teach them how to report wrongdoing. Company managers will also spring pop quizzes on employees in hallways, asking for instance, "What are three ways to report wrongdoing?" Workers who answer correctly win a coffee mug.[17]

DISCUSSION QUESTIONS AND ACTIVITIES

1. What ethical problems, if any, do you see with the basic concept behind the business of International Discount Telecommunications?

2. Why do so many people think the term *business ethics* is an oxymoron?

3. Consultant Alan Weiss says one reason we need ethics training on the job is that families today rarely have sit-down dinners at which moral behavior is discussed. What do you think of his assertion?

4. What would be a good way to disseminate information about a company code of conduct?

5. Business is not the only field in which not every person is highly ethical. Can you cite any examples of unethical behavior among physicians or lawyers?

6. Bribes are considered to be unethical, yet "dealer incentives" (bonus payments to dealers for accepting large orders of merchandise) are rarely challenged as being unethical. What do you see as the difference between a bribe and a dealer incentive?

7. Ask an experienced manager to identify the biggest ethical dilemma he or she faces. Be prepared to report your results in class.

NOTES

1. Adapted from "Rome to Bonn via New Jersey," *Business Week,* April 13, 1992; and Bart Ziegler, "Little Firm Saves Clients Big Money," Associated Press story, February 26, 1992.

2. An example is the annual Business Ethics Conference sponsored by the Conference Board.

3. Book review by Archie B. Carroll, *The Academy of Management Executive,* May 1989, p. 153.

4. "Did Microsoft Shut the Windows on Competition?" *Business Week,* September 28, 1992, p. 33.

5. James L. Bowditch and Anthony F. Buono, *A Primer on Organizational Behavior*, 2nd ed. (New York: John Wiley & Sons, 1990), p. 4.

6. Laura Nash, *Good Intentions Aside: A Manager's Guide to Resolving Ethical Problems* (Boston: Harvard Business School Press, 1990).
7. Saul W. Gellerman, "Why 'Good' Managers Make Bad Ethical Choices," *Harvard Business Review,* July–August 1986, p. 88.
8. Kenneth R. Andrews, "Ethics in Practice," *Harvard Business Review,* September–October 1989, p. 103.
9. Ibid.
10. John A. Byrne, "The Best-Laid Ethics Programs," *Business Week,* March 9, 1992, p. 69.
11. Ibid.
12. Adapted from Terence Corcoran, "Exploiting Children for Attacks on Macs," *The Globe and Mail,* November 3, 1990, p. B4. Reprinted with permission.
13. Extrapolated from data reported in Linda Klebe Trevino and Bart Victor, "Peer Reporting of Unethical Behavior: A Social Context Perspective," *Academy of Management Journal,* March 1992, p. 38.
14. Alan Weiss, "Seven Reasons to Examine Workplace Ethics," *HRMagazine,* March 1991, pp. 69–71.
15. Milton Friedman, "The Social Reponsibility of Business Is to Increase Profits," *New York Times,* September 1962, p. 126.
16. Philip M. Van Auken, "Being an Ethical Supervisor," *Supervisory Management,* October 1992, p. 3.
17. Amal Kumar Naj, "GE's Drive to Purge Fraud is Hampered by Workers' Mistrust," *The Wall Street Journal,* July 22, 1992, p. A1.

SOME ADDITIONAL REFERENCES

Beilinson, Jerry. "Ethics Rhetoric Being Replaced by Action." *Executive Forum,* August 1989, pp. 1–3.

Brown, Marvin T. *Working Ethics: Strategies for Decision Making and Organizational Responsibility.* San Francisco: Jossey-Bass, 1990.

Byrne, John A. "Can Ethics Be Taught? Harvard Gives It the Old College Try." *Business Week,* April 6, 1992, p. 34.

Gortner, Harold F. *Ethics for Public Managers.* New York: Praeger Publishers, 1991.

Harrington, Susan J. "What Corporate America Is Teaching About Ethics." *Academy of Management Executives,* February 1991, pp. 21–30.

Hitt, William D. *Ethics and Leadership: Putting Theory into Practice.* Columbus, Ohio: Battelle Press, 1990.

Jones, Thomas M. "Ethical Decision Making by Individuals in Organizations: An Issue-Contingent Model." *Academy of Management Review,* April 1991, pp. 366-95.

Kahn, William A. "Toward an Agenda for Business Ethics Research." *Academy of Management Review,* April 1990, pp. 311–28.

Sikula, Andrew, Sr. *Management in America: Crisis in Ethics.* Bend, Oregon: Daniel Spencer Publishers, 1992.

Steinberg, Sheldon S., and David T. Austern. *Government, Ethics, and Managers: A Guide to Solving Ethical Dilemmas in the Public Sector.* New York: Praeger Publishers, 1990.

Appendix to Chapter Five

AN ETHICS TEST

Many business situations are not simple right-or-wrong questions; they fall into a gray area. Here is a nonscientific test to measure ethical slippage. Put your value system to the test in the following situations:

Scoring card: Strongly agree = SA   Disagree =   D
                          Agree = SA   Strongly disagree = SD

	SA	A	D	SD
1. Employees should not be expected to inform on their peers for wrongdoing.	___	___	___	___
2. There are times when a manager must overlook contract and safety violations in order to get on with the job.	___	___	___	___
3. It is not always possible to keep accurate expense account records; therefore, it is sometimes necessary to give approximate figures.	___	___	___	___
4. There are times when it is necessary to withhold embarrassing information from one's superior.	___	___	___	___
5. We should do what our managers suggest, though we may have doubts about its being the right thing to do.	___	___	___	___
6. It is sometimes necessary to conduct personal business on company time.	___	___	___	___
7. Sometimes it is good psychology to set goals somewhat above normal if it will help to obtain a greater effort from team members.	___	___	___	___

8. I would quote a "hopeful" shipping date in order to get the order.

9. It is proper to use the company WATS (long-distance telephone) line for personal calls so long as it's not in company use.

10. Management must be goal-oriented; therefore, the end usually justifies the means.

11. If it takes heavy entertainment and twisting a bit of company policy to win a large contract, I would authorize it.

12. Exeception to company policy and procedures are a way of life.

13. Inventory controls should be designed to report "underages" rather than "overages" in goods received.

14. Occasional use of the company's copier for personal or community activities is acceptable.

15. Taking home company property (pencils, paper, tape, etc.) for personal use is an accepted fringe benefit.

0	Impeccable ethics	16–25	Average ethical values
1–5	Very high ethics	26–35	Need moral development
6—5	Good ethical values	36–24	Study this chapter again before reporting back to work

SOURCE: Adapted from Lowell G. Rein, "Is Your (Ethical) Slippage Showing?" *Personnel Journal*, September 1980. Reprinted with permission.

Chapter Six

Influence Tactics

To pursue his strategy of moving his company into exciting new product lines, the executive described below is using various influence tactics. Look for these tactics as you read the example that follows.

John Sculley, the chairman of Apple Computer Inc., is skilled at using colorful analogies. Recently, he said that for the manufacturers of personal computers, "the 1990s are a cold shower." After years of 30 percent and 40 percent increases in annual shipments, annual growth has skidded to 7 percent.

Apple has done well in comparison to the competition. The company has drastically reduced costs, and a series of fast-selling Macintoshes has enabled the company to increase market share. At the same time, profits have held steady despite much-reduced retail prices. Nevertheless, Sculley believes Apple's future will be severely constricted unless the company becomes less dependent on computers. He is concerned that if Apple remains exclusively a computer maker, the company will lose its excitement.

Sculley's solution is to move Apple Computer beyond being a computer maker. Under his direction, Apple plans to become a global electronics holding company, overseeing a variety of businesses. Sculley envisions a vast market forming as a wide range of information is converted into digital form. As he sees it, every product from high-definition television pictures to local phone calls will be converted to the zeroes and ones that computers already use. Sculley is predicting that when the conversion occurs, several industries will converge into a $3 trillion megamarket. His goal is to take a quick lead by capitalizing on Apple's leadership in making digital machines user friendly.

Sculley envisions the company building and selling consumer electronics, a full range of software, and telecommunication devices, along with computers.

Apple's first foray into this new strategy was a personal digital assistant called Newton, an electronic gadget that helps track appointments, phone numbers, and addresses. In addition, it recognizes handwriting and incorporates a built-in fax and data modem. Sculley believes Newton is the start of a revamped Apple that will include consumer electronics and digital communications.

To prepare for the future, Apple is undergoing what Sculley perceives as the most important transformation in its history. Sculley and Chief Operating Officer Michael H. Spindler are changing Apple from a one-product company with a straightforward distribution system. In its place will be a multiproduct, multibusiness conglomerate that will sell new products through new channels to new customers. To help fund the development costs of this new venture, Apple has forged partnerships with three giants in the electronics industry: IBM, Sharp, and Sony Corp. It is rumored that each one of these deals began at luncheon appointments, initiated by Sculley, with a rival executive. The Apple chairman is also engaged in cultivating potential partners in Japan and Hollywood. Sculley says he is developing relationships with entertainment, media, and publishing companies that have programming for Apple's new electronic devices. "These industries are going to bump into each other, so it's important to start building relationships today," says Sculley. An example of such a budding relationship is Apple's agreement with Random House to put an electronic version of the Modern Library books on PowerBook portables. [1]

INFLUENCE TACTICS FOR MANAGERS
AND PROFESSIONALS

To help move his company forward, John Sculley is using such influence tactics as creating a vision, forming coalitions, and networking with key people. To accomplish your objectives as a manager or professional, you too have to influence others. *Influence* in this context means securing the consent and commitment of others to work with you in accomplishing an objective. [2] Leaders, by definition, rely heavily on influence tactics because leadership is an influence process. Influence tactics are also closely linked to power, because power is the potential to influence others. Yet without the use of influence tactics, power does not lead to change.

This chapter on influence tactics deliberately follows the one addressing ethical practices. Influence tactics are usually viewed from the perspective of whether they are ethical. The influence tactics described here are classified into those that are essentially ethical and honest versus those that are essentially manipulative and devious. The ethical versus manipulative categorization is far from absolute. Except for the extremes, most of the tactics could conceivably be placed in either category depending on how they were used. For example, the tactic of "joking and kidding" can be either good-spirited or mean-spirited, and therefore could be classified as "essentially ethical" or "essentially manipulative."

Essentially Ethical and Honest Tactics

In this section, we describe ethical and honest strategies, tactics, and methods for influencing others. Used with tact, diplomacy, and good intent, they can help get others to join you in accomplishing a worthwhile objective. Because these influence approaches vary considerably in complexity, they also vary with respect to how much time is required for their development.

Display Charisma.   Charisma, or an engaging and magnetic personality, is partially based on inborn personality characteristics and on other traits that take a long time to develop. Nevertheless, some aspects of charisma can be developed with conscious effort. The characteristics of charismatic leaders described below can be developed through an effort to engage in the behaviors specified. [3]

1. *Charismatic leaders have vision.* A charismatic leader offers an exciting image of where the organization is headed and how to get there. A vision is more than a forecast because it describes an ideal version of the future of an organization or a unit.

2. *Charismatic leaders are masterful communicators.* To inspire people, the charismatic leader uses colorful language and exciting metaphors and analogies. The president of Coca-Cola tells employees and customers, "We give people around the world a moment of pleasure in their lives."

3. *Charismatic leaders inspire trust.* People believe so strongly in the integrity of charismatic leaders that they will risk their careers to pursue the chief's vision. It takes a history of being very honest with people to engender such trust.

4. *Charismatic leaders help group members feel capable.* One technique they use is to let group members achieve success on relatively easy projects. The group members are then praised and given more demanding assignments.

5. *Charismatic leaders are energetic and action-oriented.* Similar to entrepreneurs, most charismatic leaders are energetic and serve as a model for getting things done on time. Developing good work habits can contribute indirectly to your charisma.

6. *Charismatic leaders are emotionally expressive and animated.* Research has shown that people perceived to be charismatic are more animated than others. They smile frequently, speak rapidly, pronounce words clearly, and move their heads and bodies with higher than average frequency.

7. *Charismatic leaders respond to people's feelings more than to their words.* Too many leaders respond mostly to the factual content of what people say. A charismatic leader makes the effort to respond to the feel-

ings of group members. Assume a team member talks at length about how she solved an important customer problem. One response on your part might be, "Congratulations, you did an excellent job." A more charismatic response would be something to the effect, "You must be proud. Congratulations, you did an excellent job."

Charisma enables a leader to exert influence in everyday interactions with team members. The same quality is linked to influence tactics in another important way. Charisma is an essential part of transformational leadership, as described in Chapter 3 about crisis management.

Lead by Example. A simple but effective way of influencing group members is leading by example, or leading by acting as a positive role model. The ideal approach to leading by example is to be a "do as I say and do" manager. Such a manager shows consistency between actions and words. Also, actions and words confirm, support, and often clarify each other. For example, if the firm has a dress code and the manager explains the code and dresses accordingly, he or she provides a role model that is consistent in words and actions. Following the dress code provides an example that supports and clarifies the words used in the dress code. [4]

Use Rational Persuasion. Influencing people through rational persuasion is an important tactic. Rational persuasion uses logical arguments and factual evidence to convince another person that a proposal or request is workable and likely to result in goal attainment. [5] Assertiveness, along with careful research, is necessary to use rational persuasion effectively. Rational persuasion is likely to be most effective with intelligent, rational people. John Sculley used rational persuasion to help influence his board of directors that Apple should move beyond computers.

Exchange Favors. Offering an exchange of favors if another person will help you achieve a work goal is another standard influence tactic. The exchange often translates into you expressing a willingness to reciprocate later. The exchange might also be promising a share of the benefits if the other person helps you accomplish a task. For example, you might promise to place a person's name on a report to top management if he or she helps analyze the data and prepare the tables.

Another perspective on using exchange is that you are building a favor bank. You do favors for people today, with the expectation that you can make a withdrawal from the favor bank when needed in the future. A human resources manager took the initiative to help a colleague in another company recruit a physically disabled compensation analyst. Several months later, the same human resources professional called on the colleague to nominate her for office in their professional society.

Robert Dilenschneider, CEO of the worldwide public relations firm Hill and Knowlton, describes how middle managers can build favor banks: "At any level, it's a matter of knowing who needs you and whom you need," explains Dilenschneider. "You should build goodwill. If you are a middle manager, look around you. You interact with a money specialist, with a lawyer, with a variety of operations people. Use them and let them use you." [6]

Team Play.   Influencing others by being a good team player is an important strategy for getting work accomplished. A survey about influence tactics was conducted among 295 men and 228 women in managerial, professional, and sales jobs. On a one-to-five scale, both men and women gave team play a rating of about 4.2 as an influence tactic. (Only logic, or reason, received a similarly high frequency.) [7]

Chapter 10 provides details about teamwork. The tactic recommended for now is to emphasize that you are part of the team rather than a solo performer. Critical to achieving this end is to emphasize *we* rather than *I* when talking about work accomplishments. A convenient way of emphasizing the *we* concept is to share credit with co-workers for your good ideas and achievements. When you receive a compliment, explain that the group deserves most of the credit. This emphasis on teamwork will enhance your ability to influence others because you will be regarded as a team player.

Develop a Reputation as an Expert.   Becoming a subject matter expert on an important topic is an effective way to gain influence. A series of interviews conducted by Bernard Keys and Thomas Case support this observation. Managers who possess expert knowledge in a relevant field and who continually build on that knowledge are in a position to get others to help them get work accomplished. [8]

After a person establishes a reputation as a subject matter expert, the person will be treated as a true professional. Many others will grant him or her the authority to do what is best to solve a problem. One manager became the resident expert on direct marketing (selling via the mails) in his company. One day he proposed launching via direct mail a new product—simulated leather aviator jackets. Instead of top management haggling over the budget as the manager anticipated, he was told, "Go ahead. We have faith in you; just make us a profit."

Develop a Network of Resources   Networking is an important strategy for career management, including becoming an influential person. The ability to establish a network and call on support when needed helps a manager or professional exert influence. A bank branch manager used his network of resource persons when he needed additional space for his operation.

My strategy was to convince my immediate superior that the current facilities were too small to not only manage the current volume of business, but also too small to allow us to increase our market share in a rapidly growing area. First, I persuaded my manager to visit the branch more often, especially when the branch was very busy. I also solicited my accountant's help to provide statistical reports on a regular basis that communicated the amount of overall growth in the area, as well as the growth of our competitors. These reports showed that our market share had increased.

I then asked my superior to visit with me as I called on several prospects in the area. This would let him know the types of potential business in the area. During this time, I kept pushing to increase all levels of business at the branch.

Finally, I encouraged key bank customers to say favorable things about my branch when they visited with my senior managers. Eventually my boss got behind my proposal. We were able to build an addition to the building, which allowed me to add several new employees.[9]

Acquire Power.   A major strategy for becoming influential is to acquire power, because power provides the potential to influence others. Being aware of the basic sources of power guides a person toward the appropriate techniques of acquiring power. An updating of the classic types or sources of power follows:[10]

Expert power is the ability to administer to another person information, knowledge, or expertise.

Referent power is the ability to administer to another person feelings of personal acceptance or approval. Charisma is the basis of referent power.

Reward power is the ability to administer to another person things the person desires or to remove or decrease undesired things.

Coercive power is the ability to administer to another person things the person does not desire or to remove or decrease things the person does desire. (Coercive power fits into the manipulative and devious category of influence tactics.)

Legitimate power is the ability to administer to another person feelings of obligation or responsibility.

After becoming aware of the various types of power, the power seeker develops appropriate strategies and tactics to achieve his or her goal. For example, becoming a subject matter expert would help one acquire expert power. Playing organizational politics is a general strategy for acquiring power. Skill-Building Exercise 6 will help sensitize you to the importance of using political tactics appropriately.

SKILL-BUILDING EXERCISE 6
The Organizational Politics Questionnaire

Answer each question "mostly agree" or "mostly disagree," even if it is difficult for you to decide which alternative best describes your opinion.

	Mostly agree	Mostly disagree
1. The boss is always right.	____	____
2. It is wise to flatter important people.	____	____
3. If you do someone a favor, remember to cash in on it.	____	____
4. Given the opportunity, I would cultivate friendships with powerful people.	____	____
5. I would be willing to say nice things about a rival to get that person transferred from my department.	____	____
6. If it would help me to get ahead, I would take credit for someone else's work.	____	____
7. Given the chance, I would offer to help my boss build some shelves for his or her den.	____	____
8. I laugh at my boss's jokes, even if I do not think they are funny.	____	____
9. Dressing for success is silly. At work, wear clothing that you find to be the most comfortable.	____	____
10. Never waste lunchtime by eating with somebody who can't help you solve a problem or gain advantage.	____	____
11. I think using memos to zap somebody for his or her mistakes is a good idea, especially if you want to show that person up.	____	____
12. If somebody higher up in the organization offends you, let that person know about it.	____	____
13. Honesty is the best policy in practically all cases.	____	____
14. Power for its own sake is one of life's most precious commodities.	____	____
15. If I had a legitimate gripe against my employer, I woulde air my views publicly, such as writing a letter to the editor of a local newspaper.	____	____

16. I would invite my boss to a party at my home even if I didn't like him or her.   _____   _____

17. An effective way to impress people is to tell them what they want to hear.   _____   _____

18. Having a high school or skyscraper named after me would be an incredible thrill.   _____   _____

19. Hard work and good performance are usually sufficient for success.   _____   _____

20. Even if I made only a minor contribution to a project, I would get my name listed as being associated with it.   _____   _____

21. I would never publicly correct mistakes made by my boss.   _____   _____

22. I would never use my personal contacts in order to gain a promotion.   _____   _____

23. If you happen to dislike a person who receives a big promotion in your firm, don't bother sending that person a congratulatory note.   _____   _____

24. I would never openly criticize a powerful executive in my organization.   _____   _____

25. I would stay late in the office just to impress my boss.   _____   _____

Scoring and interpretation: Give yourself a +1 for each answer you gave in agreement with the keyed answer. Note that we did not use the term *correct answer*. Whether an answer is correct is a question of personal values and ethics. Each person that receives a score of +1 shows a tendency toward playing organizational politics. The scoring key is as follows:

1. Mostly agree	10. Mostly agree	18. Mostly agree
2. Mostly agree	11. Mostly agree	19. Mostly disagree
3. Mostly agree	12. Mostly disagree	20. Mostly agree
4. Mostly agree	13. Mostly disagree	21. Mostly agree
5. Mostly agree	14. Mostly agree	22. Mostly disagree
6. Mostly agree	15. Mostly disagree	23. Mostly disagree
7. Mostly agree	16. Mostly agree	24. Mostly agree
8. Mostly agree	17. Mostly agree	25. Mostly agree
9. Mostly disagree		

Based on a sample of 750 men and women managers, professionals, administrators, sales representatives, and business owners, the mean score is 10. Scores of 1 through 7 suggest a below-average tendency to play politics. Scores between 8 and 12 suggest an average tendency to play politics. Scores of 13 and above suggest an above-average tendency to play office politics, and a strong need for power.

If you have a below-average tendency to play politics you could be losing out on some of the power you will need to influence others. You are advised to study more about politics, including carefully observing people who are skillful at acquiring power. Close-to-maximum scores suggest a person is too political, perhaps to the point of being ruthless. Such a drive for power could be self-defeating because it creates too many enemies.

Empower Others.   Paradoxically, influence can be increased by sharing power with others as well as enhancing your own power directly. A truly powerful leader makes team members feel powerful and able to accomplish tasks on their own. [11] To empower others is to be perceived as a person of influence. Almost any form of participative management and shared decision making can be regarded as empowerment. Jay Conger, however, recommends specific empowering practices that will enhance a manager's ability to be influential.[12] These practices are based on direct observations of successful executives.

1. *Provide a positive emotional atmosphere.* An unusual empowering practice that emerged from the study was for executives to provide positive emotional support to team members, especially through play or drama. For example, every few months, several executives would host a daylong event devoted to building confidence. Among the activities were inspirational speeches and films about mountain climbing.

2. *Reward and encourage in visible and personal ways.* The majority of executives in the study rewarded the achievements of team members through the use of praise and by giving rewards in visible and confidence-building ways. For example, one executive established the "I Make a Difference Club." Each year, staff members who have performed in an exceptional way are invited to a company dinner in which they are inaugurated into this exclusive "Difference Club."

3. *Express confidence.* The empowering leaders in the study invested considerable time expressing their confidence in team members' abilities. Furthermore, they expressed their confidence daily through such vehicles as speeches, meetings, and chance encounters in the hallways.

4. *Foster initiative and responsibility.* By simply fostering greater initiative and responsibility in the assignments of team members, a leader can empower them. For example, one bank executive transformed what had been a constricted branch manager's job into a branch "president" role. Managers were now evaluated on the basis of deposits because these were under their control, and they were allowed to stay with one branch rather than be rotated every three years.

5. *Build on success.* The empowering executives often introduced organizational change by starting small. If the change proved successful in the pilot run, it would proceed on a larger scale. For example, a new technology might be introduced in one plant rather than organizationwide. The managers who launched these new projects reported feelings of self-efficacy.

Empowering others could be regarded as one of the most ethical and honest approaches to becoming influential. Our attention now focuses on the dark side of becoming influential.

Essentially Manipulative and Devious Tactics

The first five strategies, tactics, and approaches to gaining influence presented in this section would be considered unethical and devious by many people. In contrast, the last three tactics might be regarded by many managers and professionals as less than fully candid but still within the bounds of acceptable ethics.

Deliberate Machiavellianism. Almost five centuries ago, Niccolo Machiavelli advised that strong, ruthless, and cynical leadership is required of a prince because people are self-interested and self-serving. People in the workplace who ruthlessly manipulate others have since come to be called Machiavellians. They tend to initiate actions with others and control the interactions. Machiavellians regularly practice deception, bluff, and other manipulative tactics.[13]

A sales manager in the movie and play *Glengarry Glen Ross* epitomizes a Machiavellian manager. He announces to his staff, "We have a new sales contest [for selling undeveloped land in Florida and Arizona] this week. First prize is a Cadillac; second prize is a set of steak knives. Third prize is that you are fired."

Gentle Manipulation of People and Situations. Some people attempting to influence others are manipulative but to a lesser extent than an outright Machiavellian. By making untrue statements, or faking certain behaviors, they gain the compliance of another person. For example, an employee might imply that if given a promotion, his father's company may become a good customer. Or an employee might fake tears and talk about heavy child-rearing responsibilities when asked to work every other Saturday.

A widely used manipulative approach is the *bandwagon technique*. A manager informs his vice president he wants an enlarged budget for diversity awareness training "because all other companies are doing it." Another approach is the *always technique*. The manipulator says to his or her manager, "I always get assigned to the least important projects." Here the manipulator attempts to gain control of the discussion by indirectly prompting the boss to respond to a general accusation.

The best antidote to manipulative influence tactics is to confront the manipulator. In the last example, ask, "What do you mean by always?" and continue digging until you reach the person's true concern.

Game Playing.   People often play games to influence others. A *game* in this context is a repeated series of exchanges between people that appears different on the surface than its true motive. A game always has a hidden agenda or purposes. The game player acts in a way that is superficially plausible but has a concealed motivation. Influence is exerted in a game because the person who the game is played against is made to feel humble.

Blemish.   This is an example of a simple game often used by managers to keep team members in line. The manager finds some flaw in every assignment completed by subordinates. The game-playing boss stays one up with comments such as, "You did a great job on that report except in your conclusion. It just didn't seem to fit the body of the report."

Door-in-the Face Technique.   Closely related to game playing are one-time transactions by the influencer that have a hidden motive. One such tactic is the door-in-the-face technique. The person attempting to exert influence makes a major request that will most likely be rejected. Shortly thereafter comes a more modest request, which was the goal in the first place. [14] In rejecting the first request, the target person may feel guilty and thus be responsive to a future request.

> The manager of an internal auditing group wanted a greatly increased telephone budget for her group during a period in which the company was carefully controlling expenditures. She approached her manager and asked for a substantial increase in the auditing team's travel budget. The budget request was rejected quickly. She returned two weeks later with a request for an increased telephone budget to compensate for the limited travel. The request was granted within a week.

Undue Pressure.   Effective managers regularly use motivational techniques such as rewards and mild punishments. Yet when rewards become bribes for compliance, and threats of punishment become severe, the target person is subjected to undue pressure. An example of a bribe by a manager would be, "If you work 80 hours on this project this week, I'll recommend you for the highest pay raise I can."

A new form of threat in the workplace has been termed *office blackmail*. Many employees complain of being pushed to work unreasonably hard because of job insecurity. The thinly veiled threat is that unless the employee does the extra work, his or her job will be eliminated. [15] A threat of this type works effectively as an influence tactic when the threatened employee has limited job opportunities outside the firm.

Upward Appeal.   In *upward appeal,* the manager exerts influence on a team member by getting a person with more formal authority to carry out the influence act: "I sent the guy to my superior when he wouldn't listen to me. That fixed him." More than occasional use of upward appeal weakens the manager's stature in the eyes of group members and superiors, thus eroding effectiveness as a leader.

Upward appeal can also be applied in other ways. A person attempts to persuade you that his or her request is approved by higher management, and therefore your acceptance is automatic. Or the person appeals to higher management for assistance in gaining your compliance with the request, thus putting you in a squeeze. [16]

Ingratiation.   Getting somebody else to like you can be considered a mildly manipulative influence tactic, particularly if you do not like that person. Ingratiating tactics identified in a study about influence tactics included the following:[17]

- Made him or her feel important. ("Only you have the brains and talents to do this.")
- Acted very humbly toward him or her while making my request.
- Praised him or her.
- Sympathized with him or her about the added problems that my request caused.
- Waited until he or she appeared in a receptive mood before asking.
- Asked in a polite way.
- Pretended I was letting him or her decide to do what I wanted. (Act in a pseudo-democratic fashion.)

The ingratiator is thus a flatterer, sometimes to the point of being obsequious. Nevertheless, ingratiation is not inappropriate role behavior for many types of selling, for customer service, and for making requests of top management.

Charm and Appearance.   Managers and professionals sometimes influence others by being charming and creating a positive appearance. In the survey of men and women referred to above, men indicated they used charm one third of the way between sometimes and frequently (a frequency rating of 3.3 on a one-to-five scale). Appearance was also given a frequency rating of 3.3. The frequency ratings women gave charm and appearance were insignificantly different from those given by men. Women gave both charm and appearance a frequency rating of 3.5, partway between sometimes and frequently. [18]

Charm might be considered a contributor to ingratiation because many people like a charming person. Being charming includes such behaviors as complimenting others profusely, expressing thanks, and displaying impeccable etiquette. *Appearance* in this context means dressing professionally and fashionably.

Joking and Kidding.   Survey data indicate that joking and kidding are frequently used to influence others in the workplace. [19] Good-natured ribbing is especially effective when a straightforward statement might be interpreted as harsh criticism. Joking or kidding can get the message across while lowering the risk that the influence target will be angry with the influence agent. Joking and kidding can be interpreted as either dishonest or extraordinarily tactful because the criticizer uses humor to soften the full blow of the criticism. Here is how one manager used joking and kidding to criticize:

> A fastidious executive toured the company's office facilities. During her trip, she noticed several instances of coffeepots and small microwave ovens in the work area—a violation of safety regulations. The executive commented to the office manager, "In general, I like what I see, but why have our workers set up light housekeeping? Are you keeping them here all hours of the night?" Not long after, the gear for food and beverage preparation was not to be found outside of the employee lounge.

Evidence about the Effectiveness of Influence Tactics

Experience and common sense indicate that effective managers and professionals use influence tactics. If some form of influence tactic were not used intentionally or unintentionally, the manager or professional would be working without assistance. Experience and common sense also tell us that some influence tactics are ethically more acceptable than others. For example, rational persuasion is considered by most influence agents and influence targets to be more ethical than Machiavellianism.

At issue then is not whether influence tactics are effective, but which influence tactics are most effective. A recent study by Gary Yukl and J. Bruce Tracey provides fresh insights about the relative effectiveness of influence tactics. The study involved 120 managers along with 526 subordinates, 543 peers, and 128 superiors who also rated the managers' use of influence tactics. Half of the managers were in manufacturing companies and half were in service companies. The people who worked with the managers completed a questionnaire to identify which influence tactics the managers used. (The tactics surveyed were similar to those mentioned throughout this chapter.) Another question asked how many influence attempts by the agent resulted in completed commitment by the target respondent. Respondents were also asked to rate the managers on a one-to-nine scale. The scale ranged from "the least effective manager I have ever known" to "the most effective manager I have ever known."

The researchers concluded the most effective tactics were rational persuasion, inspirational appeal, and consultation. The least effective were pressure, coalition, and appealing to legitimate authority (formal power). Ingratiation and exchange were moderately effective for influencing subordinates and peers. The same tactics were not effective for influencing superiors. [20]

A previous study by David Kipnis and Stuart M. Schmidt also presented evidence that rational persuasion is an effective influence tactic, among other findings. According to the study, *shotgun managers* (those with high scores on assertiveness, appeal to higher authority, and coalition formation) received the lowest performance ratings. Many of these managers were apparently regarded as an annoyance. Managers classified as *tacticians* (those who emphasized rational persuasion) received the highest performance ratings. *Ingratiators* (those managers who emphasized ingratiation) received only a moderate rating. [21]

Guidelines for Action and Skill Development

A starting point in choosing influence tactics to help you accomplish your mission is to select those that fit your ethical code. For example, a person might say, "being a team player and empowering others fit my ethics, but I can't play games with people."

Another major consideration is to choose the correct combination of influence tactics. These tactics must be chosen carefully on the basis of the influence target and your objectives. For example, ingratiation might not work well with superiors. Often, it is best to begin with a gentle influence tactic and strengthen the approach as needed. Keys and Case found that most first influence attempts by managers involved gentle approaches such as requests or logical persuasion. When the influence target was reluctant to comply, later attempts included firmer tactics. [22] (Bill collectors have always used this approach!)

Influence tactics must also fit the influence objective. Kipnis and his associates observe that managers should not rely on a single influence tactic such as assertiveness to achieve both organizational and personal objectives. While it may be appropriate to insist that your boss be mindful of cost overruns, it is inappropriate to insist that you be granted time off to golf with network members. [23]

Good communication skills are required to implement influence tactics. As Keys and Case note, "Managers who choose rational ideas based on the needs of the target, wrap them with a blanket of humor or anecdotes, and cast them in the language of the person to be influenced, are much more likely to see their influence objective achieved." [24]

DISCUSSION QUESTIONS AND ACTIVITIES

1. Which of the tactics described in this chapter help explain the widespread use of business luncheons as an influence tactic?

2. Identify two exchanges of favors that you have either seen occur on the job or that you can envision might take place.

3. Managers are supposed to be generalists. How can they use the influence tactic, "Develop a reputation as an expert"?

4. How is office politics related to influence tactics?

5. Lobbyists are often referred to as *influence peddlers*, meaning they sell their ability to influence others. Which influence tactics do lobbyists use?

6. Explain how empowering others might add to rather than detract from one's power and influence.

7. Executives working for the very largest business corporations average about $2 million in annual compensation. What type of power do they possess to command such high incomes?

NOTES

1. As reported in Kathy Rebello, "Apple's Daring Leap into the All-Digital Future," *Business Week,* May 25, 1992, pp. 120–22.
2. David A. Whetten and Kim S. Cameron, *Developing Management Skills,* 2nd ed. (New York: HarperCollins Publishers Inc., 1991), p. 297.
3. Jay A. Conger, *The Charismatic Leader: Beyond the Mystique of Exceptional Leadership* (San Francisco: Jossey-Bass, 1989); Jane M. Howell and Bruce Avolio, "The Ethics of Charismatic Leadership: Submission or Liberation?" *The Executive,* May 1992, pp. 43–52; and James M. Kouzes and Barry Z. Posner, *The Leadership Challenge: How to Get Extraordinary Things Done in Organizations* (San Francisco: Jossey-Bass, 1987), pp. 123–24.
4. R. Bruce McAfee and Betty J. Ricks, "Leadership by Example: 'Do as I Do!'" *Management Solutions,* August 1986, p. 10.
5. Gary Yukl and J. Bruce Tracey, "Consequences of Influence Tactics Used with Subordinates, Peers, and the Boss," *Journal of Applied Psychology,* August 1992, p. 526.
6. "Build Power and Influence," *Executive Strategies,* June 19, 1990, p. 6.
7. Andrew J. DuBrin, "Sex and Gender Differences in Tactics of Influence," *Psychological Reports* 86 (1991), p. 640.
8. Bernard Keys and Thomas Case, "How to Become an Influential Manager," *Academy of Management Executive,* November 1990, p. 44.
9. Adapted from ibid., pp. 45–46.
10. Bernard M. Bass, *Bass & Stogdill's Handbook of Leadership: Theory, Research, and Managerial Applications,* 3rd ed. (New York: The Free Press, 1990), p. 232.
11. The discussion in this section is based on Whetten and Cameron, *Developing Management Skills,* p. 234.

12. Jay A. Conger, "Leadership: The Art of Empowering Others," *Academy of Management Executive,* February 1989, pp. 17–24.
13. Bass, *Bass & Stogdill's Handbook of Leadership*, p. 134.
14. Chad T. Lewis, Joseph E. Garcia, and Sarah M. Jobs, *Managerial Skills in Organizations* (Boston: Allyn & Bacon, 1990), p. 234.
15. Beth Sherman, "Office Blackmail," *Newsday,* May 23, 1992.
16. Gary Yukl and Cecilia M. Falbe, "Influence Tactics and Objectives in Upward, Downward, and Lateral Influence Attempts," *Journal of Applied Psychology,* April 1990, p. 133.
17. David Kipnis and Stuart M. Schmidt, "Intraorganizational Influence Tactics: Explorations in Getting One's Way," *Journal of Applied Psychology*, August 1980, p. 445.
18. DuBrin, "Sex and Gender Differences," p. 640.
19. Ibid.
20. Yukl and Tracey, "Consequences of Influence Tactics," pp. 525- 35.
21. David Kipnis and Stuart M. Schmidt, "Upward Influence Styles: Relationships with Performance Evaluations, Salary, and Stress," *Administrative Science Quarterly* 33, pp. 528-42.
22. Keys and Case, "How to Become an Influential Manager," p. 46.
23. David Kipnis, Stuart M. Schmidt, C. Swaffin Smith, and Ian Wilkinson, "Patterns of Managerial Influence: Shotgun Managers, Tacticians, and Bystanders," *Organizational Dynamics,* Winter 1984, p. 32. (Cited in Keys and Case, "How to Become an Influential Manager," p. 46.)
24. Keys and Case, "How to Become an Influential Manager," p. 48.

SOME ADDITIONAL REFERENCES

DuBrin, Andrew J. *Stand Out! 330 Ways to Gain the Edge with Superiors, Subordinates, Co-Workers, and Customers.* Englewood Cliffs, N.J.: Prentice Hall, 1993.

Halpert, Jane A. "The Dimensionality of Charisma." *Journal of Business and Psychology,* Summer 1990, pp. 399–410.

Schriesheim, Chester A., and Timothy R. Hinkin. "Influence Tactics Used by Subordinates: A Theoretical and Empirical Analysis and Refinement of the Kipnis, Schmidt, and Wilkinson Subscales." *Journal of Applied Psychology,* June 1990, pp. 246–57.

Wayne, Sandy J., and Gerald R. Ferris. "Influence Tactics, Affect, and Exchange Quality in Supervisor-Subordinate Interactions: A Laboratory Experiment and Field Study." *Journal of Applied Psychology,* October 1990, pp. 487–99.

Zucker, Elaina. *The Seven Secrets of Influence.* New York: McGraw-Hill, 1991.

Appendix to Chapter Six

IDENTIFYING INFLUENCE TACTICS

Label each influence tactic listed as being mostly an example of one of the following: I = Ingratiation; E = Exchange of Benefits; R = Rationality; A = Assertiveness; U = Upward Appeal.

Tactic	Code
1. Sympathized with person about the added problems that my request caused.	_____
2. Offered to help if person would do what I wanted.	_____
3. Set a time deadline for person to do what I asked.	_____
4. Obtained the informal support of higher-ups.	_____
5. Used logic to convince him or her.	_____
6. Made a formal appeal to higher levels to back up my request.	_____
7. Had a showdown in which I confronted the person head-on.	_____
8. Offered to make a personal sacrifice if person would do what I wanted (for example, work late or harder).	_____
9. Made him or her feel good about me before making my request.	_____
10. Explained the reasons for my request.	_____

Answers:

1. I	6. U
2. E	7. A
3. A	8. E
4. U	9. I
5. R	10 R

SOURCE: Based on information in Chester A. Schriesheim and Timothy R. Hinkin, "Influence Tactics Used by Subordinates: A Theoretical and Empirical Analysis and Refinement of the Kipnis, Schmidt, and Wilkinson Subscales," *Journal of Applied Psychology,* June 1990, p. 246.

Chapter Seven

Effective Negotiating

The marketing manager of an office furniture supply company wanted her company to implement a zero customer defection program. The president and the chief financial officer, however, did not grant her carte blanche to run her proposed program. The manager, therefore, turned to negotiation to receive the approval and funds to implement the program for zero customer defections.

Lynn Houston is the sales manager of Global Office Furniture, a company that sells office furniture and carpeting to commercial accounts. Although most of Global's customers are business organizations, the firm also has bid successfully on some government projects. Last year, Global grossed $21 million in sales and posted a $350,000 profit. Both gross revenues and profits are down about 10 percent from the previous two years.

Lynn had mixed reactions toward her 3 o'clock meeting today. She knew it would not be easy getting approval and funding for her new program. This would be her third meeting about the topic with Barry Nathan, the president, and Sara Fontaine, the chief financial officer. Lynn believed that if she failed to make substantial progress today in selling her program, the issue would be dropped until the next fiscal year.

The meeting took place in the second-floor conference room. Lynn had suggested they meet in the conference room to minimize interruptions. She also thought that meeting in the conference room would emphasize the importance of her program. Lynn took the initiative to open the meeting.

"Barry and Sara, thanks a lot for fitting this meeting into your hectic schedules," Lynn said. "I would never have asked for an hour of your joint time unless I thought we were dealing with something very important."

"Could you give us a quick rundown of your latest thinking on your customer service program?" Barry said. "I have studied your proposal, but I'm a little rusty on the details. I think Sara could use an overview also."

"Of course, I'll give you a briefing on my latest thinking," replied Lynn. "It's kind of you to ask. I'm proposing a zero customer defection program. The ultimate goal would be to stop losing customers. In a nutshell, we would research every lost customer we could to find out why they stopped doing business with us. We would teach every employee how he or she can help us hold on to customers."

"Who doesn't want to hold on to customers?" asked Barry. "But wouldn't we be better off investing more money in advertising?"

"I agree," responded Sara. "Why is spending time trying to get back former customers a good investment?"

"I have some important statistics to answer your question," Lynn said. "A study in the *Harvard Business Review* [1] showed that reducing customer defections 5 percent boosts profits from 25 percent to 85 percent. This figure applies to most businesses. The article also showed that the longer you hold on to the customer, the more profit your customer generates. One of the businesses reported on was similar to ours. It was an industrial distribution firm. In the first year, the average profit per customer was $45. By the fifth year, that profit jumped to $168."

"The statistics you quote are impressive, but we don't know that they apply to our company. How much would this program cost Global?" Barry asked.

Lynn answered, "If this program is as successful as I intend it to be, it will cost nothing. I am suggesting that we invest about $20,000 in order to reap perhaps 10 times that in profits. We would need to hire an interviewer for a month. He or she would interview every customer we have not heard from in over one year. First, we would find out if the customer was really lost. If the customer had truly defected, the interviewer would find out why. We might hire a consultant for a week to help us analyze the information.

"We would also implement a customer service training program aimed at customer retention. Every Global employee would receive the training. The zero customer defection program therefore has two parts. Analyzing why we lost customers is one key part. Training our employees to improve our retention rates is the other part," concluded Lynn.

"Why not just ask a few of our salespeople why they lost their last few accounts?" asked Sara. "We could then combine that with a customer service video for all employees. They could watch it once or twice during a long lunch hour. We'd then be talking about a program cost of a few hundred dollars."

"I agree with you strongly that your ideas represent a low-cost investment. What I'm suggesting is a bigger investment. Yet if Global does a thorough job of implementing a zero customer defection program, the financial return will be substantial.

"Another concern I have is that our salespeople lack an objective view of why we lose customers. To them, the reason is always low-price competition and terrible delivery times on our part. I think the problem is more complex."

"I'm kind of stuck in the middle here," Barry said. "Our profits are getting thinner and thinner, and so seed money is tight. Yet I do worry about the future of our firm. If our decline continues we could be facing a financial crisis.

"Lynn, is there any way you can bring this program in at about $10,000 and still do a truly professional job?" asked Barry.

"I think so. Maybe we can analyze the data ourselves, and we could hire a couple of MBA students to work as part-time interviewers.

"Consider the $10,000 one of the best investments you'll ever make in Global's future. You and Sara won't be sorry."

NEGOTIATING STRATEGIES AND TACTICS

Negotiating is required in such diverse activities as finding a job, agreeing on goals, agreeing on provisions of a contract, buying and selling, settling customer complaints, determining the size of a departmental budget, allocating resources to a project, and working out a merger agreement. As illustrated in the Global Office Furniture example, negotiation is a vital part of launching a new program.

The many negotiating strategies can be classified as either *collaborative* or *competitive*.[2] Collaborative strategies and tactics are based on a win-win (or each side wins) philosophy. The user of these approaches is genuinely concerned about arriving at a settlement that meets the needs of both parties, or at least does not badly damage the welfare of the other side. A seminar on collaborative bargaining at the Cornell School of Industrial and Labor Relations puts it this way:

> The best negotiation outcome is an agreement where all parties benefit, compliance is painless and verifiable, and relationships among the parties are built on and improved.

Competitive approaches are based more on a win-lose philosophy. Each side is trying to maximize gain with little regard for the needs and welfare of the other side. Competitive approaches also include those techniques that are more devious or deceptive than open, honest, or sincere.

The strategies and tactics described below are classified as collaborative or competitive. Two limitations to this dichotomy should be kept in mind. First, subjective judgment is used in classifying the strategies and tactics. Second, the intent of the person using a given strategy or tactic counts heavily as to whether it is collaborative or competitive. For example, one person may make small concessions gradually as a way of outsmarting the other side. Another person may rely on this tactic in a genuine attempt to arrive at a fair negotiated settlement.

Before proceeding further, obtain insight into your negotiating potential by taking the quiz contained in Skill-Building Exercise 7–1.

SKILL-BUILDING EXERCISE 7–1
The Negotiator Quiz

Directions: The following quiz is designed to give you tentative insight into your tendencies toward being an effective negotiator. Answer each statement *Mostly true* or *Mostly false* as it applies to you.

	Mostly true	*Mostly false*
1. Settling differences of opinion with people is fun.	_____	_____
2. I try to avoid conflict and confrontation with others as much as possible.	_____	_____
3. I feel self-conscious asking people for favors they have not offered me spontaneously.	_____	_____
4. I am generally unwilling to compromise.	_____	_____
5. How the other side feels about the results of our negotiation is of little consequence to me.	_____	_____
6. I think very well under pressure.	_____	_____
7. People say that I am tactful and diplomatic.	_____	_____
8. I'm known for my ability to express my viewpoint clearly.	_____	_____
9. Very few things in life are not negotiable.	_____	_____
10. I always accept whatever salary increase is offered to me.	_____	_____
11. A person's facial expression often reveals as much as what the person actually says.	_____	_____
12. I wouldn't mind taking a few short-range losses to win a long-range battle.	_____	_____
13. I'm willing to work long and hard to win a small advantage.	_____	_____

14. I'm usually too busy talking to do much listening. _____ _____

15. It's fun to haggle over the price when buying a car. _____ _____

16. I almost always prepare in advance for a negotiating session. _____ _____

17. When there is something I need from another person I usually get it. _____ _____

18. It would make me feel cheap if I offered somebody only two thirds of his or her asking price. _____ _____

19. People are usually paid what they are worth, so there is no use haggling over starting salaries. _____ _____

20. I rarely take what people say at face value. _____ _____

21. It's easy for me to smile when involved in a serious discussion. _____ _____

22. For one side to win in negotiation, the other side has to lose. _____ _____

23. Once you start making concessions, the other side is bound to get more than you. _____ _____

24. A good negotiating session gets my competitive urges flowing. _____ _____

25. When negotiations are completed, both sides should walk away with something valuable. _____ _____

Scoring and interpretation: Score yourself +1 for each of your answers that agrees with the scoring key. The higher your score, the more likely it is that you currently have good negotiating skills, *providing your self-assessment is accurate*. It might prove useful to also have somebody who has observed you negotiate on several occasions answer the quiz for you. Scores of 7 or below and 20 or higher are probably the most indicative of weak or strong negotiating potential. Here is the scoring key:

1. Mostly true	6. Mostly true
2. Mostly false	7. Mostly true
3. Mostly false	8. Mostly true
4. Mostly false	9. Mostly true
5. Mostly false	10. Mostly false

Continued

11.	Mostly true	19.	Mostly false
12.	Mostly true	20.	Mostly true
13.	Mostly true	21.	Mostly true
14.	Mostly flase	22.	Mostly false
15.	Mostly true	23.	Mostly false
16.	Mostly true	24.	Mostly true
17.	Mostly true	25.	Mostly true
18.	Mostly false		

Collaborative Approaches to Negotiation

The approaches in this category generally aim at gaining one's fair share in a negotiation without sacrificing the rights of the other side.

Use Principled Negotiation.   The Harvard Negotiation Project developed a negotiation program that encompasses many of the other approaches described in this chapter. [3] The underlying philosophy of *principled negotiation* is that you bargain over the merit of underlying issues, not personal positions or desires. Principled negotiation centers on four basic points, as described next. These points define an open and honest form of negotiation that can be used in almost any negotiating situation.

1. Separate the People from the Problem.   Human beings, unlike computers, are not entirely rational problem solvers. People have strong emotions and often have radically different perceptions of the same event. While negotiating, their emotions become entangled with the objective merits of the problem. It is important to disentangle the people problem before working on the substantive problem. At some point during negotiations, the participants should see themselves as working side by side, attacking the problem, not each other. For example, if you are negotiating with a company to repair your broken machinery, focus on the problem, but do not attack the company representative. Proceed in this manner:

> Our rotary generator that you serviced has broken down again. That is three times in the last month. The first time it was out of order for an entire week. The factory needs a functioning generator. I want your advice on how we can minimize our risk of generator breakdown. Should we change service companies, sue the manufacturer, or what? [4]

2. Focus on Interests, Not Positions.   The intent here is to overcome the drawback of focusing on people's stated positions when the true object of negotiation is to satisfy the underlying interests of both sides. A negotiating position often obscures the nature of what a person is really trying to achieve.

The standard remedy of compromise frequently produces an agreement that effectively takes care of the human needs that led people to adopt these positions. Lynn Houston communicated the spirit that she really wanted to decrease customer defections. The vehicle she chose for accomplishing this important interest was the zero customer defection program.

3. *Invent Options for Mutual Gain.* A powerful negotiating tactic is to generate several workable options before you enter into the heat of the actual negotiation session. Emotions may interfere with your thinking if you try to select an option in the presence of your adversary. When the stakes are high, the stress created by the negotiating session may dampen creativity. Thus, you may not arrive at creative alternatives.

Under ideal circumstances, the two parties can brainstorm together to arrive at options that will be mutually satisfactory. Or both parties may engage in brainstorming separately and then bring these new options to the negotiating session or bargaining table. However, a major hurdle must be overcome before a systematic search for options is possible. Both sides must realize that the outcome of negotiation is not inevitably one position winning over the other.

Lynn Houston invented an option for mutual gain that took the form of a compromise. She suggested that staff members do some of the data analysis and a couple of M.B.A. students be hired as part-time interviewers. The goal of implementing the program would still be achieved, yet the top-management goal of reducing the cost of the program would also be achieved.

4. *Use Objective Criteria.* To overcome stubbornness and rigidity on one or both sides, it helps to insist that the agreement reached reflect some fair (objective) standard such as market value, expert opinion, customary settlements, or law. For instance, if you are negotiating with a new car dealer about repairing your "lemon," you can insist the amount paid by the dealer is in line with the customary handling of the problem. Similarly, the dealer should not be forced to make a settlement with you exceeding this standard.

Regard the Other Party as a Partner. A constructive negotiating attitude is that you and the other side are helpmates in achieving your goals. Rather than the typical adversarial outlook, each party's in a negotiation needs to understand what he or she will gain from the other party is success. The president of a training and consulting firm recommends that you and the other side openly discuss what you can gain from each other's successes. Openly discussing these gains can help foster the positive negotiating climate needed for success. [5]

The partnership attitude has gained strength because many manufacturers and suppliers realize they have a common stake. Neither side can prosper without the other side also prospering. In the short range, a given manufacturer can squeeze the profit out of a supplier. Yet if all manufacturers did the same, the suppliers would vanish. The manufacturers would then have to produce their own supplies.

The partnership principle also applies within a company. If you are negotiating with the human resources department to obtain temporary workers, you
are both partners in the deal. To get your work accomplished, you need the office temporaries. If other departments throughout the organization do not make
demands on the human resources department, the department will be deemed
superfluous.

Prepare in Advance for the Negotiation Session.   A negotiation session is a meeting. As such, it will proceed more smoothly if both sides agree
on an agenda and make other necessary preparations, including searching for
mutually beneficial options. You should plan what major and minor points
you want to negotiate. The other side should do the same. Plan for the negotiation session by role-playing the opponent's most likely responses to your
suggestions.

A major part of preparing for negotiations is to set realistic and measurable
objectives. Philip L. Morgan recommends that negotiators list all their objectives. Next, the objectives should be divided into two lists: *likes* and *musts*.
Likes are things that would be nice to have but could be forgone if necessary. *Musts* are objectives one must attain for the negotiation to be successful,
such as a big enough budget to maintain an adequate level of customer service. If you are negotiating for a starting salary, a *must* item is a salary large
enough to meet your basic expenses. As negotiations proceed, the manager may
give up on many *like* items, but will persevere in trying to achieve the *must*
items. [6]

Give Yourself Time to Think.   A hasty decision made in a negotiating
session is often a poor one. If you feel pressed to make a fast decision, many
legitimate and ethical stalling tactics will give you time to reflect. You might
call for a lunch break, request time to obtain some information from your
files, demand that you first consult an expert adviser before committing yourself, or suggest that both sides resume negotiations in the morning.

Create a Positive Negotiating Climate.   Negotiation proceeds much
more swiftly if a positive tone surrounds the session. So it is helpful to initiate
a positive outlook about the negotiation meeting. Lynn Houston opened the
negotiation session with the comment, "Barry and Sara, thanks for fitting this
meeting in your hectic schedules." Nonverbal communication such as smiling
and making friendly gestures help create a positive climate. Gerard I.
Nierenberg, founder of the Negotiation Institute, maintains that by staying
positive, you'll stop a negative person cold. "It will be like a child who
throws a tantrum until the child sees that it's not working, that nobody's giving in. Then he or she will move on to something else."[7]

A positive negotiating climate can also be achieved by using noncombative language. According to talent agent Bob Woolf, aggressive language puts

people off. You are more likely to gain concessions if you use language that confers dignity. Woolf says he avoids using the word *demand*, but instead makes *suggestions, recommendations,* or *proposals.* Following are two more examples of using noncombative language during negotiations:

> Instead of "You had better accept this, because it's as far as I'm going," say, "Could you live with this?"
>
> Instead of "Absolutely not!" say, "I'm afraid we have a problem in that area." 8

In negotiating with peers for assistance, a positive climate can often be achieved by phrasing demands as a request for help. Most people will be more accommodating if you say to them, "I have a problem that I wonder if you could help me with." The problem might be that you need the person's time and mental energy. By giving that person a choice of offering you help, you have established a much more positive climate than by demanding assistance. 9

Allow Room for Negotiation. The most basic negotiating strategy is to begin with a demand that allows you room for compromise and concession. Anybody who has ever negotiated the price of an automobile, house, or furniture recognizes this vital principle. If you are the buyer, begin with a low bid. If you are the seller, begin with a high demand. If you are negotiating next year's budget for your department, begin by asking for a liberal budget—one higher than the absolute minimum required to function properly. Labor negotiators typically allow themselves negotiating room by bringing many more items into negotiation than they believe will be granted. Such optimistic items might be 100 percent dental coverage or treating an employee's birthday as a holiday. As negotiations proceed, the union drops several of these lesser demands.

Begin with a Plausible Demand or Offer.   Allowing room for negotiation does not preclude the importance of beginning negotiations with a plausible demand or offer. To begin with an unreasonable and potentially destructive demand often will be interpreted by the other side as bargaining in poor faith, thus delaying or even canceling serious negotiations. In one situation, a union negotiator initially demanded a 25 percent increase in all wage rates. Both sides realized this demand was unjustifiable. When asked to respond with a counterproposal, the company representative commented:

> I am not going to insult you and your membership with a ridiculously low initial offer. When your wage demands are more realistic, we will come forward with a specific wage package. And then we can really negotiate and come up with something we can all live with. But you have to be realistic before we will offer anything. 10

The *mini-max strategy* (or what should I give and what should I get?) leads the negotiator toward a plausible initial demand or offer. Each side may find it helpful to answer these questions.

1. What is the minimum I can accept?
2. What is the maximum I can ask for without getting laughed out of the room?
3. What is the maximum I can give away?
4. What is the least I can offer without getting laughed out of the room? [11]

Be Truthful. In many instances, laying all the cards on the table is an effective negotiating tactic. It communicates the fact that you are not game playing and that you respect the intelligence of the other party. It may also encourage the other side to make more honest demands because their distorted demands will be contrasted to a set of more honest ones. Howard Raiffa concluded from his experiments that subjects who did the best in negotiating games were the ones who simply announced the truth. [12] Most people expect negotiation to be filled with duplicity, so they may be overwhelmed by the truth.

Another way of being truthful is to never ask for something you don't want or cannot justify. In following this guideline, ethical negotiators do their homework and justify what they want. For instance, a purchasing agent might provide documentation as to why delivery of custom-made supplies is needed within two weeks: The agent's company is facing pressure for a quick delivery date from a customer.

Use Negotiation Jujitsu. It sometimes becomes necessary to parry the aggressive thrusts from your opponent. Negotiation jujitsu centers around the idea that you sidestep the attack and deflect it against the problem. [13] Here is an example:

Union representative:

Our last and final offer is a wage rate of $21.75 for machinists in this labor grade.

Company representative:

That certainly is a handsome rate of hourly pay. But what do you think that would do to the cost of our gear-cutting equipment?

Union representative:

The cost would go up, I guess.

Company representative:

You guessed right. It would raise the price so high that our foreign competition would take over our market. Or we would have to move our manufacturing overseas in order to lower labor costs. Either way we would have to close our Michigan plant, and our workers would lose their jobs.

Know Your Best Alternative to a Negotiated Agreement. People negotiate to produce something better than the result obtainable without negotiating. The goal of negotiation is thus not just to agree, but to reach an agreement more valuable than nonagreement. When you are aware of your best alternative to a negotiated agreement (BATNA), it sets a floor to the agreement you can accept. Your BATNA becomes the standard that can protect you from both accepting terms that are too unfavorable and from walking away from terms that would be beneficial for you to accept.

Knowing the other side's BATNA is also important because it helps define the other participant's bargaining zone. Understanding each other's bargaining zone makes it possible to arrive at mutually profitable trade-offs. [14]

In the situation above, the company representative may know ahead of time that if machinists are to be paid more than $18.50 per hour, it would be more cost-effective for the company to subcontract out much of its manufacturing. The company representative, therefore, can negotiate calmly and accept only an option the company can afford. In this situation, the union's BATNA might be to live with the current wages and hope for a cost-of-living adjustment in the future.

Overcome the Fixed-Pie Assumption. An underlying reason that negotiation and bargaining are necessary is that resources are fixed—the parties involved assume that what each one grants to another side represents a loss to him or her. To move negotiation away from this "fixed-pie" assumption, it is sometimes possible to choose an integrative trade-off. For example: Two business partners were in dispute over who should get which office in their new headquarters. A third party helped resolve the dispute by asking each partner what office features were the most important. One partner valued status, while the other wanted ample space. The solution was to give one partner the corner office (high status) and the other partner the central office, which was 50 square feet larger than the corner office.

Overcoming the fixed-pie assumption can also be viewed from another perspective. As a result of negotiation, it is sometimes possible to expand the resources available. A manager was given a fixed sum of money to distribute as salary increases to team members. The manager explained to his immediate superior that such an allocation would result in giving modest raises to two extraordinary performers. His immediate superior reported back three days later with good news. A few thousand dollars could be taken from a contingency budget to give above-average raises to the extraordinary performers.

Up to this point, we have emphasized fairness in negotiating. Skill-Building Exercise 7–2 gives you an opportunity to compare your sense of fairness with that of a professional arbitrator.

SKILL-BUILDING EXERCISE 7–2
If You Were the Arbitrator

Executives at Crown Industries, Inc., decided to offer a cash payment of $1,000 annually to employees who secured medical coverage on their own and chose not to participate in the company's insurance program. When the union's management learned about the company's new plan, it filed a grievance that went before an arbitrator.

The company insurance plan administrator testified that the company's offer resulted in a win-win situation for employer and employees. Workers would receive an additional $1,000, and the firm would be able to reduce the costs of medical coverage.

Union officials, however, saw themselves as a losing party if the plan were implemented. The union had negotiated the medical insurance benefit for all of its members. By offering employees a financial incentive to drop out of the plan, the company was, in effect, negotiating directly with employees rather than through the union. Also, the labor agreement stated that none of the terms of the agreement were to be changed without mutual consent of the parties. The union was not even given the opportunity to discuss the new plan before the company made its offer. After listening to both sides, the arbitrator left to consider the case.

How would you decide this case?

_____ For the union and why?

_____ For the company and why?

_____ Compromise? If so, how?

SOURCE: Earl Baderschneider, "Insurance Buyout," pp. 4, 6. Reprinted, by permission of publisher, from *SupervisoryManagement*, (May 1, 1992), American Management Association, New York. All rights reserved.

Competitive Approaches to Negotiation

The emphasis in the approaches described in this section is win-lose, or trying to maximize gain for your side even if it involves trickery and deceit. A collaborative approach is strongly recommended wherever possible. Yet a discussion of negotiation tactics and strategies would be incomplete without a description of competitive approaches. Besides, some of these competitive approaches are not particularly devious.

Establish an Appeal to Legitimacy.   People tend to respect the authority of written guidelines. Prices printed in a catalog appear more authoritative than an oral price quote, and a letter from a top executive stating the company's official position carries weight in negotiations. The advice here is "Win the advantage by carrying some kind of written support for your position. Conversely, don't believe everything you read." [15]

Frame the Outcome of Negotiations in Positive Terms. Years of experiments indicate that your mental set about negotiation can influence your success in achieving a favorable outcome. People who frame the outcomes of negotiation in terms of gains or profits are more willing to grant concessions. In addition, negotiators with a positive frame of reference completed more transactions than those with a negative frame of reference. Because they completed more transactions, their overall profitability was higher. Negotiators who frame the outcome in terms of losses or costs are more likely to take the risky action of holding out. As a result, they may lose all in an attempt to force further concessions from their adversary.[16]

All things being equal, you are likely to be more successful in negotiating when you attempt to achieve gains rather than prevent losses. This strategy is akin to raising your level of expectation or having a positive mental attitude when you enter negotiations.

Make Small Concessions Gradually. Making steady concessions leads to more mutually satisfactory agreements in most situations. Concession granting is referred to as the soft approach to bargaining. The hard approach to bargaining is to make your total concessions early in the negotiation and grant no further concessions. ("OK, you can have three of my people for your project. That's my final concession to you.")

If you are a buyer (leading from strength), start low and give in very slowly over a long time. If you are a seller (leading from weakness), just turn it around. Start higher and give in slowly over a long period. Buyer or seller, the principle remains the same—grant small concessions over the length of the negotiation session.[17]

Use Deadlines. Many deadlines are fictitious. For example, you can still obtain a specific discount after the deadline is passed. Despite these fictitious deadlines, many deadlines do force people into action. Here are examples of deadlines that often will move the negotiation in your favor:

- "Will I be receiving the promotion to senior information systems analyst by December 31? If not, I will feel compelled to act on this job offer from another firm. The promotion has become a matter of pride."
- "If we don't receive your order by February 1, you will not receive your supplies for 45 days after ordering."
- "My boss has to approve the deal, and she'll be leaving for the West Coast tomorrow."

Be Patient. A patient negotiator is often successful. If negotiations proceed at a deliberate pace, both sides learn more about the real issues involved. Patience also enables the negotiator to probe more carefully before taking a stand. An effective way of demonstrating patience is to use silence constructively. If the other side makes an offer or a demand that appears outrageous to you, just look at him or her and say nothing. You might even support your gaze with a flinch. The other side will read your message quickly and say something to the effect, "That's just an opening offer, maybe we can sweeten the deal for you." [18]

Use Impasse Breakers.   When negotiations are at an impasse, something needs to be done to get things moving. Sometimes a minor change in the nature of the deal can break an impasse. Suppose, as a manager, you are given additional responsibility but not enough new help to accomplish the job properly. An impasse breaker might be to request that you be temporarily relieved of some minor responsibility your department is now performing. Consider these other impasse breakers: [19]

1. *Try an "if, then" agreement.* For example, say, "If I can purchase 20 new PCs at less than $1,000 per unit, then will you let me go ahead with the deal?"

2. *Get the group focused on a common goal.* At times, a group decision-making session will reach an impasse because the different viewpoints and demands seem irreconcilable. To break the deadlock, search for a common goal. An example: "I don't care which path we choose out of this mess. But if we don't agree on something, we may be out of business in 60 days."

3. *Invite criticism of your ideas instead of defending them.* Ask the other side what concerns them about your proposal. Analyze their objections to help identify what their true interests are. Armed with this information, you can reformulate your own proposal. A sales representative for an industrial machinery company was at an impasse with a potential customer. He broke the impasse after he discovered the customer's true objection was the low domestic content of the equipment. The factory added more domestic components, and the company received the order.

4. *Make a last and final offer.* In many circumstances, offering the other side your final offer, or "doorknob price," will break a deadlock. A key part of the tactic is to exit from negotiations soon after making your offer. A partner in a consulting firm used this technique to advantage in negotiating a completion date for a study sought by a potential client. The potential client wanted a study done in one month. The consultant wanted the business, but did not have the resources to do the study immediately. After some thought, the consultant said, "We would like very much to conduct this study for you. However, the fastest turnaround we can offer is 60 days. If another firm can do a satisfactory job in less than 60 days, have them do it. You know where to reach me." The potential client called the consultant two days later to sign a contract for the study to be completed within 60 days.

Be Sensitive to International Bargaining Styles. A sensitivity to cultural differences in negotiating styles is important in today's global economy. Asian negotiators prefer to spend much more time at negotiations than do their American counterparts. Latin American businesspeople also prefer to prolong negotiations: They typically insist on lengthy socializing before getting to serious business. American executives typically expect to grant small concessions and receive concessions in return. French businesspeople thrive on deadline negotiations and wait until the last minute to commit themselves. And Far Eastern executives prefer to stall graciously until they are offered what they want. [20]

Rosalie Tung has compared differences among the negotiating styles of Koreans, Japanese, and Chinese. Because many Korean companies are run by the company founder and owner or his family, decision making is more centralized. As a result, the international negotiator can expect decisions to be reached more quickly in Korean companies than in Japanese or Chinese companies. Nevertheless, building relationships is very important to Korean businesspeople and that takes time.[21]

Know When to Quit. Competitive negotiations can sometimes get out of hand—conflict escalates while both sides feel committed to justify their past positions and obtain their demands. Recognizing this tendency can help the negotiator avoid bargaining beyond the point of diminishing returns. Legal fees alone can eliminate the cost-effectiveness of some types of negotiating, such as paying $40,000 in legal fees to win a $30,000 claim against another party. Prolonged negotiations can also be intellectually and emotionally draining, thus diverting attention away from more constructive tasks.

NEGOTIATING TACTICS: PRO AND CON

Improving negotiating skills has become a standard management development activity in recent years. Nevertheless, the approaches described in this chapter arouse some controversy.

Pro. An impressive argument in favor of effective negotiating skills is that they lead to increased cooperation from colleagues, subordinates, superiors, and businesspeople outside the organization. In addition, they help you achieve a reputation as a results-oriented, fair-minded problem solver. It can also be argued that negotiating skills are a requirement for managerial success because negotiating is an important role for a manager.

Despite the importance of negotiating in work and personal life, it is often conducted ineffectively. Many negotiating practices lead to long and tedious dickering that brings severe hardship to many. If more people followed the guidelines presented in this chapter, more agreements between people would be settled in an equitable fashion.

   Con.   Many of the tactics described are manipulative in nature. Some of the tactics that appear valid need to be researched more carefully. In many instances, they are based on small support from simulated negotiating sessions with college students. A person may not need to heed these strategies if he or she has good common sense and a well-developed sense of ethics. Finally, if people strived for openness and honesty with each other, there would be little need for negotiating tactics.

Guidelines for Action and Skill Development

A starting point in developing your negotiating skills is to recognize when a situation calls for negotiation. Nancy Adler explains that managers should negotiate when the value of the exchange and the relationship is important. Specifically, businesspeople should consider negotiation when:

• The other side has more power.
• The trust level is high.
• Time is available to explore both parties' needs.
• Commitment is present to ensure the agreement is carried out. [22]

   After learning to identify which situations call for negotiation, the next step in skill development is to practice negotiating in nonthreatening and relatively inconsequential situations. For instance, you might try one or two negotiating tactics when buying a piece of furniture or a home appliance. Once confidence is developed in these lesser situations, you might try negotiating for bigger stakes, such as buying an automobile or arriving at a starting salary for a new job. Incorporate several of the tactics described in this chapter into your negotiating.

   Another recommended method for improving negotiating skills is to use role-playing. Two people can first study the description of one of the many strategies described here. Next, they can develop a scenario approximating a bargaining situation they have faced on the job. Negotiation jujitsu, described in this chapter, lends itself well to role-playing.

DISCUSSION QUESTIONS AND ACTIVITIES

1. Many experienced negotiators contend they would prefer to negotiate against another experienced—rather than an inexperienced—negotiator. Why might this be true?

2. A growing trend in selling new automobiles is for the dealer to refuse to negotiate over the sticker price. Evidence suggests business volume in-

creases under this system. What do the facts just presented tell us about attitudes toward negotiation?

3. Why do people typically feel disappointed when somebody accepts their first demand or offer?

4. How can a person use negotiating skills to receive a more favorable performance evaluation?

5. Which two negotiating tactics described in this chapter do you think are the least ethical? Explain your reasoning.

6. How do you find out what is *plausible* in order to begin negotiations with a plausible demand or offer?

7. Identify a professional negotiator, such as a labor relations specialist or a trail lawyer, in your community. Interview the person to discover several of the negotiating tactics he or she thinks are the most effective. Report your results back to class.

NOTES

1. Frederick F. Reichheld and W. Earl Sasser, Jr., "Zero Defections: Quality Comes to Services," *Harvard Business Review*, September–October 1990, p. 110.
2. Robert W. Johnson, "Negotiation Strategies: Different Strokes for Different Folks," *Personnel*, May 1981, pp. 36–44.
3. Roger Fisher and William Ury, *Getting to Yes* (New York: Penguin Books, 1981).
4. Ibid., p. 26.
5. Gilda Dangot-Simpkin, "Eight Attitudes to Develop to Hone Your Negotiating Skills," *Supervisory Management*, February 1992, p. 10.
6. Philip I. Morgan, "Resolving Conflict Through 'Win-Win' Negotiating," *Management Solutions*, August 1987, p. 9.
7. "Negotiating: A Master Shows How to Head Off Argument at the Impasse," *Success*, October 1982, p. 53.
8. "Be Firm Without Being Combative," The *Pryor Report*, December 1991, p. 3.
9. Joseph D. O'Brian, "Negotiating with Peers: Consensus, Not Power," *Supervisory Management*, January 1992, p. 4.
10. Joseph F. Byrnes, "Negotiating: Master the Ethics," *Personnel Journal*, June 1987, p. 99.
11. Fred E. Jandt, with Paul Gillette, *Win-Win Negotiations: Turning Conflict into Agreement* (New York: John Wiley & Sons, 1985).
12. Howard Raiffa, *The Art and Science of Negotiation* (Cambridge, Mass.: Harvard University Press, 1983), p. 306.
13. Fisher and Ury, *Getting to Yes*, p. 114.
14. Ibid., p. 104; and Max H. Bazerman and Margaret A. Neale, *Negotiating Rationally* (New York: The Free Press, 1992).
15. Minda Zetlin, "The Art of Negotiating," *Success*, June 1986, pp. 37–38.

16. Margaret A. Neale and Max H. Bazerman, "Negotiating Rationally: The Power and Impact of the Negotiator's Frame," *Academy of Management Executive*, August 1992, pp. 42-51.
17. Chester L. Karass, *Give & Take: The Complete Guide to Negotiating Strategies and Tactics* (New York: Thomas Y. Crowell, 1974), p. 45.
18. "Negotiating Without Giving In," *Executive Strategies*, September 19, 1989, pp. 6-7.
19. "Working Fast," *Working Smart*, April 1992, p. 12; "Negotiate and Win With Players Who Won't Play," *Working Smart*, March 1992, p. 9.
20. Gerard Nierenberg, quoted in Zetlin, "The Art of Negotiating," p. 37.
21. Rosalie L. Tung, "Handshakes Across the Sea: Cross-Cultural Negotiating for Business Success," *Organizational Dynamics*, Winter 1991, p. 34.
22. Nancy J. Adler, *International Dimensions of Organizational Behavior*, 2nd ed. (Boston: PWS-Kent, 1991), pp. 183–84.

SOME ADDITIONAL REFERENCES

Gerhart, Barry, and Sara Rynes. "Determinants and Consequences of Salary Negotiations by Male and Female MBA Graduates." *Journal of Applied Psychology*, April 1991, pp. 256–62.

Griffin, Trenholme, and W. Russell Daggatt. *The Global Negotiator: Building Strong Business Relationships Anywhere in the World*. New York: HarperBusiness, 1990.

Holmes, George, and Stan Glaser. *Business to Business Negotiation*. Stoneham, Mass: Butterworth Heinemann, 1990.

Kremenyuk, Victor A., ed. International Negotiation: Analysis, *Approaches, Issues*. San Francisco: Jossey-Bass, 1991.

Mannix, Elizabeth A., and Leigh L. Thompson. "Negotiation in Small Groups." *Journal of Applied Psychology*, June 1989, pp. 508–17.

Negotiator Pro Interactive Software. Brookline, Mass.: Beacon Expert Systems, Inc., 1991.

Appendix to Chapter Seven

CHECK YOUR NEGOTIATION STYLE

To check your negotiation style, indicate which of these statements you remember making or you think you would make in the appropriate situation.

Yes	No	
_____	_____	1. You don't need to know why. Just do it the way I say.
_____	_____	2. Please, please, don't do that any more.
_____	_____	3. I need you to observe our rules. Please take that food to the break room.

_____   _____   4. Never mind. I'll do it myself.

_____   _____   5. I'd really like to give you a better raise, but this is all our budget allows.

_____   _____   6. This is an emergency. Please do it this way and I'll stop by after 5 to explain our reasons.

_____   _____   7. It's the best I can offer. Take it or leave it.

_____   _____   8. Get that food out of here. You can't eat in the lab.

_____   _____   9. What do you want me to do? I didn't make the budget rules.

If you answered yes to 1, 7, or 8, you probably have some bossy tendencies. Try lightening up a bit. Offer alternatives, avoid the accusing _you_ pronoun, and explain your reasons.

Yes responses to 2, 4, or 9 suggest your negotiating style may be a little wimpy. Don't beg— or do it yourself.

If you said yes to 3, 5, or 6, congratulations! You tend toward collaboration. People respect a boss who accepts responsibility and requires others to do the same.

SOURCE: Abridged from "Wimpy? Bossy? Check _Your_ Negotiation Style!" _Guide Lines_, 1992, Professional Training Associates Inc., 210 Commerce Blvd., Round Rock, Tex 78664-2189.

SOLUTION TO SKILL-BUILDING EXERCISE 7–2

The arbitrator agreed with the union's position. The labor agreement specifically provided that all parties would continue discussions pertaining to health coverage. Furthermore, all parties must agree mutually on the implementation of any new plan. By offering the individual $1,000 payment, the company changed the medical insurance plan without prior consultation with the union. Such action was a clear violation of the agreement.

Chapter Eight

Improving Customer Service

The automobile company described below wanted to achieve high levels of customer service and satisfaction. To achieve this goal, the company provided customer-service training to dealers and salespeople. The training emphasized a new perspective on interactions between salespeople and customers.

Jimmy Snyder carefully climbs five rungs up a ladder constructed out of 2-by-4s. After a slight hesitation, he counts to two, releases his handhold, and drops backward. He falls into the upraised arms of 17 men and women he hardly knows. For Snyder, the "trust fall" is one component of learning a new way to sell cars to the consumer.

The auto is Saturn, manufactured by a subsidiary of General Motors Corp. The weeklong training program occurs at Saturn headquarters in Spring Hill, Tennessee. The new approach to selling focuses on listening to customers and treating them with dignity and respect. Auto salespersons previously trained for their jobs by observing showroom veterans apply high-pressure tactics to customers. In contrast, Saturn teaches its *sales consultants* to hand show room visitors printed sheets of fixed prices, explain the no-haggle policy, and encourage them to comparison shop.

Most shoppers fear entering into heated negotiations while making a car purchase. Saturn attempts to erase that fear, and many customers appreciate the low-key sales approach. J. D. Power & Associates, Inc., a market research firm, recently ranked Saturn's customer-satisfaction level just below Lexus and Infiniti and above Mercedes-Benz and Lincoln. All four of those brands list for a minimum of $20,000 more than a four-door Saturn.

The Power report gave Saturn outstanding scores for its treatment of customers. Some of these customers have become such Saturn loyalists they volunteer to schmooze with shoppers on Saturdays at dealerships. "I even have my relatives buying them," says 67-year-old Ann Snyder, a Saturn owner who intends to form a Saturn-owners' club in Allentown, Pennsylvania.

Company officials think much of Saturn's future success depends on the customer-service training at Spring Hill. Based on other successful training programs, the course pinpoints 40 critical "moments of truth," such as greeting customers and listening to their requirements. Such moments of truth can make a sale and get repeat business.

Trainers facilitate discussion about how high-pressure selling alienates shoppers and customers. Sharon Smith, a trainer and experienced salesperson, tells the class, "Integrity is the key ingredient missing from the car retail business." Role-playing is used to help the trainees break bad habits. The "trust fall" aims to demonstrate how a team can protect members from landing on their heads. A team approach is a new concept for many salespeople who often compete against each other for the same buyer.

The classes prompt Saturn dealers to provide better service. For example, a salesperson from a suburban Akron, Ohio, dealership drives 100 miles to Cleveland to get a co-signature for a loan application to expedite a sale. Many Saturn dealers wash customer cars for free whenever requested. To promote esprit de corps, trainees all learn the Saturn cheer used at meetings. Salespeople are also taught to salute customers as they drive off in new cars.

To support the new training, Saturn has also made some key business decisions. To make no-haggling financially profitable, Saturn built a gross margin of 17 percent into sticker prices. Competing models typically have a 12 percent margin. To curtail high-pressure sales tactics, Saturn encourages dealers to pay salaries instead of commissions. Approximately 50 percent of Saturn dealers pay salaries only. Many others supplement salaries with bonuses tied to both sales volume and customer-satisfaction ratings.

Ron Marhofer, a Saturn dealer, is so impressed with the Saturn sales approach he is implementing it at his outlets for Lincoln-Mercury, Chevrolet, Hyundai, and Mitsubishi. As Marhofer sees its, "This is the way to do business in the future. The old way, as far as I'm concerned, doesn't work anymore." [1]

The Saturn customer-service training program illustrates that improved customer service is a major corporate goal. Improving customer service can both attract new business and retain existing business. To support this goal, managers and salespeople must take steps to improve customer service. In this chapter, we describe actions and attitudes to help managers and customer-contact people improve customer service, thus working toward total customer satisfaction. Although this chapter is aimed at external customer relationships, many of the ideas presented will also enhance internal customer satisfaction.

PRINCIPLES AND TECHNIQUES FOR MANAGERIAL ACTION

Managers must assume responsibility for implementing many of the principles, techniques, and methods that enhance customer service and satisfaction.

Eight such principles and techniques are described below. We also present a skill-building exercise that points to additional principles and techniques.

Establish Customer-Service Goals. The manager must decide how much help to give customers. Answers are needed to questions such as: Is the company attempting to satisfy every customer within 10 minutes of his or her request? Is the company striving to provide the finest customer service in its field? Is the goal zero customer defections? These goals will dictate how much, and the type of effort, the manager and team members invest in pleasing customers. An awareness of levels of customer service (see Figure 8-1) contributes to more precise customer-service goals. Goals at the highest level will move the company toward total customer satisfaction.

FIGURE 8–1   Levels of Customer Satisfaction

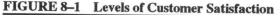

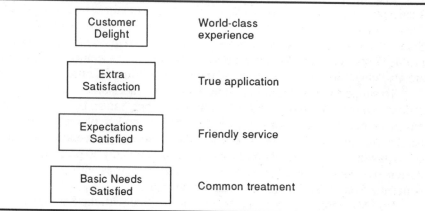

Use a Customer-Focused Organization Structure. A recent development in enhancing customer service is to use on a horizontal rather than a vertical (or traditional) organization structure. A traditional organization structure focuses attention on internal relationships but pays less attention to customers. In contrast, a horizontal structure focuses its efforts on serving the customer.

Instead of having lines of authority, the horizontal structure has strings of relationships between suppliers and their customers. Connections are drawn among people serving each other in the organization (internal customers) and external customers. As described by D. Keith Denton, a horizontal structure is similar to a hemp rope. Each strand of the organizational rope represents a customer transaction. The manager's role is to satisfy customer requirements. An external customer with a request is at one end of the strand. His or her request travels backward along the strand through various organizational units until it reaches the other end, where the customer request is satisfied.

American Express is one of several companies using a horizontal structure to improve customer service. The company observed that it was unproductive to measure the work of individual departments. Instead, it seemed important to measure the total customer transaction. Consequently, American Express began breaking down walls between departments and tracking the flow of information from start to finish. The credit card service was then divided into discrete customer transactions that were visible and measurable. These included billing customers, paying retailers, and replacing lost or stolen credit cards.

American Express then developed many performance measures based on these single customer transactions, emphasizing timeliness and accuracy. As a result of this restructuring, quality of service has improved by 78 percent, and expense per transaction has been reduced by 21 percent. The time required for processing applications has been reduced by 21 percent. American Express estimates the shift to customer-focused (horizontal) structure has saved millions of dollars over 10-years. [2]

Screen Applicants thoroughly for the Customer-Service Positions.

High-quality customer service can best be achieved by hiring high-quality people. Companies noted for their good service seek candidates who have good communication skills, project a professional image, display empathy, and appear happy. Screening for the personality characteristics of conscientiousness and extroversion is also important. As retail management expert Charles E. Cox observes, "Attract good people, and innovative marketing techniques will follow." [3]

Invest in Training.

Achieving total customer satisfaction requires a substantial investment in training. One study showed that top service companies spend between $750 and $10,000 on training per employee during the first year of employment. Training areas include problem solving, listening, communication, and stress management.[4] Workers should also receive thorough training in product knowledge. Many instances of customer dissatisfaction are attributable to sales personnel having insufficient knowledge about the merchandise.

Customer-service training needs to communicate the fact that everyone contributes to the customer's perception of service. Customers evaluate the quality of service based on their total perception of how they were treated by all people with whom they interact. For example, shabby or rude treatment by a parking lot attendant can detract from high-quality service within the store.

Empower Employees to Solve and to Prevent Customer Problems.

Customer service is enhanced when frontline workers are empowered to deal with customer problems without several layers of approval. The underlying principle to empowerment is to push decision making and complaint resolution down to the lowest possible job level. Such authority includes granting refunds, exchanges, concessions, and quick delivery dates. At Montgomery Ward, sales associates have the authority to approve checks and handle merchandise-return problems. At one time, only store managers had such authority.

In empowering customer-service workers, the organization gains the input of workers who know the customers best. Empowerment also helps customer-contact personnel focus on solving problems rather than referring to company policy. [5] A feeling of empowerment may help workers think of ways to prevent problems, such as improved packaging to reduce complaints about breakage.

Become a Customer Champion.   A *customer champion* acts as the eyes, ears, and voice of the customer. If you are a customer champion, you represent the customer in your organization.[6] The formal authority of a manager's position will often give the incumbent an opportunity to be a customer champion. Championing the customer is impressive for logical reasons. Customers rightfully believe that satisfying their needs is more important than dealing with internal administration. L. L. Bean, the esteemed catalog retailer, encourages its employees to be customer champions. Figure 8-2 presents the definition of a customer as contained on a poster the company displays at its headquarters.

FIGURE 8–2   What is a Customer?

What Is a Customer?

A Customer is the most important person
ever in this office . . . in person or by mail.
A Customer is not dependent on us . . . we are dependent on him.
A Customer is not an interruption of our work . . . he is the purpose
of it. We are not doing a favor by serving him . . . he is doing
us a favor by giving us the opportunity to do so.
A Customer is not someone to argue or match wits with.
Nobody ever won an argument with a Customer.
A Customer is a person who brings us to his wants.
It is our job to handle them profitably to him and ourselves.

SOURCE: L.L. Bean, Freeport, Maine

Maintain Direct Lines of Communication with the Customer.   An effective way of enhancing customer service is to maintain direct lines of communication with customers, particularly with respect to service problems. Courtesy telephone calls are a good way to do this. Periodically call customers and inquire about the quality of service and product reliability. Be prepared to take action on items of dissatisfaction.

A standard approach to maintaining open lines of communication is to conduct periodic satisfaction surveys, either over the phone or by mail. In contrast to a courtesy call, a survey asks a structured set of questions. If the surveys are not burdensome to answer, they will be well received by external and internal customers. Skill-Building Exercise 8 may help you improve customer service.

SKILL-BUILDING EXERCISE 8
How Well Do You Manage Customer Satisfaction?

Take a moment to look at your company (or another company familiar to you) through your customers' eyes. Your answers to the questions below will tell you about the company's ability to produce satisfied customers and identify areas for improvement.

The 12 questions asked in this customer satisfaction questionnaire also provide useful suggestions for improving your skill in achieving customer satisfaction.

	Yes	*No*
1. Is it easy for a customer to do business with your company?	____	____
If you answered yes, please list three reasons. If you answered no, please list three existing barriers.		
_____		
_____		
_____		
2. Are your salespeople professionally trained in your product knowledge and selling skills?	____	____
3. Do you regularly ask your customers to rate your product, your service, and your relationship?	____	____
4. Do you resolve customer complaints the same day you receive them?	____	____
5. Does your management make joint calls with your salespeople on a regular basis?	____	____

6. Do you invite your customers to meet your staff
    and are your customers welcome at sales
    meetings or other company events?   ____   ____

7. When your customers call your office staff for
    information, are their requests handled quickly
    and courteously?   ____   ____

8. Are all the departments within your
    organization aware of how important your
    customers are?   ____   ____

9. Have you established detailed performance
    expectations on how to achieve customer
    satisfaction?   ____   ____

10. Do your top managers visit key customers often
    check how you can improve your service?   ____   ____

11. Does your company have a program for
    ongoing improvement so you can offer yoiur
    customers even more value in the future?   ____   ____

12. Do you receive positive comments from your
    customers every day?   ____   ____

Rating scale: Assign one point to each yes and zero points to each no answer.
If you scored 10–12 points, you've reached the highest level of customer satisfaction. If you scored 7–9 points, your customers may be satisfied, but you are
overlooking room for improvement. If you scored 6 or fewer points, your company may be missing valuable opportunities for creating more satisfied customers.

SOURCE: Adapted from "How Well Do You Manage Customer Satisfaction?" PERSONAL SELLING
POWER, October 1992, p. 23. © 1992 PERSONAL SELLING POWER. Reprinted with permission.

PRINCIPLES AND TECHNIQUES FOR CUSTOMER-CONTACT WORKERS

Customer-contact workers (including sales associates and customer-service representatives) play a major role in moving an organization toward total
customer satisfaction. This section describes five major principles and techniques customer-contact workers can use to enhance customer service.

Understand Customer Needs and Put Them First. The most basic
principle of selling is to identify and satisfy customer needs. Many customers
may not be able to express their needs clearly, so you may have to probe for
information. For example, the associate in a camera store might ask, "What

uses do you have in mind for a video camera?" Knowing such information will help the associate identify which camcorder will satisfy the customer's needs.

After customer needs have been identified, the focus must be on satisfying them rather than your needs or those of the company. Assume that the customer says, "The only convenient time for me to receive delivery this week would be Thursday or Friday afternoon." The sales associate should not respond, "On Thursday and Friday our truckers prefer to make morning deliveries." Instead, the associate should respond, "I'll do whatever is possible to accommodate your request."

Focus on Solving Problems, Not Just Taking Orders.   Effective selling uses sales representatives to solve problems rather than merely taking orders. Kraft U.S.A.'s sales representatives no longer restrict their efforts to devising promotions in supermarkets. Now they also offer information for improving a store's profits, such as suggestions on store displays.[7] The focus on problem solving enables sales representatives to become partners in the success of their customers' businesses. By helping the customer solve problems, the sales representatives enhances the value of the supplier-customer relationship to the customer. The customer receives consulting services in addition to the merchandise or service being offered.

Involve the Customer in Resolving the Problem.   Mistakes and problems in serving customers are inevitable. To minimize the perception of poor service, the customer should be involved in deciding what should be done about the problem. By involving the customer in the solution to the problem, the customer is more likely to accept a deviation from the service promised originally. A sales representative for a computer outlet used this tactic successfully:

> After lengthy negotiations and many on-site visits, Shana DuVal closed a sale of 25 personal computers to an insurance agency. One week after installation, the customer was outraged. The agency had purchased some new software to help reduce the amount of paperwork in the office. After the operators had the software running, the computer screens flashed "OUT OF MEMORY." DuVal could envision a return of 25 computers, which might have to be sold as used computers.
>
> Instead of engaging the customer in an argument about whether the specifications were met, DuVal said, "Let's sit down together and work out a solution to this embarrassing and difficult problem." The director of office operations at the agency finally said, "I don't care what you do. Just give us the computers to do the job of running this new software."
>
> DuVal responded, "Thank you for a great suggestion." DuVal then proposed that her company insert memory upgrades into each computer that would enable the computers to perform the required work. The new computer boards were of-

fered to the customer at a substantial discount. As a result of the joint problem solving between DuVal and her customer, the account was retained.

Create a Bond with Your Customer.   A high-impact buzzword in selling is to bond, or form an emotional relationship, with customers. The rationale is that if you form warm, constructive relationships with your customers, they will keep buying. Such is the true meaning of *relationship selling.* Creating a bond is aimed at increasing sales, but it also enhances service. If the customer relies on and trusts the sales representative, the customer will perceive the service to be of high quality. Similarly, people perceive medical and legal services to be of high quality if they trust the physician or lawyer. Virtually all of the principles and techniques described in this chapter will help form a bond with customers. However, four key principles are: provide exceptional service, understand the customer's business, show care and concern, and make the buyer feel good.

1. *Provide exceptional service.* The best-accepted axiom about keeping customers is to provide exceptional service. Many successful companies contend their strategic advantage is good service. USAA, the fourth-largest insurer and financial services firm in the United States, has a much lower than industry average percentage of customer defectors, and its business grows primarily through referrals. USAA has no external salespeople and does not use insurance agents. Most customer concerns and inquiries are settled within minutes by calling an 800 number. Robert F. McDermott, the CEO of USSA, says, "The mission and corporate culture of this company are, in one word, service." [8]

Lands' End, the catalog clothing merchandiser, is another example of a successful organization built on exceptional service. Customer-service representatives are available 24 hours per day, and merchandise usually arrives within three days. An added feature of the good service is that the garments are sized accurately, minimizing the inconvenience of returning merchandise through the mail.

2. *Understand the customer's business.* Successful people are emotionally involved with their business, so they are more likely to bond with a sales representative who understands their business or job. Time invested in understanding the customer's business often yields a large return. Sources of valuable information about customers include annual reports, newspaper and magazine articles, and trade magazines. Speaking to employees, suppliers, and customers of the customer will also enhance understanding of the business.

3. *Show care and concern.* During contacts with the customer, the sales representative should show concern for the customer's welfare. The representative should ask questions such as, "How have you enjoyed the laser printer you bought a while back?" or "How are you feeling today?"

After asking the question, the sales representative should project a genuine interest in the answer.

4. *Make the buyer feel good.* A fundamental way of keeping a relationship going is to make the buyer feel good about himself or herself. Also, customers should be made to feel good because they bought from the representative. Compliments can be offered about customers' appearance or a report that clearly specified vendor requirements. An effective feel-good line is: "I enjoy doing business with you."

Deal Constructively with Customer Complaints and Anger. In an era when customer satisfaction is so highly valued, both retail and industrial customers are likely to be vocal in their demands. When faced with an angry customer, use one or more of the following techniques recommended by Donna Deeprose:[9]

1. *Acknowledge the customer's point of view.* Make statements such as "I understand," "I agree," and "I'm sorry." Assume, for example, a customer says, "The accounts payable department made a $1,000 overcharge on my account last month. I want this fixed right away." You might respond, "I understand how annoying this must be for you. I'll work on the problem right away."

2. *Avoid placing blame.* Suggesting the customer is responsible for the problem intensifies the conflict. With the customer who claims to have been overcharged, refrain from saying, "Customers who keep careful account of their orders never have this problem."

3. *Use six magic words to defuse anger.* The magic words are: I understand (that this is a problem); I agree (that it needs to be solved); I'm sorry (that this happened to you).

Display Strong Ethics. Ethical treatment of customers is part of providing good service because ethical treatment is a universal customer requirement. Customer-contact workers should to behave so ethically that they would not mind making their sales tactics public knowledge. Customers should also be treated in the same way the customer-contact workers would like to be treated when they are making a purchase. Conducting your business in an ethical and responsible manner may not be enough to make ethical behavior obvious. The customer-contact worker should take positive steps to let the customer know that he or she is ethical. Here are two examples:

Your customer inquires about a late order. Instead of claiming the order will be shipped immediately, you respond: "We've made some mistakes in production scheduling. Your shipment will take another three weeks. Would you like an immediate refund? I can give you the name of a supplier who might have what you need already in stock." Your customer's anger will be defused, and you will be admired for your honesty.

Your customer thanks you for having installed a billing system that is saving the company thousands of dollars per month. You respond: "I appreciate the thanks. Our billing system has improved your collection as much as we said it would. However, the real thanks belong to your new collection specialist. She's the best I've seen in the business." Your client is impressed by your ethics to the extent that you are rightfully perceived as being very ethical. As a consequence, the client's perception of high-quality customer service is also enhanced.

EVIDENCE AND OPINION ABOUT THE IMPORTANCE OF EMPHASIZING CUSTOMER SERVICE

Impressive data have been collected demonstrating that customer loyalty has positive financial consequences. A study of regional banks conducted by the consulting firm of Bain & Co. indicated the 20-year customer is worth 85 percent more in profits than a 10-year one. In addition, loyal customers spend more money, refer new customers, and are less costly to conduct business with. Profits often increase dramatically with only a 5 percent increase in retention rate. The following list reveals the profit improvement that accompanies a 5 percent customer retention increase for various industries: [10]

• Auto and home insurance, 130 percent.
• Bank branch deposits, 100 percent.
• Life insurance, 90 percent.
• Credit cards, 80 percent.
• Advertising agencies, 80 percent.
• Corporate insurance brokers, 55 percent.
• Professional publishing, 35 percent.
• Automotive services, 34 percent.

Another example of the financial consequences of good customer service is the testimonial of Dallas Cadillac dealer Carl Sewell. He reports that a lifetime customer will spend $332,000 at 1 of his 10 dealerships. Furthermore, the luxury car Infiniti was founded on the strategy that superior customer service by its dealers would differentiate it from other luxury cars. The general manager of Infiniti believes that fixing a customer's problem is more valuable than money invested in advertising. Often the person whose problem is fixed becomes a disciple of Infiniti, according to the same executive. [11]

Assume customer retention pays financial dividends. We are still faced with the issue of whether the principles and techniques described in this chapter actually influence retention rates. The fact that many business executives, consultants, and business writers support these ideas suggests they have merit.

Although few would argue that superior customer service is important, some people challenge how many sacrifices companies should make to please customers. If the service cost is too high for one customer or a group of customers, it may be unprofitable to retain them. Some customers purchase clothing or other expensive items from retailers with the intention of using them only for a brief time. For example, after wearing a $700 dress to a wedding, the customer returns the dress claiming it is a poor fit. How far should the retailer bend to please this type of customer? Should this same person be welcomed as a repeat customer?

Hal Rosenbluth, the president and CEO of Rosenbluth Travel, offers the thought-provoking argument that employee welfare should take precedence over customer welfare. He argues that if employees are not happy with their jobs (particularly in a service business) the customer will never be uppermost in their minds. Rosenbluth notes:

> We believe that only if people are first in our eyes will they be able to put the customer first in theirs. In other words, to put someone else first and mean it, you have to know what it feels like on the receiving end. [12]

A final counterargument against putting so much effort into customer service is that if you are a proud organization, with an outstanding product or service, customers will flock to you. You can dispense with customer satisfaction surveys, customer champions, and the like. Just concentrate on what you do best and demand for your offerings will continue to swell. We doubt that Tiffany jewelers, Piaget watches, or the Mayo Clinic are overly concerned about improving customer service. (Of course, few organizations are world leaders, and even Jaguar Motors has lost business because of disappointed consumers.)

Guidelines for Action and Skill Development

A strategic method of improving customer service is to create a service-driven environment. Such an environment incorporates many of the ideas presented in this chapter. Use these ideas as a checklist for action and for evaluating whether your organization is taking the right steps toward total customer satisfaction.

1. Ensure that the commitment to being customer driven begins with top management both by edict and example.

2. Obtain customer participation at the design stage to minimize the need for adjustments later.

3. Give customer-contact and manufacturing employees more authority to solve problems on the spot.

4. Gather customer satisfaction ratings and count them heavily in performance reviews and incentive payments.

5. Speak to your competitors' customers as well as your own, and discover why they are not doing business with you.

6. Make it easy for customers to reach you with complaints and questions. [13]

DISCUSSION QUESTIONS AND ACTIVITIES

1. Ask a Saturn owner his or her observations about the effectiveness of the Saturn sales techniques. Or visit a Saturn dealership yourself to make firsthand observations.

2. Many customer-contact workers are paid close to the minimum wage. How does this influence a company's ability to screen thoroughly for customer service positions?

3. Now that you have studied current approaches to improving customer-service, what do you think of the age-old philosophy "the customer is always right"?

4. What is your impression of the effectiveness of the customer-satisfaction surveys often found in hotels and restaurants?

5. What do you think of the argument that hiring so many part-time service workers is a major contributor to low-quality service?

6. How does entertaining customers lavishly fit the concept of total customer satisfaction? Of ethics?

7. It has been observed frequently that customers whose complaints are resolved satisfactorily become loyal future customers. What explanation can you give for this phenomenon?

NOTES

1. As reported in David Woodruff, "May We Help You Kick the Tires?" *Business Week*, August 3, 1992, pp. 49–50.
2. D. Keith Denton, "Customer-Focused Management," *HRMagazine*, August 1990, pp. 62–67.
3. Charles E. Cox, "18 Ways to Improve Customer Service," *HRMagazine*, March 1992, p. 72.
4. "Three Steps to Better Customer Service," *Personnel*, September 1991, p. 19.
5. Joan Koob Cannie, with Donald Caplin, *Keeping Customers for Life* (New York: AMACOM, 1991), p. 173.
6. *Ibid.*, p. 137.
7. "Smart Selling," *Business Week*, August 3, 1992, p. 48.
8. Thomas Teal, "Service Comes First: An Interview with USSA's Robert F. McDermott," *Harvard Business Review*, September–October 1991, p. 117.

9. Donna Deeprose, "Helping Employees Handle Difficult Customers," *Supervisory Management*, September 1991, p. 6.
10. "Beyond 'May I Help You,'" *Business Week/Quality*, October 25, 1991, p. 102.
11. *Ibid.*, p. 103.
12. Hal Rosenbluth, "Tales from a Nonconformist Company," *Harvard Business Review*, July–August 1991, p. 33.
13. "King Customer," *Business Week*, March 12, 1990, pp. 88–91.

SOME ADDITIONAL REFERENCES

Anderson, Kriston, and Ron Zemke. *Delivering Knock Your Socks Off Service*. New York: AMACOM, 1991.

Bell, Chip R., and Ron Zemke. "The Performing Art of Service Management." *Management Review*, July 1990, pp. 42–45.

Bowen, David E., Caren Siehl, and Benjamin Schneider. "A Framework for Analyzing Customer Service Orientations in Manufacturing." *Academy of Management Review*, January 1989, pp. 75–95.

Denton, D. Keith. "The Service Imperative." *Personnel Journal*, March 1990, pp. 66–74.

Gunsch, Dawn. "Customer Service Focus Prompts Employee Exchange."

Personnel Journal, October 1992, pp. 32–38.

Schlesinger, Leonard A., and Heskett, James L. "The Service-Driven Economy." *Harvard Business Review*, September-October 1991, pp. 71–81.

Appendix to Chapter Eight

WOULD YOU BUY FROM YOU?

One of the most effective ways to assess your effectiveness in handling customers is via the question: "If you were the customer, would you buy from yourself?" You would if you scored well on the following quiz. Answer each question by checking the appropriate blank. If you do not deal with external customers, take this quiz in relation to your handling of internal customers.

	Yes	*No*
1. Is your image one of honest and straightforward sincerity?	_____	_____

2.   Based on your experience with customers over the past year, from the buyer's point of view, would you be classified as reliable?   _____   _____

3.   Could you asy your customers obtained special benefits dealing with you they wouldn't have obtained from others?   _____   _____

4.   Do you think you come off as an expert in the eyes of your customers?   _____   _____

5.   Have you been effective helping to solve customer problems?   _____   _____

6.   Wherever possible, would you say you handled customer complaints to the buyer's satisfaction?   _____   _____

7.   Is integrity one of the most important words in your vocabulary?   _____   _____

8.   Apart from your business dealings, do you think customers believe you have their personal welfare and well-being at heart?   _____   _____

9.   Can you honestly say most of your company's customers believe you have their personal welfare and well-being at heart?   _____   _____

10. Do customers regard you as a good, reliable source of product and industry information?   _____   _____

11. Has doing business with you contributed positively to most of your customers' profit performance?   _____   _____

12. Would most of your company's customers continue dealing with you even if a competitor approached them with a price a little bit lower?   _____   _____

Total number of yes answers   _____   _____

Your rating: multiply the sum of your yes answers by 5. If you achieved a score of 55 or higher, it's a privilege to do business with you; 50 is well above average; and 40 to 45 is mediocre to fair.

SOURCE: Adapted from "Making . . . Serving . . . Keeping . . . Customers," 1992. Reprinted with the permission of customers, Dartnell, 4660 N. Ravenswood. Ave., Chicago, IL 60640, (800) 621-5463.

Improving Work Group Skills

The four techniques, methods, and programs of applied management described in the next four chapters focus primarily on the small work group. Distinctions among the individual, group, and organizational levels are not absolute. A work group is composed of individuals, and the larger organization is composed of both individuals and small work groups. Also, small-group techniques, such as problem-solving meetings, enhance organizational effectiveness.

As with most of the techniques presented in this book, those described in this part stem from a core of theory and research. Chapter 9, Conducting an Effective Meeting, is derived from both group dynamics and organizational communication. Chapter 10, Building Teamwork, is based on a number of sources including group dynamics and organization development. Chapter 11, Work Teams, describes a major new thrust in organizational design based on sociotechnical systems—an attempt to interrelate principles of organization structure with principles of motivation through job enrichment.

Chapter 12, Fun and Humor in the Workplace, has become a serious topic as managers seek new skills in reducing stress and enhancing job satisfaction. The formal literature on stress and job satisfaction provides some theoretical and research underpinnings to the intentional use of fun and humor on the job.

Chapter Nine

Conducting an Effective Meeting

The company president described below found that conducting effective meetings contributes immensely to success in business. She presents an overview of her attitudes toward meetings and some specific techniques she uses.

At age 33, Michelle Cox has been president of Prescom, a computer systems firm, for four years. She credits much of her success to knowing exactly what she wants to get out of a meeting.

"I prepare very carefully. I jot down ideas very much as if I were giving a speech. I write down a list of things I want to go over, and I detail the points I want to emphasize—down to allotting time for each one.

"I send an agenda to everybody who will attend. I ask for additional topics, and I expect people to give me input in writing beforehand. If I don't get it, I won't allow other topics to come up. I know what I want to accomplish, so I take out everything not on the agenda. As we go down the topics on my list, I make sure that the meeting doesn't stray. I don't let one thing lead to another.

"If there is time left in our allotment for a topic, I'm willing to discuss an ancillary one that grew out of our discussion. Otherwise we keep moving.

"Sometimes the meeting does not run smoothly. Conflict may flare up during the meeting. It may break up in disagreement, or a conclusion might be reached begrudgingly. If any of these happen, I put the outcome in writing. I want to be sure that whatever decision is reached is put on paper.

"Many times I participate in a meeting when I'm not the chair, such as with the parent company or with a client. Under these conditions, I'm much more deferential. I will prepare a written agenda only if I'm asked to do so. I memorize my points instead of writing them down, trying to keep them down to no more than three. If somebody else calls a meeting, I follow his or her tone and approach.

"Brainstorming sessions are something else again. I take no notes. I don't prepare. I think ideas should flow freely without a formal structure.

"I also have some other important meeting strategies that have helped me achieve success. I think it's very important to know my peers. I take the time to talk to people so I know in advance what issues they are sensitive to. I like to have a good idea of what people are likely to say at a meeting before it starts.

"It's very important not to offend the participants. Once people are offended, they stop listening—and you might as well pack up and go home.

"I believe strongly in not avoiding an issue. There's a fine line between attacking and diluting. Bending over backward so as not to appear threatening can dilute an issue so much that the point is lost.

"I look upon meetings as selling situations. You have to convince the other participants on the merit of your point of view. A smooth communication style is not enough to do well in a meeting.

"A final point is that you must understand the language people use. My experience is technical, so it is essential that I know what people want, not only what they say they want. Often they don't ask the right questions, so I have to interpret what they mean." [1]

SUGGESTIONS FOR CONDUCTING A PRODUCTIVE MEETING

The statements and suggestions made by Michelle Cox underscore an important point—effective meetings contribute to business success. Unfortunately, many meetings do not contribute to success because they are conducted so poorly they do not accomplish their intended purpose. This chapter presents suggestions for conducting productive meetings based on a mixture of experience, observation, and research. Many of the suggestions support and elaborate on the points made by Cox.

A meeting, in the sense used here, is any gathering of people with a purpose in mind, including team meetings, committee meetings, task force meetings, strategy sessions, and meetings called to practice participative management. Meetings have reached new heights of importance because of today's emphasis on the team approach to problem solving and quality improvement.

The three general purposes of meetings are to solve present problems, plan for future problems, or exchange information. We present information primarily geared toward dealing with present and future problems. The suggestions are divided into two categories: (1) those dealing primarily with the structure and administrative processes of the meeting, and (2) those dealing primarily with handling behavior, or the human element. Do not be concerned about overlap in these categories because everything about meetings is in some way related to behavior.

Although most of the suggestions are aimed at the meeting leader, many of them can be applied to other participants. For example, the leader should strive to keep others from going off on tangents. At the same time, each person should share the responsibility of staying on track. Furthermore, one participant can sometimes help another stay on track by making a polite request to that effect.

Dealing with Structure and Administrative Processes

The *structure* of a meeting includes organization and agenda, timing, and physical arrangements. The *administrative processes* refer to activities such as drawing up minutes, providing summaries, and avoiding interruptions except for emergencies. The many suggestions presented in this section reflect current thinking about improving structure and administrative processes to make meetings more productive.

Have a Valid Reason for Calling a Meeting.   Many meetings are unproductive simply because there was no valid reason for calling them. A meeting is justified primarily when there is a need for coordinated effort or interaction on the part of participants. If straightforward, factual information needs to be collected or disseminated, memos or electronic mail can be substituted for meetings.

The underlying purpose of a meeting may be different from its stated purpose. For example, the leader may use it as a political forum to gain support for a project. Or certain group members may use the meeting to publicize their accomplishments or put down another group. Almost every meeting has some undercurrent of power play. By carefully observing what is happening, the meeting becomes more informative than one might have anticipated. To sensitize you to the importance of knowing when to conduct a meeting, do Skill-Building Exercise 9–1.

Plan an Agenda and Stay on Track.   Few people who have attended meetings would deny the importance of having an agenda, distributing it in advance of the meeting, and staying on track. Yet this could be the most frequently violated principle of conducting a productive meeting. A tentative agenda should be distributed when the meeting is announced. If the agenda is revised, it can be distributed later. An effective method of obtaining additional agenda items is to gather input from participants before the meeting. Consider these suggestions:

1. Send a written or electronic, open-ended questionnaire asking all participants to identify problems, options, or positions, depending on the purpose of the meeting.

SKILL-BUILDING EXERCISE 9-1
Should I Call a Meeting?

In column A, list five valid reasons for calling a meeting. In column B, list five examples in which an exchange of paper or electronic memos would be just as productive as conducting a meeting. Discuss the results in class.

(A) Five Valid Reasons for Holding a Meeting	*(B) Five Situations in Which Memo Exchanges Can Substitute for a Meeting*
_____	_____
_____	_____
_____	_____
_____	_____
_____	_____

---

2. Put the ideas into a master list, distribute it, and ask participants for modifications or piggyback suggestions.[2]

If possible, an agenda should include at least one item of high potential interest to each participant. An exciting agenda item adds a spark to the meeting that may spill over to other topics. Examples of almost universally exciting agenda items include discussions about cash bonuses, salary increases, budgets, new hiring, and downsizings.

Decide Carefully Who Should Attend.   Considerable time is wasted in meetings because planners do not select participants carefully. The skills, authority, and motivations of the participants should be appropriate to the task. Barbara C. Palmer and Kenneth R. Palmer note that if you are orchestrating a group responsible for identifying and evaluating alternatives for toxic waste disposal, you would not want morticians and driver education teachers involved. However, you would invite chemists, biologists, physicians, and possibly urban planners.[3]

Although participants should be qualified to contribute to the group task, their knowledge backgrounds should be different enough to produce a diverse viewpoint. Heterogeneous viewpoints are useful for producing creative alternative solutions to problems.

Another source of low productivity is the failure to invite people who are prepared or authorized to act, as opposed to those who cannot or choose not to make decisions. Inviting people who regard attendance as a punishment rather than a reward can also contribute to an unproductive meeting.

It may also be important to invite those people whom you are trying to convince or whose cooperation you need. As one manufacturing manager commented, "I always invite representation from finance and engineering to our key planning meetings. It helps explain to them some of the problems we face in making a product."

The number of people should be held to the smallest number necessary to get the problem solved and achieve other purposes of the meeting. Among these other purposes might be involving a cross-section of people from the organization. If the group is too small, a diversity of viewpoints is lost. Yet large meetings often result in wasted time and extraneous conversations. Problem-solving meetings generally work the best with about five, six, or seven carefully selected members.

Schedule the Meeting at a Convenient Time and Location.   To minimize the risk of poor attendance, schedule a meeting at a time and location that will make it feasible for most people to attend. A preferred meeting time for most busy managers and professionals is at the start or toward the end of a working day. An account executive from a cellular telephone company noted: "I get edgy when I have to attend a meeting during a time I should be out with my customers." Her motivation is similar to many other salespeople: they can concentrate better on problem solving if serving customers is not disrupted.

When the people required or invited to attend a meeting are from dispersed locations, it helps to choose a central site. A related consideration is that some geographic locations are easier to reach than others, whether or not they are centralized. Time lost on ground transportation in major cities has become a concern for many businesspeople. For this reason, many business conferences today are held at hotels adjacent to airports. Teleconferencing is growing in popularity as a way of reducing time spent traveling to meetings.

Start and Stop the Meeting on Time.   Meetings that are held to their designated starting and stopping time contribute to an organizational culture of professionalism. A meeting that starts late penalizes prompt attendees and rewards latecomers. A precedent may then be established for people to arrive habitually late for meetings. Short time limits should be set on meetings whenever possible, with 50 to 90 minutes probably being the most cost-effective. Meetings follow Parkinson's Law: They tend to expand (or contract) to fill the allotted time.

Standup meetings are sometimes used to shorten meetings. If people are forced to stand, they are more likely to feel uncomfortable and will move quickly through the agenda to minimize discomfort. Standing also carries the connotation that quick action is required. Jeff Simek, a public relations manager at Xerox Corp., holds 10-to-15-minute standup meetings each Monday at 8:15 A.M. to share schedules for the week. The standup meeting was adopted to keep each staffer informed of the others' plans for the week without letting the event grow into a full-blown meeting.[4]

Despite their action orientation, standup meetings have problems. Attendees cannot take notes comfortably; they may feel so awkward that their attention will be diverted; and the meeting may not be taken seriously because it departs so far from standard business practice.

Keep Comments Brief and to the Point. One of the major challenges facing the meeting leader is keeping conversation on track. The leader can keep comments on target by responding only to targeted comments. Another method is to ask the participant: "How does your comment relate to the agenda?" As a last resort, the leader might have to respond sternly: "You've made your point about the issue, but now we have to get back to the purpose of the meeting."

Participants have an obligation to keep their comments focused on the problem at hand. Aside from lowering the productivity of meetings, irrelevant comments annoy other members. Participants can also play a leadership role by subtly asking other participants to avoid tangents.

Despite the importance of not making irrelevant comments, a manager should allow some room for spontaneity and the introduction of important ideas that might be dealt with at a future meeting. A major underlying purpose of some meetings might be to foster informal discussion.

Provide Summaries for Each Major Point. An effective way to keep a meeting focused on important issues is for the leader to provide summaries of each major point after it is made. This provides structure to the meeting and gives members the feeling that something specific is being accomplished. Placing a headline summary of key points on a flip chart adds an impressive flair to the meeting.

Set Up a Physical Structure that Encourages Communication. A meeting is typically held around a long, rectangular table. The manager occupies the central position at the head of the table. Such a configuration encourages communication primarily flowing one way—from the meeting leader to the participants. Another problem is that participants then direct most of their communication toward the head of the table rather than also interacting with other participants.

To overcome this communication barrier, participants should be seated around a circular, semicircular, or oval table. The circular configuration creates an open, conversation-inviting environment, thus encouraging wider participation. Also, the circular arrangement creates the expectation of participation and suggests that participants have good ideas to contribute.[5] A circle of chairs, with no intervening table, encourages the maximum amount of interaction.

However, some participants feel uncomfortable without a place to set their notepad. Others dislike keeping a beverage on their lap or the floor.

Another potentially important aspect of structure is the physical surroundings. It is better to meet in neutral territory such as a conference room or lounge rather than in the meeting leader's office. A neutral location, similar to a circular seating arrangement, facilitates more open communication.[6]

Use Parliamentary Procedures Only for Legalistic Meetings.   Parliamentary law, as exemplified by Robert's Rules of Order, provides specific rules for conducting a meeting, including such items as when motions can be introduced, who can second a motion, and what proportion of members have to vote affirmatively on a motion for it to be passed. These rules tend to discourage informal interaction, spontaneity, and creativity. Also, they tend to create a dreary, somber atmosphere that often detracts from group effectiveness.

Nevertheless, parliamentary procedure does have its place. Legislation (the making of rules and laws) usually requires the assistance of rules of order. The boards that oversee the activities of licensed professionals in the United States and Canada conduct their meetings according to parliamentary procedure. At these meetings, rules sometimes are formulated that govern the behavior of self-employed professionals, such as specifying the amount of job experience an architect must have to qualify for a license.

Take Minutes and Distribute them Promptly.   Minutes contribute to the effectiveness of most meetings because they serve as a summary of what was accomplished and a reminder of agreements. Minutes are especially important when:

1. Formulating policy affecting a large number of people or organizations.
2. Transacting a high volume of business.
3. Anticipating a continuing need to consult the record of the group's activities.
4. Assigning follow-up implementation activities.[7]

An effective practice is to prepare minutes that reflect an informal summary of the meeting, much like an extension of the agenda items. The minutes should be distributed within several days of the meeting to help dramatize their importance. Minutes of meetings held weeks ago receive minimal attention from busy people.

Avoid Interruptions Except for Emergencies.   A danger in holding a meeting near the work area of most of the participants is that the meeting is likely to be interrupted for routine phone calls and requests for minor information. One meeting was interrupted when an office assistant wanted to know if his boss wanted regular or caffeine-free soda with her turkey sandwich. When minor interruptions are tolerated, it creates the impression that the subject of the meeting is not as important as routine events occurring outside the meeting.

Use High Technology to Facilitate the Meeting. Advances in communication technology can facilitate meetings. Audiovisual equipment, including slides, videos, and overhead projectors, have been standard fare at meetings for years. Three important new developments are videoconferencing, electronic meetings, and software for planning meetings.

Videoconferencing, after a slow start, is gaining acceptance as a way to reduce travel costs associated with gathering people for a meeting. At a videoconference, people in different locations can talk to each other while viewing each other's image on a television screen. In addition to reducing travel costs, video conferences increase productivity because participants only have to travel to a videoconferencing center near their office.[8] A videoconference, however, may create some communication problems because it still lacks the give and take of in-person interaction. Some nonverbal communication is lost because the conference members act more stiffly than in person.

Electronic meetings allow participants to work on the same problem simultaneously by using a linked set of computers. The problem appears on each person's computer monitor. Participants can suggest a solution to the problem and enter their solution into the computer. These solutions are displayed to all the other members. Participants can also modify each other's proposed solutions. The monitors display the revised problem solutions, allowing participants to see others' solutions simultaneously. The system is particularly well suited for "what if" discussions. At the end of the meeting, all participants receive a printout of the results.

A behavioral advantage of an electronic meeting is that shy people are not dominated by forceful personalities. Each participant has an equal opportunity to submit ideas—providing the person has adequate keyboard and computer graphics skills. If the participants are struggling with the technology, operating the system takes precedent over creative thought.[9]

Software for planning meetings helps organize meetings along many of the suggestions already made. An example is *The Facilitator,* which allows the user to tell the program the objective of the meeting, the location, and the starting time. Another window allows the leader to enter the agenda and the amount of time to be spent on each agenda item. At the meeting, an alarm in the program indicates when it is time to move to the next agenda item. As ideas are generated in the meeting they are entered into the computer and categorized into buckets, or categories. *The Facilitator* also records who voted for which alternative and prints the minutes at the conclusion of the meeting.[10]

Conclude on a Positive Note. After the agenda is completed, or if the time deadline approaches, the meeting should conclude on a positive note.

The participants should leave with a feeling of having accomplished something worthwhile. If there has been much disagreement and not much visible progress, the leader should point out what went right in the meeting. For example, the meeting chairperson might say: "We didn't agree on our mission statement, but at least we did agree that we must prepare one."

Dealing with the Behavioral Aspects of a Meeting

Our suggestions for conducting an effective meeting so far have dealt primarily with structural and administrative aspects. In this section, we deal more specifically with the human aspects of leading a meeting and dealing with the behavior of meeting participants.

Serve as a Role Model. The behavior of the leader sets the tone of the meeting. If the leader is insistent, domineering, and overly quick to criticize, group members are likely to behave in the same way or retreat into silence. In contrast, if the leader is calm, reasonable, and reflective, then others—within the limits of their personality—will tend to behave similarly.[11]

The Leader Should Emphasize both Productivity and People.   Without effective leadership, most meetings are doomed to low productivity. For most situations, an effective leadership style is characterized by a high concern for both the task and the members. A high task orientation is necessary to keep the group moving toward accomplishing the goals of the meeting. A high relationship orientation is required to provide the kind of emotional support that encourages group interaction and creativity. Being people oriented also means listening carefully to the ideas and concerns of group members. A keen sensitivity to people is also necessary in running a meeting because of the many subtle interactions occurring. An example is members dragging their heels when they disagree with a given proposal.

The Leader Should Share Power and Act as a Facilitator and Collob-orator.   Participants frequently let the chairperson rule the meeting, especially if that person is also the boss. To encourage constructive ideas, the leader can share power and act as a facilitator and collaborator. In most meetings, the leader makes many statements that inhibit creative responses from participants. Accepting ideas from participants tends to spur creativity. Asking questions is an effective way of soliciting ideas. For example, the leader might ask: "How can we reduce our cycle time further?"

Although the leader may want to accept as many ideas as possible, some ideas may be unworkable. The leader needs considerable skill to constructively modify or resist suggestions from the group without inhibiting imagination or further contributions. Extraneous concerns and flaws should be acknowledged as subproblems to be worked on. Yet the group's energy should be focused on building a solution. Here is an example of what could be done in this regard (referring to the question about cycle time).

Group member:

I suggest we reduce cycle time by taking half the money we save from reduced cycle times and converting it into employee incentives. You'd see some pretty short cycle times in a hurry.

Manager and meeting leader:

I see some merit in your idea. Some kind of incentive for reduced cycle times might work. How big an incentive, however, would be up for further discussion.

Another way of sharing power is for the chairperson to encourage others to take over some leadership activity, a practice referred to as *distributed leadership*. One way of accomplishing this is to turn over a portion of the meeting to the member responsible for a particular agenda item. When that agenda item is processed, the leader can take the leadership role back gently.[12]

Create a Supportive Atmosphere to Enhance Group Discussion. By supporting members, the leader plays a major role in creating an atmosphere that fosters discussion. A supportive atmosphere is very important also for drawing out reticent members. Supportive behaviors include listening to ideas, giving verbal encouragement to worthwhile ideas, being tolerant of mistakes made by participants, and smiling frequently.

A supportive atmosphere is also important in dealing with a member who dominates group discussion. The leader might say to such a member, "Jim, you're buzzing with creativity today. But I want to make sure everybody else also has a chance to contribute."

Encourage Candid Comments. A dull, ceremonial meeting is characterized by participants offering only polite, psychologically safe comments. In contrast, an exciting, results-oriented meeting is characterized by members contributing candid comments about agenda items and related topics. Accepting criticism from group members is an important way to encourage candor.

Suppose a group member says: "It doesn't matter what machine we purchase. The real problem behind our low productivity is a group of top managers who are operating in the Dark Ages." To encourage additional candid comments, yet still preserve a sense of discipline, the leader might respond: "OK, the way you see things, if we want to improve productivity, we must examine corporate policy and top-management practices. Do you have any specific suggestions I can carry forward?"

Be Tolerant of Divergent Views. The group leader plays a key role in creating an atmosphere that encourages diverse viewpoints. Participants can play an equally significant role by showing tolerance for extreme viewpoints and controversial opinions. Toleration can be communicated by subtle behaviors such as a nod of approval or a wink after another participant has expressed an extreme viewpoint. The nod, wink, or similar behavior does not necessarily imply agreement, but it does imply acceptance of divergent views.

Act as a Mediator.   When divergent views are encouraged, differences of opinion on important issues will surface frequently. Several of the members might support an important proposal, while others might be opposed. Suppose, for example, your proposal for trimming the travel budget is meeting with both stiff opposition and acceptance at the same time. You could take a large sheet of paper, draw a line down the middle, then ask participants for the pros and cons of your proposal. Each of the arguments can be discussed briefly. Such a procedure enables all participants to hear clearly both positive and negative aspects of the proposal before taking a final stand.[13]

Encourage Group Interaction.   We mentioned the importance of the leader's encouragement of group discussion. Similarly, the leader should encourage group *interaction*. A meeting loses the advantages of two-way communication when all communication pathways are between the leader and members. It is more effective for the participants to react to each other's comments. At times, tactful challenges are in order. One member might confront another about her digressions by saying: "Janice, I, too, am concerned about the company's earnings per share, but let's deal now with our own travel budget."

Strive for Consensus, Not Total Acceptance.   Few groups composed of assertive individuals will arrive at total agreement on most agenda items. It is more realistic to strive for consensus—a state of harmony, general agreement, or majority opinion without suppression of all disagreement. When consensus is achieved, each member should be willing to accept and support the plan because it is logical and feasible. The following suggestions are designed to help the leader achieve consensus:

1. Accept the idea that different methods can be used to achieve the same goal.
2. Encourage team members to clarify and build on one another's ideas. Encourage the entire team to be sure everyone's ideas are heard.
3. Avoid vigorous or heated arguments in favor of one person's position, especially your own.
4. Avoid easy ways out—such as majority vote, averaging, and coin flipping—unless the issue is inconsequential. Such selection methods may leave team members with strong differences of opinion.

5. Shoot for win-win solutions or plans if possible. This is where you should be when you believe you have a consensus.[14]

Avoid Disruptive Behavior.   At times, it will be necessary for the chairperson to modify behavior that has a debilitating effect on meetings. The most frequent behaviors of this kind are inept humor, personal anecdotes, domination of discussion, switching topics in midstream, side conversations, unconstructive criticism, repetition of arguments, and insistence on questioning arguments already made by the group.[15] In all these instances, the disruptive person may have to be dealt with assertively by the leader (or other participants). Two specific situations calling for assertiveness are side conversations and an overbearing contributor.

An effective technique for quelling side conversations is for the leader to stare in silence at the whisperers until they stop. When one participant vents emotion and spends considerable time on his or her position, the productivity of the meeting is in jeopardy. The leader can respond to this person by inquiring, "How do the rest of you feel about this issue?"[16]

Provide Refreshments when Motivation Is a Problem.   The organizational culture prompts many employees to expect refreshments at meetings. When participants or their organizations pay to attend meetings such as conventions and professional meetings, refreshments are mandatory. For briefer meetings on company premises, refreshments are optional. Yet many people expect to be offered food and beverage during the meeting. In recent years, many participants demand low-fat, low-calorie snacks to be served along with pastries and donuts. Because eating and drinking take time away from the meeting, and a bite out of the budget, refreshments should not be served indiscriminately. Yet the lack of refreshments can dampen satisfaction and motivation. Refreshments should be served primarily when satisfaction and motivation are potential problems.

Skill-Building Exercise 9–2 will help you integrate and apply the information presented up to this point.

SKILL-BUILDING EXERCISE 9-2
Improving the Productivity of Meetings

To improve the productivity of meetings you head or attend, use the suggestions offered in this chapter as a checklist of the steps to take or factors to consider. Not all of these points, however, will be applicable to every meeting.

CHECKLIST FOR IMPROVING THE PRODUCTIVITY OF MEET-INGS

	Doing It Now	Should Do It	Not App.
Dealing with structure and administrative processes			
1. Valid reason for meeting.			
2. Stick to specific agenda.	___	___	___
3. Select attendees carefully	___	___	___
4. Convenient time and location.			
5. Start and stop meeting on time.	___	___	___
6. Brief and pointed comments.	___	___	___
7. Provide summaries for key points.	___	___	___
8. Physical structure for communication.	___	___	___
9. Restrict parliamentary procedure.	___	___	___
10. Send minutes soon after meeting.	___	___	___
11. Minimize interruptions.	___	___	___
12. Use high technology (videoconferencing, electronic meetings, planning software).	___	___	___
13. Conclude on a positive note.	___	___	___
Dealing with behavioral aspects			
1. Serve as a role model.	___	___	___
2. Emphasize productivity and people.	___	___	___
3. Share power.	___	___	___
4. Create a supportive atmosphere.	___	___	___
5. Encourage candid comments.	___	___	___
6. Tolerate divergent views.	___	___	___
7. Act as mediator.	___	___	___
8. Encourage group interaction.	___	___	___
9. Strive for consensus.	___	___	___
10. Avoid disruptive behavior.	___	___	___
11. Serve refreshments if needed.	___	___	___

During meetings you attend or lead, attempt to practice the applicable behaviors outlined in the checklist. For example, if you think group discussion is very important in your meeting, you would take note of point 8 under structure and administrative processes, "physical structure for communication." You might choose a circular or oval conference table.

THE ARGUMENTS FOR AND AGAINST FOLLOWING SUGGESTIONS FOR CONDUCTING EFFECTIVE MEETINGS

Although all of the suggestions presented in this chapter may not work all of the time, they have the potential for being cost-effective for two reasons. First, managers spend a substantial amount of time in meetings, up to two thirds of their average workday.[17] Second, it has been estimated that about half of the time spent in meetings is wasted. This waste can be translated into two types of costs. One is the cost attributed to the salaries and benefits paid to the participants while they are attending the meetings. This figure is computed as the hourly salary plus benefits multiplied by the time spent attending and traveling to and from the meetings. The other costs are opportunity costs—productive work the people might have done if they had not been at the meeting.

An argument for ignoring the suggestions in this chapter is that if rational people want to make meetings more effective, they will. Perhaps the time that appears to be wasted in meetings is really functional. The gabbing and ceremonial activity that occurs in a meeting relieves tension and helps build a sense of camaraderie. Another argument in opposition to these suggestions is that the time wasted in meetings is not a real cost, owing to Parkinson's Law. After people have wasted time in a meeting, they scurry to finish their day's work. If they did not attend the meeting, they would work at a more leisurely pace the remainder of the day.

Guidelines for Action and Skill Development

An important aspect of becoming more skilled at conducting meetings is to design the meeting carefully. Jerry McNellis, a consultant on strategy sessions, offers this advice for designing effective meetings:[18]

1. *Clearly state the topic to be discussed.* Identify the basic issue in terms all participants can understand.
2. *Supply the necessary background.* Give team members the background information they need to understand the problem to be resolved in the meeting.
3. *Clearly state the purpose of the project and the session.* Tell people why they are working on the project and what you want the group to accomplish.
4. *Determine the focus people should maintain through key questions.* Ask team members such questions as, "What do our customers like about our service?" "What improvements have you heard are needed in our service?"

DISCUSSION QUESTIONS AND ACTIVITIES

1. Why do so many people say they hate meetings?
2. Assuming that most work in organizations involves coordinated activity, what are the alternatives to conducting meetings?
3. Identify several political reasons for conducting meetings.
4. How can nonverbal communication improve the effectiveness of a meeting?
5. Why do large, bureaucratic organizations use meetings so frequently?
6. How should a person deal with the problem of having so many meetings to attend that individual productivity suffers?
7. Use the checklist for improving the productivity of meetings to analyze the next meeting you attend. Bring your analysis back to class.

NOTES

1. Adapted from "Meeting Strategies," *Executive Strategies*, August 21, 1990, p. 8.
2. "Meeting Strategies," *Executive Strategies*, January 22, 1991, p. 3.
3. Barbara C. Palmer and Kenneth R. Palmer, *The Successful Meeting Master Guide* (Englewood Cliffs, N.J.: Prentice Hall, 1993), p. 31.
4. Phil Mulivor, "Taking a Stand for Better Meetings," Rochester *Democrat and Chronicle*, May 4, 1992, p. 1D.
5. Dave Day, "More Effective Meetings," *Personnel Journal*, March 1990, p. 34.
6. "The Best Meetings Are Usually the Liveliest," *Personal Report for the Executive*, May 14, 1985, p. 5.
7. Palmer and Palmer, *The Successful Meeting*, p. 164.
8. "Rotelcom Expands Service to Meet Needs of Its Evolving Customer Base," *Rochester Tel Line*, August 1992, p. 2. (Publication of Rochester Telephone Corporation.)
9. Mulivor, "Taking a Stand for Better Meetings," p. 14D.
10. Michael Marren, "Master Your Meetings," *Success*, June 1991, p. 48.
11. "The Best Meetings Are Usually the Liveliest," p. 5.
12. Andrew E. Schwartz, "How to Get the Most from the Meetings You Manage," *Supervisory Management*, March 1991, pp. 10–11.
13. "Don't Let Discord Ruin Your Meetings," *Personal Report for the Executive*, December 15, 1989, p. 3.
14. Francis X. Mahoney, "Team Development, Part 4: Work Meetings," *Personnel*, March–April 1982, pp. 52–53.
15. Palmer and Palmer, *The Successful Meeting*, pp. 128—29.
16. Day, "More Effective Meetings," p. 39.
17. David A. Whetton and Kim S. Cameron, *Developing Management Skills*, 2nd ed. (New York: HarperCollins Publishers, 1991) p. 455.
18. Jerry McNellis, "Gaining the Edge at Meetings," *Supervisory Management*, November 1992, pp. 10–11.

SOME ADDITIONAL REFERENCES

Frank, Milo O. *How to Run a Successful Meeting in Half the Time*. New York: Simon & Schuster, 1990.

Kayser, Thomas A. *Mining Group Gold: How to Cash in on the Collaborative Brain Power of a Group*. New York: Serif Publications, 1990.

Miller, Robert F. *Running a Meeting that Works*. New York: Barron's, 1991.

The 3M Meeting Management Team. *How to Run Better Business Meetings: A Reference Guide for Managers*, 2nd ed. New York: McGraw-Hill, 1987.

Chapter Ten

Building Teamwork

A high-technology firm used a problem-solving method called the Lion's Den, developed by Brookman Resources Inc., a management consulting firm. It creates an environment in which people want to become part of the team. The Lion's Den encourages work units to spend 30 minutes of each regularly scheduled meeting "fiercely" helping own subgroup solve a pressing problem.

At a recent Lion's Den meeting, the following people were present: the marketing vice president; two representatives each from sales, manufacturing, engineering, customer service, and materials management. (Lambs are composed of the subgroup that enters the Lion's Den. Lions are the members of the larger group who intend to help the lambs.) Sales had its turn to present a problem, thus playing the role of the lambs. The problem the sales people chose had a counterpart in several previous products. They maintained marketing had overestimated the demand for a new product, a manual hedge trimmer with expandable handles.

The clipper was designed to give the yard worker a four-foot reach. Marketing had teamed with manufacturing and engineering to design the "revolutionary new clippers" without carefully consulting with sales. Initially, the product excellent acceptance by dealers and consumers. Yet when consumers used the clippers, many found them heavier than standard manual clippers, and when the handles were extended, the clippers felt even heavier. Many consumers complained they lacked the strength to manipulate the clippers when the handles were expanded. A typical complaint was that using the clippers for more than ten munutes resulted in aching arms and shoulders.

Many store customers were demanding returns. Dealers were demanding credit from the company and complaining to rep from both customer service and sales. Using the Lion's Den procedure, the sales team placed on one wallchart a paper depicting the problem from their perspective. Shown in the drawing was a sales manager at his desk. The phone was ringing incessantly and a fax machine was generating a complaint message. Customer service reps were standing nearby, pounding their heads with their fists, and pointing at the grinning face of the marketing manager who peered over them.

From the marketing manager's mouth came these words directed at sales and customer service: "Teach the dealers how to sell. We can't do the whole job for them." In another drawing, the engineering manager was telling manufacturing group, "Here's a surefire product we need for the spring gardening season. Get it ready for market as quickly as you can. These clippers are so good, they'll sell themselves. Don't worry about a small glitch here and there. We pay customer service to handle little problems."

In the opening minutes, the sales group rep explained the problem from her perspective. If marketing and manufacturing produce a faulty product, no amount of sales skill can convert it to a winner. The sales reps then lose credibility with dealers. At the end, the sales rep posed a challenge: "How can we prevent marketing, engineering, and manufacturing from putting out products with a serious built-in flaw?"

In the following five minutes the lambs offered solutions. Most dealt with pressuring the president to restrain the marketing vice president from dreaming up faulty products that created problems for sales and customer service. For 20 minutes, the lions challenged the lambs by questioning any faulty assumptions, incorrect information, and misread solutions. The lions took responsibility for playing an active role in the solution.

Within the allotted 20 minutes, the lions and lambs redefined the problem, allowing for useful solutions to surface. The breakthrough came when one of the lions suggested that the sales rep's drawing was too one sided. It failed to reflectthe enormous pressure maketing faced to introduce new products rapidly in a fickle market and achieve a specified sales volume. The comment aboutneeding sales volume prompted one lions to make another drawing. In it, the marketing vice president was saying to a team of company reps, "Please, let's all work together." All the Lion's Den members approved of this constructive, teamwork approach.

After a few more breakthrough ideas, prompted by picturing the problem, the group developed a new challenge for sales: "How can we motivate marketing and manufacturing to willingly cooperate with us in meeting the product needs of our dealers and consumers?"

Addressing this challenge, the group brainstormed and formulated an action plan designed to benefit all concerned. Sales would approach the marketing vice president with an attractive offer: "We would like to help you boost earnings by increasing the number of winning products."

It was noted that marketing and manufacturing were too self-contained and smug. Marketing relied on market research but paid scant attention to the input from sales and customer service. The implication was marketing and manufacturing were creating problems for personnel who dealt directly with customers. As a result, they were wasting resources and perhaps missing opportunities. The team reasoned that when a dealer is satisfied with the demand for a new product, he or she will not only have repeat business, the dealer will be more receptive to other new products. A product designed on the basis of input from sales and customer service was more likely to succeed.

Within half an hour, the Lion's Den technique had provided the company with a fresh approach so effective that subsequent new products were more profitable. Sales and customer service people served on a new product development committee. The heavy clippers, however, could not be sold profitably. Returned and unsold merchandise was sold below cost to deep discount stores that specialize in excess inventory. A year later an aluminum version of the long-handled clippers was introduced to the market as a "light-weight, easy to use garden tool." The product had moderate success.

The Lion's Den did not commit the lambs to implement any of the ideas that emerged. Nevertheless, sales did meet with the marketing, engineering, and manufacturing departments with the help of some Lions' Den participants from the materials handling department. The material handling department's neutral presence in these initial meetings mitigated much of the antagonism between sales and marketing.[1]

STRATEGIES AND TACTICS FOR ENCOURAGING TEAMWORK

The high-technology firm's use of the Lion's Den method illustrates a novel way of encouraging teamwork. The fact that such a firm would be concerned about developing teamwork underscores the importance of teamwork in business and industry today. As noted by Jon R. Katzenbach and Douglas K. Smith, "Managers cannot master the opportunities and challenges now facing them without emphasizing teams far more than ever before."[2] And for teams to be effective, teamwork must exist or be developed.

Approaches to developing teamwork can be divided into three categories: (1) informal strategies and tactics, (2) formal strategies and tactics, and (3) team-building experiences that occur off the job. The balance of this chapter emphasizes team building that takes place under normal operating conditions rather than off the job or through consulting programs. The Lion's Den experience is an example of a consultant-assisted program that deals with an operating problem. The interdisciplinary group (representatives from various departments) learned to work together as an effective team.

Informal Tactics and Strategies

Most of the strategies and tactics described in this section concern the interpersonal aspects of managing people, such as the team leader encouraging cooperative behavior. These approaches stand in contrast to changes in structure, policies, or procedures to encourage teamwork.

Define the Team's Mission.   A starting point in developing teamwork is to specify the team's mission. The mission should contain a specific goal, purpose, and philosophical tone. Two examples are: "To plan and implement new customer-service approaches that improve our quality image and sharpen our competitive edge"; "To boost our MIS capabilities so that we can respond more rapidly and flexibly to volatile market demands."[3]

The mission can be specified when the team is formed or at any point. Developing a mission for a long-standing team breathes new life into its efforts. During the Lion's Den meeting, the customer-service department began a new mission: helping the sales group increase sales by retaining and developing existing customers. Being committed to a mission improves teamwork, and so does the process of formulating the mission. The dialogue necessary for developing a clear-cut mission establishes a climate in which team members can express feelings, ideas, and opinions.

Develop a Norm of Teamwork.   A key strategy the team leader should use to build teamwork is to promote the attitude among group members that working together effectively is an expected standard of conduct. It is fashionable today to encourage team members to treat each other as if they were customers, thus encouraging cooperative behavior and politeness. The leader can also emphasize the norm of teamwork by making explicit statements about its desirability. Normative statements about teamwork by influential team members can also reinforce the norm of teamwork. The manager of an information systems department used the following comments (with good results) to help foster a norm of teamwork:

> My boss is concerned that we are not pulling together as a cohesive team. And I can see some merit in his argument. We are performing splendidly as a group of individuals, but I see a need for an improved united effort in our group. We need to share ideas more, to touch base with each other, to pick each other's brains more. From now on when I evaluate performance, I'm going to give as much weight to group effort as I do to individual contribution.

Serve as a Model of Teamwork.   Perhaps the most effective way to encourage the emergence of teamwork is by example. The leader must exemplify the kind of behavior that enhances teamwork. One way is for the leader to reveal important information about ideas and attitudes relevant to the work of the group. As a result of this behavior, team members may follow suit. Self-disclosure fosters teamwork because it leads to shared perceptions and concerns.[4]

The team leader can also be a model of teamwork by fully cooperating with the leaders of other groups and members of his or her own team. An even more subtle way of serving as a model of teamwork is for the leader to eliminate using the terms *superior* and *subordinate*. Both terms have come into disfavor in teamwork-oriented firms because they emphasize status differences among team members.

Practicing equality is another way the leader can be a model of teamwork. A team leader does not have to like all team leaders equally well. Yet leaders should try to make assignments on the basis of merit, otherwise they run the risk of being accused of favoritism. Equality thus means each work unit member has an equal chance of obtaining whatever rewards the leader has to offer, providing that person performs well. Playing favorites detracts from teamwork because most people do not wish to cooperate with a select one or two employees who receive undeserved rewards. The manager of a software development group at Xerox Corporation expressed this opinion about how equality contributes to teamwork:

> Equality is a cornerstone to our teamwork approach. I keep my door open to anyone who has an idea to share about an individual or group project. I believe that if each individual feels like an important and equal part of our team, more interaction will take place. The group will then be more effective in reaching its goals.

Use a Consensus Management Style. Teamwork is enhanced when the team leader practices consensus decision making (refer to Chapter 8). Contributing input to important decisions helps foster the feeling among members that they are valuable team members. Consensus decision making also leads to an exchange of ideas within the group, including supporting and refining each other's suggestions. As a result, the feeling of working jointly on problems is further enhanced. Joseph "Rod" Canion, the founder and former president of Compaq Computer Corp., practiced consensus management to foster teamwork. He explains how:

> We use a team of people to come to critical decisions. The consensus aspect has to do with striving to get them all to agree. You have a number of people who are very qualified and represent different backgrounds and disciplines. You need to get them to focus on an issue with the right attitude: they are not trying to win their own position, but are contributing to the best possible solution. That gives you the ability to get to a better answer than any one individual could by himself or herself.[5]

The consensus decision making used by Canion builds teamwork because his team members are not "trying to win their own position, but are contributing to the best possible solution."

Assign Roles to Team Members. Members of an effective team typically play different roles that are either assigned by the team leader or emerge naturally. Similar to an athletic team, the presence of various roles helps develop a spirit of teamwork. Instead of competing against each other, each member contributes in a different way as defined by the role. Roles are not necessarily fixed, and the same person will occasionally occupy more than one role simultaneously. Virginia Gemmell observed the following roles in an effective team:

1. An *ideator* is good at generating many ideas.
2. An *inventor* takes ideas and translates them into tangible realities (also an implementor role).
3. A *champion* has a passion and an impatience for seeing his or her vision become a reality. (The champion is often the team leader.)
4. A *sponsor* has the power to protect, shield, and encourage both the project and the champion.
5. A *technical gatekeeper* assimilates, accumulates, and disseminates technical information.
6. A *market gatekeeper* assimilates, accumulates, organizes, and disseminates market information.[6]

Encourage Competition with Another Group. One of the best-known ways to encourage teamwork is to rally the support of the group against a real or imagined threat from the outside. Beating the competition makes more sense when the competition is outside your own organization. When the enemy is within, the team spirit developed may become detrimental to the overall organization. A plant manager told his supervisors:

> Our sister plant in Montreal is way ahead of us in preventing lost-time accidents. We don't have to take this challenge lying down. Let's wish them the best of luck in reducing accidents, but let's create even better luck for us.

By the end of the year, the Ontario plant did reduce accidents a trifle more than did the Montreal plant. The groups worked more effectively as a team in beating the competition. In addition to competing against another plant, the plant manager capitalized on the cultural rivalry that exists between English Canada versus French Canada.

Provide and Encourage Emotional Support.   Good teamwork includes emotional support to members. Such support can take the form of voicing encouragement for ideas expressed, listening to a group member's problems, or even providing help with a technical problem. The leader can provide such support and also encourage other members to help each other. An example is the manager of a claims group at a regional Aetna office. She uses a straightforward approach to encouraging emotional support within her work unit. Should one of the claims adjusters appear stressed out on a given day, she would say to another adjuster: "Keep an eye on _____ today. She could use some positive strokes. I think she's overloaded with concerns."

Focus on the Group's Comparative Advantage.   To build a winning spirit in the work unit, the leader has to develop member pride, says former military officer and corporate executive Bill Cohen.[7] To achieve such pride, the group has to be convinced it performs some function better than others doing comparable work. If the group is truly the best in the world in performing its function, pride follows naturally. Being the world champion, however, is usually an unrealistically high standard. A more realistic tactic is to identify a specific activity the team does better compared to other groups. Among these comparative advantages are higher output per worker, lower turnover, more creative ideas per year, lower operating costs, and stronger ethics.

The comparison groups for being number one can be the company, a division of the company, the industry, the city, the state or province, or the country. If the leader makes the category small enough, any team can compare favorably to others. For example, "Our team has the best record in the company for bringing back customers who have not done business with us for five or more years." However modest the comparison, a valid comparative advantage can serve as a bedrock of group pride.

Encourage Team Members to Share Ideas.   Idea sharing is a robust tactic for developing teamwork because the exchange of information requires a high level of cooperation. David A. Stumm, the sales and training manager for Duracell Corporation, explains how a manager heightened teamwork through idea sharing:

> To get us working together, he'd say, as if in passing: "John has some ideas he wants to try. With your experience you ought to be able to help him. The two of you tell me what you want to do." Since I didn't want my boss to think only John had ideas, the situation was competitive. But the proof that I was good would be if John and I made good together—so we cooperated intensely. We became excited and committed ourselves to making things happen. We outsold all the other divisions in the company and our success ratio rose with every win.[8]

Orient New Members.   New workers should be carefully introduced to the group to give them a chance to become psychologically part of the work unit. Many companies use a big-sibling program whereby experienced workers help assimilate new workers to the formal requirements of the group and the relevant aspects of the organizational culture. Improved teamwork often results.

To improve teamwork, orienting new members should also include conditioning them to believe they are joining an elite group. Furthermore, the new members are told they would not be asked to join if they were not winners, too.[9] A key recruiting thrust at Cypress Semiconductors is to tell job candidates that only those people who want to be winners will be invited to join the company team.

Before moving on to the formal aspects of building teamwork, do Skill-Building Exercise 10–1. It will sensitize your thinking to the importance of communicating the right message about teamwork.

SKILL-BUILDING EXERCISE 10–1
A Communication Self-Assessment

In response to each item, circle the answer that reflects how well the statement applies to you: (SA) strongly agree, (A) agree, (D) disagree, and (SD) strongly disagree.

1. When people talk, I listen attentively and do not think of other things, or read, or talk on the telephone.   SA   A   D   SD

2. I provide the information the group needs, even if someone else was its source.   SA   A   D   SD

3. I get impatient when people disagree with me.   SA   A   D   SD

4. I ask for and carefully consider advice from other people.   SA   A   D   SD

5. I cut off other people when they are talking.   SA   A   D   SD

6. I tell people what I want, speaking rapidly, in short, clipped sentences.   SA   A   D   SD

7. When people disagree with me, I listen to what they have to say and do not respond immediately.   SA   A   D   SD

8. I speak candidly and openly, identifying when I am expressing opinions or feelings rather than reporting facts.   SA   A   D   SD

9. I finish other people's sentences for them.   SA   A   D   SD

10. I find it difficult to express my feelings, except when pressure builds up and I become angry.   SA   A   D   SD

11. I am conscious of how I express myself nonverbally, including facial expressions, body language, voice tone, and gestures.   SA   A   D   SD

12. When people disagree with me, I avoid arguments by not responding.   SA   A   D   SD

13. During meetings, I prefer to listen rather than talk.   SA   A   D   SD

14. When I talk, I am concise and to the point.   SA   A   D   SD

15. I prevent arguments during team   SA   A   D   SD
    meetings.

Interpretation: Agreeing (SA or A) with items 1, 4, 8, 11, and 14 and dis-
agreeing (D or SD) with all the rest, suggests you encourage openness and candor. You create a climate of trust and teamwork by involving the team in
important decisions that affect their lives. You communicate clearly and con-
cisely and balance task and interpersonal aspects of the group.

  Agreeing (SA or A) with items 2, 3, 5, 6, and 9 means you are probably task oriented and dominate the team. Such team leaders are frequently intolerant of disagreement and may squelch involvement and discussion. You would thus need to
develop a more collaborative style to build and enhance teamwork. To become better at developing teamwork, modify your approach so your behavior would be accurately characterized by agreement with items 1, 4, 8, 11, and 14.

Formal Tactics and Strategies

The tactics and strategies for building teamwork described in this section
require changes in structure, policies, or procedures. These types of changes
might also be classified as administrative because they require some administrative action to implement, such as providing group incentives.

Allow for Physical Proximity among Members.   Group cohesiveness,
and therefore teamwork, is enhanced when team members are located close
together and can interact frequently and easily. Frequent interaction often
leads to camaraderie and a feeling of belongingness. A useful tactic for
achieving physical proximity is to establish a shared physical facility, such as
a conference room, research library, or beverage lounge. These areas should
be decorated differently from others in the building and a few amenities
added such as a coffeepot, microwave oven, and refrigerator. Team members
can then use these areas for refreshments and group interaction.

Use Team Incentives.   A key strategy for encouraging teamwork is to
reward the team as well as individual members. The most convincing team incentive is to calculate compensation partially on the basis of team results.
Group incentives build teamwork because the team must perform well for individuals to receive their share of the merit pay given to the team. One bank's
experience with team incentive is described as follows:

> Executives at the bank decided that every employee in its branch system needed
> to pay attention to the quality of customer service. In the past, employees had re-
> ceived incentives for the volume of new products sold and for cross-selling (re-
> ferrals to other bank services). The old plan resulted in customer complaints that

they were being oversold and that bank employees were more interested in sales than service. A customer satisfaction survey indicated that the bank was losing more customers than it was gaining.

To stem the net outflow of customers, the bank implemented a series of initiatives to improve the quality of customer service. At the same time, the bank implemented a team incentive plan. Results are measured in terms of customer satisfaction. Current payouts are received for current satisfaction scores and deferred payouts are given for sustaining high customer satisfaction.

Although the team payouts drained some profits, the team incentives proved to be a good investment. The costs of continually selling new customers and closing out the accounts of defecting customers exceeded the small amounts of lost profits.[10]

Team incentives can be nonfinancial as well as financial. Assume a manager receives a compliment from higher management that he or she has done an outstanding job. The manager would share this praise with the group because most accomplishments of a manager reflect a team effort. Team celebrations for accomplishing milestones, such as achieving a high-quality standard, are another potentially effective form of team incentive.

Use Team Symbols. Teamwork on the athletic field is enhanced by team symbols such as uniforms and nicknames (e.g., Fighting Irish, Blue Devils, and Lady Volunteers). Symbols are also a potentially effective team builder in business. Trademarks, logos, mottos, and other indicators of products both advertise the company and signify a joint effort. Company jackets, caps, T-shirts, mugs, ballpoint pens, and business cards can be modified to symbolize a work unit.

Social symbols, such as symbolic group activities, can also identify and build team unity. Many groups use ceremonies such as award banquets to recognize group effort, thus reinforcing collaborative effort. The shared laughter at banquets, even breakfast celebrations, also creates emotional closeness and teamwork. A recommended approach here is to organize a ceremony announcing the successful introduction of a new product or service that resulted from a team effort.[11]

Use Peer Evaluations. In the traditional performance evaluation system, the manager evaluates team members at regular intervals. With peer evaluation systems, the team members contribute to the evaluation by submitting evaluations of each other. Peer evaluations frequently contribute to teamwork because team members realize that helping each other becomes as important as helping the boss. Similarly, team members recognize that pleasing each other counts as well as pleasing the boss.

Peer evaluations, however, have a downside risk. Team members might hesitate to do anything that would interfere with receiving a good evaluation, even if the action were productive. For example, for fear of receiving a negative evaluation, a team member might not confront another about an important mistake. Team members might also give high appraisals to team members they particularly liked, and vice versa.

Favorable results with peer evaluations have been reported at Digital. The group input to the appraisal is collected by a committee. In addition to each team member evaluating all other team members, each person provides a self-evaluation. A key advantage is reported as follows:

> The team member is recognized by peers. Because co-workers are usually very close to the team member, observations of performance can be more accurate than those of traditional managers. Team members respect peer analysis and are willing to change accordingly.[12]

Strive for Long-Term Membership on the Team.   Team building and attrition work against each other. A spirit of cooperation is fostered when team members recognize they will be working together relatively permanently. This approach has been one of the pillars of the Japanese strategy for achieving work group harmony. Team members should be organized so they perceive themselves spending the foreseeable future together. The result is likely to be greater commitment to the team. When new members are brought into the team, they should be advised that the work team values stability in membership.

Outdoor Training as a Method of Building Teamwork

An increasingly popular approach to building teamwork in an off-the-job setting is outdoor or wilderness training. Participants are placed in a demanding outdoor environment in which they have to rely on skills they didn't realize they had—and each other—to complete the program. The emphasis is on building self-confidence and teamwork. Outward Bound is the best known and largest of the outdoor training programs. More than 500 courses are offered in wilderness areas in 20 states and provinces. The courses typically run from three days to four weeks, with one course in North Carolina lasting 88 days. Worldwide, there are about 48 Outward Bound schools on five continents, with a total annual enrollment of about 28,000.

The Outward Bound Professional Development Program is geared toward managerial leaders because it emphasizes teamwork, leadership, and risk taking. The wilderness is the classroom, and the instructors draw analogies between each outdoor activity and the workplace during debriefing sessions. Among the courses offered are dog sledding, skiing and winter camping, desert backpacking, canoe expeditioning, sailing and sea kayaking, alpine mountaineering, mountain backpacking and horse trail riding, and cycling. The accompanying box presents a glimpse of one company's experience with Outward Bound training.

Wilderness Camp Builds Leadership

In the cold predawn light of the Rockies, a dozen executives of the Champion Spark Plug Company shiver into jogging gear. They wheeze through a 20-minute run on a winding pine forest trail, reluctantly plunge half-naked into a rushing mountain stream, and then head off to climb some rocks.

It's all in a day's work at the Colorado Outward Bound School, where hard-charging managers learn teamwork in the wild. Over the next five days the spark plug executives would discover fears they never knew they had. Among their daily feats, they clawed up a 70-foot cliff blindfolded and scaled a 13,000-foot peak, posing for photographs at the summit like an Everest assault team. Many of the exercises the Champion managers went through, such as scaling a 12-foot wall, require exceptional teamwork.

"In a couple of days I'll be back in the office saying, 'Wow, did I do all that stuff?' " said the manager of Champion's international manufacturing operations.

SOURCE: Based on information in Rick Gladstone, "Executives Take Their Insecurities Outdoors," Associated Press, September 25, 1988; and James T. Yenckel, "Bound for Adventure," *Washington Post* syndicated story, December 9, 1990.

THE CASE FOR AND AGAINST BUILDING TEAMWORK

The most cogent argument for building teamwork is that a cohesive team can consistently outperform a collection of talented individuals, both in sports and in business. On a cohesive team, the members work together in the pursuit of a common goal. A related argument for building teamwork is that the legendary success of individuals such as John Sculley at Apple Computer are really the success of teams of workers.

A new form of organization design provides indirect evidence for the importance of teamwork. *Reengineering,* as developed by Michael Hammer, organizes work around processes such as the filling of a customer order instead of by functional departments. The process teams are characterized by an emphasis on exceptional cooperation and teamwork among members of the group. ITT Sheraton Corporation has achieved exceptional success with process teams (reengineering). According to Executive Vice President John W. Herold, Jr., the typical 300-room Sheraton Hotel had required up to 40 managers and 200 employees. The hotel eliminated narrowly defined functional jobs and rethought outdated procedures. As a result, the reengineered version of the hotel could operate with only 14 managers and 140 employees, and have higher customer satisfaction. Eliminating wasteful procedures, such as managers preparing reports for their superiors, created many of the savings.[13] However, the increased emphasis on teamwork also played an important role.

An argument against the push for teamwork is that we might be too concerned about getting people to work together and like each other. Too much cohesion has some undesirable consequences such as overconformity and *groupthink,* the end point of consensus whereby group members think alike and fail to critically evaluate ideas. To be creative, many organizations need more boat rocking, more mavericks, and less mutual admiration. Organizations move forward via the individual ingenuity of a relatively few pioneers. If we rely excessively on teamwork and cooperation, these people may hold back from making their contributions.

Another argument against teamwork is that people who rely too much on teamwork will not receive recognition for their individual ideas, thus retarding their careers. Also, exploring and pursuing your own ideas can hasten self-development.[14]

Guidelines for Action and Skill Development

Quantum physicist David Bohm has concluded that *koinonia*, Greek for "a spirit of fellowship," is the key factor in creating teamwork instead of petty bickering. He has developed a five-step procedure to incorporate this high level of teamwork into an organization:

1. *Hold practice sessions.* A small pilot group of managers meets regularly to discuss anything, without an agenda. This serves as a basis for forming the relationships necessary for teamwork.

2. *Establish dialogue.* Team members exchange ideas without trying to change the other person's mind. The rules of dialogue are "don't argue," "don't interrupt," and "listen carefully."

3. *Clarify your thinking.* In this step, each person suspends all unproven assumptions and tries to look at everything with a fresh, unprejudiced eye.

4. *Be honest.* Thoughts should not be hidden, no matter how bad or controversial. If team members know what you are really thinking, they will be more comfortable around you.

5. *Koinonia.* If you diligently practice the first four steps, *koinonia* will occur. Team members will form better relationships, and they will work together more harmoniously.[14]

DISCUSSION QUESTIONS AND ACTIVITIES

1. How does the Lion's Den build teamwork?

2. How should the mission of the team relate to the mission of the organization?

3. What steps might the team leader take to purposely breed competition with another group?

4. What is the difference between a group being the best at some activity versus having a comparative advantage?

5. In what way might physical proximity of team members contribute to creativity?

6. In what way might peer appraisals lead to a surge of office politics?

7. Ask two experienced managers what they think is a good way to promote teamwork on the job. Be prepared to report your findings back to class.

NOTES

1. Adapted from Robert Brookman, "Ignite Team Spirit in Tired Lions," *HRMagazine*, June 1990, pp. 106–8.
2. Jon R. Katzenbach and Douglas K. Smith, *The Wisdom of Teams: Creating the High-Performance Organization* (Boston: Harvard Business School Press, 1992).
3. "Basic Training," Executive Strategies, October 8, 1991, p. 7.
4. Paul S. George, "Teamwork without Tears," *Personnel Journal*, November 1987, p. 129.
5. "Consensus Builder: Teamwork Tips to Make Your Company Soar," *Success*, October 1990, p. 44.
6. Virginia Gemmell, "Designing a Winning Project Team," *Supervisory Management*, April 1989, p. 27.
7. William A. Cohen, *The Art of the Leader* (Englewood Cliffs, N.J.: Prentice Hall, 1991).
8. David A. Stumm, "Teamwork and Tin Men," *Success*, October 1987, p. 22.
9. Joseph D. O'Brian, "Making New Hires Members of the Team," *Supervisory Management*, May 1992, p. 4.
10. Judy Huret, "Paying for Team Results," *HRMagazine*, May 1991, p. 40.
11. George, "Teamwork without Tears," p. 126.
12. Carol A. Norma and Robert A. Zawacki, "Team Appraisals—Team Approach," *Personnel Journal*, September 1991, p. 102.
13. John A. Byrne, "Management's New Gurus," *Business Week*, August 31, 1992, pp. 44, 51.
14. Richard Poe, "The Secret to Teamwork," *Success*, June 1991, p. 72.

SOME ADDITIONAL REFERENCES

Gatto, Rex P. *Teamwork through Flexible Leadership*. Pittsburgh: GTA Press, 1992.

Gregg, Elaine. "12 Ways to Rev Up Your Team." *Black Enterprise*, November 1990.

Hackman, J. Richard, ed. *Groups that Work (and Those That Don't): Creating Conditions for Effective Teamwork.* San Francisco: Jossey-Bass, 1991.

Horton, Thomas R. "Delegation and Team Building: No Solo Acts Please." *Management Review,* September 1992, pp. 58—61.

Olsen, Eric. "Build a Team that Never Drops the Ball." *Success,* November 1990, pp. 40–44.

Parker, Glenn M. *Team Players and Teamwork: The New Competitive Business Strategy.* San Francisco: Jossey-Bass, 1990.

Tjosvold, Dean, and Tjosvold, Mary M. *Leading the Team Organization: How to Create an Enduring Competitive Advantage.* New York: Lexington/Macmillan, 1991.

Appendix to Chapter Ten

THE TEAMWORK CHECKLIST

This checklist can serve as an informal guide to diagnosing teamwork. All members of the team, including the leader, should complete the checklist. Indicate whether your team has each of the following characteristics:

	Mostly Yes	Mostly No
1. Clearly defined goals and expectations.	————	————
2. Clearly established roles and responsibilities.	————	————
3. Well-documented guidelines of behavior and ground rules.	————	————
4. Open communication in an atmosphere of trust and mutual respect.	————	————
5. Continuous learning and training in appropriate skills.	————	————
6. Patience and support by higher management.	————	————
7. Rewards tied to individual as well as team results.	————	————
8. Desire to continuously improve and innovate.	————	————

Scoring and interpretation: The larger the number of statements answered *mostly yes,* the more likely good teamwork is present, thus contributing to productivity. The answers will serve as discussion points for improving teamwork and group effectiveness. Negative responses to questions can be used as suggestions for taking action to improve teamwork in your group.

SOURCE: Based on information in Mark Kelly, *The Adventures of a Self-Managing Team* (San Diego: Pfeiffer & Company, 1991), p. 104.

Chapter Eleven

Work Teams

> One of the world's best-known companies wanted to take back the manufacturing of one of its specialty products, if it could be done inexpensively and promptly. To accomplish these ends, the company chose to organize the work into teams of multiskilled workers rather than use the traditional assembly-line arrangement.

Some Eastman Kodak Co. managers had a problem recently, so they asked Gordon Ackley and four other factory workers to solve it. "The first thing we said was, 'Will everybody leave the room? We'll let you know how we'll do it.' " Ackley said.

Ackley is part of a *flow team* at Kodak Park, one of the world's largest manufacturing sites. Workers are grouped by what product they help make, not by what job they do. The problem assigned to this flow team (*work team* is the traditional term) was how to quckly gear up to make Ektamate paper, an ultra-thin photographic paper used to print copies of microfilm slides.

To save money, Kodak's Business Imaging Systems (BIS) unit had gone to 3M Co. for paper to be used with its microfilm machines. But BIS sales reps found that some customers preferred the old Kodak Ektamate paper. As a result, top management at BIS offered Kodak's black-and-white paper manufacturing division a chance to get the business back—but only if it could be done inexpensively and promptly.

To restart manufacturing this specialty product, BIS would have to get out machines that had been in storage for four years, find missing parts, and find substitutes for key people who had left the company. So the team—originally five people, later growing to 15—worked out the details. The schedule called for working 12-hour shifts but not disrupting vacation plans. "We didn't want any reservations canceled," Ackley said.

The team figured out what assistance it would need. Other departments had to increase their output of paper and chemicals. Machinery was modified by maintenance workers who volunteered for the project. Sometimes the project needed the help of key workers for as little as one or two hours—even though established procedures allowed only for weekly transfers outside a department.

Michael Graves, manager of development and manufacturing materials for the Business Information Systems unit, said the unit was impressed by how much these workers really wanted to bring this business back within Kodak. "They were absolutely determined to succeed," he said. "And they were up and running in 10 weeks, which is amazing in itself." Previously, workers might have taken many months to accomplish a project of this magnitude.

Ronald Heidke, manager of Kodak Park's sensitized products and manufacturing division, said the 6,000-employee division reorganized early in 1989 around flow teams. It had been organized around different jobs, such as mixing chemicals, coating film and paper, or cutting and packaging. Now the division is organized around products—black-and-white paper (including Ektamate), black-and-white film, color paper, color film for professional photographers, and so on.

The old system was what Heidke calls a "doberman" system. Accounting watchdogs would go after manufacturing units that missed targets for budget and output. Under the new system, each unit produces not only film and paper, but also a profit. The black-and-white manufacturing unit, which includes the Ektamate team, publishes its own annual report.[1]

DISTINGUISHING CHARACTERISTICS OF WORK TEAMS

The team approach to producing goods and services has become a major new thrust in organizing work. A survey conducted by *Industry Week* indicated almost 10 percent of work areas are currently organized into teams. The executives surveyed also responded that over 50 percent of their work forces will be organized into teams within five years.[2] Work teams are found in businesses as diverse as food processing, furniture manufacturing, telecommunications, and insurance.

Work teams originated as a form of group job enrichment through broadening the responsibility of team members. *Work team* is now the most frequently used term for a structure that is also referred to as *production work team, self-managing team, semiautonomous work groups*, and *autonomous work group*.

Members of the work team typically work together on an ongoing, day-by-day basis. In this sense, a work team is more similar to a department than a project or committee. The work team is often given total responsibility, or *ownership*, for a product or service, such as preparing a telephone directory.

Other times, the team is given responsibility for a major chunk of a job such as building a truck engine, but not the entire truck. The work team is taught to think in terms of customer requirements. For example, the engine makers might be told, "Think of yourself as a trucker getting up at 4 A.M. on a February day in North Dakota. Would you want an engine that might not turn over?"

To develop the sense of ownership, workers are taught to become generalists rather than specialists. Each worker learns a broad range of skills and switches job assignments periodically. Today, a worker might be installing an engine radiator, while assembling the fuel-injection system tomorrow.

Although work teams govern themselves to a large extent, they still report to a middle manager, who may have responsibility for several work teams. The work teams and their leaders, if one is assigned, coordinate the activities with the middle manager. As compiled by a team of experts, here are the distinguishing characteristics of a work team:

1. Team members are empowered to share many management and leadership functions such as making job assignments and giving pep talks.

2. Members plan, control, and improve their own work processes.

3. Members set their own goals and inspect their own work.

4. Members create their own schedules and review their group performance.

5. Members often prepare their own budgets and coordinate their work with other departments.

6. Members typically order materials, keep inventories, and deal with suppliers.

7. Members are responsible for obtaining new training they might need.

8. Members are authorized to hire their own replacements or assume responsibility for disciplining their own members.

9. Members assume responsibility for the quality of their products and services provided to internal and external customers.[3]

Work teams vary in how many of these characteristics are present; a pure work team has most of them. As a result of having so much responsibility for a product or service, team members usually develop pride in their work and the team. At best, the team members feel as if they are operating a small business with the profits (or losses) being attributed directly to their efforts.

Desirable Team Member Characteristics

The right members have to be selected for work team assignments because not every employee has the motivation or skills suited for working as a team member. The organization needs a high-quality work force for the team concept to be effective. To work effectively as a team member or team leader, employees have to be mentally flexible, alert, and possess average or better interpersonal skills. Employees must take pride in their work and enjoy working cooperatively with others.

Selection devices such as interviews and personnel tests are used to find a good match between job candidates and job requirements. Candidates for the team typically are current employees, and they, too, are carefully screened. An example of how the selection process works is the Rohm and Haas chemical plant in LaPorte, Texas. All workers in the area of the job opening participate in the interview. Candidates for team assignments are questioned about the characteristics listed below, which are known to relate to success as a self-directing team member.[4]

1. *Responsibility.* Being able to maintain a high standard of work performance, dedication to quality.

2. *Motivational match.* Finding a fit between the person's interests and needs and the work team assignment.

3. *Versatility.* Handling multiple tasks, interruptions, and diverse assignments.

4. *Learning ability.* Comprehending new job-related information such as robotics or analyzing customer needs.

5. *Honesty.* Maintaining ethical standards related to the job and admitting mistakes.

6. *Self-starting.* Staying involved in productive activity without being closely supervised.

7. *Cooperativeness and teamwork.* Showing concern about achieving team goals rather than individual accomplishment.

8. *Openness.* Possessing genuineness in dealing with others and a willingness to relate openly and deal with conflict.

9. *Tact and sensitivity.* Being responsive to the impact of one's behavior on the feelings, dignity, and performance of others.

The above characteristics are positively associated with success as a work team member, but it is unrealistic to think every team member will have high standing on all of these characteristics. Even a chief executive officer is rarely outstanding in all the characteristics described above.

Attitudes are an important aspect of personal characteristics related to team member effectiveness. Do Skill-Building Exercise 11 to examine how well your attitudes are suited for being a leader or member of a work team.

SKILL-BUILDING EXERCISE 11
Mental Readiness for Being Assigned to a Work Team

Respond to each statement on a 1 to 5 scale: (1) strongly disagree, (2) disagree, (3) neutral, (4) agree, (5) strongly agree.

1. Employees should make the majority of decisions related to their work.   ____ ____ ____ ____ ____

2. It is possible for corporate employees to take as much pride in their work as if it were their own business.   ____ ____ ____ ____ ____

3. Workers who lack advanced training and education are capable of making useful work improvements.   ____ ____ ____ ____ ____

4. Groups can work effectively without a clear-cut center of authority.   ____ ____ ____ ____ ____

5. It is worth sacrificing some specialization of labor to give workers a chance to develop multiple skills.   ____ ____ ____ ____ ____

6. Competent workers do not require too much supervision.   ____ ____ ____ ____ ____

7. Having authority over people is not as important to me as being part of a smooth-working team.   ____ ____ ____ ____ ____

8. Given the opportunity, many workers could manage themselves without much supervision.   ____ ____ ____ ____ ____

9. Cordial relationships are important even in a factory setting.   ____ ____ ____ ____ ____

10. The more power workers are given, the more likely they are to behave responsibly.   ____ ____ ____ ____ ____

Scoring and interpretation: Add the numerical value you assigned to each statement and total your scores. The closer your score is to 50, the greater your degree of mental readiness to lead or participate on a work team. If your score is 30 or less, attempt to develop a more optimistic view of the capabilities and attitudes of workers. Start by looking for evidence of good accomplishments by skilled and semiskilled workers.

Evidence about Work Team Effectiveness

Published research about the effectiveness of work teams has been consistently positive. Work teams have a good record of improving productivity, quality, and customer service. We present current evidence along with several classic studies of autonomous work groups at Shenandoah Life Insurance Co., Volvo, and Gaines Pet Foods.

Northern Telcom.   Telecommunications equipment repair had long been a money loser at Northern Telcom's Morrisville facility. Yet revenue increased 63 percent four years after implementing self-directing work teams. Sales are up 26 percent and earnings, 46 percent. Productivity per employee has increased 60 percent, and scrap has decreased 63 percent. Quality has increased 50 percent despite a 40 percent decrease in quality inspectors.

Based on these optimistic results, Northern Telcom has shifted from the usual departmental structure to work teams in many other company locations. Company spokesperson Diane Pewitt explained that one of the biggest changes in implementing self-directed work teams is transforming the roles of both managers and employees. She said, "We eliminated the terms *supervisor* and *employees* and replaced them with *coaches* and *players*."[5]

General Electric, Salisbury.   Similar results were achieved by the General Electric plant in Salisbury, North Carolina, which produces lighting panel boards. The company introduced work teams in addition to flexible automation and computerized systems. Productivity increased 250 percent in comparison to other General Electric plants producing the same products. The results were so encouraging that 20 percent of the 120,000 General Electric employees now work under the team concept.[6] The GE evidence could mean the combination of work teams and the right type of automation is especially effective in improving productivity.

Sola Barnes-Hind.   Contact lenses present unique manufacturing and marketing challenges because prescription possibilities are almost endless. It is difficult to control inventory while maintaining enough stock to meet customer demands. To deal with this dilemma, Sola Barnes-Hind of Sunnyvale, California, developed manufacturing modules responsible for lens production. The modules closely resemble work teams. A typical manufacturing module consists of about 30 employees from each of three main production areas, along with a supervisor and two work coordinators.

A module is assigned responsibility for a limited range of lenses in inventory. An important part of the module design was to give each work group greater accountability for product quality and manufacturing cost. Dividing the manufacturing floor into modules required careful planning and considerable expense. Tables, chair lathes, polishers, and various support systems such as electricity and water had to be modified.

The results of organizing into modules surpassed expectations. Improvements were found in every area of concern. The results included improved yields, cost reductions, and higher morale.

Yields. The output from each group showed substantial improvement within three to six months after the modules were formed. Production doubled for both rigid lenses and soft lenses. Quality began to be built in, rather than improved after inspection. These improvements allowed the primary goals of inventory control and customer service to be met. Back orders were reduced by 80 percent, and inventory volume was reduced by 40 percent.

Cost Reductions. Costs were reduced in several areas after converting to manufacturing modules. The direct and variable cost per lens decreased by more than 12 percent, largely because each module was accountable for the supplies it consumed. Because fewer supervisors were needed, indirect labor costs also declined. In addition, the new layout reduced space requirements by about 10 percent.

Employee Morale. Employees generally supported the module system because it meant shifting to career ladders and skill-based pay (being paid for the number of skills one possesses). The monthly turnover rate dropped to an annual range of 8 to 14 percent from a previous range of 25 to 50 percent.[7]

Aid Association for Lutherans.   An insurance company run by a fraternal society, Aid Association for Lutherans (AAL), achieved impressive results by shifting from a traditional department structure to work teams. AAL switched to teamwork primarily to process insurance cases more rapidly, thus providing better service to its field agents and policyholders. Previously, all life insurance cases were handled by one unit, health insurance by another, and support services by a third. This often resulted in some cases being bounced from one section to another, leading to embarrassing delays.

Under the new system, the insurance department is divided into five groups, each serving a geographic group of agents. Each group is composed of three or four teams of 20 to 30 employees who can carry out all of the 167 tasks formerly divided among three sections. Team members are cross-trained to learn skills that connect the tasks formerly the responsibility of only one section. Field agents in each district deal solely with one team and develop close working relationships with its members. In the eyes of the agents, working with the home office is now much more personal.

Changing to work teams has been responsible for a 20 percent increase in productivity and as much as a 75 percent reduction in case processing time. Nevertheless, the abrupt switch to teams brought mixed feelings among employees. "There was uncertainty and a lot of broken friendships when we moved to the new system. Personally I feel more tension," one worker said. Yet most employees now like the team approach because it allows them to manage themselves, but some employees prefer not to have managerial responsibility.[8]

Shenandoah Life Insurance Co. In the early 1980s, Shenandoah Life installed a $2 million system to automate processing and claims operations at its Roanoke, Virginia, headquarters. The results from computerization were disappointing. It still required 27 working days, and handling by 32 clerks in 3 departments, to process a representative claim. The delays stemmed from the elaborate maze of regulations, not from defects in the technology. To speed claims processing, and capitalize on automation, the company grouped clerks into work teams of five to seven members. Each team now performs all the functions previously distributed over three departments. Team members learned new skills that brought increased job satisfaction and pay.

As a result of organizing by teams, the typical case-handling time decreased to two days, and customer complaints about service were virtually eliminated. Within six years of installing work teams, Shenandoah was processing 50 percent more applications and queries, with 10 percent fewer employees.[9]

Volvo Automobiles. The Volvo automotive plant in Kalmar, Sweden, opened in 1974. Kalmar's work force is divided into approximately 20 production teams of 15 to 25 persons each. The team assembles a major unit of a car such as door assembly, electric wiring, or fitting upholstery in an average of 20 to 40 minutes. Members of the team can exchange jobs or change teams if they choose. Team members can also vary the work pace, keeping up with the general flow of production but speeding up or pausing as they wish. This is possible because car-carrying trolleys can be delayed for a while both before entering and after leaving each work team's area.

Production costs at Kalmar are 25 percent lower than at Volvo's plants organized on an assembly-line basis. The continuing success of the Kalmar plant has prompted management to build a new plant in Uddevalla, Sweden, following the same principles of work design.[10]

Gaines Pet Food, Topeka, Kansas. In the late 1960s, General Foods experienced negative employee attitudes and diminishing productivity at some of its manufacturing plants. To combat these problems, management began to design new plants to operate with a minimum of supervision. One well-publicized example occurred at the Gaines Pet Food plant in Topeka, Kansas. The plant was designed to permit work teams to control production, packaging, and shipping technologies rather than to let technology control people.

Production was built around teams consisting of 7 to 14 members. Three teams were used per shift: processing, packaging, and shipping and office duties. Each team was responsible for dividing its own work among team members, interviewing and hiring job applicants, establishing internal policies and decision making within their own area of responsibility. All teams were responsible for their own quality control and such diverse functions as industrial engineering, maintenance, and housekeeping. Workers were encouraged to learn and perform as many jobs on the team as possible. When workers learned more skills, they were compensated accordingly.

The early results from this experiment in self-managing teams were encouraging but not all glowing. On the positive side, about 70 people were soon operating a plant originally estimated by industrial engineers to require 110 people to operate effectively. After the first 18 months, overhead was 30 percent lower than in conventionally operated plants in the same division of the pet food operation. Turnover and absenteeism were much lower than industry norms. The plant operated for almost four years before its first lost-time accident. Altogether, an estimated annual cost savings of $1 million was achieved.[11]

Fifteen years after the experiment began, the Gaines plant still uses teamwork, both in the office and factory. Several years ago, the plant manager said Topeka produced the same pet foods as a sister plant in Kankakee, Illinois, at 7 percent lower labor costs.[12]

Despite these positive results, the Gaines plant had trouble being integrated into the larger organization. In addition to the formation of self-managing teams, other aspects of a traditional bureaucratic structure were modified. Phillip L. Hunsaker and Curtis W. Cook make this analysis:

> Because power was shifted downward within the Gaines plant, traditional functional management and professional job classifications were eliminated. Staff at the home office experienced difficulty in their attempts to communicate with unassigned counterparts in Topeka. Over time, the power shifted back to a structure that central management could control; in part, this resulted from adding on traditional management positions such as plant controller and manufacturing services manager.[13]

The organizational culture must support an innovation such as work teams, or the innovation will not endure. At Gaines, the traditional structure of the rest of the organization may have prevented the spread of self-managing teams, but it did not negate its benefits.

FOR AND AGAINST WORK TEAMS

The Argument for Work Teams

Several arguments can be advanced for work teams. Of prime importance, companies using the team approach report substantial improvements in productivity and quality. Many of these improvements can be linked directly to increased employee motivation and satisfaction. Work teams also improve productivity by giving production systems greater flexibility in meeting dynamic market demands. The team approach to organizing work is also important because teams are a major component of total quality management (TQM). Under TQM, small groups of employees become involved in making continuous improvements.

Increased job satisfaction is another important positive consequence of self-managing work teams. Many workers prefer teamwork because it offers a greater variety of tasks compared with repetitive jobs in an assembly line. A team coordinator in a GM plant makes the following comment in support of the job satisfaction argument: "Once in a while I get bored and switch jobs with someone just to relieve the tedium. I couldn't do this before we switched to work teams."[14]

Work teams also contribute to organizational effectiveness when they handle discipline problems taken care of by management in the past. If the problem is not resolved by discussion with the team leader, it is discussed openly at a team meeting. Most employees choose to resolve the problem rather than experience the embarrassment of public discussion.[15]

The Argument against Work Teams

Despite the advantages just mentioned, work teams are not suited to improving productivity and satisfaction in every work situation for the following reasons:

1.   Work teams may not fit into an organizational culture characterized by a strong belief in a bureaucratic authority structure. The traditional idea that a manager's primary function is to tell people what to do is replaced with the idea that a manager should encourage employees to use initiative. Managers who think only in terms of a top-to-bottom flow of authority would probably not allow work teams to function properly.

2.   A high-quality work force is needed to staff the teams. To work effectively as team members, employees have to be mentally flexible, alert, and possess at least average interpersonal skills. In many plants and offices, such employees are not available. Or if they are available, the employer may not be able to offer high enough wages to attract them. Also, employees must have the proper motivation to become effective team members. Employees who prefer to perform repetitive tasks, working independently, are not suited for membership in work teams.

3.   When the work force is unionized, designing jobs into teams could result in troublesome labor-management issues. Instead of multiple job classifications, a work team plant usually has only one or two. Production and maintenance work, usually two separate job categories, tend to merge into one fluid work system.[16] Other issues include: Which employees will be denied membership in the new work teams? How do you

establish wage rates for employees who can perform in six different jobs? Is the employee who interacts directly with a supervisor from another department required to be a member of the bargaining unit?

4. Employee involvement groups, including work teams, can create legal problems. The National Labor Relations Board (NLRB) has held that in one situation, work teams composed of managers and union employees violated U.S. federal labor law. The legal controversy began when a small electrical parts company, Electromation Inc., established committees to settle a wage dispute with employees. The committees were composed of six hourly workers and one or two managers. Soon after, the Teamsters began an organizing drive at Electromation and objected to the committees. An NLRB judge ruled the company had violated the Wagner Act, the National Labor Relations Act of 1935. The major legal concern is that teams may usurp the authority of labor unions. Work teams might be violating the following provision of the Wagner Act:

> A labor organization is any organization of any kind, or any employee representation committee which exists for the purpose of dealing with employers concerning grievances, wages, hours of employment, or conditions of work.

A counterargument to this concern is that the NLRB may ultimately issue guidelines for the proper use of work teams so they do not violate the Wagner Act. The key appears to be that teams must not be dominated by management. Also, the team should not address matters such as wages, grievances, hours of work, or working conditions. Furthermore, when labor unions approve of work teams, no law has been violated.[17]

5. Absenteeism and turnover tend to be higher than for comparable groups organized in a traditional way. The relatively high rate of absenteeism could be attributed to the fact that team members believe other members can cover for them because they are multiskilled. The higher turnover occurs possibly because workers were chosen for the team who prefer not to have so much responsibility for results.[18]

Guidelines for Action and Skill Development

To properly house a team operation, an organization must be redesigned and a systems point of view maintained. First, attention must be paid to the design and layout of the physical setting. Building space must allow for the product flow and for the interaction of people necessary to perform teamwork. Second, it is usually necessary to create a relatively flat organization structure whereby team members are in control of a significant amount of their work.

Similar to any significant organizational innovation, work teams require topmanagement commitment to succeed. If top management regards change to work teams as merely a "program in manufacturing," the restructuring will be short lived. The manager intending to restructure his or her area of responsibility into work teams should seek a member of top management to be the work team champion.

Work teams require *distributed leadership*, a sharing of leadership responsibility among team members. Distributed leadership occurs gradually as members come to understand each other, including their values and skills. Work teams are the most effective when the status barriers between managers and operative employees are broken down. Doing so establishes an atmosphere of trust and open communication.[19]

Employees must be carefully chosen who show pride in their work and enjoy working cooperatively with others. Self-nomination or asking for volunteers for the work teams will decrease selection errors. Be prepared to transfer employees who do not make it as team members or team leaders to more traditional jobs. Some people are not suited to self-managing work teams even though they might nominate themselves for such assignments.

After employees are selected, they must be trained thoroughly to become productive members of work teams. Essential training areas include appropriate problem-solving techniques, technical skills, and interpersonal and leadership skills.[20] One example is that team members must learn how to give constructive feedback to each other because their work is interdependent.

Encourage multifunctionalism within the team. Overspecialization isolates team members who should be able to carry out all the jobs performed by other team members.[21]

DISCUSSION QUESTIONS AND ACTIVITIES

1. What is the primary difference between a work team and the usual team of people in any other organizational unit?

2. Identify an office operation you think could be adapted well to a work team. Explain why.

3. What is the underlying reason work teams often lead to improvements in product quality?

4. Explain how the work team concept could be applied to top management in a large organization.

5. How might the information presented in Chapter 10 about building teamwork be applied to increase the effectiveness of work teams?

6. How might the organizational culture influence whether or not a work team would be successful in a given organization?

7. Find an article in a professional journal, magazine, or newspaper dealing with work teams. Discuss in class how well the article supports, or contradicts, the information in this chapter.

NOTES

1. Adapted from Phil Ebersole, "Kodak Tries Going with the Flow," *Rochester Democrat and Chronicle*, August 26, 1990, pp. 1F, 6F.
2. Richard S. Wellins, William C. Byham, and Jeanne M. Wilson, *Empowered Teams* (San Francisco: Jossey-Bass 1991), p. 225.
3. Ibid., pp. 4–5.
4. John G. Belcher, Jr., *Productivity Plus* (Houston, Texas: Gulf Publishing Co., 1990).
5. Jana Schilder, "Work Teams Boost Productivity," *Personnel Journal*, February 1992, pp. 67–71.
6. Ibid., p. 68.
7. Richard L. Bunning and Raleigh S. Althisar, "Modules: A Team Model for Manufacturing," *Personnel Journal*, March 1990, pp. 90–96.
8. As reported in "Work Teams Can Rev Up Paper-Pushers Too," *Business Week*, November 28, 1988, pp. 64–72.
9. "Management Discovers the Human Side of Automation," *Business Week*, September 29, 1986, p. 70
10. Ibid., p. 74.
11. Richard W. Woodman and John J. Sherwood, "A Comprehensive Look at Job Design," *Personnel Journal*, August 1977, pp. 384–90, 418.
12. "Management Discovers the Human Side of Automation," p. 79.
13. Phillip L. Hunsaker and Curtis W. Cook, *Managing Organizational Behavior* (Reading, Mass.: Addison-Wesley, 1986), p. 573.
14. "Management Discovers the Human Side of Automation," p. 72.
15. Donald F. Barkman, "Team Discipline: Put Performance on the Line," *Personnel Journal*, March 1987, p. 60.
16. "Management Discovers the Human Side of Automation," p. 79.
17. Aaron Bernstein, "Putting a Damper on that Old Team Spirit," *Business Week*, May 4, 1992, p. 60; and Aaron Bernstein, "Making Teamwork Work—An Appeasing Uncle Sam," *Business Week*, January 25, 1993, p.101.
18. John M. Codery, Walter S. Mueller, and Leigh M. Smith, "Attitudinal and Behavioral Effects of Autonomous Group Working: A Longitudinal Field Study," *Academy of Management Journal*, June 1991 pp. 464-76.
19. David Barry, "Managing the Bossless Team: Lessons in Distributed Leadership," *Organizational Dynamics*, Summer 1991, p. 39.
20. Constance Hamilton, "Training Is a Vital Link in the Process," *HRfocus*, September 1992, pp. 4–5.
21. "Empowered Teams," *Executive Strategies*, October 21, 1991, p. 2.

SOME ADDITIONAL REFERENCES

Bolman, Lee G., and Deal, Terrence E. "What Makes a Team Work?" *Organizational Dynamics*, Autumn 1992, pp. 34–44.

Lumsden, Gay, and Lumsden, Donald. *Communicating in Groups and Teams: Sharing Leadership*. Belmont, Calif.: Wadsworth., 1993.

Neuman, George A. "Autonomous Work Group Selection." *Journal of Business and Psychology*, Winter 1991, pp. 283–91.

Orsburn, Jack D., Linda Moran, Ed Musslewhite, and John H. Zenger. *Self-Directed Work Teams: The New American Challenge*. Homewood, Ill.: Business One Irwin, 1990.

Shonk, James H. *Team-Based Organizations: Developing a Successful Team Environment*. Homewood, Ill.: Business One Irwin, 1992.

Tjosvold, Dean. *Teamwork for Customers: Building Organizations That Take Pride in Serving*. San Francisco: Jossey-Bass, 1992.

Appendix to Chapter Eleven

IS A WORK TEAM SUITED TO YOUR WORKPLACE?

Circle the following statements yes or no. The greater the number of yes responses, the higher the probability that a work team will enhance productivity and quality in your workplace.

Workplace Characteristic	Answer	
1. My department is responsible for a task that is complex and independent.	Yes	No
2. There are workers in my firm who have the desire and ability to operate independently in a team setting.	Yes	No
3. The cost for conversion from an assembly line to a team operation would not be prohibitive.	Yes	No
4. Teamwork is valued in our organization.	Yes	No
5. Our production (or clerical) employees display initiative frequently.	Yes	No
6. Top management has a positive attitude toward power sharing.	Yes	No
7. We need to reduce our overhead costs.	Yes	No
8. Top management is accustomed to receiving suggestions from below.	Yes	No
9. Our work force is of generally high quality with respect to education, training, and skill level.	Yes	No
10. Product (or service) quality leaves something to be desired.	Yes	No
11. Much of our work could be divided into independent units without creating a major disturbance.	Yes	No

12. Union-management (or employee-management) relations are generally good in our firm.   Yes   No

13. Top management in our firm practices decentralization of authority.   Yes   No

14. Many of our employees have good interpersonal skills.   Yes   No

15. We do not have huge status differences between managers and operative employees.   Yes   No

16. Most of our supervisors could learn to cope with a decrease in their amount of formal authority.   Yes   No

17. Our basic operations could stand some productivity improvement.   Yes   No

18. Our jobs are complex enough to allow employees to make decisions and take initiative.   Yes   No

19. Top management would be willing to invest heavily in training employees for work teams.   Yes   No

20. Some of our work could be organized so teams of employees could take responsibility for entire jobs.   Yes   No

Chapter Twelve

Fun and Humor in the Workplace

> The jokes presented below were used by managers and sales representatives to help achieve an important goal, such as overcoming customer resistance or relieving tension about a serious business problem.

"Sorry, I won't consider buying any Japanese products," said the prospective customer to the sales representative whose company sold Japanese industrial products. "I feel very strongly about buying only products made in the United States for our facility. The Japanese are gaining too much market share over here."

"I can appreciate your strong patriotic feelings," responded the sales representative. "Yet, before I leave, let me tell you a short story I recently heard. There was this American original equipment manufacturer considering using Japanese components in its products. As negotiations reached the final stage between the American and Japanese executives, the Americans submitted a demanding quality standard as part of the deal. They told the Japanese that they would only accept shipments with a defect rate of one part per 1,000.

"The Japanese executives were confused by this demand, and returned to their group to discuss the quality standard proposed by the American firm. Upon returning to negotiations, they said: 'We agree to all of your terms and conditions, but why do you want us to make one bad part out of every thousand good ones?' "

The positive joke about Japanese manufacturing competence communicated an important message. After one more sales call, the original equipment manufacturer agreed to give one of the products offered by the sales representative's firm a chance.[1]

During a recession in the farm equipment business, a joke circulated through the company: "What's the difference between a farmer and a sparrow?

The sparrow can make a deposit on new John Deere equipment." By itself, this joke did not create a comeback for John Deere. Yet joking about adversity relieved tension and helped employees laugh at their own problems.

Although AT&T has a reputation for superbly high-quality telephone service, the company does receive an occasional customer complaint. In speaking to a group of stockholders, an AT&T executive said: "One of the reasons we put ZIP code maps in telephone books is so that if your call doesn't go through, you can write."[2]

Self-effacing humor of this type is highly effective. By being able to poke fun at his company's service problems, the executive defused the criticism of the petulant stockholder.

TECHNIQUES FOR INCORPORATING FUN AND HUMOR INTO THE JOB

The situation-specific jokes reported above represent but one category of workplace fun and humor used by managers and professionals to improve productivity and satisfaction. Many large firms hire humor consultants to help their managers reduce conflict and tension and enhance motivation and creativity. Among these organizations have been Hewlett-Packard, the United States Forest Service, the Internal Revenue Service, and Metropolitan Life Insurance. To help take a serious look at the subject, techniques of organizational fun and humor are classified here into five categories: jokes, witty comments, pranks, company events and programs, and enjoyable, challenging work.

Jokes

A joke is a multipurpose form of humor that is ingrained into the workplace. The key ingredient to a joke, as with any form of humor, is the element of surprise. You take people down one train of thought and then switch to another. John Cleese, a well-known producer of humorous training films, explains that a joke involves a sudden switch from one frame of reference to another. For example:

> A woman conducting a survey into sexual behavior was questioning an airline pilot. She asked him, finally, when he had last made love. He replied: "1956." She was most surprised because pilots have a reputation of being amorous. "1956?" she asked. "Well, it's only 2216 now," he replied.

Cleese explains that the sudden shift of frames of references from year to 24-hour clock is exactly the kind of lateral thinking that generates creativity.[3] Because of this link between appreciating (and formulating) jokes and creativity, developing a sense of humor is thought to enhance job creativity.

A type of joke widely used in a competitive business environment expresses hostility toward the competition by fabricating ridiculous behavior on its part. One of the oldest, and perhaps the most hostile, is: "Why does it take two (insert the name of your rival) to screw in a light bulb? "Answer: "One to hold the bulb, and another to spin him or her around."

A variation of this joke since the era of word processing is: "How can you tell when a (competitor's) executive has been using a word processor?" Answer: "There's white-out all over the computer screen."

Humor experts contend hostile jokes are not particularly effective. One problem is that they are so widely circulated, the joke teller appears unoriginal. In contrast, self-effacing humor is thought to be highly effective. A manager, for example, might tell a joke about failing at a task or being upbraided by a lower-ranking employee. A vice president of human resources who makes periodic trips to company divisions gets a positive reception with this joke:

> Sorry to be a few minutes late, but I ran into a little difficulty on the way in. One of your security guards stopped me, and wouldn't let me through. He claimed I was suspicious looking and wanted to know the nature of my business. When I said, "human resources," he responded, "Sounds even more suspicious."

Witty Comments

Rehearsed jokes lie at the bottom of the hierarchy of humor. Many people can learn a joke, but more creativity is required to size up the incongruity in a situation and make an appropriate witty comment. Such a comment can quickly defuse the tension in a meeting.

At one somber meeting, the company president talked about the possible liquidation of the organization. The silence that followed seemed to last an eternity. At that point, the director of systems development turned to the head of engineering who had just returned from vacation and was visibly sunburned. "Tell us, Peg," he said, "did you use suntan lotion or barbecue sauce while you were at the beach?" Laughter erupted, tension plummeted, and the president was able to proceed with a frank discussion of dealing with the company's problems.[4]

During a troubled period at ITT, a senior financial executive began a meeting by sketching an ocean liner on a flip chart. Next, he printed in large letters, "ITT." The other members of the team stared intently and burst into laughter when the executive added six more letters to form: "ITTtanic."

The link between the fate of the Titanic and the possible fate of ITT brought laughter and a realization that the meeting would be addressing a serious problem.

Office memos, both electronic and paper, can be another useful vehicle for expressing humor in the form of witty comments. Humor is important because workers are blitzed with memos to the point of paying scant attention to many of them. A memo containing humorous comments may receive more attention. Humor may also help turn a negative situation into a positive one and deflect hostility away from a corporate mistake. Following is the core of a memo sent to employees who erroneously received termination notices:

> Oops . . . to err is human; to really foul up things takes a computer. If you received a termination notice in your pay envelope, don't panic. Our computer decided it could operate the facilities by itself. It has since been counseled and should not attempt another unfriendly takeover.[5]

Pranks

At technology-based companies, pranks are a welcome form of humor. A noteworthy example occurred at Sun Microsystems, where a team of engineers plays a prank on top management each April Fool's Day. One year, the vice president of Sun Microsystems Laboratories Inc. found a life-size replica of his office constructed in the bottom of a shark tank at an aquarium in San Francisco. Another year, the CEO arrived at work to discover his office had been turned into a one-hole, par-four miniature golf course, complete with two sand traps and a birdbath. Yet another time, the engineers placed the co-founder's Ferrari afloat in the middle of a fish pond. A bumper sticker placed on the car read, "I brake for Pink Flamingos."

Pranks of the magnitude just described consume resources in terms of time that could be directed toward work, and possibly equipment used in setting up the prank. Nevertheless, senior management at Sun Microsystems applauds these pranks and even requests pranks for other activities. The company believes the stunts showcase the company's engineering talent and encourage teamwork and boost morale.[6]

Company Events and Programs

A widely practiced, and almost universally accepted, form of fun and humor in the workplace is company-sponsored events to encourage relaxation and enjoyment. Among the many fun company events and programs are picnics, banquets, parties, fairs, dress-down days, zoo outings, celebrations of employee accomplishments (including award banquets), and athletic olympics. Details about a few of these events and programs are described below.

Building a Playground. Bristol-Myers Squibb held a national sales meeting in Dallas, Texas, attended by all 1,253 sales representatives from the United States. Top management decided to devote one of the three days of the meeting to a fun event. The activity chosen was to build a large playground on three acres of land for the children of Cedar Hill, a Dallas community. Lumber, playground components, and tools were supplied by Squibb. Managers and sales representatives wore yellow rain parkas and hard hats that served as the uniform of the day.

Teams of 5 to 10 people were assigned to perform certain tasks. Construction experts briefed the Squibb Pharmaceutical staff before they plunged into action. Managers and sales reps shoveled sand, sawed wood, set posts, and hammered nails. John K. James, one of the participants, commented:

> Whenever I took a break from shoveling sand and looked around at my fellow workers, I saw an abundance of smiles and heard much laughter. When the final product was completed, we all felt a strong bond toward each other. And unlike our other formal national sales meetings, this one was a lot of fun. It allowed us to relax, get our hands dirty, and be ourselves.

> More importantly, management's theme, "Together we make it happen," was fulfilled by bringing the sales force closer together. A company survey conducted shortly after the meeting showed job satisfaction at an all-time high. Sales substantially increased since the event.

The Squibb national sales director also saw an important purpose being met by the fun activity. He observed: "During the playground activity, everyone was dedicated to one common goal. That feeling of teamwork can be carried back to the field. Each physician call a sales representative makes is like one more nail being hammered at Cedar Hill." Similarly, the vice president of sales, East, commented: "The camaraderie experienced at the national sales meeting will work toward keeping the sales team's morale high for a long time to come."[7]

Dress-Down Days.   A fun event gaining in popularity is to designate specific days, perhaps one Friday a month, as "dress-down" or "casual dress" day. Managers and employees who are not in direct contact with customers wear sweatshirts, jeans, and the like to the office. The basic idea is that a change from usual work attire enhances relaxation and fun. A novel example is the Keystone Ski Resort, near Denver, Colorado. Toward the end of the ski season, many of the young adult workers become tired of hearing the same comments and questions from guests such as, "The food is expensive," "Is the water free?" and "How cold is it on the mountain today?"

To relieve the monotony and boost morale, management decided to hold a beach day. In place of the regular work uniforms consisting of a polo shirt with the Keystone emblem and a fashionable pair of pants, each employee was supposed to wear beach attire. Employees showed up at work in Bermuda shorts, grass skirts, shark hats, leis, and sunglasses. The change of pace created by the beach day achieved its purpose. Tension was reduced, and staff morale jumped back to a high level for the balance of the season.

Worst Customer Contest.   Pleasing customers lies at the heart of total customer satisfaction, yet some customers are difficult to please. To help safely release some of the hostility that builds toward unruly customers, some firms have initiated worst customer contests. Each customer-contact worker submits a written or oral description of the most difficult, impossible, or obnoxious customer for a specified time period. At one bank, employees are encouraged to do an impression of the most difficult customer they served that month. To keep the contest on a constructive note, contestants must also explain how they dealt with the problem. The winner one month produced this scenario:

> My worst customer came in during our busiest time, Friday afternoon. She had been saving pennies for three years and wanted me to count them and then credit them to her account. She handed me a large plaster cat in which she had stored the pennies. The customer explained that the plug at the bottom of the bank was stuck. She wanted me to pull out the plug, but told me that she would not tolerate my breaking it.
>
> She also told me that if I broke her bank, she might withdraw all her money. The lady had $350 on deposit, and I was tempted to tell her to please take her business to a competitor bank. Instead, I smiled graciously and explained that I would give her a receipt for the cat bank and count the money later when the lines were shorter. She mumbled something about complaining to the manager, but was satisfied with my offer to count the money later.

Creating a Fun-Filled Work Environment.   A strategic way of creating fun in the workplace is to create a work environment laden with lighthearted activities. The progenitor of this approach is Ben & Jerry's Homemade Inc., the ice cream company. Each day, production workers get to choose which production task they will perform. All Ben & Jerry's employees can get a free massage and back rub during the day, three pints of ice cream a day, and a hilarious run-in with the company's Joy Gang.

The Joy Gang is a group of employees who plan companywide events and celebrations designed to ease workplace tension and promote a spirit of fun. Another Joy Gang function is to distribute joy grants to work units that develop creative ideas for bringing long-term joy to the workplace. Worth up to $500 each, the grants have been used in such morale-building ways as buying a hot chocolate machine and company roller skates. Ben & Jerry's has a cow-viewing area, games such as Legos are available at lunch, and rock music blares into the production area. Ben & Jerry employees also have the opportunity to taste test experimental ice cream flavors.

Co-founders Ben Cohen and Jerry Greenfield attribute much of their substantial growth to the pleasant work environment they have created. In addition to the fun activities, employee benefits include free health club membership, profit sharing, college tuition, and day care. Also, 7.5 percent of the company's pretax profits go to a worthy social cause. The pay scale is favorable for lower-ranking workers, with the restriction that no one can earn five times more than anyone else.[8] Executives are, therefore, limited to less than $100,000 in annual compensation.

Birthday Celebrations. Another company-sponsored fun event is a birthday club, to celebrate employee birthdays in imaginative ways. At one small company, the birthday person gets to choose what he or she would like other employees to wear on his or her birthday. The birthday person also is allowed to be manager for the day and can perform any function except for financial transactions. During the day, the birthday celebrant is given balloons, flowers, a party hat, cake, group picture, and lunch.

In a large organization, approximately one out of 365 persons would be the birthday person, including those whose birthdays fall on the weekend, so the potential for work disruption would be high.

Enjoyable, Challenging Work

The most significant type of workplace fun is providing people the opportunity to perform intrinsically enjoyable work. A program of job enrichment, including work teams, would contribute to fun on the job. Research conducted about job fun asked people, "What's exciting about your work?" and "What's enjoyable about your work?" In response to these questions, people frequently talked about situations when their work was challenging and when they had a sense of accomplishment. Many executives said challenge is one of the most fun aspects of their work.[9]

Individual differences must be recognized in assigning work intended to be fun. One employee might be ecstatic about running a new computer program, while another person might perceive the same challenge as a form of punishment. The person unable to master the new software would not feel a sense of accomplishment. Although many managers dislike conducting performance appraisals, some find the process fun.

Do Skill-Building Exercise 12 to practice your skills at making witty comments and designing fun activities in response to demanding workplace scenarios.

SKILL-BUILDING EXERCISE 12
Dealing with Demanding Workplace Scenarios

In the three scenarios that follow, imagine you are the manager of the organizational unit in which the scenario occurs. Use your creativity to develop a witty comment or design a fun activity to prevent the incident from becoming too tense or conflict-laden. Write your comment or fun activity in the space below the scenario.

Scenario A: Five minutes before entering your weekly staff meeting, you are informed by top management that all salary adjustments will be suspended for one year. You had planned to devote your staff meeting primarily to emphasizing the need for increased productivity.

_____

_____

_____

_____

Scenario B: You are discussing a new total customer satisfaction program with your store associates. An office assistant rushes into the meeting room and says, "Excuse me, but there is a screaming customer on the phone. She says the facial cream we sold her has increased her wrinkles, and she's going to sue us for a $1 million. Can you handle the call?"

_____

_____

_____

Scenario C: Your hardworking team has achieved superior results for the last 10 months. You ask your manager if the company will authorize a victory banquet. She replies, "Think of something modest. Our budget for entertainment this year is awfully tight. Your group has performed well, but the rest of the company has done poorly."

_____

_____

_____

_____

Scoring: The chapter appendix gives suggested responses to the scenarios.

POSITIVE CONSEQUENCES OF FUN AND HUMOR

Opinion, observation, and research have identified many positive consequences of fun and humor in the workplace. (The evidence is so strong that only those with comedy training may be eligible for managerial jobs in the future.) The positive consequences, advantages, and functions of fun and humor can be organized around eight points.

1. *Increases productivity.* Published information on the topic concludes consistently that when workers are having fun, they are more pro-

ductive. (Of course, fun cannot be taken to the point that work is disrupted.) A concrete example occurred at the Digital Equipment Corporation office in Colorado Springs, Colorado. After participating in a humor workshop, 20 middle managers increased their productivity by 15 percent and decreased their sick days by 50 percent in the nine months following the training. The district manager of the office explained, "If people are more relaxed, you get more out of them." A similar result took place at the Colorado Health Sciences Division in Denver. Employees who viewed humorous training films and participated in humor workshops showed a 25 percent decrease in employee downtime.[10]

Many of the other consequences of humor described below help explain why fun and humor are linked to productivity. For example, humor decreases tension and boredom and enhances creativity.

2. *Enhances creativity.* Playing around with ideas in a mirthful way encourages creativity, as described in Chapter 2. Humor is a source of intellectual stimulation because the mind has to be stretched to find the amusing element embedded in a work situation. Alice M. Isen conducted research demonstrating the link between humor and creativity. One group of subjects watched a clip of TV "bloopers" or received candy. Another group either saw a math film or did a monotonous exercise. Both groups were then given a box of tacks, a candle, and a book of matches. They were asked to attach the candle to a corkboard wall so it could be lit without dripping any wax. The "feel good" groups—the comedy audience and candy recipients—attacked the problem more efficiently and creatively. One person solved the problem by tacking the box to the wall as a candle holder.[11]

3. *Advances career.* A sense of humor can advance your career in several ways. First, demonstrating a sense of humor can help you get hired. Hodge-Cronin and Associates, an executive search firm, interviewed 737 chief executives about selection criteria. Ninety-eight percent of the chief executives surveyed said they would hire a person with a good sense of humor over a straitlaced worker.[12] Second, a sense of humor can help the leader motivate and influence team members and resolve conflict. The team performs better, and the manager is better able to achieve work unit goals, making the manager more promotable.

4. *Reduces tension.* As mentioned previously, humor helps reduce tension. A hearty laugh is physically relaxing because muscles are tightened then loosened. A small, nervous laugh, however, may actually increase tension. A hearty laugh is also much like physical exercise. It reduces stress, and accompanying tension, because laughter releases endorphins (hormones that induce a state of relaxation and heightened awareness). Humor also reduces tension because seeing the lighter side of an issue helps us place things in proper perspective. A manager said to a team member who lost an important file:

I can see why you are upset. Losing this file means that I'll fire you, then the company will fire me. Our company will go out of business. You'll never find another job in this industry, and your family will desert you. Please, redo the file and report back to me when you're ready. (The person who lost the file chuckled and started on the new file.)

5. *Defuses conflict.* Humor can be a potent tool for resolving conflict. Consultant Barbara Mackoff explains that one has to look at pressure points on a job to find an opportunity for creative comic release. For example, U.S. West was receiving flak from disgruntled callers who complained that the company—which advertised "100 years of experience"—was providing poor service. Mackoff helped customer-service representatives brainstorm a response that enabled both sides to lighten up.

"I taught them to mirror verbal humor by listening to the image the customer was creating and playing with that metaphor instead of getting angry or defensive," explains Mackoff. The group then arrived at this delivery: "I know, here we are advertising that we have 100 years of service, and you feel that we must be getting senile at this point." When the line was used, many customers laughed and were placed in a better mood to resolve the service problem.[13]

6. *Lubricates social relations.* According to W. Jack Duncan and J. Philip Feisal, *lubricant humor* facilitates relationships and reduces tensions. This type of humor keeps the machinery of human interaction running smoothly. In contrast, *abrasive humor* acts as an irritant to the machinery of interaction. Group members bring a new member into the group by joking, thus assimilating him or her into the group. Joking, more than any other behavior, makes people feel that they belong to the group.[14]

Jenny, a new member of a quality assurance team, came to her first staff meeting dressed impeccably. At lunchtime, one of the group members shot a photograph of her with an instant camera and then posted the photo on the bulletin board. The man who shot the photo said, "Jenny, this is a momentous occasion. We've never had anybody in our group with enough class to have matching shoes and attaché case." (Jenny smiled, recognizing that the group was accepting her.)

7. *Increases job satisfaction and involvement.* David J. Abramis studied 923 workers across a variety of occupations and employers. Of these people, 678 received an extensive questionnaire, and 347 were interviewed at length on many subjects including fun and humor in the workplace. People who expressed more positive humor at work, such as telling jokes and attempting to make others laugh, had higher mental

health, job satisfaction, and job involvement. The same people were also less likely to quit. The study also found that people who perceived their work to be fun scored higher on mental health, job satisfaction, job involvement, and job tenure.

Although not explicitly stated, the comparison group in Abramis' study appeared to be people who did not use humor. People who used aggressive humor, such as making fun of others, were neither more nor less mentally healthy, satisfied, or involved with their jobs.[15]

8. *Helps people cope with adversity.* A few years ago, Owens-Corning Fiberglass was forced to shut down half of its facilities and lay off 40 percent of its work force to fend off a takeover threat. Anticipating the trauma the layoffs might create, the company hired humor consultant C. W. Metcalf. Over a five-month period, Metcalf presented workshops to about 1,600 employees. He also instructed company trainers on how to maintain a humor program with the help of his videotapes on humor. The adverse psychological effects the company had feared the most—violence, sabotage, threats to management, and suicides—did not occur. The humor programs received considerable credit for helping employees manage the adversity of the layoffs.[16]

NEGATIVE CONSEQUENCES OF FUN AND HUMOR

Although fun and humor can be a powerful technique for improving interpersonal relations, inappropriate or excessive frivolity can backfire. A career trap for many managers and professionals is using fun and humor to the point of appearing emotionally immature and frivolous. Many people have been blocked from receiving a promotion into management because they develop the reputation of being an office clown.

Fun and humor can be detrimental in excess because it diverts too much time away from activities directly aimed at productivity. Some practical jokes consume organizational resources and cause considerable confusion. Following a wave of layoffs at Merrill Lynch, a bond trader sent counterfeit pink slips to other professionals in his department. The trader's joke met with a poor reception, and his manager wondered where he found the time to carry out such an elaborate scheme.

Humor that demeans or insults another individual or group of people is divisive and leads to hard feelings. People will long remember a joking insult about their appearance, thus creating strained interpersonal relations. Furthermore, racist, ethnic, or sexist humor can be interpreted as a violation of various civil rights. Donald D. Brennan, a white supervisor at a bank in Virginia, constantly barraged an African-American maintenance worker with epithets and jokes about blacks, Mexican, and Poles. The worker sued and was awarded

$521,100 by a federal court. Brennan testified that his comments were only in jest and that Robert Lee Holland, who filed the suit, was too sensitive.[17]

Sexually oriented jokes in the workplace classify as environmental sexual harassment. The person who tells jokes with sexual references or makes sexually suggestive remarks can be charged with sexual harassment. As a result, the person's career suffers and the company may become embroiled in a legal dispute.

Although ethnic jokes are now considered in poor taste, they persist. People who tell ethnic jokes despite their pitfalls should heed the advice offered by Henny Youngman. After 60 years in show business, Youngman insisted that if you tell ethnic jokes, choose those that bring people together, not divide them. His example: "A Native American woman married a Jewish man. They had a child, and to please both sides of the family, they named the child 'Whitefish.' "

To underscore the importance of not telling ethnic jokes, jokes are emerging about the poor judgment of people who tell them. An example: What's black and blue and floats in the Monongahela River?

Answer: Someone who tells Polish jokes in Pittsburgh.

Guidelines for Action and Skill Development

David J. Abramis has formulated guidelines on how to make work more playful that are particularly useful for managers, as follows:

1. *Make a conscious effort to have fun.* Incorporate goals such as "have fun" and "schedule a fun event" into your annual goal statement.

2. *Spread the word that having fun at work is often appropriate.* Explain to others how fun can be productive, as well as enhance job satisfaction.

3. *Help other managers have fun and suggest ways they can assist their team members to do the same.* Use your knowledge of fun and humor in the workplace in such a way that your effectiveness multiplies.

4. *Ask workers what they think is fun.* Fun is subjective. As one middle-age executive said, "I wish they would get rid of those blasted potato-bag races at the company picnic. I can't laugh while I'm worrying about breaking my legs."

5. *Use recognition and other rewards to let people know they are valued.* Outstanding achievements should be recognized with parties, awards, celebrations, and plenty of public pats on the back. Spontaneous praise is also helpful in creating an enjoyable, fun-filled work atmosphere.

6. *Create fun-filled events.* Suggest or implement more planned activities such as company-sponsored parties and sports that increase fun on the job.

7. *Hire people who value and are capable of having fun.* Other factors being equal, make job offers to people who can smile, make witty comments, and arouse enthusiasm.[18]

DISCUSSION QUESTIONS AND ACTIVITIES

1. What is the psychology behind the fact that self-deprecating humor is usually effective?

2. Analyze why the following one-liner by comedian A. Whitney Brown usually evokes considerable laughter: "Being a comedian is great. It's the only occupation where people don't laugh at you when you make a mistake."

3. Based on what you have studied in this chapter, would it be an effective use of humor for a manager to rehearse a new joke to use at the start of each week's staff meeting?

4. Work with three other classmates to think of a practical joke to play on your instructor that will *(a)* do no physical or mental harm and *(b)* enhance the learning environment.

5. In recent years, many employers have eliminated or severely reduced the magnitude of year-end parties to save money. What is your evaluation of this practice?

6. In one information systems department, the professional and technical staff are encouraged to play video games from 3 until 5 on Friday afternoons. What is your evaluation of this practice?

7. Find an article describing a problem faced by a company. Based on this information, prepare a witty comment a manager in the company might use to relieve employee tension about the problem.

NOTES

1. Incident contributed by Robert Barto, May 1992.
2. The AT&T and John Deere jokes are from "Corporate Jester," *Public Relations Journal*, November 1987, p. 24.
3. John Cleese, "Serious Talk About Humor in the Office," *The Wall Street Journal*, August 1, 1988.
4. W. Jack Duncan and J. Philip Feisal, "No Laughing Matter: Patterns of Humor in the Workplace," *Organizational Dynamics*, Spring 1989, pp. 18–19.

5. Wilma Davidson, "Add Humor to Workplace Memos," *Personnel Journal*, June 1992, p. 67.
6. Shari Caudron, "Humor Is Healthy in the Workplace," *Personnel Journal*, June 1992, p. 63.
7. Quote from *Sales Bulletin*, a publication for Squibb United States Pharmaceutical Group, April 1990, p. 6.
8. Caudron, "Humor Is Healthy," p. 68; and Carol Clurman, "More than Just a Paycheck," *USA Weekend*, January 19-21, 1990, pp. 4-5.
9. David J. Abramis, "Building Fun in Your Organization," *Personnel Administrator*, October 1989, p. 70.
10. Caudron, "Humor Is Healthy," p. 68.
11. Susan Lang, "Laughing Matters—At Work," *American Health*, September 1988, p. 46.
12. Karen Karvonen, "Funny Business," *USAIR*, October 1988, p. 38.
13. Ibid., p. 37.
14. Duncan and Feisal, "No Laughing Matter," p. 29.
15. David J. Abramis, "Humor in Healthy Organizations," *HRMagazine*, August 1992, p. 73.
16. Caudron, "Humor Is Healthy," p. 68.
17. Lena Williams, "Humor: Self-Censored," *New York Times* syndicated story, January 4, 1991.
18. David J. Abramis, "Finding the Fun at Work," *Psychology Today*, March 1989, p. 38.

SOME ADDITIONAL REFERENCES

Barreca, Regina. *They Used to Call Me Snow White . . . But I Drifted: Women's Strategic Use of Humor*. New York: Viking Penguin, 1991.

Kushner, Malcolm. *The Light Touch: How to Use Humor for Business Success*. New York: Simon & Schuster, 1990.

MacHovec, Frank J. *Humor: Theory—History—Applications*. Springfield, Ill.: Charles C. Thomas, 1988.

"Management with Fun." *Nation's Business*, January 1990, pp. 58–60.

Paulson, Terry. *Making Humor Work*. Los Altos, Calif.: Crisp Publications, 1990.

Raskin, Victor. "Jokes: A Linguist Explains His New Semantic Theory of Humor." *Psychology Today*, October 1985, pp. 34–39.

Zemke, Ron. "Humor in Training." *Training*, August 1991.

Appendix to Chapter Twelve

ANSWERS TO SKILL-BUILDING EXERCISE 12

Many different humorous responses are possible to the scenarios in question. Also, when making witty comments, your nonverbal communication can be as important as your verbal comments. Making a witty comment involves both good timing and the right facial expression.

Scenario A: Here is one possibility: "I have some good news and bad news today. The good news is that we are going to be talking about increasing productivity, and that top management is very interested. The bad news is that top management is so interested in improving productivity, they are beginning by withholding salary adjustments for this year. By reducing costs, productivity will be increased."

Scenario B: "How timely, gang. Our office assistant has provided us living proof that total customer satisfaction is REALLY important."

Scenario C: Here is something that has worked quite well. Hold a "Poverty Ball for Winners" in an inexpensive place such as a church or synagogue basement. Serve submarine (or hero) sandwiches, along with beer or soft drinks. To fit the decor, specify casual dress. Have a strict edict that anybody showing up in business attire will not be allowed in. Bring in boom boxes along with tapes or CDs to supply the music.

Part IV

Improving Quality and Productivity at the Organizational Level

In this part of the book, we examine four approaches designed to improve productivity and quality at the organizational level. All of these approaches involve substantial changes in the way an organization operates and in its culture. To be successful, approaches of this nature should not be considered isolated programs but part of a total commitment to high quality and productivity.

Chapter 13 describes programs to empower employees by giving them more responsibility and the authority to take initiative to improve productivity, quality, and customer service. Work teams, as described in Chapter 11, can also be included as a method of empowerment. Chapter 14 describes key components of total quality management with an emphasis on achieving high quality through the appropriate attitudes and perceptions. Information also is presented about how statistical techniques are used to achieve a total commitment to quality.

Chapter 15 describes how some firms attempt to reduce costs and hasten decision making by decreasing the number of layers of management and reducing the work force in general. Modifying the structure in this manner is based on an understanding of the theory of bureaucracy.

Chapter 16 describes how some firms are deliberately fostering product innovation within small organizational units to help the firm cope with a changing environment. The process is referred to as intrapreneuring and is based on a knowledge of individual and group creativity.

Chapter Thirteen

Employee Empowerment

The company described below reorganized to give employees more authority to solve customer problems themselves. A distribution center in Atlanta, Georgia, exemplifies a company site where the empowerment program is accomplishing its purpose of improving productivity and the quality of customer service.

In a sprawling warehouse outside Atlanta, Georgia, 31 Xerox employees ship parts, office equipment, and other products to customers in Latin America and the Far East. The warehouse shipped about $450 million in 1991. Xerox officials say the distribution center's efficiency was one reason the company has increased its business in Latin America, a tempestuous region, but one with great promise for U.S. exports.

"Productivity is extremely high," said Maury Conner, a manager of Latin American operations and international traffic for that portion of Xerox's Western Hemisphere logistics and distribution. "There's strong team spirit and work groups. People participate in the solutions. It's an informal environment resulting in a highly motivated work force."

Leading the 6 salaried and 24 union employees in Atlanta is distribution center general manager Frank Thomas, a Xerox veteran of 33 years. A slightly built man with glasses and a goatee, Thomas regards himself as a coach and not a boss. He likes to say he has 24 managers—instead of 24 employees—working with him. "*Hourly* has almost become a dirty word," said Kenny Melear, one of the 24 staff members. "We like to look at ourselves as one big happy family." At the company's monthly lunchtime barbecue, where the menu is chosen by the employees, Thomas does the cooking.

As part of a corporate reorganization announced in February 1992, Xerox is giving more responsibility to employees at lower levels, encouraging them to show initiative by solving customers' problems themselves instead of passing the problems along.

Before August 1991, when Conner's group joined the western hemisphere logistics and distribution operation, it was relatively unknown to the rest of the company. Now Xerox executives are looking more closely at the distribution operation and are studying its methods for possible duplication. "It's an efficient way of operating and making sure we do serve our customers in those countries effectively," said Paul A. Allaire, Xerox's chairman and chief executive officer.

Thomas urges employees to think like managers and take responsibility for their own jobs. He says he has been empowering employees for years because he has always been willing to surrender part of his power to team members. Thomas believes this work arrangement achieves positive results. He points to nearly nonexistent absenteeism, an almost perfect record meeting shipping deadlines, and several cost-saving ideas generated by employees as proof of high employee satisfaction in a facility that processes 4,000 orders a week.

"The only important thing to us is the customer," said Thomas. To emphasize that point, he said each shipment invoice has a section where the customer can evaluate the service Xerox provided. He calls this information their report card.

Hourly worker Ernie Bates has divided his two decades with Xerox among three locations. He says the Atlanta distribution center is the best facility he has ever worked in. One reason Bates gives is that employees take on problem solving. For instance, Thomas looked at the facility's expenses recently, saw the operation was spending $1,500 a month on trash removal, and concluded "we're doing something wrong."

So Thomas tossed the problem to the workers. Their solution was to take the huge lots of corrugated cardboard accumulated from the inventory shipments and trade the recyclable material to the trash hauler in return for free trash pickup. When the warehouse employees showed the trash hauler that the potential value of the recycled corrugated was more than the fee Xerox was paying for trash service, the deal went through.

The workers also decided to save some of the light wooden pallets that come with products and components shipped into the warehouse from Japan and use them for product shipments to Latin America. The lighter pallets saved the warehouse $30,000 in shipping costs in 1991, Thomas said.

Other freedoms exist. For example, when the group became disgruntled with Atlanta's morning and evening rush-hour traffic, the employees voted to start earlier so they could leave earlier, thus avoiding the white-knuckle time on the freeway.

A standard order is guaranteed to leave the warehouse within five days of receipt. What's more, Thomas said his team guarantees customers that any emergency order reaching the warehouse by 3 P.M. will be shipped the same day, "no questions asked." The distribution center has met that goal 99.9 percent of the time. Thomas confesses the group is a little chagrined that the record isn't perfect and says, "We're working on it."

To make sure deadlines are met, the group devised a simple coding system—one color for each of the five weekdays—which allows an employee to stroll through the warehouse and quickly spot any delinquent orders.

Thomas urges workers to "be lazy," that is, to find the fastest and easiest way to complete a task, so workers can move on to other jobs. He was recently surprised and pleased to find that his hourly staff had changed the computer coding on the shipping labels to make them easier to understand. The change was made without Thomas's approval.

Hourly worker Melears recalled how a group of company executives visiting the facility asked at the end of their tour, "What are you doing here? They all look so happy." Said Melear with a smile, "To me that's a great compliment."[1]

A SAMPLING OF EMPOWERMENT PROGRAMS

The employee empowerment program at the Xerox distribution center is one example of an important new initiative occurring in hundreds of organizations. Empowerment programs are a systematic method of granting more authority and responsibility to workers and encouraging them to make and implement decisions on their own. Empowerment programs are a form of employee involvement and participative management with an emphasis on employees taking considerable initiative in solving problems. Work teams, as described in Chapter 11, can rightfully be considered a form of employee empowerment. At IBM Kingston, the concept of empowerment is described in these terms:

- Sharing responsibility.
- Building confidence and trust.
- Building knowledge/experience.
- Working toward common vision/goals.
- Working in an exciting environment where you feel every day, "It's my business. I do make a difference."
- Challenging the status quo.
- Learning from mistakes.
- Having authority to make decisions.
- Accepting the ownership.

Next we describe several additional empowerment programs and the results they achieved. Empowerment programs are placed in this section of the text because they are typically part of an organizationwide change. Work teams are more often introduced into a smaller number of organization units.

Eaton Corporation.   A challenge faced by Eaton Corp., a manufacturer of gears, engine valves, truck axles, and circuit breakers, is to reduce costs continually. Reducing costs is crucial because Eaton's major customers are automobile manufacturers, which are committed to paring expenses. An important part of Eaton's cost-cutting strategy is to empower employees to make suggestions for reducing costs and to pay bonuses for achieving results. Teams of workers are empowered to identify opportunities for cost reduction and then implement these suggestions. Carrying such names as "The Hoods" and "The Worms," the teams ferret out bottlenecks and ways to save money.

Eaton management encourages workers to take thousands of minor steps that incrementally improve the products they manufacture and the processes they use to make them. Such small, continual steps are part of the Japanese philosophy of *kaizen,* which has become an underpinning of quality improvement. Office workers also are invited to uncover ways to trim costs.

In one year at the Lincoln, Illinois, plant, Eaton workers formally presented to management their ideas for improving operations 193 times. Among their suggestions were the following:

- One worker explained how sandblasting welding electrodes rather than machining them would save $5,126 per year.

- A team of machinery maintenance workers grew weary of fixing equipment of machines that broke down repeatedly. The alternative they offered management was to build two automated machines to perform tedious functions. Management accepted the idea, and the team built the machines for about one fourth the price outside vendors would have charged.

- Another team discovered that one press operator preheats dies before using them, extending the life of the dies. The same practice is now adopted throughout the plant, leading to $50,000 annual savings.

The savings resulting from suggestions such as the above totaled $1.4 million in one year, enabling the Lincoln plant to increase its profit 30 percent over the previous quarter. As a consequence, the employees earned $44,000 in "Eaton bucks," coupons they can exchange for merchandise in the company store. Employees also receive cash bonuses based on total plant performance. In the past decade, Eaton productivity, measured as output per hour, rose 3 percent a year. This increase exceeds the 1.9 percent average for all U.S. manufacturing. Seeking still further improvement, the company goal is now a 4 percent annual productivity increase.

At the unionized Lincoln plant, productivity increased 10 percent one year. The company rewarded the gains by offering to relocate 70 low-wage-rate jobs from Mexico. The union workers hired to fill them at half the typical company pay have advanced up the salary scale quickly.[2]

Chaparral Steel.   The best-publicized case history of employee empowerment is Chaparral Steel of Midlothian, Texas. Much of the company's recognition stems from being the world's lowest-cost steel producer. The basic elements of the company's management strategy include customer service, quality, training, working together harmoniously, and empowerment. These managerial approaches facilitate Chaparral producing steel with a record low 1.6 hours of labor per ton, versus 2.4 hours for other minimills and 4.9 hours for integrated producers.

CEO Gordon Forward, who holds a doctorate in metallurgy, is the dominating force behind the company's management style. Forward was asked by Texas industries in 1975 to help found a minimill. To become a low-cost producer, he focused on three management concepts: the classless corporation, universal education, and the freedom to act (employee empowerment).

Workers in the egalitarian philosophy receive a salary and bonus based on individual performance, company profits, and skill acquisition. No parking places are reserved for executives, and employee locker rooms are as clean and well maintained as executive offices. In return for being treated with dignity, employees are expected to take the initiative to use their problemsolving skills and achieve results. To facilitate problem solving by all, 85 percent of the company's 950 employees are enrolled in courses with an emphasis on cross-training in such field as electronics, metallurgy, and business administration.

Chapparal employees are actively engaged in making cost-savings suggestions. One example occurred when the company was designing a new mill for making wide-flange steel beams used in bridges and buildings. The employees developed a technique that manufactures a final product with just 8 to 12 passes through the system. In contrast, traditional methods require up to 50 passes.

Empowerment occurs in the office as well as the mill. Sales, billing, credit, and shipping are all housed in the same location. Workers are trained to handle each other's jobs. If a customer calls the sales department and has a credit question, the sales representative is likely to have the answer. The representative is thus empowered to solve customer problems without consulting a supervisor in most instances.[3]

Johnson & Johnson.   Johnson & Johnson, manufacturer of a wide range of products from Band-Aids to baby lotion, empowers division managers and their staffs through decentralization of authority. The company has espoused decentralization for over 50 years. CEO Ralph Larsen expects the presidents of Johnson & Johnson's 166 separately chartered companies to act independently. Heads of each company select their own staffs, choose their own products, identify their own markets, and prepare their own budgets. In addition, many oversee their own research and development. Some division presidents see corporate executives as infrequently as four times per year.

For many years, the Johnson & Johnson corporate philosophy has been that smaller, self-governing units are more manageable, more adaptable to market changes, and more accountable. The net result of this approach has been excellent, yet decentralization has contributed to some problems. Operating companies sometimes make costly mistakes because they receive so little guidance from headquarters. Overhead costs are high because of duplication in functions such as data processing.

Another problem is that some retailers have many Johnson & Johnson sales representatives calling on them. Employee empowerment is dealing with this problem. Customer-service support centers have been established to maintain good relationships with large retailers such as Kmart and Wal-Mart. Employee teams at the support centers work on-site with retailers to ease distribution and ordering problems.

The empowerment through decentralization philosophy is working well for Johnson & Johnson. In 1991, when corporate profits were generally thin, Johnson & Johnson improved earnings 15 percent, to $1.5 billion, on a sales increase of 11 percent, to $12 billion. The upward trend in sales and earnings continued in 1992.[4]

PepsiCo Inc.   With $20 billion in annual sales and 300,000 employees, PepsiCo and its products are household names. Among them are Pepsi, 7UP, Pizza Hut, KFC, Taco Bell, and Fritos. D. Wayne Calloway, the chief executive officer, believes delegation of authority and empowerment will help keep PepsiCo profitable and growing. To develop the right motivational climate for empowerment, Calloway initiated a stock purchase plan called SharePower. All 300,000 employees, including truck drivers and counter workers, receive stock options. The plan grants employees yearly options on shares equivalent to 10 percent of their compensation.

Empowerment at PepsiCo translates into pushing decision-making authority down below the middle-management level. Employees from route sales representatives to restaurant workers are encouraged to submit ideas for improving the business. For example, a 17-year-old worker at KFC in Oklahoma City helped his store increase its catering business substantially. His marketing technique was to create signs advertising the service and place them in store windows. Empowerment has also led to mistakes. At one time, the Frito-Lay sales force was given substantial latitude in granting discounts to large supermarkets. The practice was pushed so far that smaller retailers began to purchase directly from supermarkets, which hurt profit margins.

To ensure that PepsiCo is staffed with managers who believe in empowerment, Calloway interviews prospective managers. No candidate at the vice presidential level or above receives a job offer without being personally interviewed by him. (In this sense, Calloway backs off from empowering executives to make sure his philosophy of empowerment is implemented.)

In recent years, PepsiCo units have suffered from the recession and intense competition in some markets. For example, Frito-Lay Inc. laid off 1,800 employees one year. Yet Calloway believes his philosophy of empowerment will contribute to long-term growth and record profitability.[5]

Omni Hotels.   At one time, the Omni Hotels were plagued by low ratings on customer comment cards and high employee turnover. Although high turnover is typical for hotels, Omni wanted to be better than the industry average. The hotel chain addressed these problems in stages. Stage one was a program to give line employees an opportunity to tackle the problems cited in customer comment cards. Stage two was a recognition program for employees who gave exceptional service to both external and internal customers.

Stage three was an empowerment program called the Power of One. In June 1990, every Omni employee received a video, workbook sessions, and a pocket card listing 19 behaviors of empowerment at Omni Hotels. These behaviors are designed to foster independent action by frontline employees. One such behavior is "Make decisions that benefit the guests: bend the rules sometimes." Another is "Listen to the angry customer and give that person what he or she wants if it is at all reasonable." Every Omni employee was certified in a Power of One orientation. A fight song set to "Power of Love," by rock artist Huey Lewis, became the official company anthem.

During the Power of One's first month, the guest satisfaction index surged 16 percent. Employee turnover had dropped from 65 to 42 percent during the first year. The fact that each employee costs about $6,000 to replace translates this decreased turnover into substantially increased profits for Omni Hotels.[6]

Prudential Insurance Company, Group Department.   The Northeastern Group Operations of the Prudential Insurance Company faced a perplexing dilemma. Surveys indicated customers were demanding faster responses, lower prices, and more flexible product designs. At the same time, top management demanded significant and immediate cost cutting. A consulting firm hired to help resolve this dilemma advised the group that a bigger staff is not a prerequisite to improved service. Instead, they were told the key is to unleash the power of the existing staff. Empowerment of this type would spark the innovation needed to run operations more cost effectively.

Studies run by the consulting firm indicated a lack of information and authority prevented employees from responding quickly to customer requests. They also noted that a system of checks and counterchecks dampened productivity and added to higher costs. Overall, the study revealed an organizational culture in which employees who were closest to the customer and cost-reduction opportunities were powerless to resolve them. By empowering these workers with greater decision-making authority, company management believed it could enhance customer satisfaction and market success. It was also thought necessary to emphasize the existence of both external and internal customers.

Top management at the Northeastern Group Operations began the empowerment process at the top of the organization. Management had to be convinced that it was safe to relinquish power and delegate more authority to lower-ranking team members. Employees who were to be involved in the empowerment program were offered extensive training in customer service, team management, and problem solving. Forty employees were appointed as customer-satisfaction representatives. Another 16 were appointed as operational improvement consultants, whose full-time responsibility was to promote cost reduction.

Much of the empowerment centered around cross-functional groups of staff members and first-line supervisors. Each team is empowered to resolve a critical problem or provide service to a particular customer. So far, these teams have enabled management to delegate authority to lower levels, break down functional barriers, and cultivate ideas for improving service and decreasing costs.

At one location, the average claims-processing time has dropped from 10 to 3 days by forming teams of clerical support, processing, technical and quality-control specialists. Each team is empowered to approve certain types of claims, up to a dollar amount that covers 95 percent of all claim submissions. By physically locating members of the claim team in one area, claim-related decisions can be made on the spot.

Another team launched a pilot program that allows employees to process claims at home. Given the freedom to set their own hours, these claims specialists are setting new records for productivity. By processing claims 50 percent more rapidly than their office-based counterparts, they are contributing to cost reductions.

Since the empowerment program was implemented, operating costs have been reduced about 12.5 percent. Customers are noticing a substantial improvement in the quality of service and responding with new business. Gross revenues surged 40 percent over the previous year. Company officials believe the empowerment program has been instrumental in improving customer satisfaction, which in turn has increased sales revenues.[7]

We have described several programs of employee empowerment. To achieve the full potential of empowerment, managers must go beyond participating in an empowerment program to possessing the right attitudes and skills required to be an empowering manager. Skill-Building Exercise 13 provides insight into these important attitudes and skills.

SKILL-BUILDING EXERCISE 13
Becoming an Empowering Manager

To effectively empower employees, the manager has to convey appropriate attitudes and develop the right interpersonal skills. The list of attitudes and skills will help you become an empowering manager. Indicate which skills and attitudes you now have and which ones require further development.

Empowering Attitude or ehavior	*Can Do Now*	*Would Need to Develop*
1. Believe in the ability of team members to be successful.	_____	_____
2. Patient with people and give them time to learn.	_____	_____
3. Provide team members with direction and structure.	_____	_____
4. Teach team members new skills in small, incremental steps so they can easily learn those skills.	_____	_____
5. Ask team members questions that challenge them to think in new ways.	_____	_____
6. Share information with team members, sometimes just to build rapport.	_____	_____
7. Give team members timely feedback and encourage them throughout the learning process.	_____	_____
8. Offer team members alternative ways of doing things.	_____	_____
9. Exhibit a sense of humor and demonstrate care for workers as people.	_____	_____
10. Focus on team members' results and acknowledge their personal improvement.	_____	_____

SOURCE: Derived from information in Richard Hamlin, "A Practical Guide to Empowering Your Employees," *Supervisory Management*, April 1991, p. 8.

SUCCESS FACTORS FOR EMPOWERMENT AND EMPLOYEE INVOLVEMENT PROGRAMS

As with any management intervention, empowerment and employee involvement programs work best under certain conditions. When many of these conditions are present, the probability increases that employee empowerment and involvement programs will increase productivity, quality, and satisfaction. Above all, top management has to believe in employee involvement and empowerment and support the program in many ways. The CEOs at Johnson & Johnson, Chapparal Steel, and PepsiCo exemplify top-management support.

Richard J. Magjuka and Timothy T. Baldwin conducted a study of 68 employee involvement administrators and 72 employee involvement teams to identify factors contributing to the effectiveness of these programs. Actual productivity and quality data were rarely available, so effectiveness was defined in terms of how the program operators perceived the program to be functioning. The results showed that employee involvement programs are perceived to contribute the most to organizational performance when:

1. The teams operate under open and unrestricted access to information.
2. The team's membership is represented by diverse job functions and administrative backgrounds.
3. The team has a higher-than-average number of members to draw on to accomplish the program objectives. (In this study, teams ranged from 8 to 46 members.)[8]

In addition to these tangible factors, the organizational culture should favor employee involvement and empowerment. Two employee involvement consultants, Robert W. Barner and J. Jackson Fulbright, contend that certain values pervade companies in which employee involvement is successful. These values are:

Employee ownership. Employees should see themselves as owners in their companies' success and challenges.

Employee self-direction and personal growth. Employees should take the initiative to establish their own career plans.

Open communication. Fluid communications should exist between team members and managers and across work functions. Workers should have open access to the information they need to accomplish their jobs.

Risk taking and innovation. Team members should assertively look for ways to improve team performance and question outmoded or ineffective methods and procedures.

Teamwork. Team members and managers should support each other and cooperate with each other and with members of other work groups.[9]

FOR AND AGAINST EMPOWERMENT

The Case for Empowerment

Employee empowerment programs, including work teams, are a major new trend in helping organizations improve productivity and quality, reduce costs, and enhance customer service. If these programs were adding no value to organizations, astute managers would have abandoned them. Furthermore, reports in business magazines and newspapers such as *Business Week* and *The Wall Street Journal* have been quite favorable. Companies including Xerox, Eaton, PepsiCo, Chapparal Steel, Prudential, and the Omni Hotels have been pleased with their initiatives in employee empowerment.

Employee empowerment and involvement programs are also important because they fit the spirit of the times. North American employers have moved in the direction of empowering workers and away from tightly centralized control. Empowerment also fits the modern, understaffed organization. Fewer managers are available to consult with lower-ranking employees about everyday operating decisions. Also, more customers are demanding immediate resolution of their problems. When employees are empowered, they can resolve problems quickly.

The Case against Empowerment

As with other employee involvement programs, empowerment programs promise to make major contributions to productivity, quality, and employee motivation and satisfaction. As a result, the employer would stay more competitive. A recent report concludes some employers are beginning to wonder if all empowerment programs promise more than they actually deliver. A Carnegie-Mellon University study found that employee involvement programs may have hindered organizational efficiency. According to the study, large companies with employee involvement programs were 46 percent less efficient than companies without such programs. Small companies were 25 percent less efficient.[10]

Another problem is that empowerment programs require substantial change throughout the organization, and few firms may be willing to make such sweeping changes. As Edward E. Lawler III explains: "A lot of companies haven't thought empowerment through enough to know that they might have to redesign not just a small part of their work space, but also their pay systems, their training systems, and their overall work structures. A lot of errors are being made during implementation."[11]

Another potential problem with empowerment programs is the same legal issue facing work teams, as described in Chapter 11. Employee involvement programs could violate an old National Labor Relations Board rule about employer committees competing with labor unions. Empowerment programs focus on improving productivity, quality, and customer service. Consequently, they probably are not in violation of the NLRB rule.[12]

Guidelines for Action and Skill Development

To supplement the many ideas already presented about empowerment, heed the advice of Wolf J. Rinke. He argues that the most effective way to empower people is to provide them with the tools and confidence they will need to act on their own. Teach team members to ask the following four questions whenever they are not certain what to do in a specific situation:

Is it good for the customer?

Is it good for our organization?
Is it in agreement with our philosophy and values?
Is it good for me?
If the answer is affirmative to all four, team members should assume the authority to act. Tell your team members that it is easier to ask forgiveness than permission.[13]

DISCUSSION QUESTIONS AND ACTIVITIES

1. What is the difference between asking an employee's opinion and empowerment?
2. *Empowerment* has become a buzzword in business and government during the past several years. Why might this have happened?
3. Empowerment is supposed to add to rather than detract from the power of the empowering manager. How does the manager's power expand?
4. What do you think are the major complaints supervisors and other managers have about empowerment programs?
5. What controls should management put on the empowerment process?
6. What is your reaction to Omni Hotels using a fight song as part of its empowerment program?
7. Speak to an entry-level worker at a Pizza Hut, KFC, Burger King, or the like. Get that person's viewpoint on how helpful empowerment would be for him or her, and discuss your findings in class.

NOTES

1. Adapted from William Patalon III, "Xerox's Gateway to the World," Rochester *Democrat and Chronicle*, June 14, 1992, pp. 1F, 2F. Reprinted with permission.
2. Thomas F. O'Boyle, "Working Together: A Manufacturer Grows Efficient by Soliciting Ideas from Employees," *The Wall Street Journal*, June 5, 1992, pp. A1, AF.
3. "Conversation with Gordon Forward," *Organizational Dynamics*, Summer 1991, pp. 63–72.
4. Joseph Weber, "A Big Company that Works," *Business Week*, May 4, 1992, pp. 124–32.
5. Andrea Rothman, "Can Wayne Calloway Handle the Pepsi Challenge?" *Business Week*, January 27, 1992, pp. 90-98.
6. Joy Lesser, "From the Bottom Up: A Toast to Empowerment," *Human Resources Forum*, May 1992, pp. 1–2; and Joy Lesser, "Frontline Employees: Where the Action Is," *Human Resources Forum*, May 1992, pp. 2–3.

7. Peter C. Fleming, "Empowerment Strengthens the Rock," *Management Review*, December 1991, pp. 34-37.
8. Richard J. Magjuka and Timothy T. Baldwin, "Team-Based Employee Involvement Programs: Effects of Design and Administration," *Personnel Psychology*, Winter 1991, pp. 793, 806.
9. Robert W. Barner and J. Jackson Fulbright, "Set the Stage for Employee Involvement," *HRMagazine*, May 1991, p. 76.
10. Karen Matthes, "Empowerment: Fact or Fiction?" *HRfocus*, March 1992, pp. 1, 6.
11. Ibid., p. 6.
12. Larry Reynolds, "An Old NLRB Rule Threatens Quality Circles," *Management Review*, January 1992, p. 55.
13. Wolf J. Rinke, "Empowering Your Team Members," *Supervisory Management*, April 1989, p. 24.

SOME ADDITIONAL REFERENCES

Byham, William C., with Jeff Cox. *ZAPP: The Lightening of Empowerment*. New York: Harmony Books, 1991.

Lawler, Edward E., III. *The Ultimate Advantage: Creating the High-Involvement Organization*. San Francisco: Jossey-Bass, 1992.

Lawler, Edward E., III, Susan Albers Mohrman, and Gerald E. Ledford, Jr. *Employee Involvement and Total Quality Management*. San Francisco: Jossey-Bass, 1992.

Leana, Carrie R., Roger S. Ahlbrandt, and Audrey J. Murrell. "The Effects of Employee Involvement Programs on Unionized Workers' Attitudes, Perceptions, and Preferences in Decision Making." *Academy of Management Journal*, October 1992, pp. 861-73.

Mathes, Karen. "What's the Big Idea? Empower Employees Through Suggestion." *HRfocus*, October 1992, p. 17.

Simmons, John. "Participatory Management: Lessons from the Leader." *Management Review*, December 1990, pp. 54–58.

Solomon, Charlene Marmer. "Networks Empower Employees." *Personnel Journal*, October 1991, pp. 51–54.

Appendix to Chapter Thirteen

CONDUCTING AN EMPOWERMENT INTERVIEW

To be an effective empowering manager, it is important to understand the capabilities of team members. By understanding their capabilities, you will develop a clearer understanding of how much decision-making and problem-solving authority you can extend to them. For example, if a team member knew little about creditworthiness, you would not want to grant him or her considerable leeway in granting credit. You might conclude this person will be empowered to grant more credit after he or she acquires more knowledge about creditworthiness.

Conducting empowerment interviews has another benefit. As implied in Skill-Building Exercise 13, such an interview would communicate the message that you are interested in the growth and development of team members.

Practice conducting empowering interviews with a classmate, co-worker, or friend. Rely on interview techniques you may have learned in another class or through experience. As a general guideline, aim toward conducting a conversation with the other person, but do most of the listening. Following are questions to help you learn about the capabilities of a team member. Choose from among them to conduct a productive interview.

1. What type of problems do you like to work on?
2. What decisions would you like to make that you are not making now?
3. Tell me about your best job skills.
4. What job responsibilities have you handled in the past three years?
5. What work problems have you spotted on your own recently?
6. How closely do you like to check with your boss before making a decision?
7. Tell me about any ideas for improvement you have made on the job in recent years.
8. How much responsibility do you think you can handle?
9. How would you feel if you acted on your own and then made a big mistake?
10. How do you feel when your boss delegates to you?

Chapter Fourteen

Total Quality Management

The industrial company described below experienced a 50 percent drop in revenues during a recession in the industry it served. An opportunity then arose to enter into a partnering relationship with a major customer, provided the company could meet stringent quality requirements. The company responded to the challenge by embarking on a major quality-improvement program.

The Wallace Company is an industrial distributor of pipe, valves, fittings, and other specialty products for the refining, chemical, and petrochemical industries. Almost 70 percent of the company's revenues come from performing maintenance and repairs. The Wallace Company employs 280 people, and annual sales are about $90 million. A severe economic downturn in the Gulf Coast area during the mid-1980s resulted in a 50 percent drop in company revenues.

In 1985, Hoechst Celanese, a major Wallace customer, demanded strict quality requirements on delivery time and invoice accuracy from all its suppliers. Those suppliers that met Celanese requirements would be invited into a "partnering" relationship with Celanese. The Wallace Company quality-improvement program was started primarily as an opportunity to retain Celanese as a customer.

The Wallace quality-improvement program makes extensive use of statistical process control (SPC). The company information system provides extensive feedback on inventory levels, delivery schedules, pricing data, returned goods, and other critical success factors in the industry. Monthly charts related to these issues are posted for all to see. Wallace also provides on-line computer access to much of its inventory and pricing data for customers to use in making purchases. Moreover, through an electronic data interchange system, customers can directly access the system and place orders.

Statistical techniques are important to the Wallace quality-improvement program. Yet the core of the program has been an emphasis on the team approach to improving operations and service. Nine of the 16 Wallace Company strategic objectives are related to the human aspects of quality management. Examples include human resource development and on-the-job training.

Empowerment is a key theme in the Wallace approach to business. All associates (employees) are allowed to make customer-related decisions of up to $1,000 without higher approval. Customer-related decisions on values exceeding $1,000 can be made without approval when time is urgent and leadership (management) is not readily available. All associates working in the warehouse can reject shipments if the material is either defective or the shipment is incorrect. To ensure that all associates could competently perform their jobs, Wallace spent more than $2 million on formal training and education over three years.

During the same three-year period, the Wallace Company reduced its number of suppliers from more than 3,000 to fewer than 300. The remaining vendors must provide Wallace with extensive product quality information. Wallace also provides quality training programs for its vendors. The company is now requiring that all its suppliers pass its vendor certification program.

Wallace decided in 1989 to use the Malcolm Baldrige National Quality Award criteria as guidelines for its quality-improvement program and also to apply for the award. During a weekend retreat, top leadership rated itself using the award application form. Despite its considerable progress in achieving high quality, leadership rated itself only 210 points out of a possible 1,000. Sixteen quality strategic objectives were established such as quality business plan, customer/service satisfaction, suggestions system, and internal and external benchmarking.

More than 100 task forces and special quality teams were established to guide the quality-improvement process. Outside consultants were hired to help Wallace with self-examination and quality training. As a finalist in the national Baldrige competition, Wallace was visited by a team of examiners. Several months later, Wallace was declared a winner.

Because of its quality-improvement program, Wallace gained both revenue and profit growth in a still-depressed market. The company also became a leader in on-time delivery and error-free transactions. The Wallace Company's most notable accomplishments included the following:

- Received a 97.97 quality rating by Monsato—the highest rating ever attained by a vendor.
- Achieved 98 percent on-time delivery performance with partnering customers, as opposed to an industry average below 75 percent.
- Achieved a 40 percent sales increase in 1985-1989 during an industry downturn. At the same time, inventory increased only 5 percent.

- Attained sales per associate 25 percent above the average for high-performing firms in the industry.
- Reduced absenteeism and turnover 50 percent and 60 percent, respectively.

Since winning the Baldrige Award, the Wallace Company has experienced some setbacks. Revenues plunged about 20 percent in the first three quarters of 1991, and the company began losing money. More than 50 people have been laid off, and John Wallace resigned as CEO but remained as chairman of the board. A consultant was hired to help turn around the company. She believed a major source of the company's problems was that management diverted its efforts. Wallace leadership spent an enormous amount of time doing presentations for other companies and professional groups as well as conducting plant tours. When asked whether he agreed that these activities hurt company performance, John Wallace replied:

> I agree and disagree. Number one, I would like to have the money available we spent on the program now. Yet if we hadn't spent the money on the quality movement, we would not be where we are today. I don't think the company would have survived. Did we get off course somewhat as far as the time we spent on presentations and things of that nature? I think we probably put in about 75 percent focus on quality and 25 percent focus on sales. We now have switched the emphasis around, but that doesn't mean we're dropping any of our quality processes.
>
> We did get off course some. I was slow to react to some economic conditions. Would I do it again as far as the Malcolm Baldrige Award—yes.[1]

TOTAL QUALITY MANAGEMENT STRATEGIES AND TACTICS

As the Wallace Company experience suggests, achieving high quality is a comprehensive process, involving workers at every level. For many firms, the quest for high quality takes the form of total quality management. TQM is a management system for improving performance throughout the firm by maximizing internal and external customer satisfaction and making continuous improvements. Total quality management is thus a process, not merely a program with a preconceived beginning and ending.[2] The same process can also be seen as a corporate mind-set to improve customer satisfaction by continuously improving the quality of products and services. The essence of TQM is a culture that supports continuous improvements.

To explain total quality management, we describe a representative group of TQM strategies and tactics and place them into two categories. First are principles and practices related to attitudes and behavior, and second are those related to processes and technology. Our general emphasis, however, is on the *soft* (human) rather than the *hard* (statistical and technological) aspect of total quality management. The information presented in Chapter 8 about achieving total customer satisfaction can be considered an important complement to total quality management.

TQM Principles and Practices Related to Attitudes and Behavior

A system of total quality management aims to convert an entire organization toward higher customer satisfaction, continuous improvement, and employee involvement. Many TQM principles, practices, and techniques, therefore, are expressed in terms of changing attitudes, behavior, and the corporate culture.

Obtain Top-Level Commitment to Quality.   TQM must be a bottom-down process, integrated into the corporate culture.[3] A starting point in achieving TQM is for executives to give a high priority to quality. They must allocate resources to preventing as well as repairing quality problems. Quality must be included in the organization strategy, and every manager and organizational unit must be responsible for quality. The quest for quality must be perceived by workers throughout the organization as a top-management commitment. Executives should talk about quality frequently, including giving speeches on the topic and asking questions about quality at staff meetings.

Create a Corporate Culture of Quality.   Improving   quality   significantly requires an upheaval in corporate culture. According to Karen Pennar, engineers, designers, marketers, administrators, and production workers have to collaborate to ensure quality, and they all have to understand that they are critical to the process. A quality-improvement program that does not include a corporate culture that embodies quality is likely to be shallow and short-lived. "If the process is halfhearted or poorly planned, quality will become simply another fashionable word in the executive's lexicon or yet another trendy promotion vehicle for new goods."[4] World-class quality leaders such as Xerox, Motorola, and Waterman (writing instruments) operate in a culture of quality.

Focus on Customer Requirements.   The essence of quality is to satisfy the needs of both external and internal customers—at a price the customer is willing to pay. Few external customers may be willing to pay $9,000 for a personal computer, even if it is magnificently engineered. And few internal customers might be willing to wait 60 days for a report prepared flawlessly. Workers throughout the firm must get the message that the true purpose of their jobs is to satisfy customer requirements. Every action should be linked to customer satisfaction. A telemarketer might say, for example, "Is putting my customer on hold and playing music over the phone in his or her best interests?"

Corning Inc., another leader in achieving high quality, exemplifies the customer focus. The simple, yet powerful, principle "meet the customer's requirements" is the driving force behind the total quality management system. *Customer* is defined as any person with whom an employee has a job-related relationship. These people include people who buy a Corning product or service, co-workers, supervisors, supervised employees, and suppliers. Meeting the customer's requirements is the foundation of every employee's job at Corning.

To be able to meet customer requirements, employees must first understand those requirements. Also, the requirements must be documented and reviewed regularly to adjust for necessary changes and to avoid future misinterpretation. To determine how well an employee is doing, the customer is sometimes asked whether requirements are being met on time, the first time, 100 percent of the time.[5]

Emphasize Continuous Improvement.   Achieving total quality management is a gradual process as opposed to a crash program. It fits well the spirit of *kaizen*, a philosophy of continuing gradual improvement in one's personal and work life. Kaizen also means roughly, "Every day in every way, I'm getting better and better." Companies use kaizen to program themselves with positive thinking so some small improvement occurs every day.

Kaizen is a long-term gradual improvement, involving a series of small, sometimes imperceptible changes. The spirit of kaizen improves quality awareness because it prompts employees to be constantly on the lookout for small improvements. Workers are also encouraged to look for things that are not quite right, but are not yet full-blown problems. Paying attention to small details, such as checking to see if addresses on invoices are correct, fits the spirit of kaizen.

> A restaurant owner promoted the spirit of kaizen among her workers. Several of them decided to begin uncluttering the restaurant by removing some of the less attractive paintings from the wall and some of the bar decorations. Soon a few customers began to comment favorably on the cleaner decor. Given this encouragement, the owner and the workers decided to shift to an art-deco motif (characterized by a stark, clean, and modern look). Business increased substantially. The owner attributed much of this increase to the high-quality appearance of the restaurant.

Empower and Involve Employees.   To achieve total quality management, it is essential to empower employees to fix and prevent problems. Equally important, the workers have to accept the authority and become involved in the improvement process. Empowerment is one of the key principles supporting the "Leadership Through Quality" program at Xerox. The quality process revitalized the company and allowed it to compete successfully against Japanese manufacturers of photocopiers.

Empowerment is valuable because it may release creative energy. An example occurred at Advance Circuits of Hopkins, Minnesota. An empowered team eliminated pinhole defects in circuit-board film. The team discovered that a smaller darkroom eliminated many airborne particles that cause defects.[6]

Reward Employees for Achieving Quality Goals.   The principle of positive reinforcement and common sense both suggest that employees will achieve higher quality if the achievement is rewarded. Some quality gurus, such as W. Edwards Deming, are concerned that individual rewards run counter to the team concept of quality. Teams are important because most quality improvements occur as a result of linkages among people. Nevertheless, individual incentives play a role in a TQM system. American Telephone & Telegraph Co. provides a positive example of how financial incentives can enhance quality.

When AT&T introduced its Universal credit card, it faced stiff competition from established cards. The company's strategic response was to become the best customer-service company in the industry. The Universal credit card division uses 150 measures for quality. They include everything from the quality of plastic used, to the timeliness of responses, to the accuracy in letters, to the way the phone is answered. Quality indexes are tallied daily, and results are displayed on color monitors around the building. Employees receive quarterly bonuses of up to 12 percent of pay, and managers can earn bonuses of up to 20 percent of base pay.[7]

Other successful companies committed to TQM, such as Motorola, have also learned that the rewards for quality improvement must be shared with contributors to the improvement. Performance-based reward systems can accomplish this sharing of financial improvements. As indexes of quality improve, bonuses, salary increases, and gainsharing (literally sharing the gains from improvements) also increase. Other possible rewards include increased training, promotions, and the opportunity for workers to perform more challenging work. As observed by Sang M. Lee, Fred Luthans, and Richard M. Hodgetts:

> Such performance-based reward systems are a key to the difference between *talking* about quality through advertising slogans and sophisticated plans and actually *delivering* quality.[8]

Conduct Supplier Meetings about Quality.   A company needs high-quality components and materials to produce high-quality products and services. So quality awareness is also important for a company's suppliers. Wallace was a supplier to a company insisting on high quality and made similar demands on its suppliers. Sharp, the electronics firm, exemplifies the approach of upgrading quality at supplier firms. The company teaches many of its suppliers how to produce high-quality components. In this regard, part of Philip Crosby's program on quality improvement includes recommending the following policy statement: "Suppliers are educated and supported in order to ensure that they will deliver services and products that are dependable and on time." [9]

An adjunct to informing suppliers about quality specifications is to attempt to raise their general level of quality awareness. A frank discussion with suppliers about the company's TQM process will help communicate this message. Ford, Monsanto, and Motorola are three of many companies that award certificates to suppliers that meet all their quality specifications. Awards of this type are helpful in promoting quality awareness among the company's actual and potential suppliers.

Let us now examine some of the attitudes toward people and the behavior necessary to establish the right organizational culture for total quality management by completing Skill-Building Exercise 14.

SKILL-BUILDING EXERCISE 14
Do You Have the Right Corporate Culture for TQM?

To evaluate whether your company has a culture ideally suited to total quality, check whether the description in the left-hand or the right-hand column best describes your firm. Confer with another person who works for the same employer to increase the accuracy of your ratings. If you are not currently working, speak to someone who is employed and evaluate his or her company. It would be helpful to interview more than one person from the same employer.

TQM Companies	*Traditional Companies*
_____ Driven by customer needs	_____ Driven by company wants
_____ Prevention of problems they happen.	_____ Detection of problems after the fact
_____ Nothing less than 100% will do.	_____ Establishes maximum acceptable levels of error, waste
_____ Committed to quality at the source	_____ Believes inspection is the key to quality
_____ Cooperative, interdepartmental teams	_____ Autonomous, independent departments

_____ High employee participation,   _____ Top-down, management-
          empowered work force   directed work force

_____ Long-term staying power is   _____ Short-term profit is a prim-
          a primary goal   ary goal

Interpretation: Seven check marks in the left-hand column would indicate the firm you have evaluated is probably a world-class quality company. Seven check marks in the right-hand column suggests the company you have evaluated might be at a competitive disadvantage in a quality-conscious economy. Check marks to the right can also be used as indicators of need for organizational improvement.

SOURCE: "Total Quality Management: A Step-by-Step Guide to Making TQM Work for You," National Seminars brochure, 1992.

TQM PRINCIPLES AND PRACTICES RELATED TO WORK PROCESSES AND TECHNOLOGY

Total quality management began in manufacturing, so it follows that many TQM ideas are aimed at improving work processes and making optimum use of technology. Here we cover seven such key principles. However, statistical problem-solving tools are also required to support a push toward companywide quality.

Conduct Extensive Training in Quality. As part of TQM, almost every employee receives quality-related training. Each worker learns basic concepts of TQM, including problem solving and decision making, interpersonal skills, and customer service. Manufacturing operatives receive training in statistics useful for quality control such as sampling, measures of variation, control charts, and histograms.

Richard J. Schonberger, a noted authority on quality, says the quality-conscious firm emphasizes cross-training in a few jobs. Cross-training is important because the customer-focused firm requires a versatile work force. In this way, employees can readily shift to a job that satisfies current customer demands.[10]

Engage in Competitive Benchmarking. A basic TQM principle is for the firm to compare its performance to an industry standard, including a direct competitor. Competitive benchmarking is sometimes referred to as *innovation by imitation.* Senior executives at Motorola and textile manufacturer Milliken & Co. boast of taking ideas shamelessly from rivals, or from anyone who better carries out some business practice or work method. The broad approach in benchmarking is to make comparisons to the best in any industry. For example, Xerox Corporation compared its shipping capabilities to those of catalog merchant L. L. Bean.

Until several years ago, benchmarking was regarded as pirating. Fewer ethical questions are raised when benchmarking is conducted by affiliated companies. An example occurred when Ford Motor Co. intended to downsize its 500-employee accounts payable personnel by 20 percent. Ford examined the same operation at its 25 percent-owned affiliate Mazda Motor Corp. and found that Mazda employed 80 percent fewer employees, considering its relative size. As a result of the comparison, Ford reduced its accounts payable staff by 75 percent.[11]

Decrease Cycle Time.   An important goal of total quality management is for products and services to achieve a short cycle time, the interval between order and delivery of a product or service. Receiving goods promptly contributes to customer perception of quality. Working toward shorter and shorter cycle times also exposes areas of weakness that could be hurting quality, such as bottlenecks. Once the bottleneck is identified, it can be analyzed and remedied.

> A small company that produced videotapes for product demonstrations set out to reduce its cycle time. The bottleneck discovered was a cumbersome procedure for estimating production costs. Each contributor to the product would independently submit a bid on his or her input to the project. The company instituted a 30-minute group meeting attended by all project contributors. Estimates were made on the spot, and the prospective customer was notified within two days of the meeting.

Use Statistical Process Control.   A widely used quality technique is statistical process control (SPC), a method for analyzing deviations in production processes during manufacturing rather than after a part or product is completed. Similar to other methods of quality control, SPC aims to reduce variation in the finished product. You may have observed, for example, that the ink in some pens flows more smoothly than others under the same conditions. The problem is variation in the manufacturing process.

Statistical process control gauges the effectiveness of the manufacturing process by carefully monitoring changes in whatever is being produced. Potential problems are detected before they result in poor quality products. The reasons for the deviation are diagnosed, and the process is rectified to overcome the problems. Part of the turnaround of Harley-Davidson Motor Co., Inc. has been attributed to the application of statistical process control (SPC).

SPC uses a number of basic statistical techniques such as Pareto analysis, cause-and-effect of Ishikawa diagrams, and control charts. A basic control chart is shown in Figure 14–1.

Figure 14–1 A Control Chart Used in Statistical Process Control

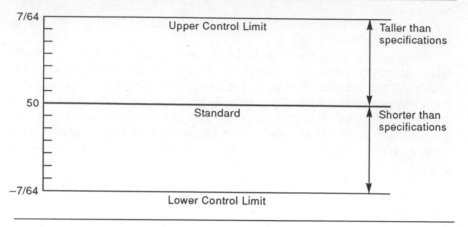

NOTE: The prescribed length of the product is 50 inches. The acceptable range of the length (tolerable limits) is plus or minus 7/64 inches, or from 49.891 inches to 50.109 inches.

Build Quality into the Process (the Taguchi Method). A widely used method to prevent quality problems is the principle of robust quality, developed by Genichi Taguchi. Robust quality means engineers must build quality into the design of a part or process so it can withstand fluctuations on the production line without a loss of quality. A major goal of robust quality is to prevent products from failing while they are being used by customers. For example, if a security system is not designed properly, it might pass inspection yet give an occasional false alarm after one year of operation.

A major thrust of robust quality is to consistently hit quality targets, rather than tolerate acceptable deviations. The classic case of Ford versus Mazda illustrates this difference. Several years ago, Ford requested that Mazda manufacture transmissions for a car sold in the United States. Both companies were supposed to build a car with identical specifications. Ford used the zero defects quality standard, while Mazda adhered to robust quality.

After the cars had been in use for a while, Ford's transmissions were creating more warranty claims and more complaints about noise. Ford disassembled and carefully measured transmissions made by itself and Mazda. Ford parts were meeting specifications (no detectable defects). Mazda gearboxes, however, showed no variability from targets. Ford was building many transmissions close to the outer limit of specified tolerances. As a consequence, minor variations in one part were creating a domino effect on other parts. The key point of this example is that Mazda managers assumed that robustness begins with meeting targets consistently. Ford managers, in contrast, assumed that staying within tolerance would prevent quality problems. [12]

Establish Stringent Quality Standards.   An organization practicing total quality management typically establishes a stringent quality standard. The standard typically has a catchy name, such as Six Sigma. The most stringent performance standard used in TQM programs is zero defects, the absence of any detectable quality flaws in a product or service. Such a standard might not appear humanly possible for complex work and would create substantial stress for those striving for zero defects. Can you imagine the Manhattan telephone directory containing no errors? Yet quality consultant Philip Crosby claims that if people are truly committed to error-free work, it can be accomplished. [13] The quality slogan, "do it right the first time," implies zero defects.

Six Sigma, a quality standard developed at Motorola, is one step below zero defects. The Six Sigma standard means that errors occur only once in 3.4 million opportunities, or 99.99966 percent free of defects. Six Sigma is also expressed as the area remaining under the normal curve, six standard deviations from the right of the mean—hardly anything! Among the few products reaching that extraordinary level are Eastman Kodak's Kodacolor film (less than 1 defect per million) and some Motorola pagers and cellular telephones. During one spring, catalog company L. L. Bean shipped 500,000 packages without an error, almost attaining the Six Sigma standard. [14]

Another quality standard less stringent than zero defects is to promote the idea "strive to do error-free work." The Corning program recognizes that errors cannot be eliminated. The principle of striving for error-free work creates an attitude that errors are not acceptable. Corning no longer operates on the basis of an "acceptable quality level" with an allowable percentage of defects. Instead, the new attitude prompts employees to ask why an error has occurred, track down the root cause, and take action to prevent a recurrence. [15]

The International Standards Organization has established a comprehensive set of quality standards known as ISO 9000, based on the standards of 91 countries. ISO 9000 presents the general guidelines for using the standards, which include five subsets. For example, IS 9003 presents specifications for final inspection and testing, and IS 9004 establishes concepts and a guide for overall quality management. The European Economic Community requires that products be made to ISO 9000 standards. Companies selling to the European Community supposedly must be accredited according to these standards. [16]

Assess the Results of Total Quality Management.   An organization should rigorously evaluate whether total quality management is achieving its intended results. Comparisons should be made between what exists now and what existed before TQM was implemented. Key variables to measure would be changes in customer satisfaction, product or service defects, sales, and profits. Objective measurement is important because a shift to TQM consumes substantial resources in terms of time, money, and equipment. Objective performance measures are also important because some companies grossly overestimate their quality performance. A customer-service representative of a TQM company was asked how well she thought her company's quality performance had improved. She replied, "Things are just as crazy as they ever were around here. We cancel customers by mistake, we can't find things, we make humongous billing errors, and business expense reimbursements to salespeople are often late."

Key results indicators (KRI) are used by Corning Inc. to measure the outcomes of total quality management. As a starting point, measures are taken of customer deliverables—those factors most critical to the customer's satisfaction. Deliverables are established with each customer, and these deliverables are tracked and improved. Customers vary in what they consider important (their deliverables). Consumer-sector customers, for example, insist on on-time delivery. For other Corning customers, such as those who purchase telescope mirrors, intact deliveries are valued the most.

Key results indicators were also established for internal company activities, illustrated as follows: Corporate communications worked toward publishing an error-free annual report; information services measured response time, systems availability, and response to internal customer problems as evaluated by the customer.

Whenever feasible, key results are expressed in parts per million. Results expressed in terms of percent sound more impressive than those using the million standard. To illustrate, a goal of 99 percent sounds close to perfection, but 10,000 defective parts per million suggests a long way to go before achieving zero defects or Six Sigma.

During one year alone, Corning used 200 key results indicators for all organizational units. A mammoth amount of paperwork and electronic mail is required to gather this information, but the company believes the effort is justifiable.[17]

The Case for Total Quality Management

A major argument in favor of total quality management is that it contributes to quality, productivity, and profitability. Many companies that have embarked on TQM have experienced an upswing in quality leading to greater customer acceptance. A stellar example is Harley-Davidson, the American motorcycle manufacturer. In 1981, the company's market share had shrunk from a mid-1970s high of about 70 percent to less than 25 percent. Harley-Davidson was moving rapidly toward extinction. By 1990, Harley's market share had surged back to 60 percent. The company's biggest challenge became producing enough motorcycles to meet demand.

Harley's comeback has been attributed substantially to a multifaceted approach to quality. Management invested in the right technology and product-design features to significantly improve the Harley's dependability and styling. The company focused on improvements that were important to customers.

Management also focused on promoting a higher-quality image for the Harley. In place of the "Hell's Angels" motif, the image shifted to a healthy outdoor lifestyle. Management also shifted to a higher quality of distribution, such as upgrading dealer training and forming a dealer advisory council. [18]

Quality consultants argue that upgrading quality is a worthwhile investment because it pays for itself. A key argument is that quality and cost are a sum, not a difference. According to Armand V. Feigenbaum, "In the old days, the myth was that higher quality meant higher cost. Now we know that when you make it better, that's the best way to make it quicker and cheaper."[19] (Many people contend, however, that quality can reach the point of pricing a product out of the market. Compaq Computer Corp. developed a low price personal computer, Prolinea, in 1992 because its regular line of high-quality computers was overpriced for the PC clone market.)

Managing for high quality is also important because it is a logical approach to competing favorably in international competition and forging ahead in domestic markets. As observed by David A. Garvin, "The quality of products presents both a problem and an opportunity for U.S. manufacturers—a problem because foreign competitors are often far ahead in offering products of superior quality; an opportunity because American consumers are increasingly concerned about the quality of goods and services they buy." [20]

The Case against Total Quality Management

The case against TQM is not that high quality is unimportant but that there are less time-consuming and cumbersome ways of achieving quality. Also, many organizational improvements should not be credited to TQM but to other managerial approaches. For example, many firms upgrade their advertising, as did Harley, but they do not consider themselves to be a total quality management organization. Another problem with TQM is that its advocates talk about TQM with a religious fervor, using cliches such as, "Either you are for TQM all the way, or you are out." No intermediate position is acceptable. The same people come to believe that quality can be achieved only through TQM, forgetting that Cadillacs, Maytag washers, Craftsman tools, and Piaget watches, among other high-quality products, existed long before total quality management.

An objective argument against total quality management is that many instances have been found in which TQM programs are ineffective. A survey of 500 manufacturing and service companies that use TQM revealed that only 36 percent believed it was boosting their competitiveness. Another survey of 95 companies working with TQM indicated that more than half had not met such goals as raising market share or increasing customer satisfaction. According to Dan Ciampa, these quality efforts often fail because the organization misuses or misunderstands what total quality tools can accomplish. Another problem he cites is that many firms are unable to incorporate a consumer-driven philosophy with the total quality management picture. [21]

Guidelines for Action and Skill Development

Many guidelines for implementing a system of total quality management have been presented throughout this chapter. Here we present a few additional implementation suggestions. A starting point is to recognize the necessity of linking quality efforts to profits or staying within budget for a nonprofit firm. Joshua Hammond, president of the American Quality Foundation, says that too often, quality proselytizers confuse means and ends. They are more concerned with TQM principles and practices, including setting up training programs, than about profits. [22]

Feedback on performance should be incorporated into all TQM efforts. Checkpoints should be built in to inform people how well quality targets are being met. Feedback devices include wall charts showing quality levels, reductions in customer complaints, and the percentage of on-time deliveries.

The manufacturing or operations process must be in control. Running a tight "operations ship" is necessary to achieve quality products and services. An in-control operations process includes such things as well-maintained machinery and office equipment, good housekeeping, and well-trained employees.

Deal openly with the problem of quantity versus quality. Many workers believe that lip service is paid to quality while high quantity (such as sales volume and meeting demanding production schedules) is what really counts. It is important to allow employees to vent their feelings about this topic, and then explain how both quantity and quality are important (if true).

DISCUSSION QUESTIONS AND ACTIVITIES

1. A popular slogan of the quality movement is that "quality is free." What does the slogan really mean?
2. In what way has the discipline of marketing always been a champion of total quality management?
3. What is your reaction to the argument of a clothing manufacturer who said, "Quality is for the big companies. Our clothing is designed for the discounters whose customers are looking for $15 shirts and blouses."
4. What happens to the status of the quality-control department in a total quality management firm?
5. Of the various quality standards cited in the text, which one do you think is the most realistic? Explain your reasoning.
6. Interview two managers, and ask them their opinion of the importance of total quality management. Be prepared to discuss your findings in class.

NOTES

1. Excerpted and adapted from Robert C. Hill and Sara M. Freedman, "Managing the Quality Process: Lessons from a Baldrige Award Winner. A Conversation

with CEO John W. Wallace," *The Executive,* February 1992, pp. 76–88. Reprinted with permission.

2. Thomas H. Berry, *Managing the Total Quality Transformation* (New York: McGraw-Hill, 1991).

3. Ibid.

4. Karen Pennar, "America's Quest Can't Be Half-Hearted," *Business Week,* June 8, 1987, p. 136.

5. William H. Wagel, "Corning Zeroes in on Total Quality,"*Personnel,* July 1987, pp. 4–5; and David B. Luther, "Advanced TQM: Measurements, Missteps, and Progress Through Key Result Indicators at Corning," *National Productivity Review,* Winter 1992/1993, pp. 23–36.

6. Del Jones, "1992 Quality Cup Finalists," *USA Today,* April 10, 1992, p. 2B.

7. Mary Rowland, "If Companies Want Quality Work, They Have to Pay for It," *New York Times* syndicated story, February 9, 1992.

8. Sang M. Lee, Fred Luthans, and Richard M. Hodgetts, "Total Quality Management: Implications for Central and Eastern Europe," *Organizational Dynamics,* Spring 1992, p. 48.

9. Philip B. Crosby, *Quality Without Tears: The Art of Hassle-Free Management* (New York: McGraw-Hill, 1984), p. 101.

10. Richard J. Schonberger, "Total Quality Management Cuts a Broad Swatch— Through Manufacturing and Beyond," *Organizational Dynamics,* Spring 1992, p. 22.

11. "Quality: Small and Midsize Companies Seize the Challenge—Not a Moment Too Soon," *Business Week,* November 30, 1992, p. 74.

12. Genichi Taguchi and Don Clausing, "Robust Quality," *Harvard Business Review,* January-February 1990, p. 67.

13. Crosby, *Quality Without Tears,* pp. 103–4.

14. Mike Zavadil, "News to Use: Perfectionists," Rochester *Democrat and Chronicle,* December 4, 1992, p. 10B.

15. Wagel, "Corning Zeroes in on Total Quality," p. 5.

16. Dan Campia, *Total Quality: A User's Guide for Implementation* (Reading, Mass.: Addison-Wesley, 1992), pp. 238–39.

17. Luther, "Advanced TQM," pp. 23–36.

18. Leonard L. Berry and A. Parasuraman, "Prescriptions for a Service Quality Revolution in America," *Organizational Dynamics,* Spring 1992, p. 8.

19. Quoted in Donna Brown, "10 Ways to Boost Quality," *Management Review,* January 1991, p. 5.

20. David A. Garvin, "Quality Problems: Policies and Attitudes in the United States and Japan: An Exploratory Study," *Academy of Management Journal,* December 1986, p. 666.

21. "Quality: Small and Midsize Companies Seize the Challenge," p. 68; and Jack Szwergold, "Why Most Quality Efforts Fail," *Management Review,* August 1992, p. 5.

22. "Quality: Small and Midsize Companies Seize the Challenge," p. 68.

SOME ADDITIONAL REFERENCES

Bhote, Keki R. *World Class Quality: Using Design of Experiments to Make It Happen.* New York: AMACOM, 1991.

Butman, John. "Quality Comes Full Circle." *Management Review*, February 1992, pp. 49–51.

Carter, Carla C. "Seven Basic Quality Tools." *HRMagazine,* January 1992, pp. 81-83.

Davis, Vicki S. "Self-Audits: First Step in TQM." *HRMagazine,* September 1992, pp. 39–41.

Harari, Oren. "Ten Reasons Why TQM Doesn't Work." *Management Review,* January 1993, pp. 33–38.

Ross, Joel E. *Total Quality Management: Text, Cases and Readings.* Delray Beach, Fla.: St. Lucie Press, 1992.

Santora, Joyce E. "Pacific Bell Primes the Quality Pump." *Personnel Journal,* October 1991, pp. 63–66.

Sensenbrenner, Joseph. "Quality Comes to City Hall." *Harvard Business Review,* March-April 1991, pp. 64–70, 74–75.

Walton, Mary. *Deming Management at Work.* New York: G. P. Putnam's Sons, 1991.

Appendix to Chapter Fourteen

DEMING'S 14 POINTS

W. Edwards Deming has been a key figure in the quality movement throughout the world. Deming formulated 14 steps that management should follow to direct the company toward the goal of high quality. These steps are used by many managers as key guidelines in their efforts to achieve total quality. The 14 steps are presented here to serve as a summary checklist for directing a TQM system.

1. Continually improve products and services in order to further the firm's competitive position.
2. Adopt the new philosophy, and do not accept delays and mistakes.
3. Do not rely on mass inspection to detect defects; use statistical controls to assume that quality is built into the product.
4. Discontinue the practice of selecting suppliers based on price. Reduce the supply base and establish long-term, trusting, single-source partnerships where both buyer and seller can pursue quality improvements.
5. Find problems—whether caused by faulty systems or by production workers—and correct them.

6. Use modern methods of on-the-job training.
7. Improve and modernize methods of supervision.
8. Drive out fear, so that everyone can work productively for the firm.
9. Open communication between departments.
10. Stop using numerical goals, posters, and slogans as a way to motivate workers without giving them the methods to achieve these goals.
11. Don't depend on work standards that assign numerical quotas.
12. Remove barriers that deprive employees of their pride or workmanship.
13. Establish a dynamic program of education and training.
14. Create an executive management structure that will emphasize the above 13 points each day.

SOURCE: Andrea Garbor, *The Man Who Discovered Quality: How W. Edwards Deming Brought the Quality Revolution to America—The Stories of Ford, Xerox, and GM* (New York: Times Books, Division of Random House, 1990).

Chapter Fifteen

Downsizing and Flat Organization Structures

The public company described below sought an alternative to the traditional approach to downsizing in which many competent and hardworking employees are involuntarily released. "Voluntary rightsizing" was the productive and compassionate alternative chosen.

Several years ago, Ontario Hydro set out on a new corporate direction to become a world-class energy company. To achieve this goal, the organization size had to be adjusted. Hydro, however, had promised employees that nobody would be terminated even though some jobs might become redundant. Working with a consulting firm, the company established a career center. All employees were invited to attend career planning workshops, on company time, to explore career opportunities both inside and outside the firm.

During the same time period, Hydro revealed its plans to employees so they would know the status of their positions. Employees whose jobs were becoming redundant were given first consideration for new openings as they occurred. Generous separation allowances were given those employees who chose to leave Hydro. During the rightsizing process, consultants provided counseling and guidance to employees at all levels.

The rationale behind Hydro's voluntary rightsizing was straightforward. Employees with sharper insights into their strengths and skills could make informed career decisions. For many, this would mean staying with Ontario Hydro in the same or a new position. Other employees would choose to leave the firm after finding a more suitable position elsewhere. They would be able to accomplish this, however, in a time frame that allowed them to develop the appropriate job search skills.

By combining voluntary separations with normal attrition, Hydro met its staffing requirements without terminating employees. Furthermore, the company ended up with employees whose skills matched the needs of the evolving organization. As Don Tyler, Hydro's director of redeployment in charge of the project, analyzed the situation: "We had gone through downsizings and major outplacement programs before, and these caused some serious employee relations problems. The difference this time was that this was not outplacement, but redeployment."

Tyler noted that previously, employees thought that management controlled almost the entire process of downsizing. "This time, they determined their futures," he said. "That's not to say that everyone found the job they'd always wanted, but they did get a realistic look at where the company was going and how they could fit into those plans."

Hydro achieved excellent results with the voluntary system. Within two years of starting the program, 620 out of 650 potentially surplus employees had been successfully redeployed. Of this group, 80 percent found positions inside Hydro and 20 percent outside. Employees took an average of about three months to secure a new position. The company's average cost per employee going through the voluntary rightsizing program was less than one month's salary. Tyler noted that a forced severance approach used in the past cost Hydro about one year's salary per employee.

Employee morale, according to Tyler, also benefited from the voluntary program. Surveys conducted before and after the project indicated high satisfaction for both managers and the surplus staff. Employees who remained did so with a renewed commitment. Many saw for themselves that Hydro was a comparatively good employer.

> "The redeployment program meant a rethinking and flexibility on the part of our managers," Tyler said. "We had to get away from viewing people in terms of narrow boxes but rather according to what they could really do. In some cases, this meant taking gambles on people but, by and large, those gambles have paid off. Interestingly enough, we found that most so-called performance problems were really relationship issues which disappeared on redeployment. The career center continues and will likely remain as part of our corporate values and culture." [1]

WHY ORGANIZATIONS ARE DOWNSIZING AND CREATING FLAT STRUCTURES

Ontario Hydro downsized its organization to prepare itself to enhance organizational effectiveness, or to become a "world-class energy company." Downsizing, or rightsizing, and creating flat organization structures (those with fewer layers) are used to achieve several other purposes. A primary reason for eliminating one or more layers of management is to reduce personnel costs. Payroll costs are important because, on the average, they represent about 75 percent of the cost of operating an organization.

Cost reduction is important for business to become more competitive with foreign rivals. In the public sector, cost reduction is necessary to cope with dwindling budgets. Reducing costs by decreasing the number of managerial layers, along with laying off other workers, is a formal turnaround strategy. As described in Chapter 3 about crisis management, reducing the number of management layers also speeds up decision making. With more layers of management, more approvals are required, thus increasing the time required to make a decision. Also, with fewer management layers lower levels of management can communicate directly to top management instead of going through a ponderous chain of command. With more rapid decision making, customer service may improve. The above reasons for downsizing are supported by a spokesperson for Xerox. In explaining a round of job cuts, he said:

> The first reason for the cuts, obviously, is the economy. The recession has been longer and deeper than we anticipated. Our second objective is to improve customer service, Xerox's stock-in-trade, by reducing management.[2] [Some would disagree with the last point. Customer service can suffer when staffing is so thin that managers are overloaded.]

Flat structures also help foster decentralization as illustrated by the French company Carrefour S.A. Carrefour is the pioneer of the hypermarket concept (a giant store selling food and other goods). The company stays lean by decentralizing as many functions as possible to its retail outlets. A headquarters staff of less than 20 employees, including secretaries, guides the business. Only one layer of management is between the central office and stores—a group of regional managers.[3]

Finally, flat structures are used by some organizations simply because a streamlined organization fits the spirit of the times. Business executive Charles Ames explains:

> "We are in turbulent times, and we must begin managing for survival in turbulent times. We must be geared to a more competitive environment, breaking apart overloaded organizational structures and streamlining, emphasizing producer people over support staff, getting our cost/profit ratio more in line. We must take the bull by the horns and do what we have to do to survive."[4]

Putting together all these reasons, it is not surprising that downsizing and creating flat structures persist even when business conditions improve. A sampling of significant downsizings in recent years follows:

- General Motors Corp. plans to close 21 plants and eliminate 74,000 jobs by the mid-1990s.
- General Electric Aerospace lost 27 percent of its work force during a three-year period.

- Digital Equipment Corporation laid off 15,000 workers during 1992.
- Eastman Kodak Company reduced its work force by 12,000 through early retirements and layoffs over a few years.
- IBM reduced its work force by an estimated 50,000 workers through early retirements and layoffs over a six-year period.
- Unisys laid off 56,000 workers, half of its work force, over several years.
- Wang Laboratories Inc. laid off 5,000 employees in 1992 while filing for bankruptcy.
- Aluminum Co. of America cut 2,100 jobs in 1992.
- Hughes Aircraft Co. laid off 17,000 workers in 1992.
- Aetna Life & Casualty Co. slashed 4,800 jobs in 1992.
- Zenith Electronics Corp. halved its payroll to 6,200 over a five-year period.

STRATEGIES AND TACTICS FOR DOWNSIZING AND CREATING FLAT ORGANIZATION STRUCTURES

Consultants and researchers have developed many strategies and tactics for downsizing, or rightsizing, organizations and creating flat structures to enhance productivity and minimize human trauma. (The term *rightsizing* implies that the organization is shrunk to its optimum size for productivity.) Such tactics and strategies are divided here into two general categories: those dealing with structure, job design, and policy, and those dealing directly with the human aspects.

Dealing with Structure, Job Design, and Policy

A substantial component of restructuring relates to revamping the organization structure, redesigning work, and developing appropriate policies and procedures.

Identify the Need for Trimming the Management Work Force.   As part of the control function of management, senior executives should stay alert to the possible need for reducing managerial layers. Michael L. Tennican, an organization planning consultant, believes many organizations are overstaffed with managers. He points out that the impressive productivity gains in factories have yet to be matched in the offices. His firm's survey of 200 representative companies indicated that from World War II to the mid-1960s they resembled pyramids, with four out of five employees working in direct production jobs. Tennican says the pyramid has since been turned upside down. There were four managers for every production worker before the current era of downsizings.

According to Tennican, poor managerial practices are responsible for much of this top-heavy structure. Diversification, for example, breeds hierarchy as headquarters adds more staff to keep senior executives supplied with information and to provide the expertise that the present managerial staff lacks. Another sign that managerial overstaffing may be occurring is when people are assigned the job title "manager" to evade pay limitations on individual contributor positions. In one case, such policies resulted in a factory where each supervisor was responsible for only 4 employees, compared with a span of control of 40 at a rival's factory. [5]

Tom Peters also recommends that senior executives examine the prevailing span of control to find out if managers are supervising too few employees. (The larger the average span of control throughout the organization, the fewer the layers of management.) He reports that many firms today have moved toward an organization structure in which the ratio of managers to nonmanagers is 1 to 100 at the bottom of the firm and 1 to 20 at the top. Peters says the traditional number of employees supervised by one manager is about 1 to 15 at the bottom and 1 to 5 at the top of the organization. [6]

Change the Organization Structure to a Simpler Design.   After the need for reducing the number of managerial layers has been identified, the next step is to simplify the organization structure. Figure 15–1 illustrates this process, with a portion of an organization chart. After downsizing, one level of management has been eliminated. The incumbents of the previous managerial positions now have been reassigned as individual contributors, invited to accept early retirement, or laid off.

Make the Changes Quickly Rather than Gradually.   The argument rages whether, in times of layoffs, to attempt to make all the cuts at once or over a protracted period. If alternative placement is not available for the workers affected, reductions in staff are much less disruptive if done all at once rather than gradually. A key argument for making the changes quickly is that the survivors deal better with the downsizing if they are reasonably assured that no further cuts will be forthcoming. The ambiguity of not knowing who will be eliminated next creates considerable stress. As many managers have said after an initial period of restructuring, "We are all waiting for the other shoe to fall."

Another human resource problem stemming from gradual cuts is that the organization may lose many competent workers who are worried about job security. Rather than wait to be terminated, some of the more qualified workers may look for better opportunities in another firm. Less competent employees may also spend work time conducting a job search and worrying about losing their jobs.

FIGURE 15–1   Contrast between a Tall and a Flat Organization Structure

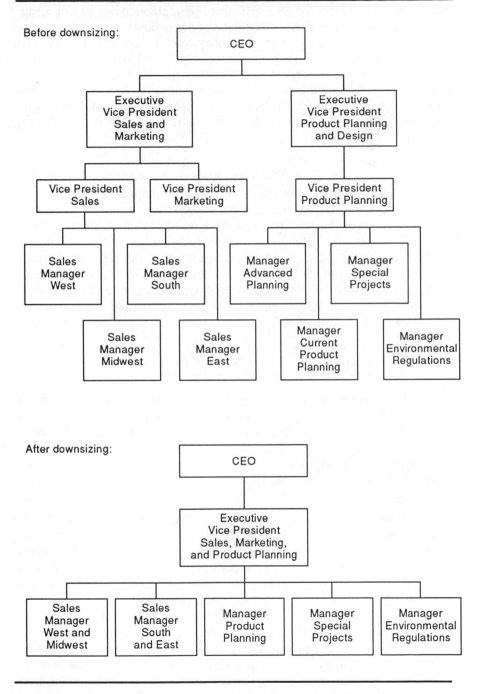

The argument for the incremental approach is that laying off workers one at a time over a period of time is less likely to be interpreted as a sign of organizational malaise than is a blitz. Shock waves throughout the organization are thus avoided. Also, it is easier for the organization to find new jobs for displaced managers and professionals several at a time than to place a large number all at once. One company that decided to eliminate two layers of management carried out the downsizing over two years. Whenever a suitable position in sales or customer service became vacant, a middle manager was invited to switch jobs. A layer of management was thus eliminated through attrition rather than through layoffs.

Streamline the Work to Match the Reduced Work Force.   Managers and other employees in a downsized organization frequently complain that the workload is excessive. To handle post-downsizing responsibilities, managers need to regularly work late at night and on weekends. The remedy to this problem is to eliminate as much low-value work as possible. Managers should justify whether every work procedure, meeting, or ceremonial activity is contributing value to the firm. For example, the number of group luncheon meetings away from the office might be cut in half, giving staff members more time during the day to conduct urgent work. Earl Landesman, a principal in the consulting firm of A. T. Kearney, expresses the problem this way:

> Too often, people focus on trying to do the same work better or more efficiently. What they should be focusing on is streamlining their work processes to include only those things that are necessary to meet customer requirements. [7]

A growing approach to streamlining work is to outsource activities to firms that can handle certain services at low cost and high quality. Among the candidates for outsourcing are payroll, benefit claims processing, printing, custodial services, and food services. The organization has to be aware, however, that the cost of these services does not exceed the costs previously paid to full-time employees to deliver these services.

Use Task Forces to Solve Special Managerial Problems.   After downsizing, restructuring, or delayering, fewer managers exist to solve problems. An antidote to this problem is for task forces, composed of top-level and first-level managers, to solve special problems. After the problem is solved, the managers return to their regular assignment full time. The task force can function part time or full time according to the magnitude of the problem.

The task-force approach makes it possible for an organization to operate efficiently with fewer managers occupying full-time, permanent positions. Special problems suitable for the task-force analysis include: whether or not to acquire or be acquired by a particular firm; how to reduce operating costs; how to create better career opportunities for the physically disabled; and how to respond to an organization crisis.

Before moving ahead to dealing directly with the human aspects of downsizings, shift your mental set to think about how you might prepare yourself for being the victim of a downsizing. Do Skill-Building Exercise 15 to gain an appreciation of steps managers and professionals can take to minimize the adverse effects of being downsized.

SKILL-BUILDING EXERCISE 15
Preparing Now to Cope with Downsizings in the Future

Downsizings, rightsizings, and restructurings appear to be a corporate way of life during business downturns. Begin preparing now to prevent a downsizing from derailing your career. Answer each of the following questions in a couple of sentences.

1. Do I keep an ongoing file of all my work accomplishments? (Give a couple of examples.)

   _____

   _____

   _____

2. Am I prepared for any contingency by maintaining a constantly updated résumé? (Also, write down the two most important skills included or that will be included in your résumé.)

   _____

   _____

   _____

3. Are my communication skills (oral, written, and nonverbal) impressive? (If your answer is negative, explain how you intend to improve these skills.)

   _____

   _____

   _____

4. Do I keep records of people I meet in business, as well as socially and in school, who could conceivably be a source of job leads or who might even be in a position to hire me? (If your answer is negative, indicate when you intend to get your Rolodex [or competitive brand] into gear.)

   _____

   _____

   _____

5. Do I strive toward becoming indispensable? (If your answer is positive, jot down what you are doing that makes you so valuable. If your answer is negative, explain how you can work toward becoming indispensable.)

_____

_____

_____

6. Do I persist in my professional education? (If your answer is negative, indicate what steps you can take to acquire important job skills and knowledge.)

_____

_____

_____

7. Do I work toward being pleasant and courteous? (If your answer is negative, describe your action plans for becoming more socially skillful.)

_____

_____

_____

SOURCE: Based on quotes from Robert Half in "Career 'Insurance' Protects DP Professionals," *Data Management*, June 1986, p. 33.

Dealing Directly with the Human Aspects

Downsizing and creating flat structures are accompanied by many human problems. Strategies and tactics have been developed to minimize the turmoil experienced by both the downsized and the survivors. As the Ontario Hydro case shows, it is sometimes possible to minimize the number of people who leave the organization involuntarily.

Deal Openly and Honestly with the Problem. The turmoil of a reduction in force intensifies when employees and other stakeholders are lied to about the timing and magnitude of the downsizing. Lies and half-truths by top management foster employee rumors and negative accusations by the media. Philip A. Greco and Brenda K. Woodlock note that no one in the firm can avoid the painful experience associated with a major downsizing. Even the survivors will be worried about their jobs and feel a sense of loss for departed work associates. Management should honestly acknowledge the widespread pain and suffering. [8]

A public statement about when, and under what conditions, the layoffs will end helps reduce anxiety. Even if top-level management is not sure of when the layoffs will end, this problem can be dealt with honestly by specifying the conditions. For example, the CEO might release a statement to the effect: "Our downsizing will end when the firm returns to profitability. With the reduction in force that has already taken place, we hope to be in the black by the end of the year."

Top management at Aetna Life & Casualty gained considerable trust from employees by being honest about the magnitude and duration of its layoffs several years ago. As an Aetna purchasing manager said, "We all knew that the industry was in trouble, and that layoffs were inevitable. Top management was so honest with us, that we trusted their ability to get us through the storm."

Use Performance Appraisal Information to Make Fair Layoff Decisions. A major strategy for making downsizing equitable is to base downsizing decisions on merit rather than seniority or political favoritism. Poor performers should be the first people to be laid off or offered early retirement during the reduction in force. Retaining people who are liked by senior management but generally incompetent damages morale and deprives the organization of needed skills.

A reliable performance appraisal system provides the information needed to objectively decide which employees will be downsized. In addition, performance appraisal data should be supplemented with other job-relevant information in the human resource information system (HRIS). The system typically contains information about an employee's work experience, special skills, and past performance appraisals.

A human resource information system improved downsizing at a 3,200-employee bank that was being purchased by an out-of-state financial institution. The new owner wanted the bank to centralize all operations of its 28 affiliates. Moving operations to headquarters meant many staff members would have to be redeployed or terminated. The bank used the HRIS program to analyze each position by title, salary grade, skills, and location. The results of this analysis revealed open positions at the main branch and the affiliates and whether an employee should be given a job offer at the main branch.

The HRIS identified 200 open jobs throughout the system, all of which were posted. Many of these positions were filled by current employees. The HRIS also provided confidential acceptance, redeployment, and termination letters. [9]

Provide Adequate Compensation and Support for the Displaced People. The managers, professionals (for example, planners and financial analysts), and other workers who lose their jobs under restructuring may need various forms of support. Middle managers often require more help than other categories of employees in coping with layoff. "We're not altogether sure that it isn't the white-collar people who suffer more," says Jeanne Gordus who has designed programs to help thousands of unemployed auto, glass, and steel workers. Managers and professionals are so attached to their jobs that they have greater stress and emotional problems. [10]

Developing support mechanisms begins with planning for layoffs in order to treat employees with dignity and respect instead of rushing them out the door. A representative severance pay guideline is one week of pay for every year of service and full retirement and health insurance payments. Eastman Kodak even pays the Social Security taxes for qualifying early retirees until they reach age 62. As many a departing Kodak employee has stated, "The company made me an offer too good to refuse."

A study of 407 downsized firms indicated 40 percent of them emphasized severance pay and extended health benefits to ease the transition out of the company. Twenty-three percent of the firms studied emphasized encouraging people to leave the firm through early retirement and voluntary separation. (The other 37 percent of firms did the best they could to prevent layoffs by redeploying the surplus people.) [11]

The next step in providing adequate support to laid-off workers is to offer each person a candid, but sympathetic statement of why he or she was chosen to be laid off. Because *every* worker is not eliminated in an organizational flattening, the person may wonder why he or she was targeted. An appropriate statement from the bearer of bad news might be: "We have decided to lay off 90 percent of the managers at your level. Your performance has been above average, but we are only retaining those 10 percent of managers with outstanding performance appraisals and who have critical skills that no other managers in the firm possess. You will receive a favorable employment reference."

A useful support mechanism for the dismissed manager is outplacement services, a systematic approach to helping the individual find new employment outside the firm (see Chapter 19).

Use Human Resource Balancing to Minimize Layoffs.   As practiced by Ontario Hydro, downsizing can sometimes be accomplished by granting options to employees to make voluntary choices. *Human resource balance* means a balance is achieved between the work force and the demand for workers. Balancing implies that if the work force is managed strategically, options exist that are less disruptive and permanent than layoffs.

A comprehensive program of human resource balancing occurred at the Loveland, Colorado, division of Hewlett-Packard. Alternative opportunities had to be found for 400 employees because top management phased out one line of business. Employees could choose among six alternatives: *Regional redistribution* allowed surplus employees to move to other divisions within the geographic region. *Relocation* gave surplus Loveland employees priority over nonsurplus employees from other divisions for positions in another Hewlett-Packard location.

A *loan program* allowed volunteers to be loaned to divisions in which short-term hiring needs existed, lasting anywhere from one day to one year. *Re-*

classification allowed employees who wanted to stay in their home location to take different jobs, often at lower pay levels. Under the *employee draft,* divisions from the same geographic region were allocated a certain number of employees from the eligible pool. Divisions with jobs to fill would choose the employees whose skills best matched the available jobs. *Voluntary terminations* were still required despite the five balancing techniques already mentioned. The major severance package offered was one year's salary and all accrued retirement benefits to employees at least 55 years old and with 15 years' seniority.

The placement of the 400 employees followed this distribution: 40 percent voluntary terminations; 27 percent regional redistribution; 12 percent reclassification; 10 percent relocation; 6 percent draft; and 6 percent loan. [12]

Provide Job Security to the Survivors. According to Robert M. Tomasko, the current demographics have been a challenge for many organizations. The baby boomers reached middle-management age when downsizing of organizations eliminated many of the positions they hoped to occupy. "Companies that have responded to this by pruning back their organizations *and* working hard to provide job security for those selected to remain will be one step ahead of the others in having loyal and committed people to deal with the demographics of the next decade." [13]

One way of shoring up the prospects of job security is to explain to the remaining managers that they are a select cadre of managers on whom the organization hopes to build its future. Words alone are not sufficient to convince the survivors that their job security is not threatened. It is equally important to manage the company in such a way that job security appears high. For example, temporary help can be used to staff certain jobs. The heavy reliance on temporary help suggests to permanent employees that the company considers them to be part of an elite work force. Also, workers believe that if further downsizing is necessary, temporary workers can be readily trimmed, thus saving the jobs of permanent workers.

Survivors of a downsizing may need emotional support to help them deal with the distress of seeing former work associates dismissed. Toward this end, some companies offer survivor workshops that function as support groups. A professional counselor may be brought in to run a few group sessions where the survivors can talk about their guilt and anxieties and encourage each other. Listening to employees is a related method of helping them deal with the adverse emotional impact of a downsizing. At the Bank of America, brown bag lunches were held between top-level managers and employees throughout the firm. Executives gave employees the opportunity to discuss their feelings about the layoff and concerns about their place in the firm. [14]

Provide Flexible Benefits to Offset Long Working Hours. The remaining employees in a streamlined organization work extra hard because they assume the responsibilities of the downsized workers. To compensate for this extra work, many companies are now creating flexible benefits to help employees blend their family and work lives. Among these benefits are dependent-care facilities, job sharing, and part-time work (see Chapter 18). Dana Friedman of the Families and Work Institute says companies see these work and family programs as survivor benefits. "Those who have survived the layoffs have low morale and feel insecure in their jobs. They've got to keep them happy." [15]

Advantages of Downsizing and Flat Organization Structures.

Downsized organizations with flat organization structures offer several key advantages, as described in the discussion about the purposes of downsizing. Downsizing pays large dividends when it results in a lean and mean organization. The reduced payroll cost may increase profits for a private company and enable a public firm to stay within budget.

Flat structures contribute to organizational effectiveness, including productivity. Ken Iverson, chairman of the profitable steelmaker Nucor Corp., makes this point about excessive layers of management: "The most important thing American industry needs to do is to reduce the number of management layers." [16] Flat structures hasten decision making because fewer managers provide input to the same decision, and top management can communicate directly with lower levels of management.

A downsized organization sometimes improves teamwork because teamwork is more important then ever in a flat structure. The thin staffing makes it important for people to work together as a team across an array of projects. [17] Customer service in a flat structure may improve because employees can resolve customer problems with fewer layers of approval. (Nevertheless, severe understaffing hurts customer service because problems go unattended.)

Downsizing sometimes performs a social good. Some of the more talented middle managers and professionals who are forced to leave the organization wind up working for smaller firms that need big-company expertise to grow. Also, the more entrepreneurial of the laid-off middle managers start businesses, thus creating jobs.

Disadvantages of Downsizing and Flat Organization Structures

Severe downsizing and flattening can create financial loss rather than gain. The confusion, inefficiency, costs of early retirement and severance pay, and legal expenses in defending against lawsuits combine to offset the gains of reduced payroll costs. A survey by the American Management Association of 547 companies that had downsized during a six-year period found that profits improved for only 43.5 percent. For example, 12 months after substantial downsizings, the following firms were showing much poorer return on equity than 12 months before the layoff: Eastman Kodak, Zenith Electronics, Sears, Westinghouse, and American Express.

Downsizing can be self-defeating in several important ways. Although payroll cuts may reduce costs, they do not produce revenue growth. Also, a severely downsized business may be too understaffed to capitalize on a recovery. Downsizing can weaken an organization by making more profitable units pay for weaknesses in other units. Westinghouse Electric Corp. is a prominent example. In response to problems in its finance subsidiary, Westinghouse cut costs by laying off workers in financially healthy divisions. [18]

The aggregate impact of downsizings is self-defeating also because it weakens the consumer sector of the economy, making a business recovery more difficult. Between 1987 and 1992, 3.5 million workers were laid off in the United States. Many of these laid-off workers cut back on making major purchases, and other workers worrying about being laid off also bought conservatively.

Downsizing often results in expensive lawsuits, especially when laid-off workers claim they were victims of age discrimination. Defending against these suits consumes considerable time, and the legal fees run about $200,000 for each case. [19] Losing a lawsuit can mean paying several million dollars in damages, along with the threat of paying for a class-action lawsuit.

An obvious negative consequence of downsizing is that many people will be forced to leave the organization. They may face the trauma of long-term unemployment or underemployment because other organizations are also trimming down. A less obvious problem of downsizing is that it may not achieve its intended result—getting rid of the fat and keeping the muscle. When early retirements are offered, the company may lose some of the people it wanted to keep and keep some of the people it wanted to lose. Many talented managers slip out the door with a financially attractive severance program because they can find new employment or start their own businesses.

Flat structures, the consequence of downsizing, have disadvantages. Most of the great organizations have been built with pyramid-shaped rather than flat structures, so the traditional hierarchy must offer some advantages. One notable advantage is the presence of a large pool of well educated, intelligent, and resourceful people at middle levels in the organization. These individuals serve important functions such as providing useful input to decision making, searching for new opportunities, and freeing the time of top management so the organization can do more than respond to emergencies. In a flat structure, many managers are stretched too thinly, often dealing with problems outside their field of expertise.

Also, the multilayered structure provides for the development of future executives. Working as a middle manager or staff person gives the aspiring executive an opportunity to manage other managers and professional workers. Without this type of experience, it would be difficult to function effectively as an executive.

Guidelines for Action and Skill Development

During a downsizing, cuts should be made selectively to avoid weakening the fabric of the organization. Across-the-board cuts are particularly damaging because they may result in eliminating some of the best producers.

Downsizing translates into wider spans of controls for managers, requiring them to spend more time supervising people and less time doing analytical work. Team members will require emotional support because many people are overworked in a downsized firm. Effective delegation (unfortunately to an already overworked staff) of nonmanagerial tasks becomes critical.

Although delegation is important, learn to develop habits of self-sufficiency because there will be less help available to perform a variety of administrative tasks and supply you with information. In many instances, the personal computer becomes your information-gathering assistant of the past.

After the major part of the downsizing has been completed, top management should communicate a believable vision to which the survivors can commit. A clearly articulated vision will help mobilize efforts toward a strengthened organization.[20]

DISCUSSION QUESTIONS AND ACTIVITIES

1. How does the trend toward flat organization structures affect your future?

2. One reason flat organization structures have become popular is that the contribution of some managerial and professional activities has been questioned. What are some managerial and professional activities you think might be wasteful?

3. How do employee empowerment and work teams fit into a philosophy of a lean and mean (downsized) organization?

4. What is your opinion of the validity of using performance appraisal results to make layoff decisions?

5. Do you think companies will remain downsized even during times of business prosperity? Explain your reasoning.

6. Find an account of a successful downsizing in a newspaper, magazine, or journal article and bring your findings to class.

NOTES

1. Robert Harris, "Canadians Replace Layoffs with Voluntary Rightsizing," *Personnel*, May 1991, pp. 15–16.
2. William Patalon III, "Xerox to Cut 800 Jobs," Rochester *Democrat and Chronicle,* December 12, 1991, p. 1.
3. Robert M. Tomasko, "Running Lean, Staying Lean," *Management Review*, November 1987, p. 46.

4. Kirkland Ropp, "Restructuring: Survival of the Fittest," *Personnel Administrator,* February 1987, p. 46.
5. "America's Leanest and Meanest," *Business Week,* October 5, 1987, p. 81.
6. The Tom Peters Group, *A World Turned Upside Down* (Palo Alto, Calif.: Excel, 1986), p. 16.
7. Donna Deeprose, "Managing a Permanently Lean Staff," *Executive Management Forum,* April 1992, p. 1.
8. Philip A. Greco and Brenda K. Woodlock, "Downsizing the Organization," *Personnel Administrator,* May 1989, pp. 105–8.
9. Jim Spoor, "HRIS Can Make Downsizing Strategic and Fair," *HRfocus,* August 1991, p. 7.
10. Tomasko, "Running Lean, Staying Lean," p. 38.
11. Anne T. Lawrence and Brian S. Mittman, "Downsizing on the Upswing," *HRfocus,* February 1991, p. 14.
12. G. James Francis, John Mohr, and Kelly Andersen, "HR Balancing: Alternative Downsizing," Personnel Journal, January 1992, pp. 71–76.
13. Tomasko, "Running Lean, Staying Lean," p. 37; and Robert M. Tomasko, *Downsizing: Reshaping the Corporation for the Future* (New York: AMACOM, 1990).
14. Harold P. Weinstein and Michael S. Liebman, "Corporate Scaledown: What Comes Next? " *HRMagazine,* August 1991, p. 36.
15. Judith Evans, "Firms Increasing Flexible Benefits to Offset Longer Hours at Work," Rochester *Democrat and Chronicle,* November 30, 1992, p. 1.
16. Tom Peters, "Revolution Needed in the Organization," syndicated column, April 5, 1987.
17. Stephenie Overman, "Managing in the Leaner Organization," *HRMagazine,* November 1992, p. 41.
18. "When Layoffs Alone Don't Turn the Tide," *Business Week,* December 7, 1992, p. 100.
19. Arthur S. Hayes, "Layoffs Take Careful Planning to Avoid Losing the Suits That Are Apt to Follow," *The Wall Street Journal,* November 2, 1990, p. 1.
20. "Executive Gold," *Executive Strategies,* September 24, 1991, p. 2.

SOME ADDITIONAL REFERENCES

Abler, Paul G., and Robert B. Marshall. "Staying Afloat During Restructuring Storms." *HRMagazine,* October 1990, pp. 68–73.

Hendricks, Charles D. *The Rightsizing Remedy: How Managers Can Respond to the Downsizing Dilemma.* Homewood, Ill.: Business One Irwin, 1992.

Skagen, Anne. "The Incredible Shrinking Organization: What Does It Mean for Middle Managers?" *Human Resources Forum,* February 1992, pp. 1–2.

Tarr, Steven C., and William J. Juliano. "Leading a Team Through Downsizing." *HRMagazine,* October 1992, pp. 91–95, 98–100.

Tjosvold, Dean. "Foolproof Your Restructuring Plan." *HRMagazine,* November 1991, pp. 79–84.

Chapter Sixteen

Intrapreneuring

The five large companies described here each faced the challenge of fostering the innovative spirit characteristic of many small entrepreneurships. Each firm chose a slightly different method of achieving product breakthroughs by way of intrapreneuring—the existence of entrepreneurial behavior and thinking within a large organization.

3M. Arthur Fry, a Minnesota Mining and Manufacturing chemical engineer, was bothered when pieces of paper that marked his church hymnal fell out when he stood up to sing. Fry was aware that Spencer Silver, a scientist working at 3M, had accidentally discovered an adhesive with weak sticking power. Under most circumstances, low adhesion would be bad, but for Fry it was good. He reasoned that markers made with the weak adhesive might stick lightly to something and then would readily detach. Because 3M allows employees to spend 15 percent of their company time on independent projects, Fry began working on the idea.

Fry made samples of the light-sticking paper and then distributed the small yellow pads to assistants within the corporation. The enthusiastic reaction by the assistants gave 3M an impetus to begin marketing the product under the name *Post-it.* The product has became a legendary success with annual sales of over $100 million.

General Electric. Jacques Robinson was given the opportunity about 12 years ago to manage GE's video products division in Portsmouth, Virginia. One of his responsibilities was to expand its product base to include a long list of products for home information and entertainment. Robinson maintained an open-door policy for anyone with fruitful ideas. One person who took advantage of this policy was Howard R. Stevenson, Jr., a technical whiz since his high school days. He had spent his entire professional life with GE, most of the time working on radar.

Although not discontent enough to leave the firm, Stevenson felt stifled. He welcomed GE's offer to transfer him to Portsmouth. Soon after, Stevenson found a creative challenge. Ordinary TV sets are much less effective than monitors in displaying numbers, letters, graphics, and images from home computers, video games, and video cameras. Working at night in his cluttered home workshop, Stevenson designed circuitry that elevated standard television sets to monitor quality. The monitor became an immediate marketing success, and Stevenson's career has become rejuvenated. He says, "I like the atmosphere of taking risks, trying things."

IBM. Fifteen years ago, International Business Machines Corporation adopted the concept of independent business units (IBUs) that operated as separate organizations. Growing in number, the IBUs each have their own miniboard of directors. An independent business unit has the authority to decide on its own manufacturing and marketing strategy, usually without asking for approval from corporate headquarters. One unit is developing a new generation of automatic teller machines; another is building industrial robots.

IBM's most heralded IBU produced the company's personal computer. A dozen executives led by Philip D. Estridge established headquarters in Boca Raton, Florida, in 1980. They were given as much money as they needed and a mandate to get IBM into the personal computer business as soon as possible. Given this latitude, the group broke some of IBM's most hallowed traditions; for example, the group supplemented the IBM sales organization with retail outlets. To control costs and hasten development, the IBU bought most of its parts from outside suppliers (among them a South Korean company), rather than from inside IBM. The PC family, including the Personal Systems/2 (PS/2) computer, has become a notable success despite intense competition from PC clones. Its only setback was the poor-selling PC Junior, which was discontinued. The dozen people in the original PC group grew into the entry systems division, which now has over 10,000 employees.

Hewlett-Packard. Over 12 years ago, this well-known electronics firm awarded engineer Charles House a medal for "extraordinary contempt and defiance beyond the normal call of engineering duty." House achieved this distinction by ignoring an order from the founder of the firm, David Packard, to stop working on a high-quality video monitor with a giant screen. Despite the admonition, House persevered and succeeded in developing the monitor. The monitor is of such high quality that it has been by NASA and also in heart transplants. Early estimates were that the market for such large-screen displays would be only 30 units. Within three years, 17,000 of them had been sold for gross revenues of $35 million.[1]

Xerox Corporation. Faced with the challenge of speeding up the development of new products, Xerox decided to sequester relatively small groups of employees in five research and development groups throughout the United States and Canada. In the Rochester, New York, "skunk works" a group of people work on special, secret products with code names like Chainsaw,

Bulldog, and Yardbird. It is called a *skunk works* because it's off in a corner, where malodorous (or devious) things are often hidden. The Rochester skunk works employs fewer than 100 people from backgrounds in engineering, research, marketing, and administrative services. From the outside, the skunk works resembles a dilapidated factory or an abandoned building. Much of the building's interior is also in a state of disrepair. The facility has been the birthplace of four major photocopiers. Two of these copiers have generated close to $4 billion in sales since 1978.

The skunk works spawned a new company that in 30 months designed, produced, and sold the first desktop copier made in the United States in eight years. It is used mostly for engineering applications. Because it is one yard wide, the copier was given the code name Yardbird.

Nearly 20 patents were achieved in developing the Yardbird. It uses no more electricity than a toaster, can be installed in a trailer at a construction site, makes copies on any kind of paper or vellum, will take copies from a variety of sources, and makes copies of copies. It can make copies a yard wide and indefinitely long—the longest one so far being 500 feet. Xerox sells the copier throughout the world. By one estimate, there's a market for as many as 100,000 machines. If this estimate were accurate, Yardbird would generate $360 million in revenue.

An industry analyst, Brian Fernandez, said: "The engineering copiers in the past have been so big and so expensive and so fixed-place. The Yardbird is smaller than anything I've heard of. I think Xerox did a fairly good job on the machine. It's different. It's unique. It demonstrates once again why the company needs a skunk works." [2]

ORGANIZATIONAL ACTIONS TO FOSTER INTRAPRENEUR-SHIP

The different aspects of intrapreneuring practiced by the five companies just described are but a sampling of steps taken by companies to encourage entrepreneurial behavior for the good of the firm. We describe 10 principles of intrapreneurship, or steps organizations are taking to encourage entrepreneurial behavior. Although Gifford Pinchot III coined the term *intrapreneurship*, the same type of activity has been referred to in the past as *divisional incorporation*, *subsidized startups*, and *venture task teams*. And intrapreneurs were labeled *corporateurs*. [3]

Develop a New Culture or Modify the Present One

The corporate culture must be compatible with intrapreneuring. Above all, authoritarian beliefs have to give way to a permissiveness that grants intrapreneurs the freedom to do things their way. The Foresight Group (founders of the training program called Sweden's School for Intrapreneurs) contends that most companies have to develop a new culture. This does not mean the existing values and myths or the traditional heroes of the old culture must be abandoned. "Rather, new values, models, and myths must be given priority. Bureaucrat and controller must coexist with, or give way to, designer and entrepreneur."[4]

When Pacific Telesis needed to develop new information services, it drew up six corporate commitments dedicated to implementing the plans at all levels. One reads like an intrapreneurial manifesto and specifies cultural values:

> We are creative, can-do people. We have the freedom to act and innovate to meet our customers' needs as though each of us owned the business. Strategy guides our direction; sound judgment guides our execution. We take prudent risks and are accountable for our actions.[5]

In most situations, revamping the organizational culture will be difficult. A realistic approach is to modify those aspects of the culture that might inhibit intrapreneurship.

Identify Intrapreneurs Early in their Careers.   Intrapreneurs are considered to be self-selecting; the organization cannot appoint people to this role. Intrapreneurs are typically people who are in the creative throes of a new idea and also have the energy and determination to pursue their own vision. They will typically follow this pursuit with or without the company's permission. Because intrapreneurs may arise from any part of the organization, a mechanism such as a multidisciplinary review board should exist to identify them as soon as possible.

Once the intrapreneurs have been identified, a formal system of assigning each one to a senior executive champion may prove valuable. The champion, or sponsor, helps facilitate the path for the intrapreneur administratively to help obtain budget approvals and other resources.

Conduct Innovative Work in Small Organizational Units.   Skunk works illustrates the important entrepreneurial principle of conducting innovative work in small organizational units. As Bill Gates, the founder of Microsoft Corp., has observed, small units are more flexible than large units in terms of spawning new opportunities.[6] The benefits of conducting innovative work in small organizational units is so well accepted that it would be unusual to find a large organization that ignores this approach. Tom Peters makes this comment about the prevalence of skunk works:

> It would not be difficult to argue that 3M, Hewlett-Packard, Digital Equipment, and Johnson & Johnson today are nothing more than collections of skunk works. I think all the evidence says that if you want to get down to the optimal size, you'll get down to the 100-person unit. The companies that push the farthest in that direction are going to be the next wave of successful companies."[7]

The decentralized units for innovation function as multidisciplinary project teams that report to an intrapreneur. It is not necessary for all the team members to be intrapreneurs, but they must be able to function in an ambiguous and dynamic environment. Team members are relieved of their regular responsibilities for the life of the project. If the project becomes successful enough to form a separate division of the company, project members usually have the option of being permanently assigned to the new division.

Reduce Physical Barriers to Interaction.   To foster intrapreneurial behavior, it helps to reduce physical barriers that could inhibit the human interaction that leads to cross-fertilization of ideas. One of Hewlett-Packard's tactics is to implement its "next bench" philosophy. "People are not isolated behind office walls," says Kitty Woodall, a communications manager. "People work in common areas by design. We go out of the way to encourage a rubbing of elbows and an exchange of ideas." [8]

Lounges for technical personnel are another way of facilitating oral interaction that could lead to the development of innovative ideas. Eliminating office walls has two potential disadvantages: (1) Many professionals will not work for an organization in which they have no hope of having a private office, and (2) innovation often requires some periods of intense concentration not possible while working in a bullpen-style office.

Grant Freedom to the Intrapreneur.   The most consistently espoused principle of intrapreneurship is that the intrapreneur needs freedom to operate effectively. *Freedom* in this context refers to such things as freedom to fail, freedom from budget restraints, freedom to make decisions without the usual multilevel approvals, freedom to pursue one's own interests, and freedom from deadlines. David Taylor, who headed the development and production of a copier developed at the Xerox skunk works, says: "Freedom is very important in this kind of environment. The freedom of the environment allows people to do things much more openly." Another employee at the same skunk works commented, "We try to create and nurture an environment where people don't feel intimidated by failure." [9]

Multilevel approvals restrict the freedom of the intrapreneur, and they also result in a distorted perception of the concept for which approval is sought. The top decision maker hears only translations of the intrapreneur's original concept and will not have the opportunity to hear the intrapreneur's enthusiastic pitch. To circumvent this problem, Pinchot recommends that a direct relationship be established between the doer and the approver. Intrapreneurs must be able to get face to face with decision makers. [10]

Allow for Some Corporate Slack.   Closely related to the principle of allowing intrapreneurs freedom is allowing slack or breathing room in resource allocation. As Pinchot observes, "When all corporate resources are committed to what is planned, nothing is left for trying the unplannable." [11] In practice, this could mean incorporating into budgets a fund for emergency allocations. It could also mean a flexible budget that overcomes the need for intrapreneurial begging or "theft" of corporate resources to pursue a new undertaking. [12]

Corporate slack can also mean the freedom to use a portion of one's time in exploring new ideas with an unknown payoff. Many organizations, including 3M, IBM, Textron, and Du Pont, allow some technical personnel to spend 5 to 15 percent of their time exploring ideas of interest to them. [13]

Avoid Traditional Controls. Tight control systems may be characteristic of a professionally managed organization, but they can also constrain innovation. It may be difficult to justify an intrapreneurial operation from the standpoint of a projected return on investment. Without the products stemming from an intrapreneurial unit, however, the organization may go out of business in the future. It makes sense not to deny funding to an intrapreneurial operation because it could not provide a convincing forecast of short-range return on investment.

Another type of control that should be avoided is transferring the old management structure onto a new operation as soon as it seems successful. A lesson in this regard comes from Exxon Corporation. After starting several new businesses in the 1960s and 1970s, the company proceeded to smother them with rules and regulations until they expired one by one. [14]

Create Changes in the Reward System. The organizational rewards should fit the preferences of intrapreneurs to keep these people with the firm. Insufficient, or the wrong type of, rewards are unlikely to decrease the effort of intrapreneurs. Rather than withdraw from work, the poorly rewarded intrapreneur will often become an entrepreneur—or an intrapreneur for another firm.

An effective reward for most intrapreneurs is the opportunity to engage in further intrapreneurial work. The more successful the intrapreneur is in developing new products, the more new products he or she is given a chance to develop. Profit sharing, or intrapreneurial pay, is another important reward for intrapreneurs. Although intrapreneurs may not be motivated primarily by money, they may look on profit sharing as a form of recognition and feedback.

Rosabeth Moss Kanter recommends that corporate employees who are responsible for new ventures should participate in its future profits. Most such pay plans pay the venture participant a base salary, generally equivalent to his or her former job level. In addition, intrapraneurs are asked to put part of their compensation "at risk." The percentage of their "ownership" is determined by the part they put at risk. Intrapreneurs under this type of pay plan would no longer receive the other type of bonuses and profit sharing they would have received in their regular job. [15]

Dual career paths are another recommended change in the reward system for intrapreneurs. Intrapreneurs may come from many different places in the organization and thus be promoted into the position of team leader or project head. After the intrapreneur starts producing, it may be advisable not to promote that person into a higher-level administrative position. It is unwise, for example, to promote an intrapreneur to a vice presidency that demands heavy administrative responsibilities, including extensive meetings. Doing so may limit the intrapreneur's opportunity to do innovative work. [16] A valued promotion for the successful intrapreneur might be to handle a bigger intrapreneurial budget or become the organization's chief intrapreneur.

End the Home-Run Philosophy.   Pinchot observes that many large organizations approach innovation with gigantic success as their single goal. The senior-level executives reason that if an innovation cannot be projected to reach from $50 millon to $500 million in sales within a decade, it cannot have a significant impact on growth or earnings per share. These businesses pursue innovation with criteria such as: (1) The business must not be risky; it must be based on proven technology and well-defined markets; (2) there must be no significant potential competition in the market.

This quest for a home run, rather than merely getting on base, is a mistake that establishes unrealistic criteria for innovations. Multimillion-dollar industries often began by serving very small markets. For example, mechanical refrigeration was first used on ships for exporting meat and later in food-processing plants. Even more convincing, the nonwoven business that dominates the textile market today began modestly as a $15,000 per year operation within Du Pont that sold lens wipers. [17]

Bill Gates observes also that many good opportunities in business lie within exploiting moderate-size markets. He says, "You can hit the home run. But somebody can become quite wealthy creating a $20 million-a-year company." [18] Similarly, large companies can capitalize on these markets through intrapreneurship.

Allow for Continuity of Responsibility.   Intrapreneurs should be allowed to continue with the innovations they have brought to fruition. Intrapreneurs are not merely inventors who are content to think of a brilliant idea and then turn it over to others for manufacturing and marketing. The intrapreneur typically has stronger interests in building an *intraprise* (an enterprise within an existing organization) than does an inventor.

INDIVIDUAL ACTIONS FOR BECOMING MORE INTRAPRENEURIAL

The presentation so far has focused on how the organization can foster intrapreneurship. For those interested in becoming an intrapreneur, it is also worthwhile to examine some skills and behaviors required of intrapreneurs. In addition, Skill-Building Exercise 16 enables you to practice the type of creative thinking required of intrapreneurs.

SKILL-BUILDING EXERCISE 16
A Grid of Possibilities

A problem facing many potential intrapreneurs, as well as entrepreneurs, is to identify which people might want to use their product or service and for what purpose. Enter the *Grid of Possibilities.*

Directions: Think of any new product or service, however farfetched it seems, and complete the following grid. Applications for your product or service might surface. Enter into the left-hand column all the categories of people who might use your product or service, such as accountants, engineers, homemakers, students, senior citizens, or computer buffs. Then enter the various attributes of your product or service, such as durability, aesthetic, large, small, washable, and portable.

Your breakthrough market and application will be found in a cell because it will pinpoint what your product or service can do for a specific group. For example, senior citizens might be interested in a shortwave radio (product) that is lightweight and durable (product attributes) because they travel frequently. Your product enables them to stay in touch with developments at home despite frequent travel.

Working in a team will give you the advantages of group problem solving and brainstorming. If stuck for a possibility, use one of these products for your grid: automobile that lasts 200,000 miles; business stationery that gives a brief verbal message when the envelope is opened; industrial packaging that decomposes into vapor within four months.

Product or Service: _____

Product or Service Attributes

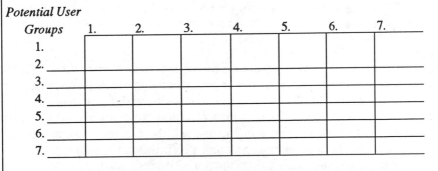

SOURCE: Based on an idea in "Breakthrough Ideas: Boost Your Company's Creativity and Blast Your Way to Success," *Success,* October 1990, p. 37.

Be Willing to Take Risks. Risk taking is characteristic of both entrepreneurs and intrapreneurs. Intrapreneuring is an insecure path that carries with it constant transition and possible failure. The innovation championed by the intrapreneur may fail, losing money for the firm and credibility for the innovator. Risk exists even when the intraprise succeeds. Once implemented, innovations eventually become standard company practice. Then the intrapreneur may feel compelled to develop another self-created innovative activity. A career path of this type does not lend itself to promotion to a senior-level executive position. [19] (If the intrapreneur is not interested in becoming a top executive, as stated previously, the risk here is small.)

The risk-averse individual is not suited for intrapreneurship. A plausible suggestion for becoming more of a risk taker is to begin taking small risks and see what happens. If you savor the rewards of success and can absorb pain from losses, your risk-taking propensity may increase.

Redefine Your Relationship with the Company. Beverly A. Potter suggests the way to become intrapreneurial is to redefine your relationship with your company. "Ask not what the company can do for you, but what you and the company can do together." However little freedom you are granted, you can perform a small intrapreneurial act. Maintain a notebook of possible areas for innovation. Formulate solutions to problems and steps to implement them. These problems could be related to product development, cost savings, or administrative efficiencies. When you identify a challenge that fits organizational goals, you might be able to incorporate it into your job function. Take the initiative to solve the problem rather than being told to proceed. This makes you more valuable to the company. The following scenario illustrates this approach:

> Bronwin McGarva, a manager in corporate financial communications, listened when Pacific Telesis publicized its commitment to attracting the best people and identified a need she could help fill. As a self-appointed talent scout and recruiter, she attends lectures, seminars, and conventions, making contact with speakers and trainers. Then, using her inside knowledge of project needs and the on-line communication system she oversees, she "markets" the speakers and trainers internally. [20]

Define a Staff Function from an Intrapreneurial Perspective. As the above example suggests, a manager or professional in a staff (support or advisory) position can sometimes function intrapreneurially. Lawrence P. Ball recommends, for example, that human resource professionals stop viewing themselves as an expense or burden. Instead, the human resource function should and can be a revenue-producing, profit-making function in its own right or in partnership with a line function. To accomplish this end, human resource managers should act as if they were running their own business with a bottom-line responsibility. [21]

An intrapreneurial perspective for a staff function would follow this logic. Assume one year's budget for the human resource department is $600,000 including compensation, administrative overhead, travel, and so forth. The human resource manager would then calculate how much money the department is earning for the company. Among the earnings might be: recruiting and training expenses saved from an improved selection system; productivity gains from rehabilitating a certain number of workers through the employee assistance program (EAP); increased sales attributable to a customer-service training program. As an example, a human resource manager at Zenith claims she gives the company a 110 percent return on investment.

Maintain a Professional Management Style. The entrepreneurs are known for their resistance to professional management techniques such as maintaining careful controls and delegating responsibility. Many entrepreneurs hire professional managers to run their operation once it achieves substantial growth. Many intrapreneurs also deemphasize professional management.

Because large, complex organizations prefer all units to be professionally managed, it is to the intrapreneur's advantage to practice professional management. In general, this refers to following the fundamentals of planning, organizing, directing, controlling, and rational decision making. Being both a professional manager and an intrapreneur gives the organization the best of both worlds. [22]

It was previously suggested that the organization should relax controls to accommodate the intrapreneur. It is a safer strategy for the potential intrapreneur to assume the organization will welcome traditional management practices.

Learn to Function with a Minimum of Structure. A successful intrapreneur has to learn to operate with less structure than a corporate employee in a more traditional role. Because intrapreneurships are not part of the mainstream of the organization, they will have fewer policies, rules, and regulations guiding them. Even the dress code may be relaxed for employees working at a geographically detached intrapreneurial unit. In some organizations, the budget for the intrapreneurship may not allow for the usual amount of staff support. To cope effectively with such an environment, the intrapreneur will have to handle ambiguity and a lack of structure.

Learn to Use Informal Influence Processes. Intrapreneurs face the same key challenge as other types of project leaders. Instead of using formal authority to get the resources and cooperation they need, they often have to rely on informal influence processes. As one skunk works leader said, "I have to charm people outside our group to get what I need to accomplish our work." In many innovative startups, the intrapreneur must cross departmental boundaries and rely on a network of allies. When the intrapreneurship is endowed with substantial support, such as the IBM group that launched the PC, informal influence processes are less necessary.

Learning to use informal influence well is important for another reason. Employees who are attracted to an intrapreneurial venture may not respond well to formal authority because they dislike hierarchy. In short, the intrapreneurial leader must rely more on personal than formal power.

The Case for Intrapreneuring

One argument in favor of intrapreneuring is that it has resulted in many products that have proved valuable to society and profitable to the corporation, and at the same time it has created excellent career opportunities for intrapreneurs and their staffs. Similarly, intrapreneuring gives large organizations the chance to be as innovative as small organizations. Furthermore, in a number of situations, being an intrapreneur is preferable to being an entrepreneur, as described by Pinchot:

- You have a burning vision that is inherently more intrapreneurial than entrepreneurial (for example, an idea that offers a way to improve the company business).
- You want to conduct new activities but your desire to stay with the friendships and security of the corporation is stronger than your desire for a chance at great wealth.
- Funding for your idea is easier to come by inside the corporation than outside.
- You want to try an innovation on the inside before risking your own funds.
- You are dependent on the company name or on its marketing channels to successfully launch your intraprise.
- You need constant access to the company's proprietary technology to stay competitive and to remain enthused. [23]

Intrapreneuring represents the best of all possible worlds for some individuals. As Albert Shapero has written:

Corporate managers who are sent off to head subsidiaries often react similarly to entrepreneurs to the exhilaration of being on their own. Our research suggests not only that many managers can be transformed into intracorporate entrepreneurs, but also that once a manager has had a taste of the entrepreneurial experience it is very difficult to lure the manager back to the corporate world. [24]

In sum, intrapreneuring can be exciting, combining the capacity and security of a large corporation with the freedom and innovativeness of the entrepreneur.

The Case against Intrapreneuring

One argument against intrapreneuring is that the organization could be hurt if too many corporate employees compete to become intrapreneurs. So many people would be spending so much time looking for interesting things to do outside of their job descriptions that the organization's regular work would not get done. (To counteract this problem, the organization could enforce a policy that a specific percent of one's time can be invested in pursuit of personal projects, such as done at 3M.)

Being too successful as an intrapreneur can create career backfire. Your new product may take business away from a major company product, which can be a political mistake. Such was the case with Andrew R. Heller, founder of HaL Computer Systems, Inc., and former IBM design engineer. Heller was assigned to design a new entry into the rapidly expanding engineering-workstation market. According to Heller's analysis, he was too successful in his venture. Company executives feared the machines might take sales away from IBM's mainframe computers. As a result, they took the division from him. Heller left the company soon after.[25]

Another problem with too much emphasis on intrapreneuring is that it glorifies the attention seeker, deemphasizes teamwork, and denigrates traditional management practices. This type of thinking is an offshoot of the current trend toward glorifying the entrepreneur and castigating the professional manager. In proper perspective, both intrapreneurism and entrepreneurism are one aspect of a professional manager's job. Organizations cannot grow and prosper on intrapreneurism alone; professional management is still vital to the long-term success of an enterprise.

Guidelines for Action and Skill Development

According to Oliver L. Niehouse, intrapreneuring is likely to work best under three conditions. First, the environment must be flexible. For instance, an intrapreneurial effort may have to be freed temporarily from bottom-line performance. Second, the decision-making procedures may need to be altered so intrapreneurs can present,
get approval for, and implement sound ideas rapidly. Third, intrapreneurs must be able to take risks without fearing the consequences of possible failure. Intrapreneurs should be reassured that their jobs are not on the line should they try and fail.[26]

The Foresight Group recommends seven initial steps for the organization that intends to embark on intrapreneurship.

1. Determine and carefully describe the kinds of entrepreneurial ideas and opportunities that top managers are interested in and willing to support.
2. Define the ground rules for the future relationship between the corporation and the intrapreneur.
3. Identify the amount of first-risk money top management is willing to invest and also possible future investments.
4. Specify the expected results from the venture, such as profitability and volume of employment.
5. Make management aware of the cultural values and rule changes that are needed to bring about innovation.
6. Inform employees about the upcoming new venture and its most important consequences.
7. Identify potential intrapreneurs.[27]

DISCUSSION QUESTIONS AND ACTIVITIES

1. How does the research and development function in an organization differ from intrapreneurism?
2. Is the term *intrapreneur* simply a modern synonym for inventor?
3. Why wouldn't large organizations be better off simply buying small companies with promising products rather than bothering to create intrapreneurships?
4. Give two examples of an intrapreneurial idea (real or not yet tried to your knowledge) not related to a new product or service. Enlist the help of a corporate employee if necessary.
5. Why not turn over the intrapreneurial function to employee involvement teams?
6. Should business schools offer courses or majors in intrapreneurship? Explain your reasoning.

NOTES

1. The first four cases are as reported in John S. DeMott, "Here Come the Intrapreneurs," *Time*, February 4, 1987; and "The Knockoffs Head for a Knockdown Fight with IBM," *Business Week*, December 21, 1987, p. 112.

2. David Dorsey, "Skunk-Working," Rochester *Democrat and Chronicle*, May 11, 1986, pp. 1F, 6F, 8F.
3. Mack Hanan, "Make Way for the New Organization Man," *Harvard Business Review*, July–August 1971, p. 132.
4. Keith Atkinson, "Intrapreneurs: Fostering Innovation Inside the Corporation," *Personnel Administrator*, January 1986, p. 44.
5. Beverly A. Potter, "Intrapreneurs: New Corporate Breed," *Business Week's Guide to Careers*, December 1985, p. 66.
6. " How Can Somebody Not Be Optimistic?': Talking to Bill Gates, Software's Billion-Dollar Man," *Business Week/Reinventing America*, 1992, p. 185.
7. Quoted in Atkinson, "Intrapreneurs," p. 46.
8. Potter, "Intrapreneurs," p. 66.
9. Dorsey, "Skunk-Working," p. 1F.
10. Gifford Pinchot, "Promoting Free Intraprise!" *Across the Board*, March 1985, p. 34.
11. Ibid.
12. Franck A. de Chambeau and Fredericka Mackenzie, "Intrapreneurship," *Personnel Journal*, July 1986, p. 43.
13. Pinchot, "Promoting Free Intraprise," p. 34.
14. Atkinson, "Intrapreneurs," p. 44.
15. Rosabeth Moss Kanter, "From Status to Contribution: Some Organizational Implications of Changing Basis for Pay," *Personnel*, January 1987, p. 22.
16. Atkinson, "Intrapreneurs," p. 45.
17. Pinchot, "Promoting Free Intraprise," pp. 36–40.
18. " How Can Somebody Not Be Optimistic?' " p. 184.
19. Potter, "Intrapreneurs," p. 71.
20. Ibid., p. 66.
21. Lawrence P. Ball, "Take Charge: Be an Intrapreneur," *Personnel Journal*, August 1990, p. 44.
22. Potter, "Intrapreneurs," p. 66.
23. Gifford Pinchot III, "The Age of the Intrapreneur," *Success*, January 1985, p. 60.
24. Ibid., p. 61.
25. "A Gallery of Risk Takers," *Business Week/Reinventing America*, 1992, p. 188.
26. Oliver L. Niehouse, "How-To Guide on Successful Care and Feeding of Intrapreneurs," *American Banker*, March 21, 1986.
27. Atkinson, "Intrapreneurs," p. 45.

SOME ADDITIONAL REFERENCES

Dyer, W. Gibb, Jr. *The Entrepreneurial Experience: Confront Career Dilemmas for the Start-Up Executive*. San Francisco: Jossey-Bass, 1992.

Kidder, Tracy. *The Soul of a New Machine*. New York: Avon, 1982.

Loveridge, Ray, and Martyn Pitt. *The Strategic Management of Technological Innovation*. London: Wiley, 1990.

Pinchot, Gifford, III. *Intrapreneuring*. New York: Harper & Row, 1985.

Polsky, Walter L., and Loretta D. Foxman. "Intrapreneurship: Charting New Courses." *Personnel Journal*, August 1987, pp. 116–18.

Russell, Peter, and Evans Roger. *The Creative Manager: Finding Inner Vision and Wisdom in Uncertain Times*. San Francisco: Jossey-Bass, 1992.

Appendix to Chapter Sixteen

HOW DO YOU RATE AS AN INNOVATOR?

On a scale of 1 (low) to 5 (high) rate your own innovation (and intrapreneurial) potential in terms of the qualities that most successful innovators and intrapreneurs have.

Innovative Quality	*Rating*
Vision	_____
Creative problem solving	_____
Action oriented	_____
Good health	_____
Emotional stability	_____
Self-confidence	_____
Persistence	_____
Motivated by achievement	_____
Hands-on involvement	_____
Persuasiveness	_____
Project-integrating skill	_____
Risk-taking judgment	_____
Realistic outlook	_____
Contingency-thinking expertise	_____
Street smarts	_____
Desire for freedom from controls	_____
Healthy lack of conformity	_____
Drive	_____
Commitment to quality	_____
Honesty and integrity	_____
Total:	_____

Interpretation:

If You Scored:	*Then You Are:*
90–100	Extremely innovative
70–89	Highly innovative

30–69	Moderately innovative
10–29	Innovative once in a while
0–9	Better off staying in your present job

SOURCE: American Management Association Extension Institute brochure, December 1992.

Part V

Human Resources Management Skills: Improving Human Potential

This part of the book describes human resources management programs to enhance human potential, improve productivity through increased job satisfaction, or help displaced employees regain career thrust. Chapter 17 describes how organizations help employees value work force diversity. Programs of this nature go beyond the minimum compliance required of affirmative action programs. Chapter 18 describes how organizations are helping employees balance successfully the competing demands of work and family. By achieving such a balance, many employees are more productive and satisfied.

Chapter 19 describes outplacement programs, a method of helping surplus employees find employment outside the firm. Outplacement programs are part of career development and are based on counseling theory and well-established techniques of conducting a job search. Chapter 20 describes telecommuting, a program for allowing selected employees to work at home yet stay in touch with the office via telephones and computers. Telecommuting has grown rapidly as many workers grapple with the problem of balancing work and family demands and attempt to minimize the hassle of commuting.

Chapter Seventeen

Valuing Diversity Training

A well-known computer manufacturer has embraced the strategic goal of valuing differences among people since the 1970s. One way the company implements this strategy is to conduct training programs to help managers and employees value differences. An excerpt from one of these training sessions is presented below.

Carmen Martinez strode into the training room with a confident stride and smile. "We've all had a chance to meet each other during our delightful buffet breakfast," Martinez began. "You seem relaxed and cheerful. That's a good sign. Yet you probably want to know why we are really here. Let me wear my executive hat for a moment. Our broadest purpose in being here is to help carry out the valuing difference vision of our division. Let me read it to you verbatim:

> Our vision is for the administrative services division to be an outstanding place to work through providing interesting, meaningful, and challenging objectives. In our workplace, differences are valued, and people are empowered to assume responsibility to develop and to creatively contribute to enable the company to become the premier supplier of information products and solutions in the world.

"Our mission statement means we want to keep being a great company where we welcome, embrace, and encourage differences. To some people, the term *differences* refers to being different in a couple of ways, such as being African American or Asian. But at our company, we mean that everybody is different. To truly value differences, you therefore have to value everybody. If employees believe that they are truly valued, the company will be able to reach its goals."

As Martinez looked around the room she saw nods of agreement and anticipation. "I want to emphasize again," she continued, "difference is broader than and encompasses more than race and sex or gender. Difference also includes but is not limited to the following: sexual orientation, physical status (being disabled or able-bodied), age, style, behavior, culture, veteran status, religious preference, marital status, dependent-care status, ethnicity and nationality, and organization and functions.

"At our company, we value a 56-year-old white male accountant as much as we do a 24-year-old customer service representative who is a woman of color. There is something wonderful about that middle-age man and that young woman. Value them both because they contribute to a beautiful mosaic called our work force."

Later in the training program, Martinez introduced the group to the *earliest-memory technique*. The participants were asked to draw pictures of both black and white people. "Don't be concerned about artistic ability," Martinez said. "We just want you to get in touch with your early recollection of differences."

"OK, OK," responded a middle-age Hispanic man. "Just give me my box of Crayolas, and I'll get to it." (Laughter from the group.) A young Native American woman said, "Please, Carmen, I can't go through with this. Any picture I draw will make me look prejudiced. I'm a horrible artist." (Louder laughter from the group.)

At first with good-natured laughter and then with serious intent, the group began preparing the drawings. Among the images depicted were the following:

- A black middle manager, male, who grew up in an all-black neighborhood in Little Rock, Arkansas, drew white police officers with German shepherd dogs and water hoses.
- A white executive, male, who grew up in an all-white neighborhood in a New York City suburb, drew a black housekeeper, dressed in a uniform, serving dinner.
- An Asian computer scientist, female, who grew up in an integrated neighborhood in Miami drew white children playing hopscotch with black children on a sidewalk.
- A Hispanic middle manager, male, raised in a mostly white neighborhood in San Francisco drew a black man batting a baseball in Candlestick Park.
- A black office manager, female, raised in a multicultural neighborhood in Toronto drew a picture of a smiling white man collecting the rent.

After the task was completed, Martinez instructed the group to gather in groups of five to discuss their drawings for 15 minutes. The participants were also told that a class discussion would be held following the small-group discussions.

COMPONENTS OF VALUING DIVERSITY TRAINING PROGRAMS

Company programs to assist workers in understanding and valuing diversity have gained in popularity for several reasons. A key factor is that the domestic work force in the United States and Canada has become more diverse, and will be even more diverse in the future. An oft-repeated prediction is that 85 percent of the people entering the domestic labor pool during the next decade will be women, minorities, and immigrants. Similarly, over half of the U.S. work force now consists of minorities, women, and immigrants. The internationalization of business has also created a climate where it is a business imperative for workers to appreciate and welcome cultural differences among co-workers.

Valuing differences goes an important step beyond affirmative action, or establishing programs to comply with goals for fair treatment of selected minorities. *Valuing diversity*, as coined by Copeland Griggs Productions, means "recognizing and appreciating that individuals are different, that diversity is an advantage if it is valued and well managed, and that diversity is not to be simply tolerated but encouraged, supported, and nurtured."[1]

Company programs to accomplish the similar goals of valuing diversity, encouraging pluralism, and enhancing cross-cultural sensitivity and awareness take many forms. The lead-in case described the earliest-memory technique. In the following pages, we describe additional components of programs aimed at valuing differences and working more smoothly with people of cultural backgrounds different than your own. Before reading ahead, do Skill-Building Exercise 17 to help identify how much you value diversity.

SKILL-BUILDING EXERCISE 17:
How Much Do I Value Diversity?

Rate yourself on your responses to the statements below. Use a scale of one to five to rate how strongly you agree with the statements, 1 being low agreement and 5 being high.

1. I regularly assess my strengths and weaknesses, and consciously try to improve myself.
2. I am interested in the ideas of people who do not think as I think, and I respect their opinions even when I disagree with them.
3. Some of my friends or associates are different from me in age, race, gender, physical abilities, economic status, and education.
4. If I were at a party with people outside my own group, I would go out of my way to meet them.

---

5. I do not need to understand everything going on around me. I tolerate ambiguity.
6. I am able to change course quickly. I readily change my plans or expectations to adapt to a new situation.
7. I recognize that I am a product of my upbringing and my way is not the only way.
8. I am patient and flexible. I can accept different ways of getting a job done as long as the results are good.
9. I am always asking questions, reading, exploring. I am curious about new things, people, and places.
10. I am interested in human dynamics and often find myself thinking, "what's really going on here?"
11. I can see two sides on most issues.
12. I have made mistakes and I have learned from them.
13. In an unfamiliar situation, I watch and listen before acting.
14. I listen carefully.
15. When I am lost, I ask for directions.
16. When I don't understand what someone is saying, I ask for clarification.
17. I sincerely do not want to offend others.
18. I like people and accept them as they are.
19. I am sensitive to the feelings of others and observe their reactions when I am talking.
20. I am aware of my prejudices and consciously try to control my assumptions about people.

Scoring: Total your answers. If your score is 80 or above, you probably value diversity and are able to manage people who are different from yourself—but you certainly have room for improvement. If your score is below 80 you probably experience much difficulty managing diversity and could benefit from further training.

SOURCE: Teacher's Trainer's Guide, *Valuing Diversity*® Part I, "Managing Differences," Griggs Productions, 302 23rd Avenue, San Francisco, CA 94121. Reprinted with permission.

Appreciating and Understanding Cultural Differences

A standard component of cultural awareness training programs is to improve participants' understanding of people from different cultures. This type of program is usually included in training for an overseas assignment, but it can also be adapted for building communication and understanding among a heterogeneous work force. After studying the type of information presented in Table 17–1, participants discuss their reactions and share their experiences.

In addition to the observations presented in Table 17–1, the trainer may introduce participants to the concept of *high-context* and *low-context* cultures. As formulated by anthropologist Edward T. Hall, high-context cultures are more sensitive to the surrounding circumstances or context of an event. High-context cultures make more extensive use of body language. Some cultures, such as the Asian, Hispanic, and African-American, are high context. In contrast, northern European cultures are low context and make less use of body language. The Anglo-American culture is considered to be medium-low context.

Most of the new entrants to the U.S. work force are high context. Members of management, however, tend to be medium-low context. Members of a high-context culture emphasize communication for interaction as well as information exchange. Members of a low-context culture emphasize words more than nonverbal behavior. [2] When people understand these differences in communication patterns, they can communicate more readily with each other.

It is important to recognize individual differences among people from the same cultural group. For example, not all Americans are impatient negotiators and not all Asians are modest about describing their accomplishments.

TABLE 17-1 Cultural Mistakes to Avoid in Selected Countries

- Insisting on getting down to business quickly in most countries outside the United States. Building a social relationship precedes closing a deal in most countries.
- Shaking hands with or hugging Asians in public. Asians consider these practices to be offensive.
- Writing on the business card of a Japanese business person. Japanese consider this insulting, much like writing across a person's photograph.
- Not interpreting "We'll consider it" as a "no" when spoken by a Japanese businessperson. Japanese negotiators mean "no" when they say, "We'll consider it."
- Giving small gifts to Chinese when conducting business. Chinese people are offended by these gifts.
- Not giving small gifts to Japanese when conducting business. Japanese people are offended by not receiving these gifts.
- Pressuring an Asian job applicant or employee to brag about personal accomplishments. Boasting about his or her professional achievements makes Asians feel self-conscious. They prefer to let the record speak for itself.
- Having a manager appearing in shirtsleeves at a business meeting in Germany. Germans believe that a person is not exercising proper authority when he or she appears at a meeting in shirtsleeves.
- Being overly rank-conscious in Scandinavia. Scandinavians pay relatively little attention to a person's place in the hierarchy.
- Appearing perturbed when somebody shows up late for a meeting in most countries outside the United States.
- Greeting a French customer or other business contact for the first time in a French-speaking country and saying, "Glad to meet you." French is a

polite language. It is preferable to say, "Glad to meet you, sir (or madame, ms, or miss).

SOURCE: Several of the above errors are based on Sandra Thierderman,"Overcoming Cultural and Language Barriers," *Personnel Journal*, December 1988, pp. 38–40; and Sylvia Overnoy, "Cet Été, Je Pars Toute Seule," *Cosmopolitan (Editions Internationales)*, Juillet 1992, pp. 91-92.

Developing Empathy.   An essential part of relating more effectively to diverse groups is to empathize with their point of view. To help training participants develop empathy, representatives of various groups explain their feelings related to workplace issues. The Snohomish County Public Utility Division followed this approach to help its employees understand and value co-workers and customers. [3] In one segment of the program, a minority group member was seated in the middle of a circle, while the other participants sat at the periphery of the circle. First, the co-workers listened to a Vietnamese woman explain how she felt excluded from the in-group composed of whites and African Americans in her department. "I feel like you just tolerate me. You do not make me feel that I am somebody important."

The next person to sit in the middle of the circle was a Muslim. He complained about people wishing him Merry Christmas. "I would much prefer that my fellow workers would stop to think that I do not celebrate Christian holidays. I respect your religion, but it is not my religion."

Exploring Cultural Assumptions.   Open discussion about exaggerated assumptions that some whites make about blacks and vice versa is another diversity training technique. The exercise aims to free the way people think about one another and help break down stereotypes. Group discussions following the exploration of these assumptions may enable relationships inside and outside of work to be based on authentic interpersonal communication rather than on distrust of differences. Following are some of the assumptions explored in this technique that block authentic relationships.

Stereotyped assumptions some whites make:

Blacks will always welcome and appreciate being included in white society.

Skin color is important in interpersonal relations.

Open recognition of color may embarrass blacks.

Blacks are trying to use whites.

White society is superior to black society.

Liberal whites are free of racism.

All blacks are alike in their attitudes and behavior.

Blacks must be controlled.

Stereotyped assumptions some blacks make:

All whites are alike.

There are no whites with strong feelings of kinship toward each other.

Whites have all the power.

Whites are united in their attitudes toward blacks.

All whites are racists.

Whites must deal on black terms. [4]

The program participants then explore each assumption to examine its validity and to determine if the assumption is blocking relationships between blacks and whites. In one training session, data were presented indicating that many black entrepreneurs and corporate executives control substantial power. Several others in the group presented examples of white people they knew who had African-American bosses. The assumption that "whites have all the power" was therefore challenged.

Using Consulting Pairs.   Approximately a dozen Fortune 500 companies are resolving interpersonal problems among diverse cultural groups by use of Consulting Pairs. The program, created by the consulting firm of Pope & Associates, trains employees from diverse backgrounds to resolve disputes and enhance cultural sensitivity. Consulting Pairs function as on-the-job diversity training.

Management selects 15 or 20 employees chosen from a group, of volunteers to represent a mix of sexes, races, ethnic groups, and job descriptions. The group receives intensive training on how cultural backgrounds shape attitudes and perspectives. In addition, cultural explanations are provided for certain types of behavior. One issue explored is *protective hesitation,* a phenomenon in which women and minorities hesitate to ask questions to avoid stereotypes about being poorly informed. By hesitating to ask questions, they may be slow to learn a new job.

Another Consulting Pairs activity involved the followed scenario: He was a black engineer eager to learn the commercial end of the business. His new boss was a white marketer, eager to teach. Conflict erupted between the two. "He questioned everything I did," reflected the engineer. "I was sure he was racist." Monsanto used a Consulting Pair to salvage the relationship. The Pair consisted of two employees who matched the racial and educational backgrounds of the engineer and the marketer. The Pair concluded the problem was marketing versus engineering, not black versus white. "Only another marketer would have spotted that my boss was trying to make me think creatively," the engineer said. "And only another black person could have persuaded me I was wrong about racism." [5]

Forming Book Discussion Groups.   Another program for valuing differences is to hold discussion groups about books dealing with cultural diversity. The discussion groups are held on company time. One firm, Web Converting Co. of Dallas, Texas, also allocates company time for reading. One approach to conducting book discussion groups is to assign workers novels that depict the struggles of people assimilating into a new culture and being accepted by peers. Another approach is for workers to read nonfiction books dealing with workplace diversity. The purpose is to provoke constructive discussion about the attitudes of people that can affect job performance. [6]

The subject matter of the book serves as a launching point to discuss personal experiences. For example, an Asian American might read *The Incorporation of Eric Chung* by Steve C. Lo. The novel tells the story of a young Taiwanese man who immigrates to the United States, and how he deals with the language barrier and a myriad of cultural barriers as well. The Asian American would then explain to the group some of the barriers he perceives in the workplace. In the process, other members of the discussion group might empathize with the Asian American, and he might realize that some of the barriers he perceived are imagined.

Maintaining an On-Line Diversity Calendar.   To heighten employee awareness about valuing differences, Digital maintains an on-line diversity calendar. The calendar is an electronic mail listing of valuing diversity events and related announcements provided by the valuing diversity office. An event might be a talk, film, discussion group, or seminar. A sampling of two recent listings follow:

DATE: Friday, October 2   SITE: Maynard, MA
PLACE: Personnel Conference Room   TIME: 12:00–1:30 p.m.

"Pink Triangles" is a documentary exploring prejudice against lesbians and gay men. The film documents homophobia and shows some of its roots and current manifestations. The film enables the audience to experience the oppression homosexuals experience and helps viewers to move beyond their own stereotypes and lack of information.

SPONSOR: PKO Cluster Valuing Diversity Team
AUDIENCE: All employees welcome. Bring your lunch!
CONTACT: For additional information contact Kendra Theriault,
             DTN 223-3728 or FDCVO6: : THERIAULT

DATE: Tuesday, October 27   SITE: Hudson, MA (HLO2)
PLACE: Cafeteria Annex   TIME:9:00 a.m.–12:00 p.m.
EVENT: "Working Together,
          Winning Together"

The objective of this workshop is to recast the subject of gender bias in a manner that does not accuse men or promote self-blame among women. We will focus on the creation of new communication channels and ways of men and women relating to each other in professional environments.

SPONSOR: Departmental Systems, Software, and SME Semiconductor
Operations

CONTACT: REGISTRATION REQUIRED. Send Name, Node, DTN: and
Affiliation to SHARE: SEMINARS, or call Janet Barry at DTN:
225-5536

THE CASE FOR AND AGAINST PROGRAMS FOR VALUING DIFFERENCES

A convincing argument for training in valuing diversity is that it contributes to harmony in an increasingly diverse workplace. Another reason is that these programs contribute toward ethical ends: egalitarianism is inherently good while discrimination is inherently evil. Programs for valuing differences are also worthwhile because they enhance productivity by reducing turnover. At Corning Glass Works, twice as many female and minority employees as males resigned between 1980 and 1987. The high turnover carried an annual cost of between $2 million and $4 million for hiring and training new employees. According to Dawn Cross, the Corning corporate director of diversity, the high turnover was caused by poor interracial communication among employees.

After Corning began mandatory antiracism training for all salaried employees in 1987, turnover dropped dramatically. Since 1987, the attrition rate for African Americans dropped from 15.1 percent to 2.2 percent in 1992. For women, turnover dropped from 16.2 percent to 5.2 percent; and for other minorities, from 16.5 to 7.8 percent. For white males, turnover dropped from 5.4 percent to 1.6 percent. (Because turnover decreased for all groups, it could be argued that economic factors also contributed to better employee retention.) Similarly, Ortho Pharmaceuticals estimates managing diversity initiatives, including diversity training, have saved the company $500,000 in reduced turnover among women and minorities.

Robert Davis, a researcher at the American Institute for Managing Diversity at Morehouse College in Atlanta, believes that antiracism training increases profits.[7] Working together harmoniously allows for better cooperation, which helps achieve corporate goals.

Taylor H. Cox and Stacy Blake reviewed the literature on managing cultural diversity, which includes educating managers on valuing differences. Extrapolating from limited data, they concluded that properly managing cultural diversity can provide a competitive advantage. One of their arguments is that companies with the best reputation for managing diversity attract the best pool of women and ethnic minorities. Another plausible argument is that firms with a good record in managing cultural diversity are at a marketing advantage. *USA Today* provides a convincing example. Nancy Woodhull, president of Gannett News Media, attributes much of the newspaper's marketing success to a diverse cultural background among people who contribute to daily news meetings. [8]

An important argument against valuing diversity training is that awareness is not enough. Unless diversity training is incorporated into an organizational strategy for valuing differences, the training will not create much change. Barbara Jerich, director of a diverse work force at Honeywell in Minneapolis, recommends against training in valuing differences. She said, "Initially, along with everyone else, we did sensitivity training. But in hindsight, that should not have been our first step. Doing sensitivity and awareness training without a strategy and a time line can set you backward. That happened to us initially." [9]

Another argument against training in valuing differences is that it can be insulting and patronizing. Many members of the work force have been raised in a culturally diverse environment and have always worked harmoniously with people from other cultures. Such people do not have to go through training exercises to sensitize them to the importance of valuing differences.

Training programs in valuing differences can sometimes trigger ill will after members of diverse groups reveal their intimate feelings about each other. At one session, a white woman said she distrusted Asians because she thought they were devious and manipulative. It took several months for her to reestablish cordial working relationships with her Asian co-workers.

Guidelines for Action and Skill Development

Lewis Griggs, a diversity consultant, offers the following suggestions for an organization interested in starting a diversity program. First, there has to be a commitment from the top and strong leadership in relation to the program. Second, every person involved in the diversity program must begin with self-examination. We all must understand that our cultural identity influences our perception, values, eye contact, and body language. After achieving self-understanding, we can recognize that another person has a set of culturally determined behaviors.

Third, workers must realize they are already adapting to different people in different settings. People behave quite differently when relating to others at a sporting event, place of worship, or school.

Fourth, after cultural awareness has been achieved, the workers are ready to speak about their own cultural differences and to perform exercises such as the earliest memory technique. [10]

DISCUSSION QUESTIONS AND ACTIVITIES

1. Why are employees in the United States and Canada more likely to receive training in valuing differences than are their counterparts in Japan and Taiwan?

2. Several employers now conduct special events to recognize gays and lesbians. What contribution do you think such events make to valuing differences in the workplace?

3. The argument is often heard that because English is the universal language of business, it is not necessary for English-speaking people to learn another language. What is your position on this issue?

4. Employees at several organizations, including the U.S. Army Corps of Engineers at Vicksburg, Mississippi, are learning American sign language to help them communicate with hearing-impaired employees. What is your reaction to this approach to learning how to value differences?

5. Digital includes people with learning disabilities as one of the many groups whose differences should be valued. Is this a sensible idea?

6. How could a company evaluate whether a valuing differences program affects the bottom line?

NOTES

1. David Jamieson and Julie O'Mara, *Managing Workforce 2000: Gaining the Diversity Advantage* (San Francisco: Jossey-Bass, 1991), pp. 187–88.
2. Jim Kennedy and Anna Everest, "Put Diversity in Context," *Personnel Journal*, September 1991, pp. 50–54.
3. Suzanne Elshult and James Little, "The Case for Valuing Diversity," *HRMagazine*, June 1990, pp. 50–51.
4. "What Is Diversity Training?" *Human Resources Forum*, February 1991, p. 3.
5. Claudia H. Deutsch, "Pairing Up for Understanding," *New York Times* syndicated story, September 2, 1991.
6. Cynthia F. Barnum, "A Novel Approach to Diversity," *HRMagazine*, May 1992, p. 69.
7. Elizabeth Atkins, "Racial 'Wall of Silence' Could Hurt Productivity," *Gannett News Service*, July 19, 1992.
8. Taylor H. Cox and Stacy Blake, "Managing Cultural Diversity: Implications for Organizational Competitiveness," *Academy of Management Executive*, August 1991, pp. 45–56; and Shari Caudron, "Monsanto Responds to Diversity," *Personnel Journal*, November 1990, p. 77.
9. Stephenie Overman, "Managing the Diverse Work Force," *HRMagazine*, April 1991, p. 35.

10. Bill Leonard, "Ways to Make Diversity Programs Work," *HRMagazine*, April 1991, p. 38.

SOME ADDITIONAL REFERENCES

Baytos, Lawrence M. "Launching Successful Diversity Initiatives." *HRMagazine*, March 1992, pp. 91-94.

Ireland, Karin. "Mastering a Foreign Acquisition." *Personnel Journal*, November 1991, p. 4.

Matthes, Karin. "Workforce 2000: Attracting and Retaining Hispanic Employees." *Management Review*, November 1992, p. 9.

Rosen, Benson, and Kay Lovelace. "Piecing Together the Diversity Puzzle." *HRMagazine*, June 1991, pp. 78–84.

Rubin, Barry Louis. "Europeans Value Diversity." *HRMagazine*, January 1991, pp. 38–41, 78.

Thomas, R. Roosevelt, Jr. "From Affirmative Action to Affirming Diversity." *Harvard Business Review*, March–April 1990, pp. 107-17.

Smith, Bob. "Diversity with a Difference." *HRfocus*, December 1991, p. 5.

Chapter Eighteen

Balancing Work and Family Demands

A needs assessment conducted by an organization revealed it was losing about $1 million in productivity costs because of child-care problems. The results were measured in terms of absenteeism and benefits, but did not include tardiness and morale. To diminish these negative consequences, the human resource department embarked on a child care program and other ways of helping employee balance the demands of work and family life.

Patrick Prince is addressing a lunchtime group of male employees at the Los Angeles Department of Water & Power. As a counselor for one of the 12 fathers' support groups at DWP, Prince begins the monthly meeting by asking, "Does anyone have questions or comments about last month's meeting?"

The men at the meeting respond proudly by exchanging information about their children, who range in age from eight months to seven years. The fathers offer stories about enduring temper tantrums and teething, developing trust, and learning to talk. Prince responds by sharing his professional insights into parenting. He explains how this information relates to the everyday life of being a father.

Children are the subject of lunchtime conversation for many of the male employees at DWP. The fathers' support group is just one of the key components of the Fathering Program at the Department of Water & Power. And the Fathering Program is just one of the offerings of Work Family Services, an ever-expanding set of programs that address the work-and-family needs of DWP employees.

The Los Angeles Department of Water & Power is the nation's largest public utility. About 76 percent of its 11,000 workers are male. The diverse job titles at the utility include engineer, physician, technical specialist, biochemist, office assistant, and underground equipment specialist.

"It's very unusual to have a program, whether you call it a work-and-family program or a fathering program, where there's a high degree of male participation," says Beverly J. King, director of human resources at DWP. "Most people think of work-and-family programs as being dedicated to women. Our program is as successful in addressing the needs of male field workers, who may work on a utility pole in the middle of some street, as it is in helping women who have office jobs." [1]

PROGRAMS AND POLICIES TO FACILITATE BALANCING WORK AND FAMILY DEMANDS

An important thrust in human resource management is to help employees balance the competing demands of work and family, or personal life in general. A survey of 1,006 major employers indicated 91 percent offered at least one work/family benefit such as dependent-care spending accounts. [2] Although work/family competing demands have always existed, they may be more intense today because of changing demographics. The work force contains more working couples with preschool children, more single parents, and more workers who must provide for both their children and elderly parents.

Organizations assume workers will be more productive and satisfied if they can resolve conflict between career and family life. Programs and policies that help balance work and family demands also help recruit and retain competent workers. Furthermore, the initiatives described in this chapter can be viewed as part of corporate social responsibility. Before reading further, do Skill-Building Exercise 18 to gauge your sensitivity to work versus family conflicts.

SKILL-BUILDING EXERCISE 18
How Do You Really Feel About Employee Caregivers?

The exercise below is designed to assess your attitudes toward employee caregivers who attempt to balance the demands of work and family life: Rather than concentrating on "right" and "wrong" responses as you go through the list, instead try to understand and reflect on your answers. Then decide whether you should reevaluate your position on any of the 25 points. For each statement, indicate whether you agree or disagree.

1. Work is a means to an end. People earn money to get what they really want out of life.
2. The company exists solely to create profit.

3. The company does not have a responsibility to its workers.
4. The company has a responsibility to society.
5. Individuals should always be personally connected to the workplace.
6. Individuals should never bring family issues to the workplace.
7. It's acceptable to call in sick for a "mental health day."
8. It's acceptable to call in sick to visit a child at school.
9. Workers should be able to use a company telephone to call elderly parents in another city.
10. It's acceptable for a worker to use company time to phone a child every day after school.
11. Managers should overlook working parents' tardiness and absenteeism.
12. Exceptions at the workplace are a way of life.
13. When neither spouse wishes to stay home and raise children, they should not become parents.
14. Individuals who play an active role in parenting will probably not rise to the top at work.
15. A working mother is bad for children under six.
16. A working father is bad for children under six.
17. The employee's value to the company depends on willingness and ability to travel, work overtime, and relocate.
18. Managers need to be understanding in periods of employee-caregiver transition (such as the birth of a child or the illness or death of a family member).
19. Family responsibilities are more important than work responsibilities.
20. Men should be the primary wage earners in families.
21. Managers have a responsibility to help working mothers succeed at the job.
22. Managers have a responsibility to help working fathers succeed at the job.
23. Employee problems notwithstanding, "business as usual" is how offices should always be run.
24. It is almost impossible to balance work and family demands.
25. Corporations have no right to get involved in family concerns.

To develop skill as a manager sensitive to work and family demands, rethink carefully some of your more traditional attitudes toward the relationship between work and family. For example, if you strongly agree with questions 13, 20, and 25 and strongly disagree with questions 9, 18, and 21, your values may be too traditional to help employees to balance the demands of work and family.

SOURCE: Adapted and abridged from Renee Magid, *The Work and Family Challenge* (New York: AMA Management Briefing, 1990), pp. 20–22.

Work and Family Life Departments

The creation of a department of work and family life is a major initiative for helping employee caregivers juggle the dual responsibilities of earning a living and managing a family. The work/family professionals who manage these departments develop and help implement the type of policies and programs described throughout this chapter. On-site child-care programs are but one example. Another aspect of the work/family professional's job is to help managers deal with a situation when a conflict exists between a team member's obligation to the company and to the family. Loretta Reiman, the work and family resource counselor at the *St. Petersburg Times*, says:

> Managers want to be flexible, but they're struggling with real issues such as how do you deal with a staffer on 12 months' leave? They need options and answers. That's the type of information people in my job and others like mine need to be delivering.[3]

Marriott Corp. houses one of the most extensive departments of work and family life. The department operates a child-development center at its headquarters in Bethesda, Maryland. The center has the capacity to provide for 60 infants, toddlers, and preschoolers, and the openings are currently only available on a lottery basis. Parents can visit their children periodically, join them for lunch, and even watch them take their first steps. The Department of Work and Family Life at Marriott also operates such programs nationwide as a family-care spending account and work and family seminars. [4] Other firms with active work and family departments include Time Warner; AT&T in Morristown, New Jersey; Bank of America; and IBM in Purchase, New York.

Child-Care and Elder-Care Programs

Assistance in dealing with two categories of dependents, children and elderly parents, lies at the core of programs and policies to help employees balance the demands of work and family. (Classifying such programs as "dependent care" is inaccurate because these programs don't provide for dependent teenagers or spouses.) According to the survey, 66 percent of major corporations offer child-care services to employees.[5] At one end of child-care assistance is a model nursery school such as the child-development center at Marriott Corp. headquarters. At the other end is simply a referral service that helps working parents find adequate child care. Many companies offer financial assistance for child care, including pretax expense accounts that allow employees to deduct child-care and elder-care expenses.

On-site child-care and elder-care centers are especially helpful because the employee can avoid the hassle of driving from home to a day-care center and then to the job—and reversing the process after work. Some employers provide funding to a privately run center, while others manage the center themselves. Still another arrangement is for several employers to pool resources to establish a centrally located child-care center. Organization-specific examples include the following:

- The Beth-Israel Hospital in Boston offers on-site day care.
- Du Pont, the chemical company, supports nearby day care.
- Fel-Pro, a supplier to the auto industry, offers on-site day care.
- HBO, the cable television company, supports nearby day care.
- SAS, a producer of computer software, offers on-site day care.

The Stride Rite Corporation, a leading marketer of high-quality footwear for children and adults, also is a leader in providing child care and elder care to employees. The Stride Rite Intergenerational Day Care Center houses 55 children between the ages of 15 months and 6 years and 24 elders 60 years and older. The program is run as a separate, nonprofit corporation. About 50 percent of the funding comes from the Stride Rite Charitable Foundation and the balance from fees paid by parents and state funds.[6]

Flexible Scheduling

Flexible work schedules facilitate the balancing of work and family demands for people with many different lifestyles. Because of family responsibility, it is often inconvenient, if not impossible, to be at work at a specific time. For example, a single parent might need to bring a child for radiation therapy treatments once a week for 10 weeks during normal working hours. Yet the employer also needs a full contribution from all employees to remain competitive. In this instance, a flexible work schedule would allow the single mother or father to work later on the days of radiation treatment. Other flexible alternatives would be to take some work home at night or work in the office on the weekend.

According to the study, 53 percent of major employers offer flexible scheduling as a work/family benefit. Flexible working hours is the most frequent type of flexible work scheduling. A flexible schedule (or flextime) allows workers to modify their starting and stopping times provided they work certain core hours. In addition, they must put in a full work week, each week. A compressed work week allows a worker to complete 40 hours in less than five days, such as 4 10-hour days. For many working parents, a compressed work week is awkward because of returning home late for dinner.

Part-time employment is an attractive option for people whose income demands are light and whose career aspirations are low. For many workers, the opportunity to work at home for all or part of the work week is the most attractive option of all (see Chapter 20). Job sharing is a modified work schedule in which two people share one job, both usually working halftime. The two sharers split the job according to their needs, such as dividing up days of the work week. The people sharing the job might be two friends, a husband and a wife, or two employees who did not know each other before sharing a job. Each of the two job sharers typically has extensive obligations as a caregiver.

At a busy dental practice, *three* dental hygienists share one job, each working three hours per day. One hygienist has a set of preschool twins, another looks after two elderly parents, and the third is so involved in theater that his lifestyle does not allow for full-time work.

Flexible Leave Policies

Over 50 percent of major employers grant employees some type of parental leave to facilitate temporarily taking care of full-time family obligations. After the obligation, such as caring for a newborn, is complete, the employee returns to his or her job.

Merck, the pharmaceutical firm, allows for a leave of absence of up to 18 months for natural and adoptive parents. The policy includes a medical leave of six weeks for a natural mother. Child-care leave is unpaid, but medical and dental benefits continue for 18 months. After an absence of up to six months, the employee returns to the former position or a comparable one. Should the employee be absent longer, Merck attempts to place the employee in a position matching his or her qualifications.

Sprint, the long-distance telephone company, offers a family-care leave of absence. The leave is designed to support family adjustments and prevent high-performing employees from quitting. A Sprint manager granted a year's leave of absence to an employee who had given birth to her third child and wanted to expand her disability leave to be home with her children. The manager justified the long-term leave on the basis of the employee's excellent record. Said the manager, "I was also motivated by her peers, who adamantly supported the leave and shared my belief that we should do whatever we could to keep her."

The manager has monthly telephone conferences with the employee, and she comes to the office once a quarter. "We don't want her to feel alienated from the company during her leave. By designing a way for her to stay connected with the work environment and be updated on the changes taking place, we also maintain our relationship with her."[7]

Another example of a flexible family-leave policy occurred at an insurance company. An underwriter won custody of his preschool child after a long legal battle. The man requested, and was granted, three months leave so he could attend to his child full time during the traumatic postdivorce period.

The U.S. Family Leave Bill of 1993 requires companies with 50 or more employees to provide up to 12 weeks of unpaid, job-protected leave each year. The leave applies to any combination of family or medical leave. Under the proposed legislation, family leave is defined as the birth or adoption of a child or the serious illness of a child, spouse, or parent.

Adoption Benefits

Twelve percent of the major corporations surveyed offer adoption benefits, suggesting that this type of work/family benefit is gaining acceptance. Adopting a child would not appear on the surface to classify as a conflict between work and family. Several factors in the adoption process, however, can create conflicts. Adopting a child is expensive and can cost more than giving birth to a child. An employee, therefore, incurs the same expenses as a biological parent, who is reimbursed through insurance for most of the costs associated with childbirth. An adoption benefit often compensates the parent for some of the legal costs associated with becoming an adoptive parent.

Adopting, similar to birthing, also takes time away from work. An adoption benefit allows employees time off from work to handle time-consuming legal and administrative aspects of adoption that must be handled during normal working hours.

Trailing Spouse Benefits

A work versus family conflict can occur when one partner is asked to relocate, and the other must sacrifice his or her job to go along with the relocation. Several companies help an employee's spouse find a new position when the employee is relocated. The *trailing spouse* (the one who accompanies the relocated partner) benefit is important because there are approximately 36 million two-income couples in the U.S. and Canadian work force.

Hewlett-Packard offers in-house job counseling and up to $500 in job search costs. In rare cases, a company will find a place on the payroll for both marital partners. Some companies are debating whether a nonspousal partner of the same or opposite sex should also be eligible for the benefit.

Trailing spouse benefit programs provide an important benefit to the employer. Some employees would not relocate unless their spouse could find a new position. When both partners have a valuable skill or other outstanding credentials, the trailing spouse program works well. For example, an accounting professor at a university in Boston was married to an executive from an energy company. He was relocated to Houston, and she readily found employment at a university in the Houston area. The professor commented, "Although I could have found the job without the help of my husband's employer, their consideration and cash allowance were both well received."

Parent Tracks

For many managers and professionals, substantial career success takes too much time away from family and personal life. For example, many executives work 60 to 70 hours per week and are away from home about 10 nights per month. Many people would prefer a less demanding managerial or professional position that would allow more time for parenting and other aspects of personal life. Some of these people reach an informal agreement with their employers placing them on a parent track.

A person choosing a parent track is not assigned positions that interfere heavily with family responsibilities, such as one requiring frequent overseas travel. The trade-off is that the person is sacrificing some promotional possibilities and income growth. The person who makes the trade-off is said to be *downshifting*, moving down to a slower speed.

A growing number of single fathers (those who have custody of a child) are choosing the parent track. Approximately 14 percent of all single-parent families in the United States are headed by a father as custodial parent. [8] A sales manager explains how he chose the parent track:

> After I was awarded custody of Jennifer, I knew that I would have to modify my career dreams. I had been a district sales manager, and the signals were that I was headed for the top. But getting there and staying there would have meant heavy travel and many nights of not being home for dinner. Under those conditions, I couldn't be a very good single parent. So I made a deal with the company. I asked to be demoted to an inside sales manager position that was opening soon. I have the job now, and my income is lower. Yet I'm at peace with myself. My job is basically 9-to-5, and I'm there for my daughter.

Compassionate Attitudes toward Individual Needs

An informal company policy that facilitates balancing work and family demands has the manager decide what can be done to resolve individual situations. But the manager cannot make arrangements with employees that would violate company policy. Being sensitive to individual situations could involve such arrangements as allowing a person time off to deal with a personal crisis with the time to be made up in small chunks of extra work time after the crisis is resolved. Another would be for the company to reimburse a new executive for trips home to visit family members who have not yet relocated.

The authors of *Managing Workforce 2000* observe that a simple act of kindness can often resolve a problem. Diane Anderson, an administrator at a medical center, allowed her secretary Dianna Jourdan to take a nap in her office during the lunch hour. "Employees must work a nine-hour day, which includes a one-hour lunch break," says Anderson. "I needed to be mindful of this work-hour policy while at the same time being aware of Dianna's special circumstance. Dianna scheduled me out of my office every day between 1 and 2 PM so that it would be available for her to rest. The hospital supplied her with a mat, pillow, and blanket.

"By allowing her to take a nap during the lunch hour, we were able to stay within organizational policy while accommodating her special need." [9]

EMPLOYER INVOLVEMENT IN WORK VERSUS FAMILY CONFLICTS

The Case for Employer Involvement

Helping employees balance the competing demands of work and family helps an organization meet its social responsibility objectives. Substantial data have been collected indicating programs and policies for balancing work and family demands also help the firm financially. Day-care centers represent an important example, according to evidence gathered by John Naisbitt and Patricia Aburdene. Intermedics Inc., a Freeport, Texas, manufacturer of heart pacemakers, has operated a day-care center since 1979. Although the center's fees do not cover expenses, the company achieved a 9 percent decrease in absenteeism among its 1,000 employees. Furthermore, it has saved $2 million in reduced turnover costs. [10]

Hechinger Co., the building-supply retailer, believes the company policy of providing day-care service and allowing for flexible scheduling has paid tangible benefits. Hechinger contracts outside for day care and allows job flexibility including part-time hours and job sharing. A company survey of employees revealed that flexible scheduling keeps them from working for competitor stores. In one situation, a competitor opened a store across the street, and not one Hechinger employee joined the competition despite active recruiting. [11]

Another positive consequence of work/family programs and policies is that they reduce employee preoccupation with family problems, thus enhancing productivity. William Lee, the chairman and president of Duke Power, says, "No worker can be productive if he or she is worrying about a sick baby at home." [12]

Elder care is another work/family initiative that appears to pay financial dividends in addition to being socially responsible. According to one estimate, employers without elder care spend $2,500 a year for each care giver in the form of absenteeism and lost productivity. Elder care, however, costs from $50 to $150 per employee. Recognizing that 20 percent of the work force cares for elderly parents, those figures translate into an annual savings of $400,000 for an employer with 1,000 employees. [13]

The Case against Employer Involvement

A major argument against employers helping employees balance the demands of work and family is that such matters are primarily an employee responsibility. As one manager commented, "Why should we have to provide baby-sitting services for our employees so they can work for us?" It could also be argued that some work/family programs, such as parental leave, can be expensive. When the employee returns to work, the company might have to create a job for that person.

Another formidable argument against employer intervention in work/family conflict is that the contribution of such involvement has not been adequately tested. Most of the evidence in favor of work/family programs and policies is derived from casual observation by people who conduct such programs. The one rigorous study of the effectiveness of these programs found that their contribution is indirect. A field study was conducted of the impact of a company-sponsored child-care center at an electronics and communications firm. The firm had converted idle production space into a fully equipped child-care center. One hundred sixty-one men and 92 women who used the center responded to a survey about work/family conflict and absenteeism.

The results provided no evidence that on-site child care reduces work/family conflict and absenteeism of employed parents. An encouraging finding, however, was that employees who were more satisfied with the quality of child care—at the company or elsewhere—experienced less work/family conflict. When employees had lower levels of work/family conflict, they had better attendance records. [14]

Guidelines for Effectiveness and Skill Development

Ray Collins and Renee Y. Magid have prepared a five-step plan for employers contemplating family-responsive programs. A task force follows these steps to develop programs and policies that will help employees create a successful balance between work life and family life.

1. *Identify options or models.* Assessing employee needs for help with work/family conflicts is a starting point. Recognize that such surveys usually overstate the need for these programs. Supplement the surveys with focus groups and work/family seminars.

2. *Spell out objectives.* After specific programs and policies have been identified based on employee needs, the task force should address the objectives and expectations of management and employees. Specify such matters as the overall goals of each program and what benefits employees expect each program to provide.

3. *Plan for implementation.* Developing action plans for implementation should involve a coordinated effort by management, employees, and the union if present. Involving community agencies is another essential part of the action plan. Operation costs and a project timetable should be included in the implementation plan.

4. *Specify outcomes and benefits.* The task force should pinpoint specific benefits and costs of each program. Outcomes should be expressed in measurable terms such as "elder-care facilities for 75 people age 70 and over." The task force should project the program's impact on recruitment, turnover, absenteeism, tardiness, productivity, and quality.

5. *Prepare to measure.* The human resource information system should be updated to accurately track employee data such as absenteeism, turnover, tardiness, job satisfaction, productivity, and quality. The union should also be involved in measuring outcomes of the program. Surveys should be taken to supplement human resource record keeping, and the accounting system should be modified to include cost/benefit information about family-responsive programs. [15]

DISCUSSION QUESTIONS AND ACTIVITIES

1. How might family-responsive programs and policies be incorporated into the strategy of a firm?
2. To some people, pets seem as important as children. Should an organization extend work/family benefits to facilitate people taking care of their pets on company time?
3. Do you believe work/family programs are cost-effective?
4. What provisions, if any, should an employer make for employees who are still nursing their babies?
5. What demographic factors are making trailing spouse benefits more important than in previous decades?
6. Find a recent newspaper article or television show about a work versus family conflict. Bring the information to class along with a recommendation as to how the employer should deal with the situation.

NOTES

1. Adapted and abridged with permission of the publisher from Charlene Marmer Solomon, "Work/Family Ideas That Break Boundaries," *Personnel Journal*, October 1992, pp. 112–13.
2. "Work/Family Benefits on the Rise," *HRfocus*, January 1992, p. 22.
3. Michelle Neely Martinez, "Making Room for Work/Family Positions," *HRMagazine*, August 1990, p. 47.
4. Charlene Marmer Solomon, "Marriott's Family Matters," *Personnel Journal*, October 1991, pp. 40–42.
5. "Work/Family Benefits on the Rise," p. 22.
6. David Jamieson and Julie O'Mara, *Managing Workforce 2000* (San Francisco: Jossey-Bass, 1991), pp. 148–51.
7. Ibid., p. 153.
8. Aaron Bernstein, "When the Only Parent Is Daddy," *Business Week*, November 23, 1992, p. 122.
9. Jamieson and O'Mara, *Managing Workforce 2000*, pp. 155–56.
10. John Naisbitt and Patricia Aburdene, *Reinventing the Corporation* (New York: Warner Books, 1992).
11. Stephenie Overman, "Workers, Families Cope with Retail's Irregular Schedule," *HRMagazine*, August 1990, p. 44.
12. Kathy Cramer and John Pearce, "Work and Family Policies Become Productivity Tools," *Management Review*, November 1990, p. 42.
13. Art Durity, "Caring for Our Parents," *Personnel*, July 1991, p. 1.
14. Stephen J. Goff, Michael Mount, and Rosemary L. Jamison, "Employer Supported Child Care, Work/Family Conflict, and Absenteeism: A Field Study," *Personnel Psychology*, Winter 1990, pp. 793–809.

15. Ray Collins and Renee Y. Magid, "Work and Family: How Managers Can Make a Difference," *Personnel*, July 1990, pp. 17–19. Reprinted, by permission of publisher, from *AMA Management Briefing*, 1990, American Management Association, New York. All rights reserved.

SOME ADDITIONAL REFERENCES

Creeden, Michael A. "Employees and Eldercare: A Growing Workplace Concern." *HR Horizons (Business & Legal Reports)*, Autumn 1991.

Friedman, Paul. "The Work-Family-Person Connection." *The Pryor Report*, November 1991, p. 5.

Hanks, Roma S., and Marvin B. Sussman, eds. *Corporations, Businesses, and Families*. Binghamton, NY: Haworth Press, 1990.

"New EEOC Ruling Warns Against Parental Leave Discrimination." *Personnel*, June 1991, p. 6.

Smith, Kerri S. *Caring for Your Aging Parents*. Lakewood, Co.: American Source Books, 1992.

Zedeck, Sheldon, ed. *Work, Families and Organizations*. San Francisco: Jossey-Bass, 1992.

Chapter Nineteen

Outplacement Programs

A company that owns and operates several groups of department stores acquired another group of stores. After sorting out the need for executives, top management decided to terminate several senior managers. To help these managers make the transition to other employment, the company contracted with an outplacement firm. One of the senior managers who was terminated describes her experiences with the outplacement program.

"Life looked pretty grim for me that unforgettable day in November, just last year. I was one of the task force members to help our company to decide whether to purchase the midwestern group of stores. My argument against the acquisition was that we would be diluting our strengths by purchasing stores that would serve the same markets we were already serving.

"I thought we would be better off rejuvenating some of our existing stores. Maybe my negative vote put me on the hit list. Whatever the true reasons, the president told me over lunch that my position would be terminated December 31. He told me not to take it personally—I wasn't being terminated, just my position. Because they had no other position to fit an executive at my level, the only sensible alternative was to dismiss me.

"Unfortunately, at age 51, I still needed all my salary and bonus. With a condominium, two children, and a Cadillac Seville, I could not live on unemployment insurance or a minimum-wage job. I had to find another top-level merchandising position. The next few days were definitely the most difficult. I knew this was the worst possible time of the year to find a retailing job. Hiring for top jobs in the industry would be postponed until the results from the holiday season were known.

"The president told me that in addition to four months' severance pay, I was entitled to receive outplacement counseling at company expense. According to Gary (President Gary Moran), the outplacement firm had an excellent reputation. They would help me overcome the trauma of being without a job, and they would help me regain employment. I showed up at Knoll and Houseman the following morning to avoid wasting time becoming reemployed. When the counselor I met with mentioned that I looked nervous and preoccupied, I told him I was frightened and humiliated, thus making me appear nervous. After a brief interview with the counselor, I was ushered into a small conference room and told to take a group of tests and questionnaires.

"After taking the tests and answering the many questions about myself, I saw the purpose in what I was doing. The questions about my experiences and accomplishments were particularly helpful. They made me think about who I was professionally and where I had been. Up to that time, I hadn't given enough serious thought to the specific nature of the contribution I was making to my company.

"My counselor told me that my test results showed I was an intelligent, resourceful person, with no outstanding hangups that would prevent me from finding a new position at the level I wanted. He also told me that the questions I was forced to answer about myself provided the information I need to prepare a good job résumé. Though I was eager to start my job search, I was sensible enough to realize that you need a good résumé to get started.

"I was referred to a slick loose-leaf binder containing models of good résumés. I found one that seemed well suited to my career, so I modeled mine after that. A résumé specialist on the staff then worked with me to perfect what I had developed. Three days later, she had 100 copies of my résumé ready, reproduced on off-white paper.

"Next, I requested another meeting with my counselor. He had many out-of-the-office appointments, so I had to wait two more days. I was getting anxious about the days rushing by. I also knew that it would be difficult to get many job interviews with the holidays coming up soon. But I was reassured by other clients sitting around the office that a job search takes longer than most people expect. A rule of thumb I heard was that finding a job takes about one month for each $15,000 of annual income.

"My counselor told me he was pleased with my progress, and that I was now ready to hone my self-marketing skills. This translated into my practicing how to speak to people over the phone about job openings and how to conduct myself in job interviews and informational interviews. The purpose of the informational interview is to speak to people about my interest but not to actually look for a job. I was pleasantly surprised to hear how well I sounded on tape and how professional I looked on videotape.

"With my pile of résumés at hand and the practice interviews behind me, I felt ready to begin my formal job search. I asked my counselor where I should start sending my résumés. He told me that sending unsolicited résumés to prospective employers is too amateurish. Instead, he told me I should use a cover letter to accompany each résumé and send both to qualified leads.

"When I asked where I could find the list of qualified leads, my counselor told me that the leads would come through my contacts. My next assignment was to draw up a list of every person I knew who could conceivably help me find a suitable position or could refer me to someone who might help me. When I asked my counselor why I needed the outplacement firm if I generated my own leads, he replied: "Our job is to help you find a job, not find a job for you. If you are looking for leads, get in touch with executive search firms and employment agencies.

"My counselor's comments sparked an important insight. The outplacement firm was a resource for helping find a new job, but it was only one resource. Fired up with that insight, I then pored over classified ads in national and local newspapers. I used the many directories in the Knoll and Houseman library to come up with a list of executive search firms that might help me. I ordered another 100 copies of my résumé.

"My job hunting had now become a 45-hour-per-week job. After having mailed about 50 résumés, I checked back with my counselor to discuss my progress. He confronted me with the fact that I was taking the easiest and least efficient approach to finding a job. He told me to concentrate more on telephoning my contacts and setting up in-person interviews.

"I lined up six people who said they would speak to me. It felt so awkward asking professional acquaintances to help me find a job. I was supposed to appear cool and polished, but I felt like I was asking for handouts. A few people were cordial, but others treated me like I was wasting their time. The most painful part was watching my contacts squirm in their chairs and look at their watches.

"Each day I checked in at the outplacement office to see if there were any mail or phone messages for me. The first six responses to my letters of inquiry were basically form letters of rejection. Gradually I began to speak to other job seekers and Knoll and Houseman about my experiences. They were helpful in cheering me up and telling me not to be discouraged, that a good job was as close as my next interview.

"Thirty days went by with no apparent progress in finding a new position. I received about 25 more rejection letters from retail firms I had written to, either by an unsolicited letter or in response to a classified ad. No executive search firm I contacted showed any interest in me. Several of them told me that they would never touch an unemployed executive because their clients wanted them to find people at the peak of their careers.

"A promising lead finally turned up from an unexpected source. When my counselor practically forced me to contact everybody I knew, I scheduled a luncheon date with the former human resources director of our company. She had since taken a job at a dress manufacturer. She told me she had no immediate leads for me but would keep me in mind. As it worked out, the administrative assistant to the president of her company called me to say the president wanted to talk to me about a key job opening.

"I went for an interview the next day. The three top marketers in the company had quit together to form a competitive company. The president said he might be suing the three managers for breach of contract, but in the meantime he needed a marketing director in a hurry. I spent three hours at the company, visiting with the other managers at headquarters.

"With great enthusiasm, I requested another meeting with my counselor. He congratulated me on my progress and told me that since I would now begin to receive job offers, I should attend the negotiation workshop. It sounded like a good idea, so I did attend the next session. We were taught how to negotiate such things as equitable compensation, perks, an employment contract, and relocation allowance if needed.

"Two days later, the president did call me. He wanted to have lunch with me to carry our discussion one step further. At lunch, he want into detail about the company's strengths and weaknesses. He told me the company needed an executive with a retailing background because large retailers were their primary market.

"Toward the end of lunch, the president offered me the job at $5,000 more per year than I had been making. Before he could practically finish his sentence, I said I would take the job. I told him I would be thrilled to give the position my full effort. I wanted to communicate my true level of enthusiasm for the job before he changed his mind.

"The job has proved to be a challenge, and the firm had more problems than even the president knew about. The pressure is tremendous, but I feel I have grown professionally by getting executive experience in directing the marketing effort of a manufacturer. With this kind of experience, I might qualify for the presidency of a manufacturer in the future.

"I was frustrated with the outplacement firm and my counselor because it didn't seem they were doing much for me. Yet they did force me to use my contacts, and they helped me to develop insight into conducting a job search. Although my counselor seemed a little impersonal, I think he gave me the type of support I needed. He forced me to rely on my own resources. Talking things over with other job seekers was also helpful. Knowing that a lot of other good people were seeking new positions made my plight seem less humiliating.

"If I were forced to lay off a manager in my firm, I think I would refer that person to the same outplacement firm. Looking for a new job is too big a task to go it alone."

OUTPLACEMENT GOALS AND SERVICES

The outcome of the outplacement program described above was successful—the terminated manager was returned to appropriate employment. She did not simply find a job; she obtained a challenging position that fit her professional background. The major goal of an outplacement program, according to the president of an outplacement firm, "should be to provide a compassionate transition for employees who no longer fit the corporate picture—for whatever reason." [1]

In the current era of downsizing, many managers and individual contributors are terminated. In response, outplacement programs and services have proliferated. The outplacement field in North America has grown from about $50 million in sales in 1980 to 230 outplacement firms with total sales of about $700 million 1992. [2] In addition, some large firms offer outplacement services through a unit within the human resources department. It would be unusual to find a large organization that did not use outplacement when laying off many employees. The lead-in case about the merchandising executive provides an understanding of the goals and services offered by outplacement firms. Here we systematize the information and present additional facts.

Goals and Purposes of Outplacement Programs

The intent of outplacement programs goes well beyond the obvious one of providing assistance to job seekers. Outplacement goals and purposes include the following:

* Minimize the trauma of termination for employees and their families.

* Help terminated individuals quickly develop a positive outlook, thus channeling energy and activity into constructive pursuits.

* Provide a structure, sense of purpose, and direction for those who otherwise might be floundering.

* Encourage participants to fully explore their skills, interests, and alternative career paths before embarking on a job search.

* Enhance the probability of finding a rewarding and challenging position more easily, faster, and more economically.

* Help outplaced employees manage their dwindling supply of financial assets.

* Improve employee morale in relation to a layoff.

* Promote a positive public image surrounding the outplacement.

* Reduce costs associated with termination. [3] (Severance pay and insurance costs are lower when terminated employees become reemployed quickly. Finding new employment also reduces the chances of the firm having to defend against wrongful discharge suits.)

Services Provided by Outplacement Firms

To achieve the above goals, outplacement firms and internal outplacement programs offer a variety of services. Not all outplacement firms offer the same range of services, and the outplaced person's job level influences the number of services received. Higher-level managers receive the most services because the fees are the highest for these people, approximately 20 percent of the manager's annual salary.

Personal Evaluation.   A counseling-oriented outplacement service provides employees a comprehensive evaluation of themselves. Using personnel and psychological tests, interviews, and sometimes feedback from co-workers and superiors, outplacement counselors identify the job seeker's strengths and weaknesses. Many outplacement firms use licensed psychologists to conduct or supervise the personal evaluations. Job seekers are taught to identify their transferrable skills and professional goals so they can seek positions that will further their careers.

Job-Search Skills and Counseling.   A basic part of all outplacement programs is to both teach job skills and provide some emotional support. The two are closely related because the outplaced person will often need strong encouragement to persist in the job search when rejections mount. Job seekers receive coaching and information about writing résumés and cover letters, uncovering job leads, interview techniques, and creating a positive appearance. Should the job search linger, job seekers may require counseling to deal with their discouragement, despair, and self-pity. In some outplacement programs, job seekers give each other emotional support as they meet regularly to discuss both progress and problems, discuss the job market, and share tips.

The counselor is the heart of the outplacement service. An effective counseling relationship has two essential components. One is sympathetic counseling to facilitate the separation and includes knowing when to be supportive and when to push the client toward certain ends such as calling a former boss. Another component is giving strategic advice and counsel on conducting a successful job search. Understanding what qualifications employers in a specific industry are seeking is critical. [4]

Institutional Support.   Another standard outplacement service is institutional support in the form of a base of operations for conducting the job search. Institutional support includes office space, clerical support, and the use of telephones, photocopying machines, fax machines, and personal computers.

Job Leads.   Some outplacement firms supply job leads to their clients by maintaining contacts with employers and sometimes with employment agencies. One outplacement firm advertises to encourage employers to consider their job seekers when filling a position, as shown in Figure 19–1.

FIGURE 19–1 Outplacement Firm Advertisement to Develop Job Leads

---

WHY PAY
RECRUITMENT FEES?

FREDERICK LANGE AND COMPANY, A LEADING
OUTPLACEMENT FIRM, HAS MANY WELL QUALIFIED
SENIOR AND MIDDLE LEVEL PERSONNEL FOR YOU TO
HIRE. WHY SPEND $10,000 TO $40,000 TO FILL A POSITION WHEN YOU
CAN PICK FROM EXECUTIVE, MANAGERIAL, ENGINEERING, AND
SCIENTIFIC PERSONNEL, OF ALL DISCIPLINES AND LEVELS, AT NO
COST TO YOUR COMPANY? WE ACTIVELY HELP OUR OUTPLACED
PERSONNEL FIND NEW POSITIONS QUICKLY.

CONTACT:

COLIN FRAGER, VICE PRESIDENT
FREDERICK LANGE & CO., INC.
101 EISENHOWER PARKWAY
ROSELAND, NJ 07068
(201) 228-8999

Financial Planning. Many major corporations are adding financial planning to their outplacement programs. Financial planning has increased in importance because the duration of job searches has increased in recent years, making it necessary for outplaced workers to maximize existing personal assets. Financial planning takes many forms. The most frequent arrangement is a half-day seminar and an opportunity for an individual session with a financial planner.

Financial planning aims to help departed employees create a financial plan that includes decisions about everything from taxes to retirement plan distributions and insurance to investments. Some workers may also need advice about unemployment benefits.[5]

SOME RESEARCH ABOUT OUTPLACEMENT PROGRAMS

A paucity of formal research has been conducted about outplacement programs or services. The two most relevant exceptions included an assessment of participants' reactions to outplacement. Information about both studies is presented below.

Career Attitudes after Outplacement

Cunis and Nolan Inc., an outplacement firm, conducted a survey of 100 outplaced employees. It found that employees who go through outplacement become more realistic about their career potential. Also, they develop a greater awareness of business and its impact on their position. Forty percent of respondents said they were acquiring specific skills to enhance their employability; 36 percent reported taking courses to improve their skills; and 24 percent said they were making only a marginal effort to improve job skills.

When questioned about how they felt about the firm that provided them outplacement services, 20 percent indicated they now were more loyal; 38 percent indicated they were less loyal; 42 percent reported ambivalence.

Almost all of the employees agreed they were now more sensitive to company politics. More women than men, 69 percent to 56 percent, respectively, indicated a great sensitivity to organizational politics. The survey results suggested that both the experience of job loss and the job search highlighted the importance of being sensitive to political factors. A specific example would be developing good relationships with powerful people. Also related to political factors, the outplacement process dramatized the importance of networking; 68 percent of the respondents said they were now making more of an effort to maintain their networks. [6]

Company Outplacement Services and Their Effectiveness

One hundred companies of different sizes from a sample of 210 firms answered questions about their outplacement services and their effectiveness as perceived by participants. Fourteen specific outplacement services were offered by the responding firms. In order of frequency, they are as follows:

1. Résumé development.
2. Interview training.
3. Benefits counseling.
4. Skill and interest assessment.
5. Job market information.
6. Out-of-area job searches.
7. Mailings and phone calls to other employers about available employees.
8. Follow-up services (offering long-term help to those in need).
9. Career resource center (including employment information, office supplies, and office equipment).
10. Counseling on personal finance.
11. Counseling on family matters.
12. Peer support groups.
13. On-site unemployment setup.
14. Remediation and basic education (including highschool equivalency exam preparation).

Large firms tended to offer more services than small firms, yet small firms were the most likely to provide job market information. Large firms were more than twice as likely to provide financial or family counseling, and they were also more likely to provide a career resource center.

Company officials said management networking with area employers to develop employment opportunities was perceived to be the most helpful outplacement service (number 7 on the above list). Networking often consisted of managers in the outplacing company calling other managers in the area to explain that the employees being outplaced were of high quality. [7]

The importance of networking in conducting a job search has been emphasized at several places in this chapter. To personalize the importance of using contacts in conducting a job search, do Skill-Building Exercise 19.

SKILL-BUILDING EXERCISE 19
Job Search Contacts

Assume you must conduct a job search. Prepare a list of 25 people you know who could possibly assist you in finding suitable employment. Each person on your list should be informed about your job availability. Also, ask each person in your network for the names of two other people whom you might contact to speak about your job search. In this way, your network expands to 75 people. For convenience, place your network contacts into the following categories.

- Friends.
- Work associates from the past or present.
- Faculty and staff from your school.
- Athletic team members and coaches, co-members of athletic clubs.
- Church, synagogue, mosque, and community group members.
- Members of trade and professional associations.
- Employees of suppliers, professionals whose services you use, and the store managers where you shop.

Interpretation: If you are unable to specify 25 sensible leads, get busy networking. Cultivate new contacts before you need to conduct a job search.

The Case for Outplacement Services

To the extent that outplacement programs achieve the goals described previously, they contribute substantially to individual and organizational welfare. How well outplacement achieves several of these goals is worth noting. A major advantage of outplacement programs is that 85 percent of job seekers find a new position that is more satisfying and pays better than the one that was lost. [8] The potential savings in human suffering, misery, and even lives, are therefore substantial.

Outplacement programs are often cost-effective because they usually cut the time required for a successful job search in half. As a result, less money is required for unemployment compensation and possibly severance pay. If the length of unemployment is reduced, the employer's unemployment tax rate is reduced. However, if the dismissed manager is given a lump-sum severance payment independent of how long it takes to find a new position, no severance money is saved.

Outplacement services are also beneficial because they provide many displaced workers with insights they can use in adding new momentum to their careers. One outplaced executive said, "The outplacement counselor helped me realize that I had lost two key jobs because my thinking is so rigid. Once my mind was made up, I blocked out any new evidence that might make me rethink my position."

The Case against Outplacement Services

Despite their merits, outplacement programs have received considerable criticism. Above all, the contribution of outplacement services may be overstated. Although they typically claim an 85 percent success rate, this figure might be inflated for two reasons. First, outplacement services often avoid taking on the most difficult-to-place managers, thus decreasing their chances of lack of placement. [9] Second is the issue of how much an outplacement service contributes beyond what job seekers could accomplish without the service. The success rate of dismissed managers in finding new employment on their own might not be significantly different from 85 percent. Some people who have been through outplacement believe they did most of the tough part on their own.

A recent survey of companies using outplacement firms indicated fairly low performance ratings of the services. On a scale of 1 to 5, with 5 indicating superior performance, the average rating was 3.17, slightly better than "average performance." Thirty-five percent of the respondents ranked cost as the biggest complaint, and 33 percent ranked the "gap between expectation and actual performance" as another major complaint. Based on their dissatisfaction, only one in eight respondents said they would increase use of outplacement firms. [10]

Another concern about some outplacement firms is the qualifications of the counselors. Many of them receive just a few hours of training to be counselors, and they attempt to be counselors while spending most of their efforts bringing in new accounts. [11] Few outplacement counselors are licensed mental-health practitioners. Lacking such credentials, they should not be dealing with such important issues as helping clients plan a comeback. Some people referred to outplacement services require psychological counseling to overcome self-defeating behavior. (In their defense, many outplacement firms do make referrals when dealing with people who are emotionally upset.)

A final important criticism of outplacement is that the services are too general. The counselors lack the intimate knowledge of specific industries that will give the job seeker a needed edge. Specific industry knowledge can help a person find a fit between his or her credentials and peculiar demands of an industry.[12] For example, a counselor pointed out to an information systems specialist that her knowledge of English and Spanish could help her translate computer programs from English into Spanish. The counselor, of course, was knowledgeable about the software field.

Guidelines for Action and Skill Development

In choosing an outplacement firm for your organization or for yourself, recognize that a program tailored to the needs of the individual candidate is the most likely to be effective. For example, a highly introverted job seeker may need to develop interview skills before being thrust into actual job interviews.

Another important way to tailor an outplacement program, according to Lewis Newman, is for the counselor to be an expert on executives, recruiters, organizations, and positions within the candidate's industry. Such expertise will give the candidate an edge over competing job seekers. [13]

Should your organization refer you for outplacement services, do not be humiliated. Being dismissed at least once during a managerial career has become common.

DISCUSSION QUESTIONS AND ACTIVITIES

1. How could a human resources department demonstrate the cost-effectiveness of an outplacement program?

2. Is it justifiable to offer outplacement as an employee benefit when it is used by so few people, yet the cost is indirectly absorbed by other employees?

3. If large organizations continue to remain lean and mean, where are all these outplaced managers finding employment?

4. If you were a hiring manager, would you look to job seekers from an outplacement firm as a source of management talent? Why or why not?

5. When a company offers outplacement services, executives typically receive a full range of services, while lower-ranking workers may be limited to group counseling and seminars for outplacement. Is this fair?

6. James Challenger, the man who founded the outplacement field, contends that offering job seekers office space and personal evaluations is counter-

productive. Instead, he says, job seekers should be out on personal interviews. What is your opinion?

7. Through library research and talking to people, derive an estimate of the current average time it takes managers to find a new job. Report your findings to the class.

NOTES

1. Richard E. Miller, "Outplacement Myths Unlock the Mystery of Its Ineffectiveness," *Personnel Journal*, January 1987, p. 26.
2. Extrapolated from 1991 data in Peter Crowden, "Outplacement Services Assessment," *HRMagazine*, September 1992, p. 69.
3. Brochure from Drake Beam Morin, Inc., 1992; and Gilbert Zoghlin, "Financial Planning Takes Lead as Outplacement Service," *Personnel*, May 1991, p. 14.
4. Miller, "Outplacement Myths," p. 30.
5. Zoghlin, "Financial Planning Takes Lead," p. 14.
6. "Career Attitudes Change for the Better after Outplacement," *HRfocus*, March 1992, p. 19.
7. Don Lee Bohl, ed., *Responsible Reductions in Force,* an American Management Association Research Report on Downsizing and Outplacement (New York: AMACOM, 1987), pp. 60–83.
8. John Stodden, "Outplacement: Starting Over after You're Fired," *Business Week's Guide to Careers*, September 1985, p. 31.
9. Ibid., p. 33.
10. Genie Soter Capowski, "Going Out with a Smile?" *Management Review*, September 1991, p. 7.
11. James E. Challenger, "When Outplacement Is a Sham," *Personnel Journal*, February 1989, p. 27.
12. William J. Heery, "Outplacement through Specialization," *Personnel Administrator*, June 1989, p. 151.
13. Lewis Newman, "Outplacement the Right Way," *Personnel Administrator*, February 1989, p. 84.

SOME ADDITIONAL REFERENCES

DuBrin, Andrew J. *Bouncing Back: How to Get Back in the Game When Your Career Is on the Line* (New York: McGraw-Hill, 1992).

Gibson, Virginia M. "The Ins and Outs of Outplacement." *Management Review*, October 1991, pp. 59–61.

Jensen, Dave. "What's All This About a Labor Shortage?" *Management Review*, June 1991, pp. 42–44.

Lancaster, Lisa L., and Thomas Li-Ping Tang. "Outplacement Offers Safety Net for Displaced Workers." *Personnel Administrator*, April 1989, pp. 60–63.

Piccolino, Edmund B. "Outplacment: The View from HR." *Personnel*, March 1988, pp. 24–27.

Chapter Twenty

Telecommuting

A profitable travel agency faced two challenges simultaneously: more office space was needed, and the turnover of the technical support staff had become unacceptably high. The agency attempted to solve these problems by implementing a telecommuting program.

Susan Lepsch and Russel Stratton, co-owners of Lepsch and Stratton Travel Agency, met for breakfast on the first Monday in July. "Sue, this is it," said Russ. "Either we take decisive action or we stop complaining about too little office space and too much turnover. We should expand from 4,000 to 5,000 square feet. We are currently paying $16 per square foot. New space in an office the size we want would cost approximately $19 per square foot. Our other overhead costs are also rising. Our volume of business isn't large enough to gamble on being able to cover that much increase in expenses."

"I get your point, Russ," Sue said. "If we expand to the amount of space we require, we'll be paying a premium rate on the entire floor space, not just the additional 1,000 square feet. My research may have uncovered a program that will take care of the space and turnover problem at the same time.

"My contacts in the human resources field tell me that one of the best ways to keep good office help is to give them a work schedule that makes life easy. We've been using flexible working hours for some time. It did reduce turnover at first, but once most small offices in the area offered flexible working hours, we lost our competitive advantage. What's hot now is letting some employees work from home. It's called *telecommuting*. *Flexplace* is now s important as *flextime*. If we had enough staffers working at home, we could get by without the additional space."

"I'm willing to try the program on a voluntary basis," said Russ. "Who should we start with?"

"The likely candidates are the five support specialists and one direct-mail specialist. Those people could do a substantial portion of their work at home if they had the right equipment. Gaining access to our files from home would be the biggest hurdle. We could meet with them about once every 10 days in the office just to coordinate activities and let them know that we still care about them." Sue and Russ identified five volunteers for the telecommuting program.

September 1 was the launching date for telecommuting at the agency. The biggest equipment problem was to supply each telecommuter with a personal computer and modum for interfacing with computers at the office and a fax machine. Two of the telecommuters volunteered to use their own personal computers; two computers were transferred from the agency to the homes of the employees.

During mid-November, Sue and Russ decided to evaluate the new system. To that date, neither partner had heard of any substantial complaint about the program either from the employees or from clients because of poor service. Sue and Russ agreed it was important to evaluate the program because the current lease would expire at the end of March. If the program were working well, the present space could be retained, thus avoiding the expense and effort of relocation.

Sue began her evaluation of telecommuting by describing her experiences in supervising the work of Kim and Betty. "I was worried about the possibility of Kim not doing her job because she wasted time on the telephone. That proved not to be a problem. If Kim was gabbing on the phone excessively, it didn't drag down her productivity. She did all the work that was required.

"A problem did arise, however, that I didn't anticipate. After the first two weeks of the plan, both Kim and Betty seemed to get their week's quota done by Thursday morning. They would then have a day and a half to do whatever they wanted. I couldn't complain because they met their quota. Yet, if they were in the office, somebody could have found something constructive for them to do."

Russ spoke to Kristin, the direct-mail specialist, about her experiences with working out of her home. Kristin replied, "My reaction has been mixed. I enjoy being treated like a true professional. Nobody has to watch over me to see that I get my work done. I like saving commuting time, so I have a little more time for reading the newspaper and taking care of errands.

"What I don't like is being so alienated from the office. I want to move up to supervisor if our agency expands substantially. If you two hardly ever see me, I could easily be passed over for promotion. Another problem I didn't anticipate is the distractions at home. My daughter asks me for rides, and my friends drop by. People just don't taking working at home as seriously as working in an office building."

Sue asked Diane, one of the support specialists, for her reaction to working out of her home. With a gleam in her eye and a smile, Diane replied, "Telecommuting has helped make my life work. My biggest problem before working at home was that I had a latchkey child. Trevor, my son, is too old for child care, yet too young to be home unsupervised. He gets home at around 3:15 in the afternoon. When he gets home he knows I'm working, but it's better than my not being on the premises. By not worrying so much about Trevor on my working days, I feel much less stressed, and much better able to concentrate on my work.

"Another great thing about having my office in my home is that the cost of working is gradually going down. Gas, lunches out with co-workers, and buying all those extra panty hose can add up. I can imagine that over a period of one year, being a telecommuter could save me about $1,400."

Russ interviewed Tony, one of the support specialists, about his telecommuting experiences. "On a scale of 1 to 10," said Tony, "I would rate teleworking a 5. I like being able to avoid commuting on a day with inclement weather. And I like getting home from work at 4:31 after having stopped work at 4:30. The pay is the same so I have no complaints there."

"What reservations do you have?" Russ asked.

"I miss the interaction with my office buddies," said Tony. "I never wanted to be a loner. If I did I would have become a forest ranger. I like people. I like taking coffee breaks with co-workers. At home, I drink my coffee at my desk. For a break, I take out the garbage. If I'm lucky I say hello to the mail carrier.

"To make matters worse, one of my neighbors brought me over some food and clothing. She thinks I've been laid off. I guess working at home doesn't give others the impression that you're a big success."

After this round of interviews, Sue and Russ expressed optimism that telecommuting could make a contribution to the Lepsch and Stratton Agency. Sue mentioned, however, "I don't know how far we will go with telecommuting. But I do know that we will always need somebody around the office to talk to our clients both in person and on the phone."

TELECOMMUTING PRINCIPLES AND PROCEDURES

The travel agency that decided to implement a program of telecommuting is not acting alone. Approximately 33 million people in the United States and Canada do some or all of their office work at home. An estimated 11 million of these people operate their own business. Over 500 large U.S. companies have formal work-at-home programs, with over 900,000 employees participating. [1] Many small businesses allow selected workers the opportunity to perform some of their work at home. Telecommuting is growing so rapidly that it has created a growth market in the personal computer industry, called the *small-office, home-office (SoHo)* package. Computer purchases to people who work at home grew 22 percent in 1992, while corporate purchases declined 5 percent. [2]

Enough experience has been gathered with telecommuting to specify principles and procedures for conducting a work-at-home program within an organization. Many of the same principles and procedures also apply to people who operate businesses out of their home.

Select the Right Jobs for Telecommuting

Any work that requires thinking, planning, writing, computer input, and no face-to-face interaction generally can be done at home. Yet as the two travel agency partners observed, not all jobs are suitable for telecommuting. According to two telecommuting consultants, a job must meet certain criteria to be suited for working at home. The following checklist covers important questions that must be answered affirmatively to determine if a job and the firm are suited for telecommuting:

1. Does the job involve information handling?
2. Does the company have significant automation?
3. Does a results-oriented style exist within the company?
4. Do management and employees trust each other?
5. Is there relatively little face-to-face contact?
6. Can terminals be employed to accomplish a large part of the job?
7. Are jobs project-oriented so tasks have an organized flow of information in a defined span of time?
8. Are there defined milestones or checkpoints in doing the work or components that can be delivered at certain times?
9. Is the job self-contained so it can be performed independently of others? If necessary, can it be integrated into the whole later?[3]

Using the above criteria as a guide, a wide variety of managerial, professional, sales, and clerical jobs can be performed independently on a location-independent basis. Among them are sales representative, telemarketer, word processing technician, computer programmer, architect, catalog order taker, insurance agent, and securities trader. Most telecommuting occurs from an office at home, but it can also be performed at small satellite locations—yachts, campsites, and recreational vehicles.

Select the Right People for Telecommuting

After the right jobs have been selected for telecommuting, the right telecommuters must be selected. A good starting point is to request volunteers, and then they must be screened. Some potentially good telecommuters may not have a home situation suited to office work. Among the unsuitable factors are too many other people present at home, no suitable place for a quiet office, and interpersonal conflict at home.

Employees who work well on site are the most likely to work well offsite.[4] A telecommuter must be an individual who has already demonstrated the self-discipline to work independently without much direct supervision. Planning ability and efficient use of time are essential. Good communication skills, including effectiveness on the telephone and with electronic mail, are important. Workers who require frequent social interaction are unsuited for working at home.

Emotionally immature people are unsuited for working at home because they may not be able to handle the responsibility of being on their own. Unless the telecommuter can concentrate on the task at hand, he or she will lose productivity because of such distractions as television, friends, and family. Skill-Building Exercise 20 will help you assess your readiness for working at home.

SKILL-BUILDING EXERCISE 20
Am I Ready for Working at Home?

Indicate the strength of your agreement with the statements below, using a 1 to 5 scale: 1 = disagree strongly; 2 = disagree; 3 = neutral; 4 = agree; 5 = agree strongly.

	DS	D	N	A	AS
1. I am effective at scheduling my own work.	1	2	3	4	5
2. I am strongly self-motivated; nobody needs to prod me to get me started working.	1	2	3	4	5
3. In comparison to most people, I procrastinate very little.	1	2	3	4	5
4. Socializing with co-workers during the day is not very important to me.	1	2	3	4	5
5. It would make me tense to interrupt my work by watching television or running errands.	1	2	3	4	5
6. I work very well without close supervision.	1	2	3	4	5
7. People who know my work would say I am very well organized.	1	2	3	4	5
8. I feel comfortable working for up to eight hours at a stretch on the same project.	1	2	3	4	5
9. Commuting to work is a waste of time.	1	2	3	4	5

10. I can get work accomplished over   1   2   3   4   5
the phone as well as I can in person.

Scoring and interpretation: Total your score by adding the circled numbers. A score of 45 or higher suggests your work habits and temperament are ideally suited to working at home. A score of 11 to 44 suggests moderate suitability for working at home. If your score is 10 or lower, you are better suited for now to work in a traditional office. The statements that you circled as 1 or 2 suggest areas for personal growth if you want to become more self-sufficient and productive.

Establish Appropriate Salaries

Salary administration is another important consideration in planning and implementing a telecommuting program. The organization must decide whether work will be paid according to a normal work week, with an annual compensation equivalent to the current income for on-site employees. An issue raised by Carol Ann Hamilton is whether a telecommuter who finishes an assignment in half a week should be expected to produce twice as much as office workers in order to be paid for a regular work week. [5] An office-bound worker can more readily do fill-in assignments when he or she has completed a major assignment.

It is easier to establish wages for employees exempt from overtime than for nonexempt employees. Whether or not overtime is justified is more apparent for office workers than for those employees working out of their homes. Because telecommuters do not have to spend time commuting to the office, it is easier for them to work long hours. The general principle here is to resolve thorny policy issues before employees begin working at home. Administratively, the easiest alternative is to continue paying teleworkers the same salary and benefits they received as office workers.

Many telecommuters are part-time workers who are typically paid by the amount of work produced, such as the number of insurance claims processed. Part-timers also receive some benefits. For example, the NPD Group, Inc., a national market research firm, employs approximately 50 part-time telecommuters for an average of 20 hours per week. These workers receive several benefits including vacation pay and health insurance. Another category of telecommuter is contract workers who take on temporary assignments for a fixed fee and receive no benefits because they are not company employees.

Train the Telecommuters

Consultant Joanne H. Pratt recommends that telecommuters and their managers receive training, individually and in groups. Managers may need to develop confidence in managing people they do not see regularly. [6] Employees should be trained in the fundamentals of telecommuting. For example, the state of California covers these topics: organization and time management; dealing with interruptions by family and friends; office organization; communicating with co-workers; safety and security.[7] (Security is an important issue because telecommuters maintain or access important files at home.)

Introduce Telecommuting on a Trial Basis

A principle that applies to telecommuting, as well as to most human resources programs, is to begin on a trial basis. Computer programmers and word processing technicians are two occupational groups well suited to launching a telecommuting program. Both jobs require relatively little face-to-face contact with other people, and the work can be divided into deliverable milestones such as a completed program. Several companies' experiences with teleworking have validated the wisdom of starting with as few as three or four employees. A trial sample of this size usually provides sufficient data to evaluate the effectiveness of telecommuting, yet is manageable enough to be monitored regularly.[8]

Create Opportunities for Interaction with Co-Workers

Feelings of isolation and alienation may arise when telecommuters are rarely seen in person, so telecommuters should spend some time at the regular office. A rule of thumb is to require teleworkers to return to the office at least one day per week. At Traveler's insurance company, for example, several hundred employees work at home from one to three days per week, thus allowing time for interaction with co-workers.

According to William Atkinson, employees "need to plug back into co-worker relationships, catch up on gossip, be apprised of company policy changes, discuss work progress and problems with their managers, and even be involved in birthday parties, company outings, and the like."[9] Spending time in the office also helps telecommuters gain the visibility they may need for future promotions. Among the frequently used methods of getting together with teleworkers are regularly scheduled department meetings, business/social functions, and special meetings to discuss the concerns of teleworkers.

Encourage Telecommuters to Use Ergonomic Office Design

Home workers should be given assistance in designing an office that follows basic principles of *ergonomics,* the science of making machines and equipment compatible with human requirements. A properly designed office can help prevent such problems as VDT stress and repetitive motion disorder from overuse of wrist muscles. Here are some basic suggestions based on ergonomics that can be implemented by most workers at home:

1. A proper chair is essential and should allow the worker to sit with thighs parallel to the floor and feet flat. The back of the chair should support the spine.
2. Workers who keyboard and talk simultaneously should use a phone with a headset.
3. The computer should be positioned so the video display terminal is at eye level, and the keyboard at elbow level.
4. A wrist rest should be used to help prevent wrist strain.
5. Telecommuters should avoid glare from sunlight or electric light by using blinds and the appropriate amount of artificial light.
6. Workers should be encouraged to take frequent rest breaks and make frequent small movements while seated. [10]

Establish Clear Criteria for Measuring Performance

A successful telecommuting program establishes standards for measuring the output of the home worker. Supervisors of teleworking activities have had to abandon measures of performance such as attendance, punctuality, and attitude. The more tangible the output, the more readily it can be measured. A recommended approach is to establish specific goals related to quantity and quality and completion times for each work-at-home project.

Molly Tyson, the manager of instructional products at Apple Computer, supervises 58 employees who work at home at least one day per week. In regard to measuring work, Tyson says, "It's been a significant step forward in my maturation as a manager to become more focused on objectives, rather than how the work is accomplished." [11]

Inform Employees of the Tax-Deductible Aspects of the Office at Home

Income tax rulings about the office at home concern many telecommuters. Because many people anticipate generous tax deductions for their office at home, it is important to communicate accurate written information about this topic. A company tax accountant should provide an interpretation of current tax legislation regarding working at home.

The government provides some tax relief for working at home with write-offs for offices at home, under strict guidelines. According to a 1993 Supreme Court decision, taxpayers may not take tax deductions for offices at home if they spend the majority of their workdays elsewhere. Coopers & Lybrand, the accounting firm, caution that an office must be the principal place of business and used only for business to be deductible. [12] If this is the case, telecommuters can deduct a portion of their mortgage interest or rent, utilities, real estate taxes, repairs and painting, and depreciation. The percent of the deduction is calculated by dividing the amount of square feet used exclusively for office purposes by the total square feet of the house or apartment.

Professional tax advice is particularly important because there are many debatable deductions in relation to working at home. One telecommuter wanted to deduct a mileage allowance for trips to the company office claiming these trips were a travel expense. The teleworker's tax advisor ruled against him, emphasizing that trips to the company office are a normal part of the job.

Provide for Security of Information

Computer terminals off the company premises represent a potential security risk. Some companies resist telecommuting programs because they do not want employees using company files outside the office. The organization must ensure that telecommuters can access only the system or files they are authorized to work with. A general recommendation is to take the same security measures in an office at home that would be taken at the traditional office. [13]

ADVANTAGES OF TELECOMMUTING

Telecommuting offers many potential advantages to both the organization and the individual. Of primary importance to the organization, telecommuting programs typically contribute to productivity increases, as supported by the following company examples. The Traveler's insurance company cites productivity increases of 20 percent in terms of the amount of code generated by computer programmers. U.S. West Communications Inc. reported a productivity increase of up to 40 percent.

A study conducted with data-entry specialists at the NPD Group indicated that when eight different projects were switched from in-house to in the home, productivity increased an average of 30 percent. The researchers cautioned, however, that the in-house and work-at-home groups were not comparable. The telecommuters worked an average of 20 hours per week and were younger and better educated. In a telecommuting project undertaken by AT&T and the state of Arizona, 80 percent of the supervisors thought telecommuting increased employee productivity.

Another productivity advantage is that office-space rental usually decreases with a telecommuting program. Cost savings also occur when employees are taken off the regular payroll and hired part time because they receive reduced benefits. Furthermore, the company gains under telecommuting when new labor pools are opened. Among the people who might not be able to attend a full-time office job are people with very young children and some disabled people with impaired mobility.

A telecommuting program can also be a potential recruiting incentive to those candidates who would prefer to work out of their homes rather than in a company office. Any company advertising for work-at-home employees is flooded with applicants. Similarly, the opportunity to work at home can help retain valuable employees who prefer not to relocate. The chairman of the board of the largest home mortgage firm in the world works almost exclusively out of his home.

Telecommuting also supports a variety of lifestyle and environmental advantages. Telecommuting makes some aspects of child care easier because the parent can be at home to at least lightly supervise the child. (Nevertheless, taking care of children while working can be stressful and unproductive.) Telecommuting also helps workers avoid the discomfort of close supervision, interruptions from co-workers, and lengthy commuting. [14] As indicated in the opening case, telecommuting decreases expenses for commuting, lunches out, and clothing. The environment gains because telecommuting helps reduce pollution from crowded highways.

DISADVANTAGES OF TELECOMMUTING

Every potential advantage of telecommuting can be matched by a potential disadvantage for organizations and individuals. A potential disadvantage for the organization is that it is difficult to build teamwork when a large number of workers rarely come to the office and do not interact much with co-workers. This problem is particularly acute for firms pursuing total quality management, because TQM depends on teamwork and interaction. Telecommuting may not be suited for workers who are not performing measurable work and who require close supervision to stay focused on the job.

A substantial number of potential disadvantages to the individual stem from telecommuting. Similar drawbacks were found in two separate studies, including the following:

Not having necessary supplies or equipment.

Having too many family interruptions.

Mixing work with family life too much.

Experiencing limited benefits and advancement opportunities.

Receiving low earnings or unpredictable earnings.

Not having interactions with co-workers.

Not having a regular routine.

Blurring of distinction between work and home. [15]

A final disadvantage of telecommuting is that it fosters workaholism. Many telecommuters claim that having an office at home allows them to take a dinner break with the family. If they worked many miles from home, it would not be practical to come home to dinner before returning to work at night. Similarly, a corporate worker who has an office at home can readily return to work after dinner. The same situation leads to a work addiction because it is easy to return to the project sitting in an office at home. Many people with offices at home work 70-hour weeks.

Guidelines for Action and Skill Development

To tie together the principles and procedures for telecommuting already presented, we offer some summary guidelines to the individual and the organization. First, here are six keys to managing telecommuters:

1. Show faith in your telecommuter, and stand ready to give additional training and encouragement.
2. Take the concept of telecommuting seriously by affording it the time and planning it requires.
3. Organize and plan your objectives, but monitor results more closely than the players.
4. Keep the team spirit alive by making sure there is a team. Keep your off-site workers attuned to what is happening in the office.
5. Focus on objectives, such as the amount of work produced, not activity, such as the number of hours worked.
6. Stay in touch with your telecommuters. Give off-site workers first priority when they call. Keep in touch by telephone, voice-mail, E-mail, or pager.[16]

Beginning telecommuters should take the following steps: First, create a work environment separate from the living area and get a separate telephone. An office in a living area makes it difficult to separate oneself mentally from work. Second, set up a daily work schedule and stick to it the same as you would if working an in off-site office. Third, fully equip the office including personal computer, modem, laser-quality printer, answering machine or voice mail, copying machine, fax machine, pencil sharpener, and postage scale.

DISCUSSION QUESTIONS AND ACTIVITIES

1. In what way have corporate downsizings contributed to a growth in the number of offices at home?
2. What is the difference between a true telecommuter and anybody who works out of his or her house, such as a sales representative in a remote territory?
3. Identify five jobs you think would be well suited to telecommuting.
4. Identify five jobs you think would be poorly suited to telecommuting.

5. What similarities do you see between telecommuting and the cottage industries that preceded the industrial revolution?

6. Develop a policy a company might use to decide how many office supplies to allow telecommuters to bring to their home office.

NOTES

1. Deborah Fineblum Raub, "No Place Like Home to Get the Job Done," *Rochester Democrat and Chronicle*, January 1, 1993, p. IF; Donald C. Bacon, "Look Who's Working at Home," *Nation's Business*, October 1989, p. 21; and Dennis Hayes, " 'Commute' by Computer," *USA Weekend*, March 27-29, 1992.

2. Catherine Arnst, "PC Makers Head for 'Soho'," *Business Week*, September 28, 1992, p. 125.

3. Marcia M. Kelly, "The Next Workplace Revolution: Telecommuting," *Supervisory Management*, October 1985, pp. 5-6.

4. Karen Matthes, "Telecommuting: Balancing Business and Employee Needs," *HRfocus*, December 1992, p. 3.

5. Carol Ann Hamilton, "Telecommuting," *Personnel Journal*, April 1987, p. 97.

6. Matthes, "Telecommuting: Balancing Business and Employee Needs," p. 3.

7. Shari Caudron, "Working at Home Pays Off," *Personnel Journal*, November 1992, p. 49.

8. Hamilton, "Telecommuting," p. 99; and Matthes, "Telecommuting: Balancing Business and Employee Needs," p. 3.

9. William Atkinson, "Home/Work," *Personnel Journal*, November 1985, p. 108.

10. Pam Black, "A Home Office That's Easier On the Eyes—And on the Back," *Business Week*, August 17, 1992, p. 113.

11. Caudron, "Working at Home," p. 44.

12. Jan M. Rosen, "IRS Is Losing Tax Court Cases on Deduction of Home Office," *New York Times* syndicated story, April 15, 1990; and Rob Wells, "What You Want to Know about Home-Office Tax Ruling, Associated Press story, January 17, 1993.

13. J. A. Young, "The Advantages of Telecommuting," *Management Review*, July 1991, p. 21.

14. Caudron, "Working at Home," p. 40; Young, "The Advantages of Telecommuting," p. 20; Andrew J. DuBrin, "Comparison of the Job Satisfaction and Productivity of Telecommuters versus In-House Employees: A Research Note on Work in Progress," *Psychological Reports* 68 (1991) pp. 1233-1234.

15. Thomas R. King, "Working at Home Has Yet to Work Out," *The Wall Street Journal*, December 22, 1989, p. B1; Andrew J. DuBrin and Janet C. Barnard, "What Telecommuters Like and Dislike About Their Jobs," *Business Forum*, Winter 1993.

16. Phillip Mahfood, *Homework: How to Hire, Manage and Monitor Employees Who Work at Home* (Chicago: Probus Publishing, 1992).

SOME ADDITIONAL REFERENCES

Arden, Lynie. *The Work-at-Home Sourcebook*. Boulder, Colo.: Live Oak Publications, 1988.

Cross, Thomas B., and Marjorie Roaizman, *Telecommuting: The Future Technology of Work*. Homewood, IL: Dow Jones-Irwin, 1986.

Farmanfarmaian, Roxane. "Worksteading: The New Lifestyle Frontier." *Psychology Today*, November 1989, pp. 37–52.

Scordato, Christine, and Julie Harris. "Workplace Flexibility." *HRMagazine*, January 1990, pp. 75-78.

Shamir, Boas, and Ilan Salomon. "Work-at-Home and Quality of Working Life." *Academy of Management Review*, July 1985, p. 461.

Organization Index

Name Index

Subject Index